In *Towards A New Theory of Adjudication*, former Justice of Appeal Andrew Phang provides an insightful critique of the major theories of legal reasoning and adjudication, and building on that analysis, propounds his own theory of adjudication. The unique perspective of this book is that it comes from someone who has combined a career as an academic with a long-standing interest in legal theory with the practical experience of being a judge of the Singapore High Court and Court of Appeal. The theoretical issues discussed are illustrated by reference to decided cases, in many of which the author wrote or contributed to the court's reasoning. The result is a book which manages to bridge the divide between theory and practice, and which I strongly recommend.

Mr Justice David Foxton, High Court Judge, King's Bench Division and Judge of the Commercial Court

Justice Phang's deft analytical skills, honed as a scholar and a jurist, make his new theory of adjudication particularly profound. It is a theory developed through eagle eyed analysis and a deep understanding of both legal theory and adjudicative method. A must read for anyone seeking to make sense of common law adjudication.

Professor Liz Fisher, Faculty of Law, University of Oxford

Justice Phang has written a masterful work on jurisprudence that should be read by law students, legal practitioners and judges. Drawing on his vast experiences and deep insight as a Professor and a Judge, he provides a rare blend of a strong philosophical foundation for the practice of judicial adjudication and a practical edge to jurisprudential theory. His analysis of the major works of the jurisprudential giants of classical jurisprudence is accessible, illuminating and compelling. His work on a new theory of adjudication, is rich in values, deep reflections and practical utility. It is worth returning to constantly, for those who seek to improve as judges, in the pursuit of justice.

Justice Kwek Mean Luck
Supreme Court, Singapore
Chairman, Singapore Judicial College

In this invaluable treatise, the author embarks on an ambitious project to present a new and compelling model of adjudication encompassing a line of reasoning that reconciles legal theory with the realities of judicial practice. He achieves the difficult goal of bridging the often-divergent realms of legal theory and judicial practice. The model is particularly convincing, given the author's extensive and renowned experience and expertise in both the judicial and academic fields of law. In brief, *Towards A New Theory of Adjudication* affords an influential new contribution to legal scholarship for academics, adjudicators and jurists attracted to the dynamics of judicial reasoning and decision-making.

The Honourable Justice Tan Sri Datuk Nallini Pathmanathan, Judge, Federal Court of Malaysia

Drawing on legal theory and philosophy, and referencing decided cases as touchpoints, in *Towards A New Theory of Adjudication* Justice Phang seeks to fill the gap in the extant literature by offering a robust new theory of adjudication that provides practical guiderails for the reader. By focusing on judicial attitude, as informed by judicial values, the theory of adjudication posited in this book is directed ambitiously at achieving both procedural and substantive fairness. In Justice Phang's inimitable style, the book is well-structured and logical with a delightful mix of informal conversational flair and intellectual rigour.

Professor Natalie Skead, Dean, Singapore Judicial College and Professor of Law, the University of Western Australia

Justice Phang calls this book a 'labour of love'. But it is more than that. Part intimate memoir and part academic treatise, this is both Justice Phang's most introspective and his most analytical work to date. It is analytical in the way that Justice Phang critically evaluates various modern theories on the nature of law. It is introspective in the way that Justice Phang repeatedly asks himself whether the theories actually reflect his almost 20 years of experience as a Singapore judge. In the end, Justice Phang concludes that it is Dworkin's theory that, with suitable modification, comes closest to capturing how judges decide. It is Justice Phang's modified theory, focusing on the strengths and (especially) limits of practical adjudication, that will be of interest, not merely to judges, but also to law students, academics and lay readers.

Justice Anselmo Reyes, International Judge, Singapore International Commercial Court and former Judge of the Court of First Instance in Hong Kong

This book is a brilliant and fresh vision of what judges do and why it matters. I learned so much from it, not only because of its extraordinary intellectual range, but because it was so compellingly written. It's a great contribution to the judicial literature, and will quickly become a magnetic classic.

Rosalie Silberman Abella, Retired Justice of the Supreme Court of Canada and currently the Pisar Chair at Harvard Law School

TOWARDS A NEW THEORY OF ADJUDICATION

This book explores the major theories of common law adjudication and presents a new theory of adjudication.

It shows that the existing major theories of common law adjudication each capture only part of what occurs in actual court proceedings. It presents a new theory of adjudication that incorporates both useful and modified elements of these theories. The new theory itself comprises two parts: first, an attitudinal aspect based on institutional values; and second, a number of practical and theoretical factors which give concrete expression to those values. Throughout the book, the author draws on his prior experience both as a law professor and as a judge in his country's highest appellate court in order to provide a unique perspective that illustrates this new theory.

Towards a New Theory of Adjudication

Integrating Theory and Practice

Andrew Phang

• HART •
OXFORD • LONDON • NEW YORK • NEW DELHI • SYDNEY

HART PUBLISHING

Bloomsbury Publishing Plc

Kemp House, Chawley Park, Cumnor Hill, Oxford, OX2 9PH, UK

1385 Broadway, New York, NY 10018, USA

Bloomsbury Publishing Ireland Limited, 29 Earlsfort Terrace, Dublin 2, D02 AY28, Ireland

HART PUBLISHING, the Hart/Stag logo, BLOOMSBURY and the Diana logo are trademarks of Bloomsbury Publishing Plc

First published in Great Britain 2025

A catalogue record for this book is available from the British Library.

A catalogue record for this book is available from the Library of Congress.

Library of Congress Control Number: 2025030850

ISBN: HB: 978-1-50997-695-9
ePDF: 978-1-50997-697-3
ePub: 978-1-50997-696-6

Typeset by Compuscript Ltd, Shannon

For product safety related questions contact productsafety@bloomsbury.com

To find out more about our authors and books visit www.hartpublishing.co.uk. Here you will find extracts, author information, details of forthcoming events and the option to sign up for our newsletters.

To the memory of my parents, Mr and Mrs Phang Sing Eng,
and to my wife, Sock Yong and
my daughters, Rachel and Christine

FOREWORD

The nature of adjudication has taken on renewed significance in contemporary times. Many courts worldwide are facing a mounting trust deficit, fuelled in part by misconceptions and misgivings about how judges decide cases. This erosion of public confidence is particularly acute in disputes that raise socially polarising issues, where judges sometimes face accusations of allowing extra-legal or partisan considerations to influence their judgments. Compounding this challenge is the disturbing claim that 'AI judges' might one day come to replace human judges, which carries the implicit premise that there is nothing inherently or inextricably human about the institution of judging. In a climate of growing scrutiny over the very nature of adjudication, the need for a normative *theory* of adjudication has never been more pressing.

In this groundbreaking work, Justice Andrew Phang responds to this need with a compelling and original theory of adjudication. Central to his theory is the fundamental spirit of the adjudicative enterprise – that of good faith judging in accordance with objective procedure to achieve fair and just results. The author's focus on the *attitudinal aspect* of judging is a pioneering attempt to construct a more holistic and accurate picture of judicial practice, one informed by his own deep and storied experience as a long-serving judge. The theory will therefore no doubt resonate with many judges as it speaks powerfully to the foundational institutional values that anchor and animate the adjudicative process.

The proposed theory is remarkable not only for what it stands for, but also how it builds and improves on existing scholarship. With his characteristic modesty, the author claims that his work is 'new' only in its emphasis on the attitudinal aspect, but not insofar as it endorses several major theories of adjudication (save for the most sceptical ones). Yet this belies the work's thoughtful design and broader significance, which extends beyond the novel theory proposed in its final chapter.

After laying the conceptual foundations for the book, several chapters are dedicated to a systematic critique of major theories of law and adjudication. Each theory is situated in its jurisprudential context, carefully unpacked, and rigorously evaluated against the realities of judicial practice. Rather than set up a contest between theories, the author identifies useful elements from each theory and masterfully synthesises them into a coherent and integrated whole. Thus, the endorsement of the major theories arises not from uncritical acceptance, but from a considered process which recognises that each theory offers valuable insights, even as no single theory can fully capture the complexity of adjudicative practice.

Each chapter offers readers an analytical, comprehensive and faithful treatment of the original theories. The author also draws seamlessly upon an impressive array of cases that bring his theoretical analysis to life, including many that he was personally involved in and can speak to authoritatively. The chapters on Professor Ronald Dworkin's theory of adjudication are especially noteworthy. Tracing the evolution of his theory over some three and a half decades, they offer an excellent companion and commentary to Dworkin's major works. These chapters contain rich insights that can only be derived from a close study of Dworkin's scholarship, ranging from the pervasive but understated influence that Professor Walter Bryce Gallie has had on Dworkin's theory, to the intriguing question of whether lawyers and judges are best characterised as hedgehogs, foxes or eagles.

The book culminates in a final chapter where the author advances his proposed theory of adjudication. In my view, the theory is immensely significant for two key reasons. First, it finds its moorings in the institutional values that underpin the adjudicative process, giving expression to essential qualities such as impartiality, wisdom and humility. Such qualities are sometimes absent from more abstract or positivist theories of adjudication which, as a result, fail to account for the sense of professional responsibility and humanity that profoundly influence the practice of adjudication.

Second, the author has deliberately designed his theory to provide practical guidance to judges. He explains how institutional values shape adjudicative practice by translating them into specific factors that judges should consider when deciding cases. Bridging theory and practice can be a formidable challenge, but it is an enterprise that is eminently worthwhile – a point that the author consistently emphasised in his scholarship and brilliantly demonstrated in this book.

Above all, the book is a remarkable reflection of the jurist and person that the author is. He describes it as a labour of love, and indeed, no project could more perfectly encapsulate the present chapter of his professional life. After spending nearly a quarter century as a highly regarded academic, followed by an extraordinary 18 years as one of our nation's most eminent and influential judges, the author could be said to have returned to his first love – legal theory and jurisprudence. Yet those familiar with his work would know that his passion for theory never once waned, and I am delighted to see this take shape in this monumental book.

In preparing this foreword, I was reminded of a passage from one of his earlier articles:[1]

> If I may interpose briefly (albeit informally and personally), when I hear the corrosive – and disorientating as well as dispiriting – sounds of scepticism and cynicism [about the nature of the law], I am reminded that, often, what is unseen is more important

[1] A Phang, 'Doctrine and Fairness in the Law of Contract' (2009) 29 *Legal Studies* 534, 537.

> than what is seen. In particular, I am reminded of the values that are embodied in the law – in particular, the nobility of the quest for justice and the weighty responsibility we bear (whether as students, lawyers, academics or judges) to pursue this noble aim. These cannot be seen but nevertheless constitute the ideals that are the foundation of the enterprise of the law itself. I am also reminded that, on a deeper level, nobility and goodness in general is not something that we should take lightly. On the contrary, these are qualities which we should treasure. They are the true 'anchors' that will prevent us from being cast adrift in troubled (and troubling) times such as we are experiencing at the moment …

Although this passage appeared as a brief interposition in an article on contract law, its emphasis on legal values shines through with great clarity and conviction. What is perhaps most striking is the consistency this reveals in the author's approach to the law (and, I would add, to his life). In this respect, his proposed theory of adjudication is far from 'new' – it is one that he has wholeheartedly embraced and lived out throughout his professional life.

Andrew Phang has produced an excellent and consequential treatise that deserves close study. The work represents an outstanding contribution to the academy and fills a vital gap in the scholarship, while simultaneously offering a practical and inspiring resource for judges at all stages of their careers. The analysis is nuanced and incisive, and yet it remains accessible to students and readers without a background in jurisprudence. I would unhesitatingly recommend this exceptional work to all with an interest in the law and adjudication.

Sundaresh Menon
Chief Justice
Supreme Court of Singapore

PREFACE

My career in the law may be divided into two (approximately equal) halves. The former half was spent in legal academia, whilst the latter half was spent on the Bench. Roughly speaking, legal academia focuses more on 'theory', whereas court work focuses (instead) on 'practice'. There is a popular view that there is a gap between the two, and some extreme views go so far as to state that never the twain shall meet. Indeed, I do know of many legal academics who immerse themselves in theory and are unconcerned with the practical effects and implications of their academic writings. The contrast just mentioned is particularly stark when dealing with academic writings in the context of jurisprudence and legal philosophy.

At this particular juncture, I have a confession to make. Even as a student, jurisprudence was my favourite subject. Indeed, I waited until my final year to read it, as I wanted to be as mature as I could when I took the course in order to garner the most from it. Indeed, I enjoyed the course and all the theories taught as well as discussed in it tremendously. And of all the prizes on offer in law school, the prize for jurisprudence was the one that – if it was at all possible – I wanted most to receive. Needless to say, I was overjoyed (and relieved!) when I did in fact receive it (not, I hasten to add, because of any egotism on my part but because, as mentioned, I truly loved the subject). It was also a wonderful experience when I had – many years later – the opportunity to write a biographical essay on the jurist after whom that particular prize had been named. After graduation, I joined legal academia immediately. I loved theory. Then I learnt to love – and write on – legal history. I also taught legal method and legal doctrine (specifically, contract law). I still believe that a sound grounding in theory, history and doctrine is essential for every law student. However, before I digress further, I should return to my interest in 'theory'. It never went away. On the contrary, I read more and more books – not only in jurisprudence and legal theory but in general philosophy as well. And so it was an honour and privilege when I was finally tasked after some years to teach the jurisprudence course. Alongside the law of contract, it became part of my teaching and research interests for a great many years.

Then, after approximately a quarter of a century, my legal career took a *radical* turn: I was invited to serve on the Bench. As I have recounted elsewhere, this invitation came like a bolt from the blue. Indeed, as I have also recounted, the transition from legal academia to the Bench could not have been more contrasting; as I have observed elsewhere:

> Indeed, after joining the Bench, I recall being in Hong Kong to deliver a public lecture. One of the first questions I was asked was what it was like to be a judge after having been a legal academic for such a long time (close to a quarter of a century in point of fact). I still recall my response vividly. It was unscripted and instinctive but quite picturesque. I likened the initial transition as follows: being a legal academic was like wearing a glove that was crafted by its maker who knew not only the size of my hand but also the material that fit so well that it felt like it was a part of me, whereas being a judge was like climbing up a wall with a near perpendicular gradient and with no safety harness! I am grateful that after a decade and a half on the Bench, the experience generates much less apprehension.

After joining the Bench, I had to change my writing style drastically – no footnotes with the analysis of even very difficult or novel points of law being set out in as simple (albeit not simplistic) a manner as possible. It also seemed to me that my predilection for theory would have to take a backseat to my now very practical job – or even be discarded altogether lest it muddy practical thinking and analysis. On the contrary, however, I began to discover two closely related things. First, I found that theoretical reflection and analysis – particularly from a conceptual perspective – was in fact not only useful but, on occasion, even imperative from a very *practical* perspective. This was the case, for example, in the context of clarifying legal analysis by understanding the theoretical distinction between the descriptive and the prescriptive, between the 'is' and the 'ought'. Another situation where theoretical analysis was imperative was – perhaps not surprisingly – in the context of novel (or hard) cases. Yet another situation related to the need to distinguish between principle and policy and (relatedly) when a certain conception of the concept of 'policy' had to be harnessed. Second, I discovered that much of the theoretical material that I was enamoured of in the past, whilst intellectually challenging and interesting, was of little – or even no – use to legal practice. On the contrary, they were, with respect, rife with convoluted reasoning which, whilst impressive in form, led to only obvious points at best and confusion at worst. We often forget that legal academics have no ultimate practical responsibility for their writings. Indeed, a change of mind is often perfectly acceptable (in the spirit of intellectual discovery and discourse) and might even lead to additions to one's publications record. In sharp contrast, actual cases concern parties' livelihoods, liberty or even their very lives. Whilst it is true that courts of law are not infallible (and that is why there is, amongst other things, a system of appeals), it is also true that they strive to do their best to achieve a just decision in the case at hand and that every effort is made to ensure that mistakes (whether in law and/or fact) are avoided.

Given the fact that theory *is*, on occasion at least, useful – and even imperative – in the context of *actual* adjudication, it seemed to me that a book that attempted to *integrate* what was best in the existing theories of adjudication into a *new theory* of adjudication that reflected (as far as is possible) what *actually* transpires in practice would be a worthwhile project: hence, the present book.

As I describe in the first chapter of this book, I devote the second and third chapters of this book to important theoretical concepts as well as the issues of theoretical frameworks and objectivity, respectively. They set the stage for the discussion of specific theories of adjudication. These are the subject of the fourth to ninth chapters, and an overview of all these chapters may be found in the first chapter of the present book.

The tenth – and final – chapter attempts to set out a proposed (and new) theory of adjudication. It comprises two main parts. The first focuses on the *institutional values* that are fundamental to the adjudicative process, whilst the second sets out the *practical and theoretical factors* that courts ought to consider in arriving at their respective decisions. It is perhaps appropriate at this particular juncture to note that my proposed theory of adjudication is unlike any of the theories considered in the preceding six chapters. In particular, it does not attempt to posit a comprehensive substantive theory based on metaphysical objectivity but, instead, focuses (as just alluded to above) on a *procedural* theory based on procedural (or epistemic) objectivity. It subscribes to the view that there is no perfect theory that enables lawyers and judges to predict precisely the *substantive outcomes* of cases (if nothing else, because the possible fact situations are myriad). I nevertheless emphasise the need to avoid artificially (and unhelpfully) distinguishing procedure from substance. At appropriate junctures in the present book (in particular, and not surprisingly, in this final chapter), I am at pains to point out how procedure and substance *interact* and that the proposed theory of adjudication, which focuses on procedure, will aid in achieving just and fair *substantive outcomes* as well. Indeed, this is precisely what takes place in *practice*. It is important, however, to reiterate that the proposed theory of adjudication *does* take into account aspects of the *other* theories which are both theoretically sound and practically useful, and these are acknowledged at appropriate junctures in this final chapter.

It has been a labour of love producing the present book. As mentioned at the outset of this *Preface*, I have always been fond of as well as intensely interested in theory. This project enabled me to revisit the legal literature that I had hitherto been familiar with and (perhaps more importantly) catch up, so to speak, with the voluminous literature that had been published since I last engaged seriously with jurisprudence and legal theory. It has nevertheless been a 'painful' experience as well. I had to literally review as well as read literally tens of thousands of pages from hundreds of books and articles. In many ways, though, little had changed. With respect, the bulk of the literature concerned was still too abstract and abstruse and consequently did not reflect accurately the true adjudicative process. This is not to state that they were not interesting (on occasion, even intensely interesting) theoretical chestnuts that exercised one's mind. However, on a practical level, there was, with respect, much to be desired. I have therefore sifted through the material to locate what seemed to me were of particular importance to the *practice* of adjudication.

I have also sought to be simple – albeit not simplistic. To this end, I have focused – first and foremost – on the actual primary writings of the respective jurists themselves. This was especially important because too much attention to the secondary writings would not only have increased the length of the respective chapters inordinately but would have also (and more importantly) muddied the main points sought to be explored in the chapters themselves. Even the chapters on Professor Dworkin's theory of adjudication are – in my view at least – quite compact despite being the lengthiest part of this book. Indeed, many doctoral dissertations (at least potential books in themselves!) could be (and in fact have been) written on various aspects of Dworkin's theory of adjudication (as well as his political theory). In order to retain the focus of the present book, I have had to be particularly attentive to the need to prevent unnecessary 'clutter' and to ensure that the roadmap that I had set out in the very first chapter of this book was adhered to in a reasonable fashion in order to 'transport' the reader to the ultimate 'destination' that is the focus of the final chapter of the present book.

It is hoped that this book will be of interest to students, lawyers and judges. Indeed, jurisprudence and legal philosophy is not, I believe, a popular subject in law schools (and all the more when it is a compulsory subject). This is probably due – in part at least – to the fact that it is viewed as too abstract and abstruse, having little to do with the practice of law, which is the reason why they enrolled in law school in the first place. It is also hoped that the present book will be of special interest to aspiring judges as well as judicial colleges.

In completing this project, I have incurred several debts of gratitude to a great many individuals (many of whom are or were eminent judges). I express my gratitude to all of them in the *Acknowledgments*. I would like, in particular, to express my deepest gratitude, first, to Kate Whetter and her team at Hart Publishing for endorsing this project. I would also like to express my deep gratitude to the Honourable the Chief Justice Sundaresh Menon for all his encouragement as well as for writing the *Foreword* to the present book. Perhaps my deepest debt of gratitude is, first, to the Lord for providing me the wisdom, strength and insight to complete a book that also acknowledges the very pluralistic nature of the project itself, as well as to my wonderful family who encouraged me at every step of the way. In particular, I would like to thank my wife, Sock Yong, for her love and tangible care as well as for her wise advice (rendered even more precious as well as remarkable by the fact that she is not a lawyer). I would also like to thank my elder daughter, Rachel (now herself a legal academic in her own right), who provided me with valuable comments and suggestions not only on substance but also on the presentation of specific arguments. My younger daughter, Christine (a wonderfully gifted artist who has combined her artistic talents together with psychology to minister to others in need), provided the wonderful cover illustration to this book, capturing the pith and marrow of the project in a striking and marvellously designed image.

However, all substantive faults and infelicities in language remain my own.

Andrew Phang
October 2025

ACKNOWLEDGEMENTS

The present book would not have been possible without the support and encouragement of a great many individuals.

My family, as always, has been an amazing pillar of support. As detailed in the *Preface*, each one of them has in fact contributed directly to this book – in relation to both its spirit and content (including the cover image itself).

I would also like to express my gratitude to the Honourable the Chief Justice Sundaresh Menon for his encouragement and support as well as for writing the *Foreword* to this book.

I am also grateful to a great many individuals who provided much-needed information and/or who read various parts of this work and provided many valuable comments and suggestions, which greatly improved this work. In particular, Justice David Foxton provided many detailed and helpful comments; this was all the more remarkable given the rapidity with which he read and analysed the manuscript. Likewise, Professor Liz Fisher was not only equally rapid in her response but also made several valuable suggestions in relation to the structure of the book itself – all of which have made this book much more accessible to the reader. Many other individuals also contributed substantially to the book, but the constraints of space will not permit me to set out their invaluable help in detail; they are (in alphabetical order): Mr Goh Yihan, Justice Michelle Gordon, Justice Kenneth Hayne, Justice Kwek Mean Luck, Professor Lee Pey Woan, Professor James Lee, Mr Keeron Lee, Ms Angela Lim, Justice Nallini Pathmanathan, Justice Anselmo Reyes, Professor Natalie Skead, Professor Sandy Steel, Associate Professor Tan Zhong Xing, Mr Damien Teo, Professor Tham Chee Ho, and Ms Carol Yap.

I would also like to thank Mr Ezra Lim Pin and Mr Neo Yu Fan for excellent research assistance.

I would like to express my gratitude to Ms Kate Whetter, Ms Verity Stuart, Ms Linda Goss and their wonderful team at Hart Publishing. I thank them for the foresight and encouragement that they displayed in taking on this book project and for all the professionalism and hard work that went into bringing this book to fruition.

Last but not least, I would like to thank Mr Chris Harrison, whose able editing made the book much better than it would otherwise have been.

CONTENTS

PART III
TOWARDS A NEW THEORY OF ADJUDICATION

PART I

Introduction and Fundamental Concepts

1

Introduction: An Overview of this Book

I. The Impetus for this Book

The impetus for this book arose from the fact that I have almost uniquely been on both sides of the fence, so to speak. Indeed, my career in the law may be divided into two (approximately equal) halves. I was a legal academic for close to a quarter of a century and during that time, taught jurisprudence and legal philosophy (which, as I elaborate upon in the Preface, was also my favourite subject in law school). For the next 18 years or so thereafter, I was on the Bench and, contrary to what I had initially thought, discovered that theoretical reflection and analysis – particularly from a conceptual perspective – was (as I also elaborate upon in the Preface) not only useful but also, on occasion, even imperative from a *practical* point of view. However, there was a second discovery as well – that much of the theoretical writings I had been enamoured of in the past as a student and then as a legal academic, whilst intellectually interesting and even challenging, were rife with convoluted reasoning that had, with respect, no practical value whatsoever (and which perhaps explains in large part why many law students do not enjoy jurisprudence and legal philosophy and/or do not see any practical value in them).

Recognising that theory *is*, on occasion at least, useful and even imperative in the context of *actual adjudication*, it seemed to me that a book that attempted to *integrate* what was best in the existing theories of adjudication as well as some theoretical propositions derived from my own experience as a judge into a *new theory* of adjudication that reflects (as far as is possible) what *actually* transpires in *practice* would be a worthwhile project. Whilst I realise that there is no *perfect* theory of adjudication, most of the existing theories on offer are not wholly off the mark. However, as I hope to demonstrate, most (unfortunately) capture only one aspect of judging as it occurs in *practice*.

It also occurred to me that insufficient focus has been placed on what seems to me to be one of the key practical concepts when one engages in actual judging – the *attitudinal aspect*. Put simply, what ideals underlie the judicial process, and how does that impact the manner in which judges approach the tasks at hand? The present work therefore focuses on this aspect as a vital element in the adjudicative process and demonstrates how it makes up for any *theoretical* deficit that necessarily arises from the fact that no perfect theory of adjudication is possible.

In summary, I hope to *integrate* both theory *and* practice in order to posit a *new theory* of adjudication that is at once both theoretically sound *and* practically useful. In particular, I will (especially in, albeit not limited to, the final chapter of this book) illustrate the salient points from *actual cases* (I was, in fact, part of many of the panels concerned which rendered these decisions[1]). To the best of my knowledge, this last-mentioned approach is unusual (perhaps even unique) in the context of books on theories of adjudication.

Before turning to a brief summary of the chapters in the present book, a short note on the continuing importance of theory might be apposite.

II. The Continuing Importance of Theory

There have been numerous *theories* of adjudication in the common law context. There is, understandably, some skepticism – especially amongst *practising* lawyers and judges. However, there continues to be great interest, particularly in the search for an ideal theory of adjudication, and this is rightly so for a number of reasons.

The first is that a particular *theory* is, by definition, not only *normative*[2] in nature but also *universal*. Put simply, it furnishes us with a central organising principle which aids us in the *practice* of adjudication. However, the fundamental difficulty is that, given the complexity of the world in general and the myriad facts to which any given legal rule or principle[3] might be applied in particular, it is (at least in my view) *impossible* to postulate an even close to *perfect* theory. That having been said, the present book is an attempt to set out a theoretical framework for adjudication that, whilst imperfect, makes up for any theoretical deficit by laying down guidance that is *practical* and, hence, useful to both judges and lawyers who go about their daily work.

The second – and closely related – reason is that, try as we might, there is no way of avoiding theory. Put bluntly, even an approach which avows that a

[1] However, all discussion will be based on the text of the respective judgments themselves, the judgments being documents of public record.

[2] Though *cf* certain theories proffered by, for example, legal positivists and legal realists who insist that their respective *theories* are nevertheless only *descriptive* in nature. I would respectfully disagree with such an approach and deal with this point at appropriate junctures in the present book (see, especially, chs 4 and 9 in this volume).

[3] The distinction between rules on the one hand and principles on the other is an important one that will be explored in a future chapter (when we deal with the theory of adjudication propounded by Professor Ronald Dworkin, as to which see, especially, ch 6 whilst reference may also be made to chs 7 and 8 in this volume).

theoretical framework is not possible is *itself* a theoretical framework. If the argument is that this is a purely *logical* process, my simple response is that all *intelligible* discourse is *necessarily* logical and that whilst logic is not the only consideration, it is a necessary and integral prerequisite to intelligible discourse.

However, arriving at the aforementioned theoretical framework requires patience. It involves, as the reader will soon note, a step-by-step approach – beginning with the most basic concepts. Before proceeding to do so, perhaps a short note on the approach adopted in the present book might be appropriate.

III. A Note on the Approach Adopted in this Book

Whilst I have been – and will always be – fascinated by legal theory and philosophy, there is a sense in which this fascinating branch of legal studies must also serve a more general as well as practical purpose. Most of the writings in this field are (perhaps understandably and with respect) extremely involved at best and turgid as well as confusing at worst. The present work attempts to steer a middle course between the Scylla of theoretical abstruseness and the Charybdis of simplistic legal formalism. It is a truly formidable task indeed – to be simple without being simplistic.

To this end (and given the constraints of space), I will attempt to focus on the common law in general and the main legal theories that appear to be most relevant to legal practice in particular. I will also endeavour to outline the basic contours of each theory *as they apply to the specific task of adjudication*. I will specifically address the respective strengths and weaknesses of the relevant elements of the theory concerned. In the process of fulfilling this task, I have (as is to be expected) read very widely as well as comprehensively but will cite only those academic works that are the most relevant to the task at hand. In this regard, I have focused on extracting the very essence of each theory as it applies to adjudication and have attempted to set it out in as comprehensible a fashion for the reader as possible. This serves two purposes.

The first has in fact already been mentioned – to facilitate the reader's understanding. This leads to the second – having laid down the foundation of the theory in question, I then proceed to extract the most useful (especially *practical*) elements that will constitute part of the *separate and new theory of adjudication*, which is the main focus of the present book.

It should be noted, however, that I also refer to scholarly work in other fields – principally in the field of philosophy. This is not surprising in view of the fact that theoretical as well as conceptual discourse necessarily entails a multidisciplinary perspective. This is especially true for the next two chapters, which deal with basic and general concepts (which I elaborate upon briefly in the next part).

Let us now turn to a summary of the chapters in the present book.

IV. A Summary of the Chapters in the Present Book

A. Part I – Introduction and Fundamental Concepts

The very first chapter in this first Part (Part I) of the book is, of course, the present chapter. The remaining two chapters in this Part deal with the vital building blocks that will inform the discourse in the remaining parts of this work.

Hence, in the next (and first substantive) chapter (chapter two[4]) of this work, I deal with *various elements and concepts* that are traditionally part of the adjudicative process. I first examine the distinction between the normative[5] and the descriptive.[6] This distinction finds expression most notably in the court's *application* of the relevant *rules and principles* (which are *normative*) to the relevant *facts* of the case (which are *descriptive* in nature). Indeed, even at this early point in the book, I will also demonstrate – through illustrations from the case law – how *practical* the aforementioned distinction is.

I also examine the distinction between *procedure or process* on the one hand and *result* on the other. As I have observed elsewhere, '[t]he rules and principles which constitute the *doctrine* of the law are not ends in themselves but are, rather, the means through which the courts arrive at *substantively fair* outcomes in the cases before them in *every* area of the law'.[7] This is an important distinction because, as I have further observed:[8]

> [N]either is more important than the other. In other words, the desire to arrive at a fair outcome does not mean that the courts can manipulate legal doctrine in an arbitrary fashion. … [a]ny attempt to manipulate them in order to arrive at a predetermined result would be both artificial as well as unacceptable, and would instead lead to a loss of legitimacy in the law in the eyes of both the legal profession as well as the public alike. … On the other hand, legal doctrine is not an end itself. Its primary function is to guide the court, in a reasoned fashion, to arrive at a *fair result* in the case before it.

Indeed, as we shall see, different theories of adjudication tend to emphasise either procedure or process on the one hand or result on the other. In point of fact (as I have observed):[9]

> I would prefer viewing doctrine and fairness as an *interactive* process, although the attainment of a fair result in each case is the ultimate aim of the court.

[4] See ch 2 in this volume.

[5] Colloquially referred to as the 'ought'.

[6] Colloquially referred to as the 'is'.

[7] See A Phang, 'Doctrine and Fairness in the Law of Contract' (2009) 29 *Legal Studies* 534, 535 (emphasis in the original text). I should add that by the reference to 'doctrine', I refer not only to the rules and principles of the law *per se* but also to their *application* to the facts of the case at hand.

[8] ibid 535–536 (emphasis in the original text).

[9] ibid 537 (emphasis in the original text).

Put simply, the process of legal reasoning and the sense of the justice of the case at hand, whilst part of the *judge's experience*, are simultaneously *quite different* but must, in the final analysis, somehow be *integrated* together in as holistic a fashion as possible.

I next deal with the (*closely related*) concept of *fairness* and explain why it is so intractable, inasmuch as it is, in my view, impossible to capture in any one theory of adjudication. Yet, it is fundamental because it is crucial to the entire point of judging in the first place. However, the *justificatory problems* are numerous and multifarious, as I hope to demonstrate in the next chapter.

Finally, I deal with what I consider to be a fundamental part of any theory of adjudication – the *attitudinal* aspect (which one author has described as an attitude of *good faith*[10]). Indeed, I view this to be *the key concept* in the theory of adjudication proffered in the present book because it helps *to make up for the theoretical deficits of the various theories of adjudication*. This will, in fact, be the focus of the final chapter of the present book.

Whilst still on the topic of general concepts, I deal (in the next chapter (chapter three[11])) with the topics of *theoretical frameworks as well as the concept of objectivity*. In this latter regard, I deal head-on with the issue as to whether objectivity in the law is possible to begin with. My first basic thesis in this chapter is (as already alluded to above) that whilst it is impossible to achieve a *perfect* theoretical framework, such frameworks are nevertheless still necessary. The second basic thesis is that objectivity in the law is not only possible but also utterly necessary. On a related note, I deal with the distinction between 'concepts' on the one hand and 'conceptions' on the other and attempt to ascertain whether this distinction aids in the quest for objectivity amidst controversy as to what the right answer is in the case at hand. Indeed, this is, as we shall see, a key element in Professor Ronald Dworkin's theory of adjudication.[12]

I then proceed, in the subsequent six chapters, to describe what I consider to be the major theories of adjudication currently on offer in the common law world. This constitutes Part II of the present book.

B. Part II – Theories of Adjudication Considered

The first chapter in Part II of the present book (chapter four[13]) deals with adjudication in the context of *legal positivism*, primarily as encompassed within the arguments by that great doyen of legal philosophy, Professor HLA Hart. This

[10] See SJ Burton, *Judging in Good Faith* (Cambridge, Cambridge University Press, 1992). Reference may also be made to RH Fallon, 'Arguing in Good Faith about the Constitution: Ideology, Methodology, and Reflective Equilibrium' (2017) 84 *University of Chicago Law Review* 123.

[11] See ch 3 in this volume.

[12] See generally chs 6, 7 and 8 in this volume.

[13] See ch 4 in this volume.

particular chapter examines Hart's basic thesis that the legal system comprises a system of rules and that, when the rules do not furnish the court with an answer to the issues at hand, the court is entitled to exercise its discretion in order to arrive at its decision. The emphasis appears to be on *procedure or process* as opposed to the result. Legal positivism is not without benefits: in particular, its quite correct emphasis on rules in the context of the role they play in legal doctrine (a staple, indeed essential, legal diet of both lawyer and judge). However, I also point out the difficulties with legal positivism – especially its insistence (pursuant to the theory that is the focus of that chapter at least (ie, that of Professor HLA Hart)) on a rigidly descriptive view of the law.

The next chapter (chapter five[14]) examines various theories of adjudication premised on *natural law*. In *contrast* to legal positivism, a natural law approach towards adjudication appears to emphasise *the result*. This is not surprising because natural law theories tend to emphasise *morality and fairness*, and, hence, a moral and fair *result* is often paramount. Further, a *religious* natural law theory would *also differ* from legal positivism inasmuch as it would be premised not (at least solely) on human reasoning as such but would involve guidance from *God* as well. I should add, though, that apart from, perhaps, Professor Lon L Fuller, most of the natural law theories do not really deal with adjudication as such, although each theory does implicate the judicial process (albeit on a more macro level[15]). At this juncture, I should also mention that I will be touching briefly on the natural law theory of Professor John Finnis. I acknowledge the benefits of natural law – in particular, its emphasis on the need to achieve a just and fair result in the case concerned as well as its focus (especially in its modern form) on the rule of law (especially per Fuller). However, I also consider the difficulties with that theory, in particular, during the present (pluralistic) times in which we find ourselves (I have in mind, in particular, classical natural law theory, which requires one to acknowledge, first and foremost, the concept of God).

In chapters six, seven and eight, I consider one of the most influential modern theories of adjudication – that of Professor Dworkin.[16] His theory is interesting because it not only constitutes a trenchant critique of legal positivism but also avoids a wholly natural law approach as well. Put simply, Dworkin attempts to *straddle* both of the aforementioned legal theories. Whether he does so successfully will be the focus of these particular chapters in the present work. Even at this very preliminary juncture, however, I will point to two specific points that Dworkin makes that are of vital importance to the judicial process. The first is his vigorous as well as rigorous defence of the concept of objectivity (which, as we shall see, is attacked by jurists that are the subject of chapter nine). The second relates to the distinction he draws between principle on the one hand and policy on the other.

[14] See ch 5 in this volume.

[15] With perhaps the possible exception of what I term 'Classical Natural Law Theory' where God is the ultimate source of wisdom and guidance, which wisdom and guidance would, I assume, extend to the more specific sphere of adjudication as well.

[16] See chs 6, 7 and 8 in this volume.

I must confess that, as a law teacher, I was rather critical of this distinction only to find (later as a judge) how vital a role it played in the judicial process. Indeed, I arrive at the conclusion in this book that Dworkin's theory is closest to what occurs in practice today. Not surprisingly, therefore, it is the lengthiest part of the present book. In particular, Dworkin's emphasis on the concept of 'principles' as well as his equally strong emphasis on objectivity in general and the concept of a uniquely correct answer in every case in particular are both noteworthy and practically useful. However (and as to be expected), there are many difficulties with his theory as well. Even so, there are still benefits to be gleaned: for example, his rejection of one conception of the concept of 'policy' is persuasive, although I argue that there is another conception of that concept that may nevertheless be (and has in fact been) utilised by the courts. I should mention that there are two reasons why I deal with Dworkin's theory of adjudication in three separate chapters (which, collectively, constitute a major part of the present book). The first is (as just mentioned) that his is the theory of adjudication that comes closest to depicting what occurs in practice. The second is that his theory was developed and modified as well as refined over a period of almost three and a half decades through several books and essays. This necessitated a detailed as well as careful unpacking and analysis of Dworkin's various concepts and theory as they unfolded over the years.

In chapter nine, I examine three main branches of theories, two of which stem from the *American* context.[17] The first is *Legal Realism* and the second (and more modern one) is *Critical Legal Studies* – and both stem from movements in legal philosophy in America. The third is *Marxian Theory*. What all these theories have in common is what I would term *a total skepticism of (even cynicism towards) the law in general and legal adjudication in particular*. I will seek to demonstrate why, in the final analysis, despite persuasive points of critique of the legal system as it currently operates, all these theories are, in the final analysis, too abstract as well as too corrosive, disorientating and dispiriting and should therefore be rejected. In fairness, though, one theory – American Realism – is nevertheless useful in reminding us of the importance of the role of *facts* but, for the most part, it and the other two theories considered in this chapter are far too negative and disempowering to be of any practical use. However, they needed to be considered not just for completeness but also to furnish the reader with a balanced account of the various theories of adjudication.

C. Part III – Towards a New Theory of Adjudication

In the final chapter of this book (chapter ten[18]), I propose a 'new' theory of adjudication. The word 'new' is in quotation marks for two reasons.

[17] See ch 9 in this volume.
[18] See ch 10 in this volume.

First, my proposed theory is *not*, strictly speaking, 'new' inasmuch as it endorses all but the most skeptical of the theories of adjudication presently on offer. However, it does not seek to reconcile them because they cannot be reconciled. Yet, most of them offer us an accurate snapshot of the judicial process (albeit only from a single and thus limited angle).

Second, my proposed theory is, looked at in another light, 'new' because it emphasises (in the first part of the theory itself) the *attitudinal approach* that (as alluded to earlier in the present chapter) can *make up for the theoretical deficits* in the other theories of adjudication. Indeed, to the best of my knowledge, there is only one work that adopts something akin to this approach.[19] However, it is also of the first importance to emphasise that the aforementioned attitudinal approach is simultaneously undergirded by *substantive content* (this is dealt with in the second part of the theory). Nevertheless, because (apart from the so-called easy cases) of the myriad facts that are part of each case, *traditional* theories tend to be too straitjacketed inasmuch as they posit a comprehensive solution that simply does not ring true in the practical sphere. That having been said, because the line between procedural justice and substantive justice is (as we shall see in a subsequent chapter[20]) a *very fine* one *and* that, *in practice, both* indeed *interact* with each other, the theory that is mooted in this book is *not* one that is *merely process-oriented*. Indeed, the proposed theory of adjudication which focuses on procedure will aid in achieving just and fair *substantive outcomes* as well.

As already alluded to earlier in this chapter, I will also be *illustrating* my proposed theory by reference to *actual decisions*.[21] It is hoped that such an approach will lend a real practical bent to what might otherwise be perceived as mere abstract propositions (which is indeed the principal general criticism of theoretical work).[22]

[19] See Burton (n 10).
[20] See ch 2 in this volume.
[21] See also the text to n 1, above.
[22] Though *cf* EW Thomas, *The Judicial Process – Realism, Pragmatism, Practical Reasoning and Principles* (Cambridge, Cambridge University Press, 2005). Reference may also be made to A Barak, *Judicial Discretion* (New Haven, Yale University Press, 1989) and, by the same author, *Purposive Interpretation in Law* (Princeton, Princeton University Press, 2005) as well as *The Judge In A Democracy* (Princeton, Princeton University Press, 2006).

2

Fundamental Concepts

I. Introduction

In the present chapter, I deal with two pairs of fundamental concepts. They are fundamental because they are not merely theoretical in nature but also constitute the basic building blocks not only in a theoretical context but also in a practical one as well.

The first pair of concepts is one that distinguishes between the *descriptive* on the one hand and the *prescriptive or normative*[1] on the other. The former relates to the sphere of an *existing* state of affairs, which, by its very nature, ought to be susceptible of description. On the other hand, the latter relates to propositions that have *universal* application. Not surprisingly, therefore, *theoretical concepts* are *necessarily* normative in character. It might also be noted that this distinction is also popularly referred to as one that distinguishes the 'is' from the 'ought'.

The second pair of concepts is one that sets out the relationship between *procedure* on the one hand and *result* on the other. In this regard, the distinction is often drawn between procedural justice on the one hand and substantive justice on the other.

II. The Descriptive and the Prescriptive

Although seemingly obvious, the distinction between the descriptive and the prescriptive[2] is not only theoretically important but also practically useful as well. Put simply, this distinction states that one cannot derive a prescriptive or normative proposition (that, *ex hypothesi*, applies *universally*) from a *specific descriptive or factual set of circumstances.* As Professor Max Black put it, 'no

[1] The general literature on the concept of 'normativity' is (understandably) enormous: see, eg, JJ Thomson, *Normativity* (Chicago, Open Court, 2008); J Stelmach, B Brożek and M Hohol (eds), *The Many Faces of Normativity* (Kraków, Copernicus Center Press, 2013); and G Marchetti and S Marchetti (eds), *Facts and Values: The Ethics and Metaphysics of Normativity* (New York, Routledge, 2017). For a valuable collection in the specific context of the law, see KE Himma, M Jovanović and B Spaić, *Unpacking Normativity: Conceptual, Normative and Descriptive Issues* (Oxford, Hart Publishing, 2018). Reference may also be made to S Bertea, *The Normative Claim of Law* (Oxford, Hart Publishing, 2009).

[2] Often also described (as noted above) as the distinction between the 'is' and the 'ought'.

normative statement can follow from exclusively factual premises'.[3] This distinction is popularly referred to as 'Hume's Guillotine' (after the views of the famous Scottish philosopher, David Hume).[4] It is important to note that the distinction is based on *logic* and, viewed from that perspective, is a powerful one. To take a simple illustration, just because a specific action results in the same outcome nine hundred and ninety-nine times, it nevertheless does *not necessarily* follow (as a matter of *logic*) that there is therefore a *universal* rule (that, *ex hypothesi*, is prescriptive or normative in nature) that that action *will* result in the same outcome on the thousandth time. One way around 'Hume's Guillotine' is to derive a prescriptive or normative proposition from prescriptive or normative (as opposed to descriptive or factual) premises. That is, for example, the approach adopted generally by natural law. However, the natural law approach itself engenders (as we shall see) difficulties of its own.[5]

As already alluded to, the distinction between the descriptive and the prescriptive is also *practically* useful. I will illustrate this particular point by way of a few examples from both case law and legal scholarship.

In Singapore, the less serious criminal cases are tried in the State Courts. There is an appeal as of right to the General Division of the High Court. However, for reasons of finality, no further appeal is permitted to the Court of Appeal (which is the highest appellate court in Singapore). An exception is made, however, where there is a question of law of public interest that is required to be clarified by the Court of Appeal. A further condition is that this point of law must simultaneously affect the decision in the case concerned. In order to prevent, amongst other things, backdoor appeals, the Court of Appeal distinguishes between questions of 'law' of public interest and what are cleverly (or often not so cleverly) disguised questions of 'fact'. One sees here the importance in this particular context of the distinction between the prescriptive on the one hand and the descriptive on the other. And this is how the Court of Appeal set out the distinction in order to provide guidance for both courts and counsel alike:[6]

> As a matter of principle, the courts must determine whether there is sufficient generality embedded within a proposition posed by the question which is more than just descriptive but also contains normative force for it to qualify as a question of law; a question which has, at its heart, a proposition which is descriptive and specific to the case at hand is merely a question of fact.

[3] See M Black, 'The "Factual" and the "Normative"' in K Kuypers (ed), *Human Sciences and the Problem of Values* (The Hague, Martinus Nijhoff, 1972) 56.

[4] This term appears to have been coined by Professor Max Black: see M Black, 'The Gap Between "Is" and "Should"' (1964) 73 *The Philosophical Review* 165, 166. See also Black (n 3) 56.

[5] See ch 5 in this volume. See also generally B Donnelly, *A Natural Law Approach to Normativity* (Aldershot, Ashgate, 2007).

[6] *Public Prosecutor v Teo Chu Ha* [2014] 4 *Singapore Law Reports* 600, [31].

Another illustration – this time in the sphere of private law – relates to that vexed topic of contractual illegality.[7] As I have observed elsewhere, the law relating to illegality and public policy is 'confused (and confusing)'.[8] A key difficulty which faces the courts is the fact that no one legal structure (whether theoretical or doctrinal) can wholly eradicate the intractable problems that bedevil this particular area of the common law of contract. Indeed, the very doctrine of illegality and public policy itself rests on the theoretical premise that where the illegality concerned is such as to result in actual harm to the wider public interest, this justifies the court concerned in overriding the parties' individual contractual rights. At the risk of oversimplification, the community's welfare surpasses the contracting parties' individual rights, and, at the risk of further oversimplification, it would appear that utilitarian considerations defeat individual rights.

There has – not surprisingly, perhaps – been doctrinal disagreement as well. For example, the majority in the UK Supreme Court, in *Patel v Mirza*,[9] adopted an entirely new approach towards contractual illegality (albeit only in relation to common law illegality) by adopting a 'range of factors approach', whereas the minority adopted a rule-based approach. The former approach confers discretion on the court to decide whether to permit recovery notwithstanding the presence of an illegal contract. The minority would not permit recovery pursuant to the illegal contract but may permit recovery under established exceptions. In the Singapore Court of Appeal decision of *Ochroid Trading Ltd v Chua Siok Lui*,[10] the Court did not follow the approach of the majority in *Patel v Mirza*.

It is not my purpose in the present chapter to revisit these decisions[11] – save on one specific point about the meaning to be attributed to the concept of *reliance*. The understanding of reliance in the context of an illegal contract may have implications for other areas of the law, such as the law of trusts.[12] The understanding of reliance in this context is a specific illustration of how useful an apparently simple theoretical distinction may operate in the practical sphere. This is, of course, the distinction between the descriptive on the one hand and the prescriptive (or normative) on the other.

Put simply, the concept of 'reliance' can be used in either a descriptive or a normative sense. To elaborate, the proposition that, even when the claimant is relying on an independent legal course of action (for example, pursuant to the law

[7] I draw here from my article: see A Phang, 'The Importance of Theory and History in Understanding and Developing the Common Law of Contract – Some Preliminary Reflections' (2023) 1 *Contract and Commercial Law Review* 67, 84–87.

[8] See A Phang, 'Of Illegality and Presumptions – Australian Departures and Possible Approaches' (1996) 11 *Journal of Contract Law* 53, 53.

[9] *Patel v Mirza* [2017] AC 467.

[10] *Ochroid Trading Ltd v Chua Siok Lui* [2018] 1 *Singapore Law Reports* 363.

[11] See generally A Phang, 'Illegality and Public Policy' in ch 13 of A Phang (gen ed), *The Law of Contract in Singapore*, 2nd edn (Singapore, Academy Publishing, 2022) vol 1, especially paras 13.015–13.018, 13.124–13.132, 13.170–13.175 and 13.186–13.189.

[12] See, in particular, the House of Lords decision in *Tinsley v Milligan* [1994] 1 AC 340.

of tort) to recover by way of restitution amounts paid under the illegal contract, that claimant is nevertheless still to be taken as having 'relied' on the illegal contract because reference must be had to the illegal contract is a proposition that, whilst literally true, is not necessarily true when viewed from a normative perspective. Insofar as this last-mentioned point is concerned, whilst it might be stated that the claimant, in pursuing an independent legal cause of action (in, say, tort), must necessarily refer (literally and descriptively) to the illegal contract, he or she is not 'relying' on the illegal contract insofar as his or her legal cause of action is concerned. The claimant is 'relying' – insofar as the legal (or normative or prescriptive) claim is concerned – on a cause of action in tort law, and not on the illegal contract as such. Such an approach is helpful because the courts (and legal academics) need no longer be mired in the concern that there is 'reliance' even though the claimant is not founding his or her legal cause of action on the illegal contract itself. Whilst there might be literal or descriptive reliance in this last-mentioned regard, that is wholly irrelevant and immaterial from the perspective of 'reliance' in the prescriptive or normative sense.

To take this illustration further, suppose that the claimant has no legal recourse other than 'reliance' on the illegal contract itself; then the result is that that claimant would be 'relying' not only literally on the illegal contract but also prescriptively and normatively on the same as well. And it is this latter sense of (prescriptive or normative) 'reliance' that is proscribed simply because that would, in substance if not form, be an enforcement of the illegal contract itself – which would be entirely inconsistent with the prohibition of the contract under law in the first instance.

Indeed, the approach (which rests on the distinction between descriptive or literal 'reliance' and prescriptive or normative 'reliance') was one that was adopted in the *Ochroid Trading* case.[13] Specifically, in the *Ochroid Trading* case,[14] the court drew a useful distinction between the concept of 'reliance' in a formal or procedural manner and the concept of 'reliance' which is to be properly understood in a normative or substantive sense. As the court observed:[15]

> In our view, much of the confusion in this area can be avoided if it is recognised that there are, in fact, two different conceptions of 'reliance' which must be disengaged. First, there is reliance in the procedural or formal sense, as applied in the cases of *Bowmakers* [*v Barnet Instruments Ltd* [1945] 1 KB 65] and [*Tinsley v Milligan* [1994] 1 AC 340], which is triggered whenever the plaintiff has to assert, whether by way of pleading or evidence, the illegal acts and therefore (literally) rely on the illegal contract. This is a wholly separate and looser concept of 'reliance' from the distinct conception of the reliance principle as a normative or substantive principle which is only engaged when a plaintiff seeks to enforce, and thereby profit from, the illegal contract through his claim. Such a claim is legally impermissible, in our judgment, because it offends

[13] I draw here gratefully from Phang (n 11) paras 13.171 and 13.173–13.175.
[14] [2018] 1 *Singapore Law Reports* 363.
[15] [2018] 1 *Singapore Law Reports* 363, [128]–[129] (emphasis in the original text omitted).

> the fundamental principle that that there can be no recovery under a contract that is prohibited on the basis of illegality.
>
> However, when the plaintiff 'relies' on an independent cause of action in order to successfully establish a restitutionary claim, such 'reliance' is inoffensive from a normative point of view, even if it could be said that the plaintiff needs to 'rely' on his illegal conduct (in a loose and indirect sense). The claim does not offend the principle underlying the illegality doctrine as restitution does not allow the plaintiff to profit from the illegal contract but simply puts the parties in the position they would have been if they had never entered into the illegal transaction. Indeed, as noted earlier, (restitutionary) recovery through an independent cause of action is the flipside of the 'reliance principle' (in the normative sense) as it involves a situation where the illegal contract is *not* being invoked or 'relied on' in any substantive legal manner.

Put simply, a claim in unjust enrichment[16] would not offend the principle underlying the illegality doctrine, even if it could be said that the plaintiff needed literally to 'rely' on his or her illegal conduct (in a loose, indirect, and literal sense), as the claim would not allow the plaintiff to profit from the illegal contract but would simply put the parties in the position they would have been if they had never entered into the illegal transaction.[17] Indeed, the distinction referred to in the preceding paragraph was also supported by the views expressed by Lord Mance and (especially) Lord Sumption in *Patel v Mirza* – a point emphasised by the court in the *Ochroid Trading* case.[18]

That the above distinction conduces towards clarity cannot, it is submitted, be doubted. Once it is understood that only a normative or substantive 'reliance' on the impugned contract would suffice to cause the claimant to fall foul of the reliance principle, the fact that a claimant 'relies' in a procedural or formal sense on the impugned contract in order, for example, to establish its claim pursuant to an independent cause of action is legally unobjectionable. Indeed, if such an approach is adopted, there is no need to have to accept what has been termed the 'no reliance theory'[19] and, still less, feel that an alternative explanation is required to reconcile that theory with the endorsement of what is essentially an independent legal course of action.[20]

The approach just considered would also, it is submitted, serve to rationalise the otherwise seemingly controversial nature of cases such as *Tinsley v Milligan*[21] and *Bowmakers v Barnet Instruments Ltd.*[22]

[16] Or, indeed, any other independent legal cause of action (for example, pursuant to the law of tort).
[17] See generally [2018] 1 *Singapore Law Reports* 363, [128], [129] and [139].
[18] [2018] 1 *Singapore Law Reports* 363, [134]–[137].
[19] See N Enonchong, 'Title Claims and Illegal Transactions' (1995) 111 *LQR* 135, 135.
[20] As was the case in Enonchong (n 19).
[21] *Tinsley v Milligan* [1994] 1 AC 340.
[22] *Bowmakers v Barnet Instruments Ltd* [1945] 1 KB 65. See, eg, B Coote, 'Another Look at *Bowmakers v Barnet Instruments*' (1972) 35 *MLR* 38; and *cf* JW Carter, W Courtney and G Tolhurst, '*Bowmakers* Revisited – Independent Causes of Action for Restitution' (2023) 1 *Contract and Commercial Law Review* 3.

I turn now to a final illustration – this time from legal academia. And it concerns a quite different area – that of trade mark law. In particular, it has been argued that the focus in this particular area of the law should be not so much on the empirical realities (of actual consumer association and confusion) but more on the normative character of trade mark law.[23] In this way, we might avoid the 'fetish of empiricism'.[24] Such an approach is not only understandable but also laudable insofar as there is a danger that preoccupation with the empirical facts might conflate (or, worse still, even obscure) the 'broader normative concerns'[25] underlying trade mark law. Nevertheless, a note of caution is necessary inasmuch as I do not understand the learned author to be arguing that the facts of cases are unimportant simply because, at a practical level, courts are engaged in applying what they understand to be the relevant law to the relevant facts of the case concerned in order to arrive at a just and fair decision.[26]

III. Procedural Justice and Substantive Justice

The distinction between procedural justice on the one hand and substantive justice on the other is not only important from a theoretical perspective but is also of the first importance from a *practical* one as well. As I had occasion to observe in a judicial capacity:[27]

> 4 It is axiomatic that every party ought to have its day in court. This is the very embodiment of *procedural* justice. The appellation 'procedural' is important. Procedural justice is just one aspect of the holistic ideal and concept of justice itself. In the final analysis, the achievement of a substantively just result or decision is the desideratum. It is more than that, however. It is not merely an ideal. It must be a practical outcome – at least as far as the court can aid in its attainment.
>
> 5 However, the court must be extremely wary of falling into the flawed approach to the effect that 'the ends justify the means'. This ought never to be the case. The obsession with achieving a substantively fair and just outcome does not justify the utilisation of any and every means to achieve that objective. There must be fairness in the *procedure or manner* in which the final outcome is achieved.
>
> 6 Indeed, if the procedure is unjust, that will itself taint the outcome.
>
> 7 On the other hand, a just and fair procedure does *not*, in and of itself, ensure a just outcome. In other words, procedural fairness is a necessary but not sufficient condition for a fair and just result.

[23] See GB Dinwoodie, 'Trade Mark Law As A Normative Project' [2023] *Singapore Journal of Legal Studies* 305.
[24] Dinwoodie (n 23) 306, 319. And see ibid 329 (where the term 'empirical fixation' is used).
[25] ibid. See also ibid 309.
[26] See also ibid 321–322.
[27] *United Overseas Bank Ltd v Ng Huat Foundations Pte Ltd* [2005] 2 *Singapore Law Reports (Reissue)* 425, [4]–[9] (emphasis in original).

8 The quest for justice, therefore, entails a continuous need to balance the procedural with the substantive. More than that, it is a continuous attempt to ensure that both are *integrated*, as far as that is humanly possible. Both *interact* with each other. One cannot survive without the other. There must, therefore, be – as far as is possible – a fair and just procedure that leads to a fair and just result. This is not merely abstract theorising. It is the *very basis* of what the courts do – and ought to do. When in doubt, the courts would do well to keep these bedrock principles in mind. This is especially significant because, in many ways, this is how, I believe, laypersons perceive the administration of justice to be. The legitimacy of the law in their eyes must never be compromised. On the contrary, it should, as far as is possible, be enhanced.

9 It is true, however, that in the sphere of practical reality, there is often a *tension* between the need for procedural justice on the one hand and substantive justice on the other. The task of the court is to attempt, as I have pointed out in the preceding paragraph, to *resolve* this tension. There is a *further* task: it is to actually attempt, simultaneously, to *integrate* these two conceptions of justice in order that justice in its fullest orb may shine forth.

The reader would notice that, in a *practical* sphere at least, the relationship between procedural justice and substantive justice as embodied in the above quotation is one of *interaction and integration*. This is in contrast to the bright lines that are often sought to be drawn in a theoretical context. Indeed, as I hope to demonstrate in the chapters that follow, this is due in no small measure to the fact that courts are faced with an almost infinite number of fact situations to which the relevant law is to be applied and that this entails the need for the court concerned to grapple with both procedure and substance as it attempts to arrive at a just and fair outcome in the case at hand. Hence, whilst the ultimate decision that is substantively fair is the desired aim in every case, there are limits as to how far any *one* particular theory can take us. This issue is closely related to the problem of *theoretical frameworks*, which I deal with in the subsequent chapter. For present purposes, it will suffice to note that it is not so much 'substantive' theory that will aid us in understanding how courts arrive at a substantively just and fair result but, rather, the *attitudinal approach*, which consists in the court attempting its level best to decide in *good faith*.[28] This is in fact the *key concept* in the theory of adjudication proffered in the final chapter of the present book.[29] Although it is indeed a 'theory', it is much more flexible since (as just mentioned) it does not purport to set out a substantive set of conditions but focuses instead on the attitudinal approach that the court ought to adopt, regardless of the fact situation concerned (bearing in mind the fact that, as already mentioned, fact situations are *myriad* and that it is therefore difficult (if not impossible) to predict in advance what theory would *always* lead to a substantively just and fair outcome in the case concerned). It should also be emphasised that such an approach is *not merely procedural*. As just mentioned,

[28] It is important to emphasise that this is not mere empty rhetoric. As we shall see, judges are guided by qualities such as independence and impartiality (which I will touch on in the next chapter).

[29] See ch 10 in this volume.

the line between procedural justice on the one hand and substantive justice on the other is a fine one, and both *interact* with each other. The theory of adjudication that is proffered in this book is therefore one that is, when viewed holistically, *not* one that is *merely process-oriented.* This should come as no surprise because, as already mentioned, the purpose of adjudication is to arrive at an ultimate decision that is *just and fair.*

IV. Conclusion

We have considered two pairs of fundamental concepts in the present chapter. The first – which distinguishes between the descriptive and the prescriptive, is important on two significant levels. First, it serves as a caveat as to what (in particular) cannot be done when we are developing theoretical frameworks (at least where this is dependent on logic). Second, it serves – in and of itself – as a very practical tool in aiding the courts in arriving at a clear legal analysis in developing the relevant area of the law.

We also considered the relationship between procedural justice on the one hand and substantive justice on the other. Each cannot be construed – let alone applied – mechanistically, alone and apart from each other. On the contrary, they *interact* with each other, and this is something that courts and jurists must constantly bear in mind. In particular, the latter must not be too optimistic of arriving at an overarching theory that has even close to a perfect predictive effect simply because the myriad instances of factual situations and circumstances mandate a more flexible approach that has as its focus the *attitudinal* approach of the courts themselves (bearing in mind that such an approach is not merely process-oriented and that there would be a natural integration of both procedural as well as substantive justice). This particular relationship segues into larger issues that centre on the development of theoretical frameworks as well as the extremely important issue of whether or not objectivity exists (and/or ought to exist) in the adjudicative process (and, if so, how it can be achieved). These will in fact constitute the content of the following chapter – to which we now turn.

3

On Theoretical Frameworks and Objectivity

I. Introduction

The present chapter considers two vitally important theoretical issues that have a direct bearing on the core of this book.

The first relates to the issue of *theoretical frameworks*. Put simply, is it possible to arrive at a (general or universal) theory that would aid one in making sense of the myriad (specific or particular) facts in the real world? Viewed in the context of adjudication, is it possible to posit a theory of adjudication that is at once both conceptually sound (or at least persuasive) *and* practically relevant?

The second relates to the issue of *objectivity*: Is it possible to conceive of objectivity in the law? Or, as more skeptical commentators would have it,[1] is such objectivity a myth since (to put it somewhat crudely at this particular point) everything is subjective and depends, in the final analysis, on the personal (and perhaps even idiosyncratic) preferences of the judge concerned?

The ostensible simplicity of both issues belies complex (and even perplexing) questions – and it is to these questions that our attention must now turn. However, before proceeding to do so, it should be noted that one of the key concepts considered in the previous chapter – that relating to the relationship between procedural justice and substantive justice – ought to be borne in mind, as it is (as we shall see) inextricably connected to both the aforementioned issues that are considered in the present chapter.

II. The Problem of Theoretical Frameworks

As already alluded to at the outset of this chapter, is it possible to posit a theory of adjudication that is at once both conceptually sound (or at least persuasive) *and* practically relevant? It is not immediately clear that a clear answer is possible.

On the one hand, most *theories* are – by their very nature – general and abstract. If, therefore, a theory is pitched at too general a level, it might become too abstract

[1] See, in particular, ch 9 in this volume.

to be of any practical use. On the other hand, without a general theory to act as an organising framework, a court might not be able to make sense of (let alone analyse and decide on) the specific *facts* before it. This perennial tension between the general and the particular, between universals and particulars, is nothing new and may indeed be traced back to early Greek philosophy.

Lest the reader arrive at the view that the tension just mentioned is merely 'theoretical', the following illustration from an actual decision might prove instructive.

In the Singapore Court of Appeal decision of *Mühlbauer AG v Manufacturing Integration Technology Ltd*,[2] the claimant sued the defendant for infringement of its Patent. The Respondent acknowledged that its machine infringed all ten claims of the Patent. In its counterclaim, however, the Respondent contended that the Patent lacked novelty as well as any inventive step vis-à-vis the state of the art and should therefore be found to be invalid. The Court considered an important preliminary point, which it characterised in the heading of the judgment concerned as 'the importance of logic and rational argument as well as the danger of over-generalisation and over-abstraction'; in particular, it elaborated on the point as follows:[3]

> 40 The present appeal illustrates the very important *general* point to the effect that no area of the law (including that relating to patents) is exempt from the general principles of logic and rational argument. Indeed, this point is so obvious that it is often taken for granted. In this appeal, it is illustrated (especially during oral submissions before this court) by the argument by counsel for the Respondent, Mr Foo Maw Shen ('Mr Foo'), that, because the use of pick up heads was nothing new and (more importantly) because his client's patents had, in fact, more pick up heads, the Appellant's claim that the Patent was novel and embodied an inventive step must fail. Such an argument is, at first blush, admittedly persuasive. However, it is our view that Mr Foo (albeit unintentionally) has pitched the argument on behalf of his client at *too high a level of abstraction* (reference may also be made, in this regard, to the interesting paper by Tun-Jen Chiang, 'The Levels of Abstraction Problem in Patent Law' (George Mason University Law and Economics Research Paper No 09-33

[2] *Mühlbauer AG v Manufacturing Integration Technology Ltd* [2010] 2 *Singapore Law Reports* 724.

[3] ibid [40]–[43] (emphasis in the original text). See also ABL Phang, 'Constructing Theoretical Frameworks' (1988) 30 *Malaya Law Review* 211 and, by the same author, *The Development of Singapore Law – Historical and Socio-Legal Perspectives* (Singapore, Butterworths, 1990) 8–13. Reference may also be made to A D'Amato, 'Can Any Legal Theory Constrain Any Legal Decision?' (1989) 43 *University of Miami Law Review* 513 and J Husa, 'Kaleidoscopic Cultural Views and Legal Theory – Dethroning the Objectivity?' in ch 10 of J Husa and M Van Hoecke (eds), *Objectivity in Law and Legal Reasoning* (Oxford, Hart Publishing, 2013). Reference may be made, further, to Z Bańkowski and J MacLean (eds), *The Universal and the Particular in Legal Reasoning* (Aldershot, Ashgate, 2006) (which, however, despite the general title, focuses more on Professor Neil MacCormick's legal theory). And on the importance of facts and fact-finding, see KO See, *Fact-Finding and Reality: A Judicial Decision-Making Primer* (Singapore, Academy Publishing, 2022).

For more general works, see, eg, MJ Loux (ed), *Universals and Particulars: Readings in Ontology* (New York, Anchor Books, 1970) (an excellent collection) and JP Moreland, *Universals* (Montreal & Kingston, McGill-Queen's University Press, 2001).

<http://ssrn.com/abstract id=1434465>) (accessed 12 January 2010), exploring the 'correct' level of abstraction in view of the tug-of-war between a patentee's claim to a broader level of abstraction (to promote incentives) and limiting the patentee to specific embodiments (to reduce the monopoly cost of each patent)). Put simply, whilst the proposition advanced is not factually incorrect, it does not include that degree of specificity which is required under the particular principles embodied in the current law (as to which see generally [15]–[25] above). Indeed, if Mr Foo's argument is correct, *any* novelty and/or further inventive step would, literally, be (virtually, if not wholly) *impossible*. A moment's reflection would reveal that this is incorrect simply because it is *always possible* for there to be novelty and/or a further inventive step – particularly if we view the inquiry from a *qualitative* point of view. Everything would depend, in the final analysis, on the particular facts and (more importantly) the impact (if any) that the patent concerned has on the existing state of the art in that particular sphere. Indeed, one of the Respondent's arguments, as we have just seen, centred really on the *quantity* of pick up heads, rather than (as we think ought to be the case) *the overall qualitative difference (if any) between the Patent on the one hand and the patents relied on by the Respondent on the other.*

41 It is important to emphasise, at this juncture, that the use of the general principles of logic and rational argument do *not*, in any way whatsoever, undermine the *legal* principles that are germane to a particular area of the law (in this case, that relating to patents). Indeed, on one view, the legal principles themselves are the product – in part at least – of the process of logic as well as rational argument. It is no surprise, therefore, that the application and/or development of general principles of logic and rational argument must (as we shall see) be *integrated with* the particular legal principles as well. In other words, the general principles of logic and rational argument and the particular legal principles (here, in relation to the patent law) are *complementary* in nature.

42 Turning, then, to the perspective of general principle and logic, there is an irreducible tension between universality and particularity (or, to use equally clear terminology, between generality and specificity; *cf* also the decision of this court in *Spandeck Engineering (S) Pte Ltd v Defence Science & Technology Agency* [2007] 4 SLR(R) 100 at [28] (in the context of liability in negligence for pure economic loss)). However, as we shall see, this is not a tension that necessarily leads to paralysis or inaction; on the contrary, it (as we shall attempt to demonstrate in a moment) is, in fact, mediated via an *interactive process* that defines what the law and decision-making are all about in the *practical* sphere. Indeed, the unique combination (or, perhaps more appropriately, integration) of the universal and particular, of the general and the specific, and of the normative and the descriptive, produce not only decisions for the case at hand but also precedents for the future.

43 To elaborate, when an argument is pitched at too high a level of abstraction, it will probably attract no controversy (and may even achieve consensus) but, because it is at such a 'rarefied' level, it is actually unhelpful in most cases (for example, virtually all persons will agree that it is desirable to 'do good', but, of course, once we descend into the *specifics* (*ie*, what 'doing good' means to each person), the opposite extreme will be reached, with little (if any) agreement amongst all concerned). Indeed, such an approach is *especially* unhelpful in cases involving *patents*, simply because, in many cases (such as this), a necessary step involved in the court's decision entails a *comparison* of the competing patents. At this point, *specific details* must *necessarily* come into

> play. However, it is also acknowledged that the court cannot go to the other extreme in focusing only on the trees and missing the wood. This is, however, unlikely to happen in practice because the court must perforce come to *an overall conclusion*, and that would entail gathering together all the relevant (and *specific*) details *and analysing* them in the context of the applicable legal rules and principles *before* arriving at *an overall conclusion*. Here, we see the *interaction* between the universal and the particular, between generality and specificity, as well as between the descriptive and the normative. It is *not* something which can be reduced to a mechanistic formula simply because life in general and the decisions of courts (as a consequence) in particular are too complex to admit of a rigid formulaic approach. However, that does not mean that there are no *general principles* that ought to guide the court. As already mentioned, there are, of course, the general principles of logic and argumentation. More importantly, each area (as well as sub-area) of the law will also embody general legal rules and principles which are to be applied to the facts at hand. In the specific sphere of patent law, we would think that, in addition to the general legal rules and principles (embodied in ss 13, 14 and 15 of the Act; see also generally [15]–[25] above), the court would *also need to apply* those rules and principles (as well as those relating to general logic and argumentation) to the *specific claims which are contained within the patent(s) concerned*. Indeed, these claims constitute the *specific factual matrix as well as context* which the court takes into account in arriving at its decision. Again, however, it is of the first importance to emphasise that this is an *interactional* process that is not susceptible of mechanical application. Put crudely, it entails *an exercise of judgment by the court concerned in applying the general principles of law as well as logic to the facts concerned, and as understood in the context in which they occur.*

Consistent with the judicial observations just quoted, the problem of theoretical frameworks remains an intractable one – particularly at the conceptual level. The main aim must surely be to posit a theory (here, of adjudication) that achieves a *balance* between the general on the one hand and the particular on the other, between the universal and the particular, simply because one cannot simply throw one's hands up in the air in despair at the enormous magnitude of the task at hand (although such enormous magnitude is in fact true). This is, of course, easier stated than accomplished. I attempt, in the final chapter of the present book,[4] to tread (and thread) this very fine line by drawing from the best (and most practical) elements from many of the existing theories in order to posit just such a theory. As I shall argue, one of the *key* considerations is *to accommodate the very practical reality that facts will vary from case to case*[5] *and that, as a result, apart*

[4] See ch 10 in this volume.

[5] It should be noted that the 'facts' referred to here comprise *not only actual* 'facts' *but also relevant* facts, viz, facts which fall *within* the *factual parameters* that *constitute an integral part of* the *legal rule* itself. In this last-mentioned regard, it should be noted that part of the content of the *legal rule* itself would comprise the factual parameters just referred to. Hence, when we refer to the *application* of the law to the (*actual*) facts of a given case, we are referring only to those facts which are *relevant* inasmuch (as mentioned at the outset of the present note) as they fall *within* the *factual parameters* that are *part of* the *legal rule* itself. I should add that I am not here concerned with the actual jurisprudential nature of such (relevant) facts themselves – in particular, whether they are descriptive or normative in nature (see generally M Greenberg, 'How Facts Make Law' in ch 10 of S Hershovitz (gen ed), *Exploring Law's*

from the easy cases, we need a theory that will simultaneously be sufficiently flexible to effect the aforementioned accommodation. This, in turn, entails a theory that focuses more on attitude and process (in the judge's quest for a fair and just result or outcome) as opposed to one that looks solely (or even primarily) at outcomes that, ex hypothesi, *cannot be predicted in advance (again, in all but the easy cases).*[6] *However, because the line between procedural justice and substantive justice is (as we have seen in a previous chapter*[7]*) a very fine one and that, in practice, both indeed interact with each other, the theory that is mooted in this book is not one that is merely process-oriented. More generally, it does bear adding that the theory would, by its very nature, apply in an* a fortiori *manner to easy cases.*

In the meantime, it is also important, nevertheless, to view the existing theories that are discussed in the following chapters through the lenses of this particular issue of theoretical frameworks in order to gauge whether or not they are too abstract or achieve the purpose of being amenable to practical application. As already mentioned, I will endeavour to ascertain *elements* in those theories that are indeed practically useful as well and integrate them into my proposed theory of adjudication.

III. Is there Objectivity in the Law?

A. The Necessity for, as Well as Inevitability of, Objectivity in the Law

I wish to state right at the outset that objectivity in adjudication is of the first importance. Indeed, without it, adjudication would become a wholly meaningless exercise, and disputes could just as well be settled in any other arbitrary fashion (for example, by the toss of a coin[8]) – a point that I shall return to as well as underscore

Empire: The Jurisprudence of Ronald Dworkin (Oxford, Oxford University Press, 2008) and, by the same author, 'Hartian Positivism and Normative Facts: *How Facts Make Law II*' in ch 11 of the same book (the former chapter was originally published in (2004) 10 *Legal Theory* 157)). My own view is that as the relevant facts of a given case necessarily fall within the factual parameters that are an integral part of the *legal* rule itself, whilst they are (on one view) *descriptive* in nature (particularly when viewed in isolation), when the legal rule concerned is *applied* to such facts, they also take on a *normative* nature as well (a view that is consistent with that advocated by Greenberg in the essays just cited). Needless to say, this is a uniquely jurisprudential or conceptual issue which (based on my own practical experience as a judge at least) does not impact the process of adjudication in the *practical* context.

[6] It might, for example, well be the case that the *actual* facts of a given case fall *outside* the factual parameters that constitute an integral part of the relevant legal rule (as to which see above, n 5) – and vice versa. That is why the *specific facts* are *crucial*.

[7] See ch 2 in this volume.

[8] I exclude here any reference to supernatural elements because ostensibly arbitrary procedures might well be undergirded by an absolute justification (for instance, the belief in the ancient procedure of trial by battle or the casting of lots during Old Testament times). And see, in this last-mentioned regard, the fascinating article by HL Ho, 'The Legitimacy of Medieval Proof' (2003-2004) 19 *Journal of Law and Religion* 259. Though *cf* the discussion of classical natural law in ch 5 in this volume.

below.[9] It is *precisely* because adjudication is perceived to be both objective in nature and productive of objective outcomes that it maintains its *legitimacy* not only in the eyes of the legal profession itself but also (and more importantly) in the eyes of the public whom the law ultimately serves.[10] Undergirding this is the idea that a just and fair result is one that is *objective* in the sense that it ought to be accepted by all concerned, *regardless* of one's own *personal or subjective* desires or predilections.

On a related note, as one learned writer perceptively observes:[11]

> [O]bjectivity is a very powerful idea, one that we could, perhaps, put to good use in criticizing what merits criticism and praising what merits praise.

All this raises a *prior* question: Is there in fact objectivity in the law to begin with? The straightforward answer – at least from a *logical* point of view – must be in the affirmative. Put simply, any argument to the *contrary* is *necessarily circular as well as self-defeating or self-refuting*. Let me elaborate.

In order to underscore the importance – and, indeed, inevitability – of objectivity, it may (perhaps ironically) be appropriate to consider its *converse*. This last-mentioned view is in fact a popular one and holds that everything is subjective and that the pursuit of objective truth is doomed to failure. In its most extreme form this would constitute 'external skepticism', as described by Professor Dworkin.[12] Dworkin argues, instead, in favour of 'internal skepticism',

[9] See the text to nn 17 and 18, below.

[10] As Professor Postema also succinctly put it, 'In law, objectivity matters because legitimacy matters.': see GJ Postema, 'Objectivity Fit for Law' in ch 3 of B Leiter (ed), *Objectivity in Law and Morals* (Cambridge, Cambridge University Press, 2001) 115. The learned author then proceeds to observe thus (ibid 116):

> Why, then, do we demand objectivity in legal reasoning? Because we want law to make good on its offer to provide a forum and a language for, and a structured and disciplined practice of, public practical reasoning in conditions of coercive pluralism of modern political societies. The stakes are high. Without a credible claim to objectivity, we could not hope to sustain the legitimacy of law and the modern political society it serves.

See also G Villa-Rosas and JL Fabra-Zamora, 'Introduction: The meanings of "objectivity"' in ch 1 of G Villa-Rosas and JL Fabra-Zamora (eds), *Objectivity in Jurisprudence, Legal Interpretation and Practical Reasoning* (Cheltenham, UK, Edward Elgar Publishing 2022) 2. Indeed, these same authors persuasively observe thus (ibid 11 (emphasis added)):

> Without the quest for objectivity, empirical science would become a fanatical machination, history and journalism would turn into propaganda or sheer delusion, *and the law would be nothing more than an irrational coercive mechanism.*

Reference may also be made to T Bustamante, 'Why do Legal Philosophers (perhaps correctly) Insist on Moral Objectivity While Dismissing Metaethical Inquiry?' in ch 12 of G Villa-Rosas and JL Fabra-Zamora (eds), *Objectivity in Jurisprudence, Legal Interpretation and Practical Reasoning*, above, 237–238. But *cf* the legal thought considered in ch 9 in this volume.

[11] See HL Feldman, 'Objectivity in Legal Judgment' (1994) 92 *Michigan Law Review* 1187, 1188. See also G Villa-Rosas and JL Fabra-Zamora, 'Introduction: The Meanings of "Objectivity"' (n 10) 1 and 6–7.

[12] On the distinction between internal and external scepticism, see generally RM Dworkin, *Law's Empire* (Cambridge, Harvard University Press, 1986) 78–85. See also, by the same author, 'Law, Philosophy and Interpretation' (1994) 80 *Archiv fu¨r Rechts-und Sozialphilosophie* 463,

that is, that even though there may be uncertainty as to what the objectively correct answer is, all parties nevertheless agree that there *is* an objectively correct answer. 'External skepticism', in contrast, holds that no objectively correct answer is ever attainable. Dworkin also expresses this distinction through his use of Professor Gallie's idea of 'essentially contested concepts'[13] (which I will consider in the next part of this chapter).

It is clear that – even from the standpoint of pure logic – the extreme stance taken by 'external skepticism' is (as already alluded to) circular and self-defeating or self-refuting. Indeed, one could even go so far as to characterise such an approach as being incoherent. We begin from the premise that the assertion of a belief necessarily implies a truth-claim. As Professor Dworkin so succinctly put it:[14]

> [External skeptics] purport to stand outside a whole body of belief, and to judge it as a whole from premises or attitudes that owe nothing to it. Of course they cannot stand outside thought altogether, to deny real truth to every thought. For even archimedeans need some place to stand … They must assume that some of what they think (at an absolute minimum, their beliefs about good reasoning) are not just their own or their culture's invention but are true or valid – indeed 'objectively' so. Otherwise they could only present their views as 'subjective' displays in which we need take nothing but a biographical interest. Skepticism, in the sense of disbelief, must be built up from belief of some kind; it can't be skeptical, as we might put it, all the way down.

Hence, even the argument that there are no objective truths – which is in fact the thrust of 'external skepticism' – is *itself* a *truth*-claim. However, if this is the case, then *that* particular argument, if true, is *itself* suspect, since no argument can (on *its* terms) be objectively true. The circularity and self-refutation are clear for all to see.

The (here, external) skeptic may seek to argue that his or her argument is merely a personal opinion, but if that is so, then there are no reasons for taking *seriously* the argument in the first place. On the other hand, if the external skeptic is attempting to persuade others as to the cogency of his or her argument

especially 474–475 and 'Objectivity and Truth: You'd Better Believe It' (1996) 25 *Philosophy and Public Affairs* 87; see also his 'Darwin's New Bulldog' (1998) 111 *Harvard Law Review* 1718, especially 1719, 1732–3, 1736 and 1738 (which is in fact a response to R Posner's Oliver Wendell Holmes Lectures, 'The Problematics of Moral and Legal Theory' (1998) 111 *Harvard Law Review* 1637; see now, by the same author in booklength form, *The Problematics of Moral and Legal Theory* (Harvard University Press, Cambridge, Massachusetts, 1999), and demonstrating (convincingly, in my view) that Posner (despite his arguments to the contrary) is himself an absolutist; see also, in this regard, MC Nussbaum, 'Still Worthy of Praise' (1998) 111 *Harvard Law Review* 1176, especially 1787 (this also being a response to Posner, above).

[13] See WB Gallie, 'Essentially Contested Concepts' (1955-1956) 56 *Proceedings of the Aristotelian Society* 167 (reprinted in ch 8 of WB Gallie, *Philosophy and the Historical Understanding* (New York, Schocken Books, 1968). References hereafter will be the original article.

[14] Dworkin, 'Objectivity and Truth: You'd Better Believe It' (n 12) 88. See also ibid, especially 94–99, 128 and 134–139. See also J Waldron, 'On the Objectivity of Morals: Thoughts on Gilbert's *Democratic Individuality*' (1992) 80 *California Law Review* 1361, 1371.

(ie, that he or she *is* engaging in *serious* discourse), then that statement necessarily contains an implicit recourse to *the universality and truth* of the argument itself. Indeed, it would be odd for a person to claim belief in an argument while simultaneously denying that it is true. One can, of course, never prove the *absoluteness* of one's argument; to that extent, there is room for a number of differing views, each claiming to represent the correct and objective answer. Different conceptions exist with respect to a concept that is held in common.[15] As it is the concept that is itself essentially contested, it falls within the sphere of 'internal scepticism' (utilising Dworkinian terminology). As Professor Dworkin himself puts it, 'uncertainty' (which he accepts) is quite separate and distinct from 'indeterminacy'.[16] Again, it bears reiterating that the idea of 'essentially contested concepts' will be dealt with in the next part of this chapter.

At this juncture, however, I would like to turn to an important issue – if (as I think we must) we accept that objectivity in the law is not only fundamental and crucial but also inevitable, what *precisely* do we mean by objectivity in the law? In particular, what specific *theoretical* framework can *simultaneously* provide *practical* guidance in the enterprise of adjudication? This is the issue to which our attention now turns. However, before proceeding to do so, it is pertinent, in my view, to note that the approach from subjectivity mooted by the external skeptic is, in the final analysis, discouraging as well as disempowering. As one learned author observed:[17]

> Its ubiquity notwithstanding, subjectivism is a troubled and troubling philosophical stance. Whatever one's metaphysics, subjectivism eats away at our aspirations for law.

And I have observed, in a similar vein, thus:[18]

> [I]n some quarters at least, there has – particularly with the advent of post-modern legal thought – been an increased (and, unfortunately, increasingly) sceptical view

[15] See Gallie (n 13). And see RM Dworkin, *Taking Rights Seriously,* rev edn (Cambridge, Harvard University Press, 1978) 103 n 1.

[16] Dworkin, 'Objectivity and Truth: You'd Better Believe It' (n 12), especially 135 and 138. See also Postema (n 10) 104. Professor Kramer draws the same distinction as well as a distinction between 'indemonstrability' on the one hand and 'indeterminacy' on the other: see MH Kramer, *Objectivity and the Rule of Law* (Cambridge, Cambridge University Press, 2007) 17–18, 19–21 and 35.

[17] See D Patterson, 'Normativity and Objectivity in Law' (2001) 43 *William and Mary Law Review* 325, 340.

[18] See A Phang, 'Doctrine and Fairness in the Law of Contract' (2009) 29 *Legal Studies* 534, 536–537 (emphasis in the original text). Reference may also be made to the following observations by Chief Justice Owen Dixon, 'Concerning Judicial Method' in The Right Honourable Sir Owen Dixon, *Jesting Pilate and Other Papers and Addresses*, 2nd edn (Australia, The Law Book Company Limited, 1997 (collected by His Honour Judge Woinarski)) 152–165, 155 (I owe this very pertinent reference to Justice Michelle Gordon of the High Court of Australia):

> It is taken for granted that the decision of the court will be 'correct' or 'incorrect', 'right' or 'wrong' as it conforms with ascertained legal principles and applies them according to a standard of reasoning which is not personal to the judges themselves. It is a tacit assumption. But it is basal. The court would feel that the function it performed had lost its meaning and purpose, if there were no external standard of legal correctness.

taken of the law in general and legal objectivity in particular. Such an approach is, on any view, both corrosive as well as destructive.

...

Indeed, the view that the law is subjective (and, consequently, arbitrary) would cause an irreparable loss in the legitimacy of the law in the eyes of the public. And ... it would also dispirit as well as disempower lawyers, judges and students alike. And, from just a logical perspective, the very view that all law is subjective is *itself* an 'absolute' proposition that thus involves circularity and (more importantly) self-contradiction.

B. Towards a Framework with Regard to Objectivity in the Law

Not surprisingly, there is a veritable plethora of literature with regard to the topic of objectivity in the law.[19] Equally unsurprising is the fact that most of them not only approach the topic quite differently but also in what, it is respectfully suggested, is too theoretical and abstract a fashion. Given that the present book is concerned with integrating both theory and practice in the context of a new theory of adjudication, such a state of affairs is, to say the least, unfortunate.

Consistently with the general approach adopted in this book, I proffer what I consider to be the most theoretically grounded framework that is nevertheless simultaneously reflective of what takes place in practice in the context of adjudication before the courts. In order to accomplish this, I will draw from the most useful elements in the theories espoused in the relevant literature.

Given the theoretical thicket engendered by the many writings on the topic of objectivity in the law, it is suggested that the basic distinction drawn by two learned authors between *procedural (or epistemic) objectivity* on the one hand and *metaphysical objectivity* on the other is an excellent starting point.[20] Given the

[19] See, eg (and for just a sampling of just the books that are available), K Greenawalt, *Law and Objectivity* (New York, Oxford University Press, 1992); N Stavropoulos, *Objectivity in Law* (Oxford, Clarendon Press, 1996); Leiter (n 10); Kramer (n 16); Husa and Van Hoecke (n 3); and G Villa-Rosas and JL Fabra-Zamora, *Objectivity in Jurisprudence, Legal Interpretation and Practical Reasoning* (n 10).

[20] See JL Coleman and B Leiter, 'Determinacy, Objectivity, and Authority' (1993) 142 *University of Pennsylvania Law Review* 549, 595. However, to the extent that the learned authors advocate a wholly *descriptive* approach as their proposed *normative* framework (see, eg, ibid 549). I would respectfully beg to differ (see also n 23). See also B Leiter, 'Introduction' in Leiter (n 10), especially 1–3 as well as E Bulygin, 'The Objectivity of the Law' in ch 19 of E Bulygin, *Essays in Legal Philosophy* (Oxford, Oxford University Press, 2015). I have dealt with this particular approach briefly in the previous chapter, and will deal in more detail with it in ch 4 in this volume.

It should be noted that there are *other* concepts of objectivity proffered by other authors. For example, Professor Marmor distinguishes between semantic objectivity, metaphysical objectivity and discourse objectivity: see A Marmor, *Positive Law and Objective Values* (Oxford, Clarendon Press, 2001) ch 6. Reference may also be made to P Pettit, 'Embracing Objectivity in Ethics' in ch 6 of Leiter (n 10), where the learned author refers to semantic objectivism, ontological objectivism and justificatory objectivism and to Kramer (n 16), who refers to ontological objectivity, epistemic objectivity and semantic objectivity. However, viewed particularly from the practical perspective, it is suggested that

fact (already made at several points in the present book) that given the myriad factual situations, it is virtually impossible for any *theory* to come even close to covering (save perhaps for the so-called easy cases) all cases insofar as the *outcome* is concerned. This last-mentioned theory (purporting to cover all or most *outcomes*) would appear to endorse *metaphysical* objectivity instead. As the aforementioned learned authors note:[21]

> According to metaphysical objectivity, *there are correct answers* to pressing legal, political, and moral questions: answers whose correctness is independent of people's beliefs about them and are ... objectively correct.

In *contrast*, however, *procedural (or epistemic)* objectivity is *not* concerned with the *outcomes* of cases. As the same authors aptly observe:[22]

> These procedures are defensible, *not because they provide correct answers to legal and political disputes, but because they resolve such disputes in a fair and impartial, that is, objective manner*. This is a rough and ready formulation of the classic conception of procedural or epistemic objectivity.

Looked at in this light, all that is required is objectivity in the *process* of adjudication.[23] It is submitted that this is a much more feasible approach that is simultaneously a realistic depiction of what actually happens in practice in the adjudicative context. It also reflects the idea of *procedural* justice, which is often contrasted with the idea of *substantive* justice – to which I will return in a moment.

How, then, does 'objectivity' *manifest* itself in *concrete and practical terms*? From an *adjudicative perspective*, 'objectivity' manifests itself in *impartiality* in relation to the entire court process.[24] Indeed (and this is, in fact, the mirror

the distinction referred to in the main text between epistemic objectivity and metaphysical objectivity is the best way forward as it is clear and (as, if not more, importantly) reflects most accurately what *actually* takes place in the context of *adjudication* in the sphere of the common law.

[21] See Coleman and Leiter (n 20) 597 (emphasis added). Insofar as uncertainty with regard to *facts* is concerned, see Greenawalt (n 19) 44–48.

[22] ibid 596 (emphasis added). See also ibid 600, on the importance of not confusing 'objectivity' with 'determinancy'.

[23] For an account of objectivity that, inter alia, eschews a metaphysical approach but is, instead, grounded in *action* (by legal professionals), see Patterson (n 17) (*cf* also AA Leff, 'Law and' (1978) 87 *Yale Law Journal* 989, especially 989 and 1011). However, inasmuch as Professor Patterson's approach appears to align itself with a purely *descriptive* approach as his proposed *normative* framework, I would respectfully beg to differ (see also n 20).

[24] And see generally W Lucy, 'The Possibility of Impartiality' (2005) 25 *OJLS* 3. See also ibid 7, where the learned author observes that 'impartiality is appropriate where there exists a conflict of interests between two or more parties, with a third party being involved to either police the conflict or to resolve it'. See also Kramer (n 16) 53, who observes as follows:

> Another epistemic variety of objectivity is impartiality, which consists of disinterestedness and open-mindedness, and which can be designated as 'detachedness' or 'impersonality'. It is to be contrasted with bias and partisanship, but also with impetuousness and whimsicalness (though sometimes not with genuine randomness).

image of what has just been stated), many writers characterise 'objectivity' as involving the *absence of partiality*.[25] Professor Leiter also observes that 'the demand to be objective is the demand to be free of *bias* or other factors that distort judgment'.[26]

To take a concrete example (which I, like many other judges, have experienced), if a claimant has a right to win, then the fact that he or she may appear to the judge to be an unpleasant and even otherwise exploitative person does not alter the fact that the decision must be given in his or her favour. Likewise, a witness who is extremely unpleasant on the witness stand but who is nevertheless telling the truth must be believed regardless of how repugnant he or she presents himself or herself on a personal level to the court. The reader will immediately discern – even with these very simple, yet commonplace, examples – how fundamentally important an objective and impartial approach is. Putting aside for the moment the actual decision of the court, without an objective and impartial *process*, a just and fair *result or outcome* would not (save for the occasional happenstance) be possible. Indeed, the concept of 'process' is, in my view, also helpful in understanding 'objectivity *in action*', so to speak. This is an important point, not least because adjudication in the real world involves courts and judges deciding real-life cases based on actual facts. In this regard, I would like to consider briefly a specific illustration in the context of the concept of 'objectivity' in the law of contract.

To take, then, another concrete example, the issue of 'objectivity' in the law of *contract* was the subject of a series of learned articles in the *Law Quarterly Review* commencing from around the mid-1980s.[27] In the first of these articles, Professor Howarth proffers three options in relation to 'objectivity' in the law of

See also generally ibid 53–68. And Professor Greenawalt observes (see Greenawalt (n 19) 197):

> A judge's reliance on a form of reasoning is itself not enough to establish that the reasoning is objective. The reasons offered must be something other than an expression of the particular judge's feelings and attitudes.

See also ibid 100. Reference may also be made to J Raz, 'Notes on Value and Objectivity' in ch 5 of Leiter (n 10) 196, where the learned author observes thus:

> Not infrequently official action is based in part not on the beliefs of the officials concerned, but on the basis of propositions that are accepted by them as a reasonable basis for action in the circumstances of the case. Objectivity as impartiality can characterize deliberation and decisionmaking based on accepted – rather than believed – premises as well. This requirement of objectivity is a requirement of impartiality in all the stages of the decision-making process.

[25] See, eg, Coleman and Leiter (n 20) 596, n 85.

[26] Leiter (n 20) 1 (emphasis in the original text). See also G Villa-Rosas and JL Fabra-Zamora, 'Introduction: The meanings of "objectivity"' (n 10) 9 and 22.

[27] See W Howarth, 'The Meaning of Objectivity in Contract' (1984) 100 *LQR* 265; JP Vorster, 'A Comment on the Meaning of Objectivity in Contract' (1987) 103 *LQR* 274; W Howarth, 'A Note on the Objective of Objectivity in Contract' (1987) 103 *LQR* 527; and A de Moor, 'Intention in the Law of Contract: Elusive or Illusory?' (1990) 106 *LQR* 632.

contract – promisor objectivity, promisee objectivity and detached objectivity.[28] This approach stems clearly from the concept of *perspectives*. However, even then, there is a yet further question: how do we ascertain, insofar as the first two perspectives are concerned, the promisor's or the promisee's perspectives, respectively?

Professor Howarth refers to the perspective of *a reasonable person* placed in the position of the promisor or promisee, respectively.[29] The third option – detached objectivity – connotes a 'reasonable "fly on the wall" theory'.[30] Whilst all these options are interesting from a *theoretical* perspective, it is suggested that, in the *actual practice* of adjudication, courts adopt a much more *holistic* approach (or, rather, *process*), which requires them to look at *all the relevant evidence in order* to arrive at a final decision.[31] This approach from detached objectivity is perhaps the closest and most accurate description of what actually takes place in the courts, although it is still somewhat different inasmuch as it permits courts to arrive at a view that 'may differ from the actual or reasonable perspective that either the promisor or promisee might have of the situation'.[32] It is submitted that the approach I have just suggested is, as already mentioned, more *holistic* inasmuch as it ultimately results in a finding in favour of *one* of the parties.[33] Such an approach is also consistent with the endorsement (in the present part of this chapter) of *procedural (or epistemic) objectivity*. Put simply, the focus is more on the *actions* of the court concerned in relation to the *process* of ascertaining the relevant facts and circumstances of the case in as *objective* a manner as possible *in order to* arrive *at a fair and just result*.[34] At this juncture, it would be apposite to refer to an important essay that *supports* the approach that I have just advocated,[35] and which was jointly written by Professor JW Carter and the late Professor Michael Furmston (two of the foremost experts in the common law of contract). Significantly, perhaps, this was probably Professor Furmston's final

[28] See Howarth, 'The Meaning of Objectivity in Contract' (n 27).

[29] ibid 270–271. *Contra* Vorster (n 27) 276, who argues that Howarth's views in this regard are 'seriously flawed by his misleading use of the terms "promisor objectivity" and "promisee objectivity"' as 'each party to a synallagmatic contract is both a promisor and a promisee'. See also ibid 281. Reference may also be made to ABL Phang and YH Goh, 'Offer and Acceptance' in ch 3 of ABL Phang (ed), *The Law of Contract in Singapore*, 2nd edn (Singapore, Academy Publishing, 2022) vol 1, para 03.015. For Howarth's response to Vorster (n 27), see Howarth, 'A Note on the Objective of Objectivity in Contract' (n 27).

[30] See Howarth, 'The Meaning of Objectivity in Contract' (n 27) 276.

[31] See also Phang and Goh (n 29) para 03.020.

[32] See Howarth, 'The Meaning of Objectivity in Contract' (n 27) 280–281.

[33] See also Vorster (n 27) 283–284. It should, however, be noted that, under Singapore and Indian law, there is a concept of 'not proved' (see, eg, s 3(5) of the Singapore Evidence Act 1893 (2020 Rev Edn); see also the Singapore Court of Appeal decision of *Loo Chay Sit v Estate of Loo Chay Loo* [2010] 1 *Singapore Law Reports* 286). Even then, the court would still arrive at a decision in favour of one of the parties in the final analysis.

[34] See also de Moor (n 27) 648. Reference may also be made to Postema (n 10) 137, where the learned author emphasises the *practical* aspect of objectivity.

[35] In the discussion of this joint essay that follows, I draw gratefully from A Phang, 'Book Review of *The Future of the Law of Contract* by Michael Furmston' (2021) 37 *Journal of Contract Law* 145.

published work in his final edited work.[36] In chapter five of this book, simply entitled 'Objectivity', Professor Carter and Professor Furmston tackle this thorny topic of 'objectivity' in an interesting and innovative fashion. It is, in fact, the main chapter which analyses the general role of theory in the law of contract in that particular book.[37]

Professor Carter and Professor Furmston are obviously aware of the scholarship (including the aforementioned articles,[38] which are in fact cited in the first footnote of the essay, amongst many other pieces). However, their essay seeks to go *beyond* the existing literature. They acknowledge the well-established approach (alluded to above) that courts adopt an objective approach, with a starting point that looks at the relevant evidence through the lenses of a reasonable person – although (as they pertinently observe) the objective evidence is itself subject to the process of construction as well as to the relevant rules of evidence. Interestingly, throughout their essay, the learned authors are constantly aware of the interaction between the objective and the subjective. They therefore focus on the *means* by which courts strive to give effect to the actual intention of the parties (this is an important point to which I shall return to in a moment). To this end, they explore various aspects in which the search for objectivity in the law of contract operates – ascertaining the meaning of a contract, its existence, as well as the somewhat thorny area in relation to implied terms. Not surprisingly, ascertaining the meaning of a contract does involve, inter alia, a focus on language. However, insofar as the latter two areas are concerned, the authors unpack the role that objectivity plays in them through a detailed examination of the leading cases. The reader is required to follow the analyses closely because the focus is really on the *means or process* of analysis by the courts. It is therefore difficult to capture – precisely at least – in a freeze-frame, so to speak, the thesis or theses of the authors. Perhaps this is not surprising as, in my view at least, what the authors are attempting to do is to demonstrate the law 'in action' in situations where the objective and the subjective are not only in tension but also *interact* with each other. And this demonstrates simultaneously how difficult it is to harness theory for practical uses, although litigators reading the present essay will be enlightened as to how the *process* of arguing one's case can be made in an effective manner. However, this is not to state that the authors leave us hanging without any resolution or point of reference. There is an attempt to draw the central threads of their chapter together; in their words:[39]

> Our argument is not that the objective approach should be abandoned, far from it. The objective theory is clearly fundamental to the common law of contract. It has also been a successful approach. Equally, to say that the common law is concerned exclusively

[36] See M Furmston (ed), *The Future of the Law of Contract* (Abingdon, Oxon, Informa Law, 2020).
[37] See JW Carter and M Furmston, 'Objectivity' in ch 5 of Furmston (n 36).
[38] See above, n 27.
[39] See Carter and Furmston (n 37) 92 (emphasis added).

> with 'objective intention' is clearly wrong. An ingredient of success is that objectivity is *tempered by* subjective elements.
>
> That the approach is not always purely objective can be traced to the fact that *the objective theory operates* at the *level of process*. The purpose or object is to arrive at reliable conclusions about actual intention. While the approach relies heavily on a presumption that people mean what they say, it is clear not only that courts are guided by subjective indicia of intention but also that contract law includes mechanisms which ensure that decisions remain faithful to the purpose of the process. Of course, the fact that in the construction of written contracts the search is for a common intention means that there is rarely room for consideration of individual beliefs and intention. A contract in writing is not the sum of two unilateral intentions.

Although I have spent some time summarising the basic arguments made by both these learned authors, I cannot do it justice. It has itself to be read – and carefully at that. Suffice it to state that that particular chapter *supports* the approach that I proffer in this chapter with regard to the concept as well as uses of 'objectivity' in the *adjudicative process*. Put simply, whilst it might be arguable whether or not the court has applied the concept of objectivity correctly in a given case,[40] it cannot be gainsaid that every court endeavours its level best to arrive at the correct answer based on an objective ascertainment of all the relevant facts at hand. This approach (which might be termed 'judging in good faith'[41]) cannot be underestimated. Indeed, this is one of the central themes as well as elements in my proposed theory of adjudication (which is the subject of the final chapter of the present book[42]).

To summarise the approach towards objectivity advocated in the present part of this chapter, it is one that centres on *procedural (or epistemic) objectivity* (in *contrast* to *metaphysical objectivity*). *However*, this does *not* mean that such an approach is unconcerned with arriving at the just and fair *outcome or decision* in the case at hand. In this regard, it is hoped that the reader would also note the (*closely related*) importance of the relationship between procedural justice and substantive justice, which was discussed in some detail in the previous chapter.[43] At this juncture, it is also important to underscore a crucial point that was also made in the preceding chapter – that a focus here on *procedural (or epistemic) objectivity* (which is the analogue of *procedural* justice discussed in the previous chapter) is *not merely process*-oriented but is *integrated* with *substantive* justice (which is related to *metaphysical objectivity*, and such integration having also been

[40] *Cf* Gallie (n 13) as well as (in a more general vein) the copious case comments that are to be found in the relevant legal literature. And see the discussion of Gallie's idea of 'essentially contested concepts' in the following part of this chapter.

[41] Drawing from the title of the book by SJ Burton, *Judging in Good Faith* (Cambridge, Cambridge University Press, 1992).

[42] See ch 10 in this volume.

[43] See ch 2 in this volume.

discussed in the previous chapter). As, for example, Professor Kramer observes (in the context of impartiality (a concept already discussed above)):[44]

> One major reason for insisting on legal officials' impartiality ... is focused on the *outcomes of* their *processes* of decision-making. Impartiality *markedly increases* the probability that those *outcomes* will be *correct*.

There are yet more *specific* aspects or elements that would be an integral part of such a process. As this is a more general chapter, I will deal with them in detail in the final chapter (where I set out my proposed theory of adjudication).[45]

Given the fact that my preferred concept of 'objectivity' is, in the main at least, procedural (or epistemic[46]) in nature because it is (in the vast majority of cases) impossible to posit a substantive or metaphysical concept of 'objectivity' coupled with the corresponding result that reasonable judges can differ reasonably as to the outcome in relation to the same fact situation,[47] how then do we engage with such a result? In this regard, the next part attempts to deal with this issue by focusing on the idea of 'essentially contested concepts'.

IV. 'Essentially Contested Concepts'

As mentioned, this part of the present chapter follows, in fact, from the preceding one. Put simply, given the virtual inevitability (except with the exception of the easiest of cases) of controversy as to what (objectively speaking) the right or correct decision in a given case is (particularly given the myriad fact situations that could arise), how does one maintain fidelity to objectivity whilst simultaneously providing coherent *theoretical* guidance? One possibility is to utilise a

[44] See Kramer (n 16) 65 (emphasis added).

[45] See ch 10 in this volume. See also Lucy (n 24), whose work I shall also be drawing upon in this chapter.

[46] For similar approaches, see, eg, Postema (n 10). In particular, the learned author emphasises both method and process (ibid, especially 117, 121, 125, 132–133 and 136); his proposal of 'objectivity as publicity', he states, 'has *no metaphysical* pretensions or commitments' and is 'a *methodological* conception of objectivity' (ibid 129 (emphasis added)). He also advocates the 'willingness [of all concerned] to engage in the process *in good faith* with the hope that others are also engaging *in good faith*' (ibid 120 (emphasis added)). As the learned author puts it, '[w]e look to objectivity, not to clinch the case for this or that legal judgment in the course of debate about its correctness, but to give us the assurance we need to carry on with the argument for its correctness with others who persist in disagreement' (ibid 131). Such an approach, as we shall see, is wholly consistent with my proposed theory of adjudication in ch 10 in this volume.

[47] *Cf* Raz (n 24) 198, where the learned author observes thus:

> People who are epistemically objective judges of certain matters are not free from error in those matters. They are merely free from errors arising out of biases and an emotionally blinkered inability to respond to the evidence and evaluate it.

Even this particular observation distinguishes between the epistemic from the metaphysical and emphasises the importance (both theoretical *and* practical) of *epistemic* objectivity (which is also endorsed in the present chapter).

theoretical approach first mooted by Professor Gallie close to seven decades ago – the idea of 'essentially contested concepts'.[48] Indeed, as we shall see in subsequent chapters, this idea forms a crucial element in Professor Ronald Dworkin's theory of adjudication.[49] As Professor Gallie put it:[50]

> I want to show that there are apparently endless disputes for which neither of [the] explanations *need* be the correct one. Further, I shall try to show that there are disputes, centred on … concepts …, which are perfectly genuine: which, although not resolvable by argument of any kind, are nevertheless sustained by perfectly respectable arguments and evidence. This is what I mean by saying that there are *'concepts'* which are *'essentially' 'contested'*, concepts the proper use of which inevitably involves endless disputes about their proper uses on the part of their users.

At the risk of oversimplification, the idea of 'essentially contested concepts' involves the proposition – in the context of legal adjudication – that whilst there is necessarily one objectively right answer to the case concerned, it is controversial what that answer is as two or more sets of analysis are premised on perfectly respectable arguments and evidence. It should, however, be pointed out at this juncture that – from a strictly *theoretical* perspective – such an approach is, with respect, not very satisfactory. From a *practical* perspective, though, there is (as I shall argue[51]) much to be said for this approach.

However, even if we accept the idea of 'essentially contested concepts', there is (potentially at least) a *prior* problem. Put simply, the 'concept' concerned has to be defined with sufficient clarity.[52] As Professor Gallie observed, in order for the idea of 'essentially contested concepts' to apply, it is important that

> each party recognizes the fact that its own use of [the concept] is contested by those of other parties, and that each party must have at least some appreciation of the different criteria in the light of which the other parties claim to be applying the concept in question.[53]

[48] See Gallie (n 13).
[49] See chs 6, 7 and 8 in this volume.
[50] Gallie (n 13) 169 (emphasis in italics in the original text; emphasis added in quoted italics).
[51] Particularly in the final chapter: see ch 10 in this volume.
[52] And see DH Ruben, 'W.B. Gallie and Essentially Contested Concepts' (2010) 39 *Philosophical Papers* 257, 259, where the learned author observes as follows (emphasis added):

> If the contest only showed us that the parties to the dispute meant different things by 'X', then 'X' would be ambiguous and the dispute easily resolved by distinguishing *two concepts* where one thought initially there was only one.

[53] Gallie (n 13) 172. See also ibid 190 (emphasis in the original text), where it is observed that 'a certain piece of evidence or argument put forward by one side in an apparently endless dispute can be recognized to have a definite logical force, even by those whom it entirely fails to win over or convert to the side in question' and that 'when this is the case, the conversion of a hitherto wavering opponent of the side in question can be seen to be *justifiable* – not simply expectable in the light of known relevant psychological or sociological laws – given the waverer's previous state of information and given the grounds on which he previously supported one side and opposed the other'. The learned author proceeds to add that '[i]t is for this reason that we can distinguish more or less intellectually respectable conversions from those of a more purely emotional, or yet those of a wholly sinister kind'.

This is in fact the fifth of five initial conditions of 'essential contestedness'[54] – to which the learned author added two more later in his essay.[55] It seems to me at least that, insofar as the discipline of law is concerned, the practice as well as the context contained therein would be useful in providing us with the necessary clarity.[56] The concept of an 'interpretive community' (here, of the legal community) may be useful in this particular regard.[57] However, it should be noted that the concept of an 'interpretive community' is equally consistent with an ostensibly subjectivist approach, as evidenced in the work of literary theorist as well as legal scholar, Professor Stanley Fish.[58] I use the description 'ostensibly' because, as I have argued in the preceding part of this chapter,

[54] The first four are as follows (see Gallie (n 13) 171–172): first, that the concept concerned must be '*appraisive* in the sense that it signifies or accredits some kind of valued achievement' (emphasis in the original text); second, that '[t]his achievement must be of an internally complex character, for all that its worth is attributed to it as a whole'; third, '[a]ny explanation of its worth must therefore include reference to the respective contributions of its various parts or features'; and, fourth, '[t]he accredited achievement must be of a kind that admits of considerable modification in the light of changing circumstances; and such modification cannot be prescribed or predicted in advance'. The learned author also adds that he 'shall call the concept of any such achievement "open" in character'.

[55] The sixth is that 'the derivation of any such concept from an original exemplar whose authority is acknowledged by all the contestant users of the concept' and the seventh is that 'the probability or plausibility, in appropriate senses of these terms, of the claim that the continuous competition for acknowledgement as between the contestant users of the concept, enables the original exemplar's achievement to be sustained and/or developed in optimum fashion': see Gallie (n 13) 180.

[56] But *cf* W van der Burg, 'Law as a Second-Order Essentially Contested Concept' (2017) 8 *Jurisprudence* 230, especially 253–255. With respect, however, the learned author's reference to law as a *second*-order essentially contested concept would lead (as the author himself appears to suggest) to endless dispute. However, he does not proffer this particular argument as being a definitive one. It should also be noted that his reference to positivists and non-positivists may itself be accommodated within Gallie's framework of conceptions of the essentially contested concept of (here) the law. On a more practical level, he does not refer to the practice and context contained within the discipline of law and (as discussed immediately below) the concept of an 'interpretive community'. Reference might also be made to KM Ehrenberg, 'Law is not (best considered) an essentially contested concept' (2011) 7 *International Journal of Law in Context* 209 which, whilst correct in pointing to the confusion that might arise as a result of the difficulties inherent in the many ways of (and concomitant levels of abstraction involved in) defining the concept of 'law', tends, with respect, to ignore the practice and context contained within the discipline of law just referred to. And, in allowing that the idea of essentially contested concepts might be more useful with regard to the related concept of the rule of law, he might well agree that the same idea might be equally useful with regard to the central focus of the present book in the context of theories of adjudication (bearing in mind the practice and context just mentioned). And, as Ehrenberg himself argues, any use of the idea of essentially contested concepts must yield a greater understanding of the uses of the concept to which it is applied and, looked at in this light, it is suggested that whilst not, as I argue, a panacea, this idea is both interesting and helpful. And *cf* (at a more general level) G Rey, 'Concepts and stereotypes' (1983) 15 *Cognition* 237 and EE Smith, DL Medin and LJ Rips, 'A psychological approach to concepts: Comments on Rey's "Concepts and stereotypes"' (1984) *Cognition* 265.

[57] See generally OM Fiss, 'Objectivity and Interpretation' (1982) 34 *Stanford Law Review* 739. Reference may also be made to Greenawalt (n 19) 14, 33, 48, 71, 72, 74 and 233 (referring, more generally, to the importance of shared assumptions about linguistic meaning as well as social contexts and practices). Professor Greenawalt does, in fact, refer expressly to the concept of an 'interpretive legal community' as well as to Professor Fiss's article that is cited in the present note (see ibid 211–212).

[58] See, eg, his classic book, *Is There A Text in this Class? - The Authority of Interpretive Communities* (Cambridge, Harvard University Press, 1980).

objectivity is imperative if (amongst other things) we are even to begin to engage in meaningful discourse. My proposed theory of adjudication,[59] however, does acknowledge – in part at least – the difficulties which Professor Fish has with the more traditional theories inasmuch as they tend to adopt an overly rigid theoretical framework that does not (amongst other things) take into account the myriad fact situations that occur in the real world, so to speak, of adjudication. I hasten to add, however, that I do *not* endorse the subjectivity that constitutes the core of Professor Fish's theory – as is evident from the discussion earlier in this chapter.

It will suffice for the purposes of the present chapter to note that the idea of 'essentially contested concepts' is nevertheless a useful one that we will have occasion to return to, in particular when considering Professor Dworkin's theory of adjudication[60] as well as my own proposed theory of adjudication.[61] Indeed, as I shall elaborate upon in the final chapter of this book, the idea of 'essentially contested concepts' is not (in the main at least) inconsistent with my proposed theory of adjudication. There are at least two aspects in this regard.

More generally (and on the level of which *theory* of adjudication is most persuasive), it is worth noting that in addition to Professor Dworkin's theory of adjudication, each of the theories considered in the other chapters also constitutes a conception of the concept of 'adjudication' and, indeed, will also be assessed accordingly – together with both Professor Dworkin's theory as well as mine.

More specifically, the idea of 'essentially contested concepts' is also applicable in the context of the *particular process of adjudication* in general and *the interpretive choice of the correct answer to the case concerned* in particular. For example, in a given case, there may be equally persuasive arguments as to *which interpretation* would yield the correct answer.[62] Put simply, the interpretive issue is 'essentially contested'. Once again, we will encounter precisely such an issue in the chapters that follow – in particular (and yet again) with regard to Professor Dworkin's theory of adjudication[63] as well as my proposed theory of adjudication.[64]

[59] See ch 10 in this volume.

[60] See chs 6, 7 and 8 in this volume. See, in particular, Dworkin (n 15) 103 n 1.

[61] See ch 10 in this volume.

[62] Putting to one side the so-called 'easy case' where there is unanimity as to what the correct interpretation (and, hence, outcome or decision) should be.

[63] See chs 6, 7 and 8 in this volume. Reference may also be made to Professor Greenawalt's observation that, in contrast to 'an ideal judge' (whom, as we shall see in a later chapter, Professor Dworkin calls 'Hercules'), '[a]ctual lawyers and judges may disagree about what the answer is, but judges strive to find such an answer, and the answer does exist' (see Greenawalt (n 19) 209). This observation is, as we shall see, consistent with both Dworkin's theory of adjudication as well as my proposed theory of adjudication (in the final chapter of this book), and does rely (to some extent at least) on the idea of 'essentially contested concepts' first mooted by Professor Gallie (see Gallie (n 13)). Reference may also be made to Greenawalt (n 19) 213 (but *cf* the doubts of Professor Greenawalt with regard to whether there is a right answer to questions of *political morality* (as opposed to legal questions), save to the extent that 'questions about sound morality have correct answers': see ibid; see also 213, 220–221, 226 and 234).

[64] See ch 10 in this volume.

V. Conclusion

In the present chapter, we considered, first, the problem of *theoretical frameworks.* I suggested that this problem remains an intractable one – not least because of the very practical reality that facts will vary from case to case and that, apart from the easy cases, it will be difficult to posit a theory that accommodates this. I therefore suggested that the best way forward would be a *flexible* theory that focuses more on *attitude and process* in contrast to one that looks, instead, solely (or even primarily) to *outcomes.* Such an approach would not *necessarily* be divorced from substantive justice and outcomes simply because both procedural justice and substantive justice *interact* with each other.[65] I develop this proposed theory of adjudication in the final chapter of this book in accordance with the approach just mentioned.[66] I will also be viewing the various theories considered in the subsequent chapters of the present work through the lenses of this particular issue of theoretical frameworks. In particular, I will draw upon specific *elements* in those theories that are practically useful and that can be usefully integrated into my proposed theory of adjudication.

I also considered the extremely important – even vital – issue of *objectivity in the law* in general and in the context of adjudication in particular. As I was at pains to emphasise, objectivity in adjudication is of the first importance as it goes to the very heart of the *legitimacy* of the law, particularly in the eyes of the public. I also argued that the converse view – that everything is subjective and that the pursuit of objective truth is doomed to failure – is necessarily circular as well as self-defeating or self-refuting. This last-mentioned approach is also discouraging as well as disempowering. I proffered, instead, an approach towards objectivity in adjudication premised upon *procedural (or epistemic) objectivity* – with the caveat that such an approach is not merely process oriented but is *integrated* with *just and fair outcomes in the sphere of substantive justice* as well. This approach also reflects best what *actually takes place* in the *adjudicative* sphere. I also discussed briefly Professor Gallie's idea of 'essentially contested concepts'[67] and its relevance (in particular) to Professor Dworkin's theory of adjudication[68] as well as to my proposed theory of adjudication.[69]

Bearing in mind the various theoretical issues discussed in both the present and the previous chapter, it would now be appropriate to turn to the *specific* theories of adjudication (which will, inter alia, be examined utilising the various theoretical 'tools' discussed in both these chapters) – commencing with legal positivism in the context of the adjudicative process.[70]

[65] See ch 2 in this volume.
[66] See ch 10 in this volume.
[67] See Gallie (n 13).
[68] See chs 6, 7 and 8 in this volume.
[69] See ch 10 in this volume.
[70] See ch 4 in this volume.

PART II

Theories of Adjudication Considered

4

Legal Positivism and the Adjudicative Process

I. Introduction

In spite of legal positivism's *theoretical* 'battles' (especially with natural law), its focus (by Professor Hart) on law as a system of *rules*[1] is one that most of us can readily accept. This is particularly the case with practising lawyers as well as judges, for whom the rules of law are a vital part of the litigation process. It is customary, for example, for judges to ascertain what the relevant rules of law are before applying them to the facts.[2] However, what is more controversial is whether or not there is a *necessary* connection between the rules of law on the one hand and morality on the other.[3] A closely related debate – principally between Hart and Dworkin[4] – is whether, in addition to rules, principles also constitute part of the law.

As the principal task of the present book is to posit a *new* theory of *adjudication*, it is unnecessary for me to resolve the abovementioned theoretical controversies. Indeed, to even attempt that would require a book or even several books. The reader will nevertheless discern what my views – at least implicitly – are. The main task, nevertheless, of this chapter is to draw what is useful to the new theory of adjudication, which I set out in the final chapter of this book.[5]

Legal positivism[6] itself encompasses the work of a number of jurists. However, my focus in the present chapter will be on the work of Hart.[7] This is because Hart's concept of law comes closest – as we shall see – to what we find in practice.

[1] See HLA Hart, *The Concept of Law*, 3rd edn (Oxford, Oxford University Press, 2012).

[2] See also above, ch 2 in this volume for the distinction between the applicable rules and the application of the same.

[3] See also below, ch 5 in this volume.

[4] See below, ch 6 in this volume.

[5] See ch 10 in this volume.

[6] For the avoidance of doubt, I refer to the terms 'legal positivism' and 'positivism' interchangeably not only in this but in all other chapters in this book.

[7] The other main jurist in this regard is Professor Hans Kelsen, who has been described by Professor Neil MacCormick as 'the greatest of modern European jurists': see N MacCormick, *HLA Hart*, 2nd edn (Stanford, Stanford University Press, 2008) 9. See also, eg, H Kelsen, *Pure Theory of Law* (M Knight, translator) (Berkeley, University of California Press, 1967) as well as JE Núñez, G Villa-Rosas,

II. Hart's Concept of Law

As already alluded to above, Hart's concept of law is one that views the law as *a system of rules*. The basic structure of such a system is to be found in his seminal book, *The Concept of Law*.[8] In his view, a legal system comprises two types of *rules* – primary rules and secondary rules, respectively. The former relate to rules that – as their very terminology suggests – concern obligations and duties which must be generally obeyed, whereas the latter concern the primary rules themselves. Primary rules relate to the regulation of order within society and would typically focus on areas such as the criminal law as well as tort law. Insofar as secondary rules are concerned, these comprise secondary rules of adjudication, change and (most importantly) the rule of recognition. Secondary rules are – unlike primary rules – power-conferring in nature. Hence, the secondary rules of adjudication prescribe who can pass judgment on cases, whilst the secondary rules of change concern the powers of individuals to, for example, transact with each other pursuant to the law of contract. The rule of recognition is the most important because it sets out the criteria that determine the validity of all the other rules in the legal system concerned. It is itself, therefore (and as Hart argues), neither valid nor invalid. A legal *system* consists of the *union* of primary and secondary rules.

An important – and closely related – concept which Hart introduces in *The Concept of Law* concerns *the internal point of view*. Indeed (and as we shall see), this particular concept is also important in the context of *adjudication*. Indeed, the concept is, in my view at least, an insight of the first importance, as it has practical implications as well. Hart describes the internal point of view in the following terms:[9]

> What is necessary is that there should be a critical reflective attitude to certain patterns of behaviour as a common standard, and that this should display itself in criticism (including self-criticism), demands for conformity, and in acknowledgments that such criticism and demands are justified, all of which find their characteristic expression in the normative terminology of 'ought', 'must', and 'should', 'right' and 'wrong'.

Indeed, the internal point of view aids in distinguishing Hart's concept of law from Austinian command theory.[10] Put simply, people obey rules not only because of the threat of (Austinian) sanctions being imposed upon them but also because they voluntarily *accept* that they *have an obligation* to obey those rules – as

JL Fabra-Zamora (eds), *Kelsen's Legacy: Legal Normativity, International Law and Democracy* (Oxford, Hart Publishing, 2025).

[8] Above, n 1.

[9] Hart (n 1) 57. For an interesting discussion of the internal point of view in the context of contract law, see ZX Tan, 'Deconstructing the Internal Point of View in Contract Law and Theory' (2018) 34 *Journal of Contract Law* 260.

[10] As propounded by John Austin. And see generally WL Morison, *John Austin* (Stanford, Stanford University Press, 1982).

opposed (under Austinian command theory) to *being obliged* to obey the same under threat of sanction in the event of disobedience. It is suggested that this is a valuable insight and can also apply – in the context of the present book – to *judges* as well. As I argue in the final chapter of this book,[11] judges ought to engage in *good faith judging*, and that requires individual acceptance of the values embodied in, inter alia, the oath of judicial office which they have taken.

Insofar as Hart's own concept of a legal system is concerned, he is realistic enough to acknowledge that, in *practical* terms, it is unfeasible to expect the *general population* to accept the *primary* rules from an internal point of view (although that would, presumably, be ideal). Looked at in that light, the role of sanctions for disobedience of the primary rules remains significant. *However*, in Hart's view, the *personnel administering* the *secondary* rules (including *judges*, albeit *not* (by definition) the general population) *must* accept them from an internal point of view. It is only if the aforementioned conditions are satisfied that the union of primary and secondary rules gives rise to a proper legal system in the Hartian sense.

It suffices to note at this point that there are – as to be expected – numerous points that one can take issue with in relation to Hart's concept of law and legal system. However, it is not necessary – in the context of *this* book (which deals with the specific topic of adjudication) – to canvass most of these various issues.[12] There are nevertheless a few specific issues that bear directly on the topic of *adjudication*.

First (and as just alluded to above), there is the role of the internal point of view. However, I will reserve discussion of it until the final chapter when I attempt

[11] See ch 10 in this volume.

[12] A comprehensive, yet succinct, critique of the various aspects of Hart's concept of law may be found in MacCormick (n 7) (these include, amongst many other issues, questions raised with regard to the distinction between primary and secondary rules, the possible circularity in relation to secondary rules, as well as various problems with the rule of recognition (not to mention other more general issues such as the nature of morality as well as of punishment)). And as expected, the general literature is enormous. For a sampling of (just) the books on Hart's work, see, eg, M Martin, *The Legal Philosophy of HLA Hart: A Critical Appraisal* (Philadelphia, Temple University Press, 1987); R Gavison (gen ed), *Issues in Contemporary Legal Philosophy: The Influence of H.L.A. Hart* (Oxford, Clarendon Press, 1987); P Leith and P Ingram (gen eds), *The Jurisprudence of Orthodoxy: Queen's University Essays on H.L.A. Hart* (London, Routledge, 1988); MD Bayles, *Hart's Legal Philosophy: An Examination* (Drodrecht, Kluwer Academic, 1992); J Coleman (gen ed), *Hart's Postscript: Essays on the Postscript to The Concept of Law* (Oxford, Oxford University Press, 2001); N Lacey, *A Life of HLA Hart: The Nightmare and the Noble Dream* (Oxford, Oxford University Press, 2004); MH Kramer, C Grant, B Colburn and A Hatzistavrou (gen eds), *The Legacy of H.L.A. Hart: Legal, Political, and Moral Philosophy* (Oxford, Oxford University Press, 2008); AWB Simpson, *Reflections on The Concept of Law* (Oxford, Oxford University Press, 2011); LD d'Almeida, J Edwards and A Dolcetti, *Reading HLA Hart's The Concept of Law* (Oxford, Hart Publishing, 2013); and MH Kramer, *H.L.A. Hart* (Cambridge, Polity Press, 2018). Lacey's book provides us with the most personal account of Hart's life whilst Simpson's furnishes us with the academic backdrop and context to Hart's work. As already mentioned, the legal literature on Hart's work is enormous. Of special interest – at least to the present author – are L Green, 'The Concept of Law Revisited' (1996) 94 *Michigan Law Review* 1687 (reviewing the second edition of *The Concept of Law*; Professor Green was, in fact, to write the Introduction to the third edition (n 1)); AWB Simpson, 'Herbert Hart Elucidated' (2006) 104 *Michigan Law Review* 1437; and J Finnis, 'H.L.A. Hart: A Twentieth-Century Oxford Political Philosopher' (2009) 54 *American Journal of Jurisprudence* 161.

to draw the various threads of the relevant theories together into a proposed theory of adjudication.[13] Suffice it to state at the present juncture that it is (as very briefly alluded to above) a valuable insight, as it goes to the very heart of the judge's *personal* conception of his or her duty to discharge his or her office in the best way possible. There are – not surprisingly – possible difficulties with the concept of the internal point of view when viewed from a more *general* perspective. These have been dealt with in a simple (albeit not simplistic) manner by Professor MacCormick in his most valuable book on Hart's work.[14] In this regard, he raises a couple of points that might be usefully noted at this juncture. The first is that the internal point of view might apply even in a context where there is in fact no social rule.[15] However, this does not impact the point that the internal point of view nevertheless remains a valuable perspective when considering the adjudicative process. Second, MacCormick does argue persuasively that the internal point of view ought to incorporate the element of emotion as well.[16] For the judge, however, the duty to focus, instead, on the objective truth as well as justice of the case is all-important.[17]

Third, there is the debate between legal positivists (such as Hart) and other jurists (including natural lawyers[18] as well as Dworkin[19]) as to the role of *morality* in the context of the law in general and adjudication in particular. Put simply, is there a *necessary* connection between law and morality? I will have occasion to deal with this issue in the context of the other chapters just mentioned and will therefore deal with only a few specific issues in the present chapter (which arise from the Hart-Fuller debate, which is considered in the next part of this chapter[20]).

Fourth (and this seems to me to be the most important issue that Hart considers in the context of adjudication simply because of the very nature of the question itself), there is the issue as to what a judge ought to do when faced with a 'hard case' (where there is no clear answer to the case that is before the judge). Hart's views in this regard were to generate the famous Hart-Dworkin debate. In a sense, it would be difficult to consider this particular issue fully in the present chapter simply because much of the relevant material itself emanates from Dworkin. However, I will endeavour to set the stage, so to speak,[21] for the fuller discussion as well as analysis that follows in relation to this particular debate in the chapters after next.[22]

[13] See ch 10 in this volume.
[14] See, especially, MacCormick (n 7) ch 4, entitled 'Social Rules'.
[15] ibid 45–46.
[16] ibid 48–49.
[17] And see ch 10 in this volume.
[18] And see ch 5 in this volume.
[19] And see chs 6, 7 and 8 in this volume.
[20] Section III.
[21] See section IV below.
[22] See chs 6, 7 and 8 in this volume.

Finally (and this, as we shall see, is another very important point in the context of adjudication), there is the very strict line which Hart (and other legal positivists) draw between the descriptive on the one hand and the normative on the other. I have in fact dealt with this particular point more generally in an earlier chapter and have demonstrated (by way of actual case law examples) that this distinction can be useful in the practical sphere in relation to *specific legal reasoning*.[23] However, when this distinction is applied in the larger and more general context of the *process of adjudication* itself, the question arises as to whether or not this is justifiable from both theoretical and practical points of view. I deal with the various difficulties in this regard in the penultimate part of this chapter.[24]

I turn now to the Hart-Fuller debate on whether there is a *necessary* connection between law on the one hand and morality on the other.

III. The Hart-Fuller Debate

On a personal note, the Hart-Fuller debate is, literally, as old as I am.[25] However, it is such a fundamental one that it continues to resonate even today.[26] This is not surprising because it impacts an intensely basic question: is there a *necessary* connection between the law on the one hand and morality on the other? Hart answered this question in the negative, whilst Fuller responded in the positive.

In maintaining his thesis, Hart was clear that a clear line should be drawn between the descriptive (the 'is') and the prescriptive (the 'ought'). Morality lay in the realm of the latter. In particular, he was concerned with analytical clarity.

In contrast, Fuller was of the view that morality was an integral part of the law. This led him to formulate his eight principles of legality, which I will be considering in the next chapter.[27]

For the purposes of the present chapter, my own view with regard to the role of morality in the context of adjudication in general and the Hart-Fuller

[23] See ch 2 in this volume.

[24] Section V below.

[25] See HLA Hart, 'Positivism and the Separation of Law and Morals' (1958) 71 *Harvard Law Review* 593 (this was the Oliver Wendell Holmes Lecture delivered at Harvard Law School in April 1957) and LL Fuller, 'Positivism and Fidelity to Law – A Reply to Professor Hart' (1958) 71 *Harvard Law Review* 630. The debate in fact continued over the ensuing years: see, eg, HLA Hart, *The Concept of Law* (Oxford, Clarendon Press, 1961; 3rd edn, 2012); LL Fuller, *The Morality of Law* (New Haven, Yale University Press, 1963; rev edn, 1969), especially 133–145, 184–186, and 187–242 (the last-mentioned citation constituting a post-publication reply to his various critics (in which the legal positivists in general and Hart in particular are the principal 'targets' of critique); and HLA Hart, 'Book Review: *The Morality of Law*' (1965) 78 *Harvard Law Review* 1281.

[26] See, eg, P Cane (ed), *The Hart-Fuller Debate in the Twenty-First Century* (Oxford, Hart Publishing, 2010) and AC Hutchinson, *Hart, Fuller, and Everything After* (Oxford, Hart Publishing, 2022).

[27] See ch 5 in this volume.

debate in particular is (with *the important qualification* set out at the end of the present paragraph and in the next paragraph) that *because courts strive to attain what they perceive is the just and fair decision in the case at hand after having applied the relevant law to the relevant facts, there is a connection between law and morality (the latter being signified by the search for the just and fair decision).* I would in fact venture so far as to state that such a connection is (on the face of it) even *necessary* – if nothing else, from a *causal* perspective. Let me elaborate. It is true that an alternative approach, which views the relationship between law and morality as being merely *correlative*, would be consistent with Hart's approach inasmuch as Hart does not disavow the role of morality; his point is that there is no *necessary* connection between law and morality as such. However, the difficulty with this last-mentioned approach is, first, that it is too vague and really posits nothing practically concrete or useful. Second, if in fact courts strive to achieve or attain what they perceive is the just and fair decision in the case concerned, such an approach is (in substance at least, if not also in form) at least premised on the assumption (or even belief) that there is a *necessary* connection between law and morality. It is my belief that courts do proceed, in such an *attitudinal spirit*, in deciding cases in the *practical sphere*.

I would like to pause at this juncture to take stock of what has been stated thus far. This is because if the actions of the courts in the *practical sphere* are (more) *attitudinal* in nature, there is a sense in which such an approach might not – *wholly* at least – be at odds with Hart's approach. Let me elaborate.

In seeking to arrive at the just and fair decision in the case at hand, a court must – first and foremost – adopt a just and fair *procedure*.[28] It is suggested that this is *entirely consistent with objective morality*. Hart might himself have no (or at least less vigorous) objections to such an approach inasmuch as it might enable him to still maintain the distinction between the *existence* of legal *rules* (which is amenable to a purely *descriptive* undertaking) and the *content* of the same (which might require an excursus into *normative as well as moral* arguments as well as considerations). If so, then the approach which I have suggested (which is *attitudinal as well as procedural* in nature) might *not* be – *wholly* at least – inconsistent with Hart's insistence that there is no *necessary* connection between law and morality. I will return to this point in the concluding part of the present chapter.

IV. Judicial Discretion and Hard Cases

As mentioned earlier in this chapter, this is probably the most important part of the chapter, given the focus of the present book (which is on theories of

[28] As to why I do *not* endorse a *substantive* (as opposed to a *procedural*) approach towards objectivity as well as theory, see ch 3 in this volume.

adjudication). The main question considered in this part is deceptively straightforward: what ought a judge do when faced with a 'hard case' (where there is no clear answer to the case that is before the judge concerned)? Hart's answer was deceptively simple. In essence, there would be no problems if the rule concerned was clear. However, Hart also referred to the 'open texture' of rules and famously drew the distinction between what he termed the 'core' and the 'penumbra', respectively, of a given rule. The 'core' of a rule (or, more accurately, the language within the rule itself) would be such that the court would have no difficulties in deciding that the fact situation before it was covered by the relevant language of that rule. In contrast, however, there might be situations which are not clearly covered by the language of the rule concerned. These would be situations which, in Hart's view, were in the 'penumbra'. This approach is not surprising in view of Hart's focus on linguistic philosophy.[29] But what about the situation where the court has literally 'run out' of rules? This would constitute a 'hard case'. In such a situation, Hart would be prepared to accept that the judge concerned would be free to have regard to *extra*-legal considerations and *make new law*. As we shall see in the chapter after next,[30] Dworkin takes issue with such an approach. As already alluded to above, this generated the very important debate between Hart and Dworkin. More importantly, Dworkin's critique of Hart's views almost inevitably 'forced' him to formulate his *own* theory of adjudication. As we shall also see, it was much more philosophically complex than Hart's approach. For present purposes, however, it can be stated (by way of a preliminary view (until Dworkin's theory of adjudication is considered)) that Hart's approach towards a 'hard case' is indeed an attractive one. Most practising judges and lawyers would, I believe, tend to agree with it. The immediate reason is simple: the tools of trade for judges and lawyers lie primarily in ascertaining what the law is before applying the relevant law to the relevant facts of the case before them. In the former regard, the search for law is (in substance) the search for the relevant legal doctrine or (more specifically) the relevant legal *rules* that would (potentially at least) apply to the facts of the case at hand.[31] It therefore follows that when the legal rules 'run out', the judge, in particular, would *necessarily* need to have recourse to at least the *extra*-legal *context* in order to formulate a *'new' rule* in order to enable it to *decide* the case at hand.

However, Dworkin proffers an *alternative approach*. To run a little ahead of the relevant chapter, he argues that when the judge concerned 'runs out' of rules, that is not the end of the matter. He argues, in particular, that '*principles*' are also part of the law and that the judge ought to have recourse to them in order to decide a 'hard

[29] See, eg, MacCormick (n 7) ch 2, entitled 'Hart: Moral Critic and Analytical Jurist', 23–30.

[30] See ch 6 in this volume.

[31] But *cf* Simpson, 'Herbert Hart Elucidated' (n 12) 1456, where it is observed that 'it is entirely possible for rules to exist without being codified in text at all'. Whilst this is possible, it is suggested that legal rules *are* almost always embodied in *text* as that would be the medium which communicates their content for the purposes of analysis as well as application.

case'. Attractive as it is to continue the analysis at this point, it is suggested that it would be more appropriate to take up this point relating to judicial discretion in a 'hard case' when we consider Dworkin's theory of adjudication in detail in the chapter after next.[32] I would like to turn, instead, to the more *general* difficulties with *legal positivism* itself – in particular, the insistence by Hart on the *descriptive* nature of the judicial enterprise. And it is to those difficulties that our attention now turns.

V. The Difficulties with Legal Positivism

As just mentioned, this part of the chapter deals with the more *general* difficulties with legal positivism. In particular, legal positivists in general and Hart in particular posit a *theoretical framework* that is *purely descriptive* in its *content*. This approach appears to be consistent, for example, with the Singapore Court of Appeal decision in *Ma Hongjin v SCP Holdings Pte Ltd*,[33] where the Court endorsed 'the proposition that *the court* can indeed *confer normative force* on *a test*, the *content* of which might turn on a *factual* determination'.[34] *However*, it should be noted that this endorsement related to a *specific* legal test in the context of the doctrine of consideration in the law of contract. Put simply, that particular legal test held that the *legal* requirement relating to the doctrine of consideration would be satisfied if it could be proven that a *factual* benefit or detriment was present. *However*, there might be a *counterargument*, at least insofar as the aforementioned approach is applied – as Hart does – in a *much broader context* that relates to *theoretical frameworks*.[35] Let me elaborate.

One might argue that although it is possible to have a *theoretical framework* that has as its *content* mere *descriptive material*, both the framework *and* its content are *necessarily two sides of the same coin, or at least have to interact*. If so, then a *theoretical* framework such as that which Hart posits would, on one view, be a *practically ineffectual (and, hence, dilute) one since* the *only* guidance it would provide would be to *merely describe and record what has happened in the past as well as present – but which would furnish no (normative) guidance with regard to the future*. Indeed, 'Hume's Guillotine' (which provides that 'no normative statement can follow from exclusively factual premises'[36]) would apply insofar as the last-mentioned argument is concerned. Put simply, Hart's approach would, with respect, be a theoretical framework with very little (if any) *normative* content

[32] See ch 6 in this volume.
[33] *Ma Hongjin v SCP Holdings Pte Ltd* [2021] 1 *Singapore Law Reports* 304.
[34] ibid [69] (emphasis in the original text).
[35] As to which, see also ch 3 in this volume.
[36] See M Black, 'The "Factual" and the "Normative"' in K Kuypers (ed), *Human Sciences and the Problem of Values* (The Hague, Martinus Nijhoff, 1972) 56. See also the discussion in an earlier chapter of this book: see ch 2 in this volume.

(which is, in fact, precisely his point). However, the result is that such a framework would be one that is 'theoretical' only literally speaking and in name, albeit *not* in *substance*.

On yet *another* view, it might be argued that since (as I have suggested in the preceding paragraph) both the theoretical framework and its content *necessarily* (and at the very least) *interact*, it might be argued that a merely *descriptive content* might result in the *theoretical framework itself becoming descriptive* – that would (in turn) result in that framework *thus ceasing to be a theoretical framework since it would be (in substance and possibly form as well) one that would be devoid of all normative content as well as force*.

Even if we reject the objections just proffered in the preceding couple of paragraphs, it is submitted that Hart's approach, with respect, *still comes up short as a suggested theoretical framework*. This is because whilst the external observer may (in good faith) strive to divest himself or herself of all bias in describing what is observed, he or she would nevertheless (and necessarily, in my view) possess a *normative framework* which *cannot but introduce an evaluative element into what Hart claims is a mere descriptive exercise*. That this occurs – more often than not – on a *subconscious* level merely *exacerbates* the problem. Put simply, even the attempt to merely '*describe*' would *necessarily* be carried out through the *specific lenses* of *the observer* concerned. This is especially the case when one is not – as is the case with regard to *the law* – engaged in describing, say, a physical object (such as an apple or a chair) but *human and social conduct as well as institutions instead*.

It is nevertheless understandable why Hart adopts the position he does. If he concedes that his theory goes *beyond* mere description, he would be *contradicting* himself in relation to a controversy on which he has already taken a stand to the effect that there is no *necessary* connection between law and morality. In other words, in order to maintain that particular stand, Hart's 'theoretical' approach *must preclude all elements as well as references to morality (which, by definition, is normative) – hence, his insistence on mere description, and nothing more*. Indeed (and relatedly), if he adopted any *other* stand, he would, by adopting a *normative* stance, be necessarily drawn into 'theoretical battle' with *other (normative) theories* – with the result of having to *justify* why his theory is the *objectively correct* one. All this is, of course, precisely what Hart is trying to *avoid*.

Notwithstanding the reasons as to why Hart adopted the position he did, it is, with respect, submitted that, for the reasons I have already set out above, it is both *practically (and I would submit theoretically) impossible to implement his theory*. Put simply, evaluation is a necessary element of the process of description, whether we like it or not. *Every* evaluator will evaluate from his or her perspective (which *necessarily includes a personal theoretical framework*). The 'pure' descriptive project which Hart proffers is, with respect, an impossibility. The conclusion in this part of the chapter of this present book is also *consistent* with my conclusion in the preceding part of the same, in which I argue – for the reasons stated therein – why

I do *not* accept (*at least wholly*) Hart's thesis that there is no necessary connection between law on the one hand and morality on the other. Indeed, Professor Guest (very importantly, in my view) identified legal positivism as not only *not* being value-free but *also* as possessing its own theoretical agenda that resulted (in turn) in its focus on description; in his words:[37]

> It is *not* a *value-free* metaphysical explanation at all of law but *a largely implicit proposal for promoting, amongst others, the values of certainty and the independence of the citizen.*

And, on a more general level, the same author put it well when he observed that Hart's approach 'overlooks the possibility that we might *undetachedly* choose to look at law from a detached viewpoint'[38] and that '[t]here is *moral judgment involved* in putting to use the detached eye of the camera'.[39]

As importantly, perhaps, there is *another* reason why, *even if* we *accept* Hart's approach, it would be of *no practical use* in the context of *adjudication*. As already

[37] See S Guest, *Ronald Dworkin*, 3rd edn (Stanford, Stanford University Press, 2013) 30 (emphasis added). See also ibid 39 and 40.

[38] ibid 30 (emphasis added).

[39] ibid (emphasis added). See also J Finnis, 'Law and What I Truly Should Decide' (2003) 48 *American Journal of Jurisprudence* 107, 119, where the learned author observes (very perceptively and persuasively in my view) as follows (emphasis added):

> What the long march through contemporary jurisprudence (as it extended from Bentham to the late 1970s) made manifest can be summarized in two propositions: (1) any plausible theory that results from an effort to describe law, a subject-matter considered as something transcending any local history *has not and will not be normatively inert*; (2) this is in large part because, *given that any general theory of law, however merely descriptive in its ambition, necessarily prefers one concept of law over countless others – given (that is to say) that the theorist's is always a more or less distinctive concept, one that the theorist considers a superior concept, better fitted to answer the questions people have about how law relates to other things and why its various elements hang together as they do – explanations of why this concept is an improved one, to be preferred to other concepts, are designed to show that this concept, this theory, makes better sense of the complex idea that law is something there is reason to have.*

Indeed what has just been quoted would apply *equally* to *Hart's* so-called *descriptive* theory which, it might be added, as '*theory*', *necessarily* possesses as well as embodies a *normative claim*. As Finnis proceeds to observe, Hart's theory is 'not normatively inert' but possesses both 'reason' and 'value' (ibid 120). Indeed, he also points out (again, very persuasively, in my view) that 'a theory does not have comprehensive normative inertness unless it holds that contradictory legal norms can coexist, each equally valid' (ibid 124). Presumably, however, Hart would argue to the contrary (that is, if he desires his theory to be both persuasive and, *ex hypothesi* (ie, *qua theory*), as being universal in application). At that point, however, the claim to 'normative inertness' must necessarily fall away; its claim to 'theoretical neutrality through mere description' is itself a *non*-neutral *theoretical* claim. As Professor Finnis himself incisively observes in another essay, Hartian 'descriptive social theory will be unable to get beyond an endless video of social histories – or a merely statistical ordering of them – unless it makes the judgments about reasonableness that are fundamental to practical social theory': see J Finnis, 'On Hart's Ways: Law as Reason and as Fact' (2007) 52 *American Journal of Jurisprudence* 25, 52 (see also ibid 28 and 46–53 (a version of which was also published in ch 1 of Kramer, Grant, Colburn and Hatzistavrou (n 12)). Reference may also be made to B Edgeworth, 'Legal Positivism and the Philosophy of Language: A Critique of H.L.A. Hart's "Descriptive Sociology"' (1986) 6 *Legal Studies* 115, especially 133–134 and A Phang, '"The Concept of Law" Revisited' (1995) *Tydskrif Vir Die Suid-Afrikaanse Reg (Journal of South African Law)* 403, 406–407.

mentioned above, a theory of adjudication that has as its *sole content* a merely *descriptive* observation of how judges decide cases in the jurisdiction concerned (what an author has described as 'Hartian reportage'[40]) will furnish or provide *no normative guidance* to the court. It would – at best – be an *historical record* of what the court concerned has *already done*. Indeed, any argument to the effect that such an historical record might nevertheless furnish normative guidance (for example, in aiding a court in looking to past decisions in order to decide the case before it) would bring us back full circle to the critique just considered – that Hart's approach is *not* value-free but possesses its own theoretical agenda that results (in turn) in its focus on description.[41]

It is apposite at this particular juncture to conclude the present chapter. Although I have disagreed with many of the theses that characterise Hart's theory insofar as the adjudicative process is concerned, there are nevertheless many (if I may be permitted to put it this way) 'positives' that can be drawn from legal positivism in general and Hart's theory in particular.

VI. Conclusion: The 'Positives' from Legal Positivism

It will be clear to the reader that I do not accept – wholly at least – Hart's thesis that there is no necessary connection as such between law and morality. *However*, I also do not think that there is a clearly persuasive argument as to *which* natural law theory ought to prevail. This is, in fact, an issue which I will deal with in the following chapter.[42] There are, nevertheless, 'positives' which we can glean from positivism that will form part of my *new* theory of adjudication.[43]

As I alluded to at the outset of this chapter, lawyers and judges in the common law world operate daily on the basis of legal *rules*.[44] The Hart-Fuller debate (and, as we shall see, the Hart-Dworkin debate[45]) impacts the *content* of those rules (for example, as part of the latter debate, whether in addition to legal rules, there exist legal *principles*). However, if we put this last-mentioned issue to one side for the moment, it is almost a truism to say that legal rules are part and parcel of everyday legal life – what we would popularly refer to as 'doctrine'. Indeed, a perceived overemphasis on such rules is what jurists such as Dworkin and (as we shall see) schools such as American Realism and Critical Legal Studies took issue with.[46]

[40] MacCormick (n 7) 205.
[41] See the text to n 37, above.
[42] See below, ch 5 in this volume.
[43] As to which see below, ch 10 in this volume.
[44] Despite its title, for an excellent overview that, on balance, argues in favour of rules, see CR Sunstein, 'Problems with Rules' (1995) 83 *California Law Review* 953.
[45] See below, ch 6 in this volume.
[46] For these two schools, see below, ch 9 in this volume.

That having been said, the fundamental – and, indeed, practical – importance of legal rules cannot be gainsaid. If I may lapse temporarily into less scholarly language: try telling a lawyer or a judge (or even a law student) that legal rules do not really exist, and you would receive startled and disbelieving looks, which might even imply that you had taken leave of your senses – and perhaps even from laypersons as well. I should add that this insight from legal positivism should not be gainsaid. It bears reiterating that legal rules are *an indispensable and fundamental* part of the practice of law: they constitute the legal framework for such practice. Indeed, there is a sense in which jurists and legal philosophers can miss this utterly fundamental – and practical – issue when (ironically) discussing their respective theories of *adjudication*.

I should add that, given what I at least perceive to be the intractable controversy surrounding the various debates, it might – as a *provisional* step in endorsing the benefit of legal positivism (as an element in a proposed new theory of adjudication) – be wise to view this particular legal theory as being *procedural* (rather than substantive) in nature.[47] Hart would, I think, have approved of this characterisation simply because, by drawing a distinction between the existence of the rule and its substance (which for natural lawyers, would encompass moral content), his legal theory would continue to (simultaneously) distinguish the descriptive from the prescriptive (or normative), the 'is' from the 'ought'. Looked at in this light, this is why I utilised the term 'provisional' above, for this corresponds to the fact that I do not endorse – *fully* at least – this very strict dichotomy which legal positivism in general and Hart in particular draw between the descriptive and the prescriptive. Indeed, most lawyers and judges in practice would *not* settle (in the main, let alone solely) for a *procedural* theory of law. Insofar as the latter is concerned, courts and judges strive to achieve a *just and fair decision* based on the application of the relevant law to the relevant facts at hand. This involves *more* than a mere procedural conception of law but also a *substantive* one as well.

What, then, ought to be – if at all – the *(substantive) content* of legal *rules*? This would be an appropriate juncture at which to turn to the next chapter (which deals with theories of adjudication premised on *natural law*).[48]

However, before proceeding to do so, a brief note on the relatively short length of the present chapter is in order. Compared, for example, to Dworkin, Hart's focus was on the nature of a legal *system* (of which adjudication formed a small and, in many ways, peripheral or marginal role). His views, however, on adjudication nevertheless formed the jurisprudential platform from which Dworkin built a systematic as well as nuanced theory of adjudication (this also explains, in contrast, the *lengthiness* of the chapters on Dworkin[49]). It is curious, in my view at least, that this particular point has not really been raised (more often at least)

[47] See also ch 3 in this volume.
[48] See ch 5 in this volume.
[49] See chs 6, 7 and 8 in this volume.

in the vast literature that surrounds the Hart-Dworkin debate. Not surprisingly, perhaps, the only notable occasion when it has was by a scholar who was greatly influenced by Hart and who wrote the classic book surveying the entire body of Hart's work; in his words:[50]

> It is worth remarking, however, as others have,[51] that Hart offered *at most a sketchy or skeletal theory about the character of adjudication and of legal reasoning* in [*The Concept of Law*], *and did not subsequently develop any extended account of these matters.* The direction of his inquiry was always more toward a structural explanation of the elements of a legal system and of its systemic character as such. *It is perverse to read his book as though it centrally addressed questions that are somewhat peripheral to its main concerns – and this is perverse, even if the critic thinks these are the most urgent issues jurisprudence should address.* Most of what Hart had to say about adjudication was developed as a part of his attempt to steer a course between formalism and rule-scepticism, and was *not a main topic of his writing.* In response to criticisms by L. L. Fuller and his followers *and by Ronald Dworkin, Hart indeed confessed that there was need to develop a more elaborate theory of legal reasoning than he was ever able himself to do.*

Professor Simpson also furnishes us with a further possible clue as to why Hart's work was not really focused on *adjudication* as such:[52]

> It was quite clear that Hart was not in the least interested in the form of the common law judicial opinion, and indeed did not even see that there was anything to be explained.

Indeed, in a separate essay, Simpson was even more explicit:[53]

> Since Herbert's time, the emphasis in western legal philosophy has been on the analysis of the process of adjudication … Thus *Dworkin's* legal theory is concerned *with little else, and not even with adjudication in some general sense, but only with adjudication by the Supreme Court of the United States. But Herbert's The Concept of Law does not explicitly have a great deal to say on adjudication as such.* It does, however, have a great deal to

[50] MacCormick (n 7) 212 (emphasis added).

[51] Citing F Schauer, '(Re)taking Hart' (2006) 119 *Harvard Law Review* 852 and WL Twining, 'Schauer on Hart' (2006) 119 *Harvard Law Review* 105. See also SJ Shapiro, 'The "Hart-Dworkin" Debate: A Short Guide for the Perplexed' in ch 1 of A Ripstein (gen ed), *Ronald Dworkin* (Cambridge, Cambridge University Press, 2007) and N Stavropoulos, 'The Debate That Never Was' (2017) 130 *Harvard Law Review* 2082, especially 2085–2086 and 2092–2095. Indeed, Hart's written engagement, so to speak, with Dworkin was fairly limited (at least until his posthumously published postscript in *The Concept of Law* (n 1)): see, eg, HLA Hart, 'American Jurisprudence Through English Eyes: The Nightmare and the Noble Dream' (1977) *Georgia Law Review* 969, 978–989 and, by the same author, 'Between Utility and Rights' (1979) 79 *Columbia Law Review* 828, 836–846 (the former (also reprinted as Essay 4 in HLA Hart, *Essays in Jurisprudence and Philosophy* (Oxford, Clarendon Press, 1983)) addresses Dworkin's theory of adjudication, whilst the latter (also reprinted ibid as Essay 9) addresses Dworkin's broader political theory).

[52] See Simpson, *Reflections on The Concept of Law* (n 12) 12. See also ibid 165–168 (notably, this section of this chapter of the book is entitled 'The Absence of the Common Law'). Indeed, in a separate essay, the learned author notes this lack of attention to the common law in Lacey's book on Hart as well: see Simpson, 'Herbert Hart Elucidated' (n 12) 1456.

[53] See Simpson, 'Herbert Hart Elucidated' (n 12) 1452 (emphasis added in italics; final emphasis in italics in the original text). With respect, however, I think that Dworkin's theory of adjudication went *beyond* adjudication by the Supreme Court of the United States.

> say on a further question … – what is meant when we say that a legal *system* exists? In what sense do laws form a system, and what is meant by existence when predicated on such a system? Can laws exist without forming part of a system?

Indeed (and as also emphasised in the preceding quotation), it bears reiterating that Hart was interested more in the nature of a legal *system*. As Simpson aptly put it, Hart was a 'hedgehog' and not a 'fox'.[54] The learned author also observed thus:[55]

> To be sure Hart did not have a great deal to say about the concept of law in general, for his book[56] ended up as a book about the concept of a legal *system*.

This would be an appropriate juncture at which to turn to a theory that is – in many ways – the antithesis of legal positivism: natural law theory, which, as we shall see in the next chapter,[57] has been cast in both classical and modern forms.

[54] Simpson, *Reflections on The Concept of Law* (n 12) 138–140. And see the line from the fragments of the Greek poet Archilochus, which states: 'The fox knows many things, but the hedgehog knows one big thing.' – quoted, famously, by Professor Isaiah Berlin: see I Berlin, *The Hedgehog and the Fox – An Essay on Tolstoy's View of History*, 2nd edn (London, W&N Essentials, 2013) 1. See also R Dworkin, *Justice for Hedgehogs* (Cambridge, Belknap Press, 2011) 1–2 as well as (especially) ch 7 in this volume. Indeed, Simpson himself describes Dworkin as '[t]he leading hedgehog': see Simpson, *Reflections on The Concept of Law* (n 12) 150.

[55] See Simpson, *Reflections on The Concept of Law* (n 12) 204–205 (emphasis added). See also above, n 51.

[56] Viz, *The Concept of Law* (n 1).

[57] See ch 5 in this volume.

5

Natural Law and the Adjudicative Process

I. Introduction

As already witnessed in the previous chapter,[1] in contrast to legal positivism, natural law posits a *necessary* connection between law on the one hand and morality on the other. Put simply, in order to constitute a valid rule or principle[2] of *law*, that particular rule or principle *must* be consistent with *morality*. Given that morality is often associated with being consistent with justice and fairness, it is not surprising that natural law focuses more on *substantive* justice (which, in turn, centres on the *result* of the case concerned). Looked at in this light, a natural law approach towards the adjudicative process is an attractive one simply because of our natural inclination towards the attainment of just and fair results or decisions.

A natural law approach is also attractive because it circumvents the problem of the 'Humean guillotine' which we had considered in an earlier chapter.[3] This problem precludes the derivation of an 'ought' from an 'is'. However, pursuant to a natural law approach, the 'ought' is (as we shall see) not derived from an 'is'; put simply, the prescriptive rule or principle of law does *not* purport to be derived from an existing state of affairs (ie, the 'is'). On the contrary, the prescriptive rule or principle of law is derived from a source that is *itself prescriptive or normative*. It is suggested, however, that by bypassing or circumventing one problem (in this case, that of the 'Humean guillotine'), one nevertheless encounters (as we shall see in a moment) yet *another* problem – the need to *justify* the *source* of the prescriptive rule or principle of law.

Before proceeding to consider the issue just stated, it might be apposite to set out the traditional classification of natural law theory. The first is what has often been termed 'classical natural law'. It is – as the very term suggests – a natural law theory that has its roots in a so-called bygone age. In particular, the specific theory I have in mind is that of Saint Thomas Aquinas. The foundations of this

[1] See ch 4 in this volume.

[2] I deal with the distinction between 'rules' and 'principles' in the next chapter: see ch 6 in this volume. For the purposes of the present chapter, I will use these terms interchangeably.

[3] See ch 2 in this volume.

particular theory rest upon *God* as the ultimate source as well as justification of both divine and human laws. As we shall see, given the gradual erosion – and even disintegration – of religion (in particular, the Christian religion in the context of Aquinas), problems arise with the reliance on Aquinian classical natural law.

A second classification of natural law theory is what I would term 'modern natural law' (which, unlike classical natural law, is not linked to religion as such). In this regard, I will be considering Professor Lon Fuller's theory of law, principally as expounded in his classic book (that was based on his famous Storrs Lectures), *The Morality of Law*.[4] The other work I will be considering is Professor John Finnis's important treatise, *Natural Law and Natural Rights*.[5] As we shall see, the main problem with both these works centres (as is the case with 'classical natural law', albeit understandably in a different way) on that of justification.

Let us now proceed to consider each of the natural law theories in turn and the accompanying lessons (if any) we can learn from them in the context of the adjudicative process.

II. Classical Natural Law[6]

A. The Classical Natural Law Theory of Saint Thomas Aquinas

As already mentioned, my focus in this part of the present chapter will be on Saint Thomas Aquinas's theory of natural law. In particular, he developed, amongst other things, the classical natural law tradition and invested its ultimate source (as also briefly noted above) in God.[7] This last-mentioned point is of the first importance in the context of this book in general and the present chapter in particular, and we shall therefore have occasion to return to it in a moment.

[4] New Haven, Yale University Press, 1963. I will be referring hereafter to the Revised Edition published in 1969.

[5] Oxford, Clarendon Press, 1980. The second edition was published in 2011 by Oxford University Press. I will hereafter be referring to the latter.

[6] See also A Phang, 'Security of Contract and the Pursuit of Fairness' (2000) 16 *Journal of Contract Law* 158, 174–183 (which, however, concerns larger issues relating to the attainment of fairness in the law of contract).

[7] See generally AH Chroust, 'The Philosophy of Law of St Thomas Aquinas: His Fundamental Ideas and Some of His Historical Precursors' (1974) 19 *American Journal of Jurisprudence* 1. See also generally, eg, RJ Henle, SJ, *St Thomas Aquinas – The Treatise on Law* (Notre Dame, University of Notre Dame Press, 1993); AJ Lisska, *Aquinas's Theory of Law – An Analytic Reconstruction* (Oxford, Clarendon Press, 1996); and J Finnis, *Aquinas – Moral, Political, and Legal Theory* (Oxford, Clarendon Press, 1998). And for a good *general* overview of natural law (including classical natural law), see G Duke and RP George (eds), *The Cambridge Companion to Natural Law Jurisprudence* (Cambridge, Cambridge University Press, 2017).

It suffices for present purposes to note that Aquinas distinguishes amongst four types of law.[8] First, he posits a free-standing divine law that constitutes direct revelation from God Himself. Eternal law, natural law and human law (the three other types of law) are interrelated: eternal law, according to Aquinas, is 'the type of Divine Wisdom' that directs all actions and movements; natural law is the participation by rational creatures in the eternal law; and human law comprises the 'particular application of natural law to local communities'.[9] Aquinas also argued that the law is enacted for the common good.[10] In Thomistic theory the 'common good' may, stemming as it does from Christian premises, be distinguished from the utilitarian conception of the same.[11] It is interesting to note, though, that whilst Thomistic theory provides the conceptual foundation for a comprehensive (here, classical) natural law theory, it does not *completely* bridge the gap between the universal and the particular.[12]

[8] See generally *Summa Theologica*, 1a2ae. Q 91. All references to this work are hereinafter to the Dominican translation, originally published in America by Benziger Brothers, and which is now available in a five-volume reprint by Christian Classics, Westminster, Maryland – to which reprint I refer in the present chapter (for a shorter (and well-annotated) version of the *Summa Theologica* based on the same translation, see P Kreeft, *A Summa of the Summa* (San Francisco, Ignatius Press, 1990); and for ease of reference, the citations of the main parts of the *Summa Theologica* may be correlated as follows (I follow the former mode of citation, the second being in parentheses): 1a (I); 1a.2ae (I–II); 2a.2ae (II–II); and 3a (III)). See, further, 1a2ae. Q 93 ('Of the Eternal Law'; see esp Art 1 thereof, where it is stated that 'the eternal law is nothing else than the type of Divine Wisdom, as directing all actions and movements'), Q 94 ('Of the Natural Law'; it should be here noted that Aquinas observes, in Art 2, that the 'first precept of [natural] law' is 'that good is to be done and pursued, and evil is to be avoided' and that '[a]ll other precepts of natural law are based upon this'); Q 95 ('Of Human Law'; at this juncture, an important point should be noted: in Art 1, Aquinas, whilst arguing that 'man has a natural aptitude for virtue', nevertheless admits that 'since some are found to be depraved, and prone to vice, and not easily amenable to words, it was necessary for such to be restrained from evil by force and fear, in order that, at least, they might desist from evil-doing, and leave others in peace, and that they themselves, by being habituated in this way, might be brought to do willingly what hitherto they did from fear, and thus become virtuous. Now this kind of training, which compels through fear of punishment, is the discipline of laws. Therefore, in order that man might have peace and virtue, it was necessary for laws to be framed …'. Further, in Art 2, Aquinas states that 'every human law has just so much of the nature of law, as it is derived from the law of nature. But if in any point it deflects from the law of nature, it is no longer law but a perversion of law'); reference may also be made to Q 92, Art 1, Reply Obj 2 ('It is not always through perfect goodness of virtue that one obeys the law, but sometimes it is through fear of punishment, and sometimes from the mere dictates of reason, which is a beginning of virtue …'); Q 96 ('Of the Power of Human Law'); and Q 97 ('Of Change in Laws').

[9] See NL Geisler, *Thomas Aquinas – An Evangelical Appraisal* (Grand Rapids, Michigan, Baker Book House, 1991) 41 and, generally, ch 12. See also the preceding note.

[10] See *Summa Theologica*, 1a2ae. Q 90, Arts 2 and 4. It should also be noted that the central ideas of Aquinas, whilst endorsed by Catholicism, are nevertheless consistent with Protestantism: see Geisler (n 9) ch 1 – although the learned author's endorsement of Aquinas does not blind him to the ideas of Aquinas which he disagrees with: see generally the 'Epilogue', ibid 177–178.

[11] In the context of general and political philosophy.

[12] It is unnecessary for the purposes of this book as well as this chapter to deal with how the relevant *historical* arguments (centred on Christian apologetics) could possibly bridge this gap in what might become a new Christian natural law theory, as to which see A Phang, 'American Jurisprudence Through Christian Eyes – Beyond the Nightmare and the Noble Dream' (2004) 81 *University of Detroit Mercy Law Review* 867, 902–920. Broadly speaking, invoking arguments from Christian apologetics centring on the death and resurrection of Jesus Christ, the reliability and veracity of the Bible, and the person as well as work of the Holy Spirit could possibly aid in resolving the problem of objectivity as well

Whilst Aquinian classical natural law theory is attractive since its ultimate source (as well as source of justification) is itself normative and is located in God, it is nevertheless subject to several significant objections.

B. The Difficulties with the Natural Law Theory of Saint Thomas Aquinas

The most obvious objection centres on a fundamental controversy as to the existence of God. In fairness to Aquinas, he did proffer arguments for the existence of God, which arguments in fact extend beyond their Christian origins and could possibly be applied in the context of most mainstream religions that contain a conception of God.[13] Two of his arguments are of especial significance:[14] the cosmological argument and the argument from design, respectively.[15] Aquinas

as in providing (through the guidance of the Holy Spirit) the necessary guidance when applying the relevant law and in reconciling individualism and communitarianism (through the application of the self-sacrificial *agape* love of Christ that resolves the problem of human nature and human self-interest). For an early statement of these ideas and arguments, see Phang (n 6) 178–181.

In a related vein, it is also interesting to note that Geisler is of the view that Aquinas provides us with the foundation in theistic apologetics that is 'the logical prerequisite of historical apologetics': see Geisler (n 9) 21. Indeed, it is of further interest to note that (and this is a point not often stressed by scholars, in particular, Christian critics of Aquinas) that Aquinas emphasised in no uncertain terms that the Holy Bible or Scriptures are the inspired and inerrant Word of God: see, eg, *Summa Theologica*, 1a. Q 1, Art 1; 1a. Q 1, Art 2 ('[S]acred doctrine is a science'); 1a. Q 1, Art 3 ('Sacred doctrine is one science … because Sacred Scripture considers things precisely under the formality of being divinely revealed, whatever has been divinely revealed possesses the one precise formality of the object of this science; and therefore is included under sacred doctrine as under one science'); 1a. Q 1, Art 10 ('The author of Holy Writ is God, in whose power it is to signify His meaning, not by words only (as man also can do), but also by things themselves'; also, 'it is plain that nothing false can ever underlie the literal sense of Holy Writ'); 3a. Q 1, Art 3; 1a. Q 1, Art 1; 2a2e. Q 1, Art 9 ('The truth of faith is contained in Holy Writ'); and 2a2ae. Q 173, Art 4; see also 3a. Qq 27-59 (on the life of Christ). See, further, Geisler (n 9) 37 and esp ch 4; see further, 43, where the learned author observes that 'Aquinas had a deep respect for Scripture and made extensive use of it in his writings'; and at 56, the author observes, in similar vein, that 'the hundreds of citations of Scripture reveal the thoroughly biblical nature of his theology as well as his vast knowledge of Scripture'. Reference should also be made to J Van der Ploeg, 'The Place of Holy Scripture in the Theology of St Thomas' (1947) 10 *Thomist* 398, where the learned author observes (at 398) that '[a]ccording to Pope Leo XIII, St Thomas Aquinas was the leading exegete of Holy Scripture among the theologians of the Scholastic age'; (at 400) that '[i]n the last seventeen years of his life, from his graduation as a Master of Theology in 1256 until his death in 1273, St Thomas wrote commentaries on a number of biblical books'; and (at 401) that '[i]n his other theological works St Thomas cited a great number of scripture-texts and has interpreted separately very many of them'. Nor, to take another important and related point, did Aquinas gloss over the problem of human nature in general and sin in particular, which might prevent proper knowledge of God Himself: see, eg, *Summa Theologica*, 2a2ae. Q 2, Art 4. See also the very significant point made by Aquinas in 1a2ae. Q 95, Art 1. On sin generally, see 1a2ae. Qq 71-89. And, on grace, see, in particular, 1a2ae. Q 109.

[13] It is equally true, however, that the *content* of the various religions may be quite different and that some religions conceive of an immanent rather than a transcendent God. Aquinas, though, adopts a Christian approach that views God as both transcendent *and* immanent.

[14] See generally *Summa Theologica*, 1a. Q 3, Art 3.

[15] See generally *Summa Theologica*, 1a. Q 2, Art 3 (on the five ways in which Aquinas states the existence of God can be proved) and 1a. Q 44 as well as *Summa Theologica*, 1a. Q 2, Art 2 (on whether it can

argues that God created the universe ex nihilo.[16] Insofar as he is concerned, God is the source of all truth.[17]

It is also pertinent to note – in a related vein – that a central motif in Aquinas's work is the reconciliation of faith and reason.[18] As Aquinas himself observed:[19]

> Now, although the truth of the Christian faith … surpasses the capacity of the reason, nevertheless that truth that the human reason is naturally endowed to know cannot be opposed to the truth of the Christian faith. For that with which the human reason is naturally endowed is clearly most true; so much so, that it is impossible for us to think of such truths as false. Nor is it permissible to believe as false that which we hold by faith, since this is confirmed in a way that is so clearly divine. Since, therefore, only the false is opposed to the true, as is clearly evident from an examination of their definitions, it is impossible that the truth of faith should be opposed to those principles that the human reason knows naturally.

Aquinas's reconciliation of faith and reason is based on the concept that the faculty of reason is unique to human beings and is given by God Himself.[20] Pursuant to

be demonstrated that God exists). For more modern works arguing for the existence of God, see, eg, JP Moreland, *Scaling the Secular City – A Defense of Christianity* (Grand Rapids, Michigan, Baker Book House, 1987); Geisler (n 9) ch 9; and R Swinburne, *The Existence of God*, rev edn (Oxford, Clarendon Press, 1991).

[16] See generally *Summa Theologica*, 1a. Qq 44–46.

[17] See generally *Summa Theologica*, 1a. Q 16, Arts 1–8 and 1a2ae. Q 109, Art 1 (where it is stated that 'for the knowledge of any truth whatsoever man needs Divine help, that the intellect may be moved by God to its act. But he does not need a new light added to his natural light, in order to know the truth in all things, but only in some that surpass his natural knowledge. And yet at times God miraculously instructs some by His grace in things that can be known by natural reason, even as He sometimes brings about miraculously what nature can do').

[18] See, eg, *Summa Theologica*, 2a2ae. Q 2, esp Art 10 (where, inter alia, first referring to 1 Peter 3:15, Aquinas proceeds to observe that 'reason does not diminish the merit of faith'); reference should also be made to *Summa Theologica*, 2a2ae. Q 2, Art 2 (reason can be used to prove that God exists but cannot be used to force persons to believe in that fact, which requires an act of will (in faith) on the part of the persons concerned; see also *Summa Theologica*, 2a2ae. Q 6, Art 1 (where there is also reference to 'some supernatural principle moving in him [the person concerned] inwardly; and this is God. Therefore faith, as regards the assent which is the chief act of faith, is from God moving man inwardly by grace'; this is, it is suggested, the work of the Third Person of the Trinity, viz, The Holy Spirit). See also *Summa Contra Gentiles*, Bk IV, chs 21 and 22 (the translation of Bk IV is by CJ O'Neil (Notre Dame, University of Notre Dame Press, 1975) and is the translation referred to in this chapter); *Summa Theologica*, 2a2ae. Q 2, Art 1 (a reasonable faith, where it is stated, inter alia, that 'it is proper to the believer to think with assent'); 2a2ae. Q 4, Art 8 ('[S]cience is not more certain than faith; nor is anything else'); as well as 2a2ae. Q 4, Art 2 (faith resides in the intellect); and *Summa Contra Gentiles*, Bk I, ch 4, paras 2–5 (on the limitations of reason; the translation of Bk I is by AC Pegis (Notre Dame, University of Notre Dame Press, 1975) and is the translation referred to in this chapter; and *cf* the main text to the next note; see also, in this regard, Aquinas's *De veritate*, Q 14, Arts 5 (this particular article emphasising the supreme importance of love in relation to faith) and 10 (this translation is by JV McGlynn SJ, *Truth – St Thomas Aquinas*, vol 2 (Indianapolis, Indiana, Hackett Publishing Company Inc, 1994)). See, further, Geisler (n 9) ch 5; the learned author pithily observes thus (57): 'Aquinas holds that faith and reason are interrelated. Faith uses reason, and reason cannot go it alone without faith. Both are necessary, but each in its own order'.

[19] *Summa Contra Gentiles*, Bk 1, ch 7, para 1.

[20] See, eg, *Summa Theologica*, 1a. Q 79, esp Art 8 and Ia2ae. Q 1, Art 1. In a more specific vein (insofar as the law itself is concerned), Aquinas stresses that 'law is something pertaining to reason': see *Summa Theologica*, 1a2e. Q 90, Art 1; the law itself 'is nothing else but a dictate of practical reason': see *Summa*

the foregoing, an argument that places law on an objective natural law basis would not, *ex hypothesi*, be premised on blind faith.

However, Aquinas's views have – as briefly alluded to above – not been immune from critique. One major factor that has contributed towards diminishing the persuasiveness of the classical natural law argument in general and the view that God exists in particular has been the rise of pluralism and the loss of a belief in religion as well as universal values. Whilst pluralism does not necessarily entail subjectivity or relativism, the latter attitude has – particularly in the more recent era of postmodernism – led to the erosion of (or even abandonment of) a belief in God. That seems to me to be the biggest stumbling block in adopting classical natural law as a theory in the context of the adjudicative process. It is indeed the case that judges embrace different worldviews and faiths, and some may hold either agnostic or atheistic worldviews; other judges may believe in God, but the content of their respective beliefs may be quite different. However, that does not mean that they do not administer justice. After all, the law applies to everyone, regardless of his or her religious persuasion. Legal rules and principles are not – and cannot be – coterminous or in any way linked with a single religious belief or viewpoint, especially in common law countries[21] which are multi-cultural and religiously plural in their nature. Indeed, personal religious and ethical beliefs are not necessarily inconsistent with the general sense of justice and fairness that is embodied in the general rules and principles of the law itself; there is, in fact, every reason to believe that the converse would be the case. Even when viewed from a Christian perspective, it cannot be said that courts which do not subscribe to a Christian natural law theory do not dispense justice. Indeed, the Christian faith itself acknowledges that God can ensure that justice is dispensed by common grace, consistently with what the apostle Saint Paul has termed 'the law written on the heart'.[22] And that is why even committed Christian judges like Lord Denning never, at least expressly, espoused his religious beliefs in his judgments; such views are to be found, instead, in his extra-judicial writings.[23] More generally, that is also why one does not find – regardless of the jurisdiction concerned – courts in common law (or even civil law) jurisdictions referring to divine, eternal, and/or natural law in the manner posited by Aquinas (and as referred to briefly above).

Theologica, 1a2e. Q 91, Art 1. Again, he states that 'a law is a dictate of the practical reason': *Summa Theologica*, 1a2e. Q 91, Art 3. See also *Summa Theologica*, 1a2e. Q 91, Art 2, where Aquinas observes that 'because the rational creature partakes thereof in an intellectual and rational manner, therefore the participation of the eternal law in the rational creature is properly called a law, since a law is something pertaining to reason … Irrational creatures, however, do not partake thereof in a rational manner, wherefore there is no participation of the eternal law in them, except by way of similitude'.

[21] And even civil law countries for that matter.

[22] See Romans 2: 14–15.

[23] See A Phang, 'A Passion for Justice – Lord Denning, Christianity and the Law' in ch 15 of M Hill and RH Helmholz (eds), *Great Christian Jurists in English History* (Cambridge, Cambridge University Press, 2017) 320.

Let us turn now to consider the more 'modern' natural law theories as embodied within the work of Professors Fuller and Finnis, respectively.

III. Modern Natural Law

A. Fuller's 'Internal Morality of Law'[24]

i. Fuller's Theory

As already alluded to above, Professor Lon L Fuller's theory does not rely upon God as its ultimate source of justification. The roots of his theory may be traced to the famous 'Hart-Fuller debate',[25] and, as already mentioned, my focus in this part of the present chapter will be on his book, *The Morality of Law*.[26] Before proceeding to consider it briefly, it is interesting to note that Fuller's theory, having lain relatively dormant for many years in the context of Anglo-American jurisprudence, has recently witnessed a renewed interest and even a revival of sorts.[27]

Fuller commences by drawing a distinction between what he calls 'the morality of aspiration' and 'the morality of duty'.[28] The former 'is most plainly exemplified in Greek philosophy' and 'is the morality of the Good Life, of excellence, of the fullest realization of human powers', whereas the latter 'lays down the basic rules without which an ordered society directed toward certain specific goals must fail of its mark'; as Fuller puts it, 'the morality of duty' 'does not condemn men for failing to embrace opportunities for the fullest realization of their powers' but, instead, 'condemns them for failing to respect the basic requirements of social living'.[29]

[24] See generally RS Summers, *Lon L Fuller* (Stanford, Stanford University Press, 1984). Indeed, Professor Summers wrote a comprehensive and insightful review essay on Fuller's book (Fuller (n 4)) almost two decades before: see RS Summers, 'Professor Fuller on Morality and Law' (1965) 18 *Journal of Legal Education* 1. Somewhat surprisingly, perhaps, Fuller himself went to the trouble of compiling a list of book reviews of his book: see Fuller (n 4) 243–244. And for some possible at least (general) hint at Fuller's possible motivation in this last-mentioned regard, see N Lacey, 'Out of the "Witches" Cauldron?' in ch 1 of P Cane (ed), *The Hart-Fuller Debate in the Twenty-First Century* (Oxford, Hart Publishing, 2010) 16–22 (in particular with respect to Fuller's sensitivity towards critique of his work).

[25] See HLA Hart, 'Positivism and the Separation of Law and Morals' (1958) 71 *Harvard Law Review* 593 and LL Fuller, 'Positivism and Fidelity to Law: A Reply to Professor Hart' (1958) 71 *Harvard Law Review* 630. The debate, as Fuller himself noted, continued over the ensuing years: see, eg, HLA Hart, *The Concept of Law* (Oxford, Clarendon Press, 1961; 3rd edn, 2012); Fuller (n 4), especially 133–145, 184–186, and 187–242 (the last-mentioned citation constituting a post-publication reply to his various critics (in which the legal positivists in general and Hart in particular are the principal 'targets' of critique); and HLA Hart, 'Book Review: *The Morality of Law*' (1965) 78 *Harvard Law Review* 1281.

[26] Fuller (n 4).

[27] See, eg, Cane (n 24); K Rundle, *Forms Liberate: Reclaiming the Jurisprudence of Lon Fuller* (Oxford, Hart Publishing, 2012); and AC Hutchinson, *Hart, Fuller, and Everything After: The Politics of Legal Theory* (Oxford, Hart Publishing, 2023).

[28] Fuller (n 4) 4.

[29] ibid 5–6.

In his view, 'the morality of *duty* finds its *closest cousin* in *the law*'.[30] It is (not surprisingly perhaps) also the case that '[i]n the morality of duty it is understandable that *penalties* should take precedence over rewards'.[31]

He then proceeds to outline – in relation to a legal system proper – *eight principles of legality*. These principles comprise 'eight kinds of legal excellence toward which a system of rules may strive'.[32] Not surprisingly, they constitute the *core* of Fuller's '*internal morality of law*'. Although he is of the view that this internal morality of law 'embraces [both] a morality of duty and a morality of aspiration',[33] the learned author (somewhat surprisingly, in my view at least) concludes that 'the inner morality of law is condemned to remain *largely* a morality of *aspiration* and not of duty' and that '[i]ts primary appeal must be to a sense of trusteeship and to the pride of the craftsman'.[34] In my view, this last-mentioned observation is surprising because, as we shall see, the *very nature* of the internal morality of law seems, to me at least, *so basic and fundamental* to the *existence and operation* of *any viable legal system* that it should be viewed as a morality of *duty*. It should be noted, though, that Fuller does observe that one particular principle of legality is nevertheless imperative – 'the desideratum of making the laws known, or at least making them available to those affected by them'.[35]

The eight principles of legality themselves comprise the following.

The first relates to *the generality of law*. As Fuller puts it, 'there must be rules'.[36] So, for example, agencies fail in this particular respect when 'they have failed to develop any significant rules at all'.[37] He nevertheless acknowledges that there may in fact be rules that are *unfair*.[38] This appears to be, therefore, *not inconsistent* with a *legal positivist* approach towards the law, for, as we have seen in the previous chapter,[39] one of the fundamental tenets of legal positivism is that there is *no necessary* connection between law on the one hand and morality on the other. It is suggested that this is an important point to which we shall return below. That having been said, this particular requirement of legality is so *basic* that it is often taken for granted. However, its importance cannot be gainsaid. This is because a system cannot be a *legal* system if it is devoid of rules that are, by their *very nature, normative and universal* – and which therefore form the foundation for *objectively just and fair outcomes, regardless* of the fact situation concerned.

[30] ibid 15 (emphasis added).
[31] ibid 30 (emphasis added).
[32] ibid 41.
[33] ibid 42.
[34] ibid 43 (emphasis added). See also ibid 45 (emphasis added), where Fuller refers to 'the *utopia* of legality'.
[35] ibid 43.
[36] ibid 46. As the learned author also observes (ibid 49): '[T]he requirement of generality rests on the truism that to subject human conduct to the control of rules, there must be rules.' He also observes (ibid 155) that 'law is a precondition of good law'.
[37] ibid 47.
[38] ibid.
[39] See ch 4 in this volume.

Put simply, without rules, any decision by a court would be *necessarily arbitrary* in nature. Not surprisingly, therefore, Fuller observes that '[i]n *actual* systems for controlling and directing human conduct a *total failure* to achieve anything like a general rule is *rare*'.[40]

The second principle of legality consists in *promulgation*. This principle that entails *publishing* laws is related to education in order that a citizen should know what he or she can (and cannot) do. However, Fuller does acknowledge that there is a prior problem as to what should count as 'law' for the purposes of this particular principle.[41]

The third principle relates to the prohibition of *retroactive laws*. Indeed, as Fuller puts it:[42]

> Taken by itself, and in abstraction from its possible function in a system of laws that are largely prospective, a retroactive law is truly a monstrosity.

He nevertheless does acknowledge – in fairness – that there might be situations 'when things go wrong', at which point 'the retroactive statute often becomes indispensable as *a curative measure*'.[43] Fuller also raises the important issue of the inherent (yet wholly necessary) element of retroactivity that accompanies every decision by *a court*; as he puts it, '[i]f the judge decides the case, he inevitably engages in an act of retrospective legislation'.[44]

The fourth principle relates to *the clarity of laws*. Indeed, the necessity for clear laws seems to me to be an obvious requirement. Again, however, Fuller is fully cognisant of logic and common sense in general and the *nature* of *the common law process* in particular. Hence, he accepts that '[t]o put a high value on *legislative* clarity is *not* to condemn out of hand rules that make legal consequences depend on [common law] standards such as "good faith" and "due care"';[45] on the contrary, Fuller notes that '[s]ometimes the best way to achieve clarity is to take advantage of, and to incorporate into the law, common sense standards of judgment that have grown up in the ordinary life lived outside legislative halls'.[46] And as he aptly puts it, '[a] specious clarity can be more damaging than an honest open-ended vagueness'.[47] Indeed, '[i]n *commercial law*, for example, requirements of "fairness" can take on *definiteness of meaning* from a body of commercial practice and from the principles of conduct shared by a community of economic traders'.[48]

[40] Fuller (n 4) 48 (emphasis added).
[41] ibid 50.
[42] ibid 53.
[43] ibid (emphasis added).
[44] ibid 56 (though *cf* jurists such as Professor Ronald Dworkin (see also generally chs 6, 7 and 8 in this volume)).
[45] ibid 64 (emphasis added).
[46] ibid.
[47] ibid.
[48] ibid (emphasis added).

The fifth principle states that there are to be *no contradictions in the laws.* Fuller perceptively observes that in order to ascertain whether or not there is such a contradiction, 'we must often take into account a host of considerations extrinsic to the language of the rules themselves'.[49] This is eminently correct because the *context* in which language is used is also an extremely important consideration.[50]

The sixth principle *prohibits laws requiring the impossible.* Fuller does raise the issue as to whether or not '[t]he question may be raised … whether most of the other desiderata that make up the internal morality of law are not also ultimately concerned with the possibility of obedience'.[51] In response to (and in defence of having separate requirements as components or elements of the internal morality of law), he states as follows:[52]

> But in justification for the separation effected … it should be observed that my concern is not to engage in an exercise in logical entailment, but to develop principles for the guidance of purposive human effort. The logician may, if he wishes, view a law that contradicts itself[53] as a special case of the impossibility of observance, though in adopting this view he may … find it difficult to define what he means by a 'contradiction'. From the standpoint of the lawmaker, in any event, there is an essential difference between the precautions he must take to keep his enactments consistent with one another and those he must take to be sure that the requirements of the law lie within the powers of those subject to them. Essential differences of this sort would be obscured by any attempt to telescope everything under the head of 'impossibility of obedience'.

Whilst Fuller acknowledges the (broader) need for strict liability, he also notes that '[w]hat the internal morality of law demands of a rule of strict liability is not that it cease commanding the impossible, but that it define as clearly as possible the kind of activity that carries a special surcharge of legal responsibility'.[54] And whilst he also acknowledges that *contractual* liability is also, generally speaking, strict, it does not pose any problems insofar as he is concerned:[55]

> It scarcely requires demonstration that this … form of strict liability presents no problem for the internal morality of law; the law ought not itself to impose an impossible burden on a man, but it is not bound to protect him from contractually assuming responsibility for an occurrence that lies beyond his powers.

[49] ibid 69.

[50] This is indeed the case in the law of contractual interpretation where both text *and* context are of the first importance: see, eg, the Singapore Court of Appeal decision of *Y.E.S. F&B Group Pte Ltd v Soup Restaurant Singapore Pte Ltd (formerly known as Soup Restaurant (Causeway Point) Pte Ltd)* [2015] 5 *Singapore Law Reports* 1187, [2], [30] and [35].

[51] Fuller (n 4) 70 n 29.

[52] ibid.

[53] This, it will be recalled, is the fifth principle.

[54] Fuller (n 4) 75.

[55] ibid 77.

However, his view of strict *criminal* liability is somewhat more negative.[56]

Fuller's seventh principle of legality requires the *constancy of the law through time.*

His eighth – and final – principle of legality is the need for *congruence between official action and declared rule.* This is, in his view, 'the most complex of all the desiderata that make up the internal morality of the law'.[57] In order to ensure that this particular principle is met, various procedural devices taking 'a variety of forms' are necessary, and that, in his view, '[w]e may count here most of the elements of "procedural due process"'.[58] Significantly, 'it is *chiefly to the judiciary* that is entrusted the task of preventing a discrepancy between the law as declared and as actually administered'.[59] However, Fuller acknowledges that such an approach also carries with it 'serious disadvantages': including 'the willingness and financial ability of the affected party to take his case to litigation'.[60]

Having set out the abovementioned eight principles of legality that constitute the internal morality of law, Fuller observes (importantly, in my view) that 'the stringency with which the eight desiderata as a whole should be applied, as well as their priority of ranking among themselves, will be affected by the branch of law in question, as well as by the kinds of legal rules that are under consideration'.[61]

It is clear that Fuller's internal morality of law is *quite different* from classical natural law theory. And he helpfully clarifies what the precise relationship is in *The Morality of Law*[62] itself. He first responds to the question as to whether his internal morality of law represents some variety of natural law thus:[63]

> The answer is an emphatic, though qualified, yes.

However, as just mentioned, it is nevertheless quite different from classical natural law theory. As Fuller puts it:[64]

> What I have tried to do is to discern and articulate the natural laws of a particular kind of human undertaking, which I have described as 'the enterprise of subjecting human conduct to the governance of rules'.[65] These natural laws have nothing to do with any 'brooding omnipresence in the skies'. Nor have they the slightest affinity with any such proposition as that the practice of contraception is a violation of God's law. *They remain entirely terrestrial in origin and application. They are not 'higher' laws; if any metaphor of elevation is appropriate they should be called 'lower' laws. They are like the natural laws of*

[56] ibid 77–78.
[57] ibid 81.
[58] ibid.
[59] ibid (emphasis added).
[60] ibid.
[61] ibid 93.
[62] Fuller (n 4).
[63] ibid 96.
[64] ibid (emphasis added).
[65] See also ibid 106 and 122.

carpentry, or at least those laws respected by a carpenter who wants the house he builds to remain standing and serve the purpose of those who live in it.

Indeed, Fuller *contrasts* the internal morality of law with what he terms 'the *external* morality of law'.[66] He proceeds to observe as follows:[67]

> As a convenient (though not wholly satisfactory) way of describing the distinction being taken [between the internal morality of law and the external morality of law] we may speak of a *procedural*, as distinguished from a *substantive*[68] natural law. What I have called the internal morality of law is in this sense *a procedural version of natural law*, though to avoid misunderstanding the word 'procedural' should be assigned a special and expanded sense so that it would include, for example, a substantive accord between official action and enacted law. The term 'procedural' is, however, broadly appropriate as indicating that we are concerned, not with the substantive aims of legal rules, but with the ways in which a system of rules for governing human conduct must be constructed and administered if it is to be efficacious and at the same time remain what it purports to be.

In his view, the internal morality of law is *facilitative* of 'enabling men to live a satisfactory life in common'.[69]

In a related vein, Fuller observes thus:[70]

> But a recognition that the internal morality of law may support and give efficacy to a wide variety of substantive aims should not mislead us into believing that *any* substantive aim may be adopted without compromise of legality.

Of significance, too, are his following observations:[71]

> I have attempted to show that the internal morality of law does indeed deserve to be called a 'morality'.[72] I hope I have demonstrated that an acceptance of this morality is

[66] ibid 96 (emphasis added). See also ibid 102.

[67] ibid 96–97 (emphasis added). The following heading in the same book (entitled 'The Neutrality of the Law's Internal Morality toward Substantive Aims') is also very significant: see ibid 153.

[68] And see the reference to Saint Thomas Aquinas in this particular regard: ibid 98. Indeed, Fuller later observed that one writer had pointed out that 'Aquinas in some measure recognized and dealt with all eight of the principles of legality' (referring to Lewis, 'The High Court: Final … but Fallible' (1968) 19 *Western Reserve Law Review* 528, 565): see Fuller (n 4) 242. However, he nevertheless also observed that '[i]t may be stretching things a bit to say that Aquinas recognized the principle of congruity between official action and declared rule': ibid 242, n 52. *Quaere* whether Fuller at least implicitly conceded that Aquinas had in fact recognised and dealt with the *remaining seven* principles of legality.

[69] Fuller (n 4) 223 (citing with approval HM Hart, 'The Relations between State and Federal Law' (1954) 54 *Columbia Law Review* 489, 490).

[70] Fuller (n 4) 153 (emphasis in the original text).

[71] ibid 168 (emphasis added). And he also observes that 'law is a precondition of good law': see ibid 155.

[72] In response to critics who viewed the internal morality of law not as a morality but, instead, an instrument to achieve efficacy, Fuller observed thus (ibid 205):

> What is generally missing in these accounts [by the critics] is any recognition of the role legal rules in making possible an effective realization of morality in the actual behavior of human beings. Moral principles cannot function in a social vacuum or in a war of all against all. To live the good

> *a necessary, though not sufficient condition* for the realization of justice, that this morality is itself violated when an attempt is made to express blind hatreds through legal rules, and that, finally, the specific morality of the law articulates and holds before us a view of man's human nature that is indispensable to law and morality alike.

Finally, the following statement (towards the very end of the book) is also thought-provoking:[73]

> If I were asked, then, to discern *one central indisputable principle* of what may be called *substantive natural law* – Natural Law with capital letters – I would find it in the injunction: *Open up, maintain, and preserve the integrity of the channels of communication by which men convey to one another what they perceive, feel, and desire.*

Insofar as his many *concrete illustrations* are concerned, his argument in relation to the then-situation in South Africa (where, inter alia, legislation prescribed racial discrimination) is interesting inasmuch as he attributes the situation then not to substantive injustice as such but, instead, to failure to meet the requirements of legality embodied in the internal morality of law.[74]

The above contrast described briefly above between the internal morality of law on the one hand and the external morality of law on the other constitutes an extremely important point – which I shall consider in a moment as we now turn to both the benefits from, as well as difficulties with, Fuller's theory.

ii. The Benefits from, and Difficulties with, Fuller's Theory

Before considering briefly the difficulties with Fuller's theory centring on the internal morality of law, it would be apposite to first consider the *benefits* arising from that theory itself.

For anyone who is even remotely familiar with the concept of the Rule of Law, it is clear that the eight principles of legality embodied in Fuller's internal morality of law constitute a large part of what we understand by the Rule of Law. This is underscored by Fuller's emphasis – mentioned above – on the fact that the internal morality of law is *procedural* in nature. Indeed, the concept of the Rule of Law is often associated with the idea of 'due *process*' – a point that is also stressed by Fuller himself.[75] In my view, this is the principal *benefit* that is to be derived

> life requires something more than good intentions, even if they are generally shared; it requires the support of firm base lines for human interaction, something that – in modern society at least – only a sound legal system can supply.

Fuller's view was, in other words, 'an interactional view of law' (see ibid 221; see also ibid 238). Reference may also be made to his observations at ibid 207.

[73] ibid 186 (emphasis added).

[74] ibid 160.

[75] See the text to n 58, above. See also LL Fuller, 'A Reply to Professors Cohen and Dworkin' (1965) 10 *Villanova Law Review* 655, 656, where Professor Fuller states: 'I embrace and accept what may be called the concept of an institutional or *procedural* morality; they reject it.' (emphasis added). And as

from Fuller's internal morality of law. Admittedly, this still leaves us with the issue of source (and justification). Unlike, for example, classical natural law, there is no clear source of justification for the eight principles of legality. As we have seen, classical natural law finds its ultimate source of justification in God, although that particular justification also raises difficulties of its own.[76] What is clear, however, is that the Rule of Law nevertheless remains foundational to the very idea of a just and fair legal system – a point that is wholly consistent with Fuller's internal morality of law. As I will argue in the final chapter of this book,[77] my proposed theory of adjudication posits that *judges* will indeed – in judging in 'good faith' – ensure that they observe (as far as is possible) the Rule of Law and, looked at in this light, Fuller's internal morality of law is indeed directly relevant to the approach I advocate.

Turning now to the *difficulties* surrounding Fuller's theory, one might quite legitimately inquire whether the two moralities he refers to (that of aspiration and that of duty) really add anything to the theory itself. There is another – and more specific – point: we have already noted that Fuller characterises the internal morality of law largely as a morality of *aspiration*.[78] As I have already suggested earlier in this chapter, this is a surprising characterisation, as the internal morality of law is *so basic and fundamental* to the *existence and operation* of *any viable legal system* that it should be viewed, instead, as a morality of *duty*.[79] And this is, a fortiori, the case if, as I have just argued, we view Fuller's internal morality of law as being consistent with *the Rule of Law* itself.

More specifically, the relationship amongst the eight principles of legality appears to be rather fluid. For example, Fuller states that the second, third and fourth principles may diminish in importance if there already exists a public consensus with regard to extralegal morality.[80] We have also seen that the learned author has stated that the stringency with which the eight principles of legality as a whole should be applied 'will be affected by the branch of law in question, as well as by the kinds of legal rules under consideration'.[81] This statement is, with respect, quite vague, although it might be argued that, in the nature of things, there can be

one learned author put it, despite his powerful critique of *The Morality of Law* itself (see Summers, 'Professor Fuller on Morality and Law' (n 24) 27):

> It is the best discussion of the demands of the rule of law in existing literature. And, it establishes beyond doubt that compliance with 'principles of legality is essential if we are to order our daily lives.

Reference may also be made to D Sturm, 'Lon Fuller's Multidimensional Natural Law Theory' (1966) 18 *Stanford Law Review* 612, 613.

[76] See the text to nn 20–23, above.

[77] See ch 10 in this volume.

[78] See the text to n 34, above. Fuller does make one exception though: see the text to n 35, above.

[79] See the text to nn 34–35, above. Though *quaere* whether the view just proffered is itself, at least arguably, culturally biased: see, eg, H Gross, 'Book Review of The Morality of Law' (1965) 40 *New York University Law Review* 1220, 1222. For further critique of the distinction between the two moralities, see Summers, 'Professor Fuller on Morality and Law' (n 24) 4 and 5–12.

[80] Fuller (n 4) 92.

[81] ibid 93. See also above, n 61.

no precise answer – which raises, once again, the perennial problem that besets theoretical frameworks.[82]

Finally, a more general – and fundamental – difficulty is this: given Fuller's demarcation of the procedural from the substantive, it does appear that he at least implicitly (if not explicitly) concedes that there is no such thing as an objective *substantive* morality.[83] If so, then the question that arises is whether or not Fuller's internal morality of law is a *true* natural law theory since it appears to be confined to the *procedural* only. Indeed, in an earlier chapter, I argued (in the context of *adjudication*) in favour of a *procedural (or epistemic)* version of objectivity as a *metaphysical* version of objectivity was beset with all manner of problems (in the main because the facts of most cases were myriad in nature).[84] I suspect that Fuller also adopts a *procedural* approach for similar reasons. There ensue at least three implications if this reading of Fuller's theory is correct.

First (and as already alluded to above), Fuller's internal morality of law is *not* a true (or 'complete') natural law theory. And this leads to a closely related point.

Second, it also means that Fuller's critique of Hart's legal positivism is greatly weakened. Indeed, given the first point just made, it would be problematic for Fuller to argue that there is a *necessary* connection between law and morality or, at best, that if there is such a connection, it lies in the *procedural* – as opposed to substantive – context.

Third, as I have argued in an earlier chapter,[85] the line between procedural justice on the one hand and substantive justice on the other cannot often be demarcated clearly, and that, on the contrary, both *interact* with each other, particularly in the *practical* sphere where *actual* adjudication takes place.

It is nevertheless the case that Fuller's theory is still useful and, as already mentioned, resonates with practical reality insofar as our understanding as well as practice of the Rule of Law is concerned – particularly with regard to their emphasis on *procedural* justice. It also bears reiterating that his theory underscores in large part what judges and courts actually do in practice. That having been said, it

[82] See generally ch 3 in this volume.

[83] And as one learned author put it (see BR Burrus, 'Book Review of The Morality of Law' (1966)17 *Hastings Law Journal* 861, 864), '[a]t the end of *The Morality of Law* one still might wonder, what does the author mean by "morality"?'. And see, to like effect, Summers, 'Fuller on Morality and Law' (n 24) 3–5. However, in fairness to Fuller (and consistently with my own views in ch 3 in this volume)), Fuller may himself have realised the impossibility of proffering a theory that supported a *metaphysical* (in contrast to a *procedural or epistemic*) objectivity. As a learned author perceptively observed, 'I would urge, however, that his works over the years would clearly reveal that he *has* considered a *substantive* theory *but has rejected* such *as epistemologically and generally unworkable; man's reason is not capable of formulating a viable substantive natural-law theory*' (see RJ Savarese, 'Book Review of The Morality of Law' (1964) 53 *Georgetown Law Journal* 250, 257 (emphasis added)). *Cf* also PP Nicholson, 'The Internal Morality of Law: Fuller and His Critics' (1974) 84 *Ethics* 307, 319.

[84] See ch 3 in this volume.

[85] See ch 2 in this volume. To the extent that procedural justice on the one hand and substantive justice on the other interact with each other, Fuller's internal morality of law is not merely 'form' (though *cf* F Jacobs, 'Book Review of The Morality of Law and Legalism' (1966) 75 *Mind* 605, 606; reference may also be made to Rundle (n 27)).

also bears reiterating that, notwithstanding the rough *correlation as well as interaction* between procedural justice and substantive justice (as just noted above), it is entirely possible (from a *theoretical* standpoint at least) for a legal system to fulfil all eight requirements of legality in Fuller's internal morality of law and yet be capable of engendering substantively *immoral* results (a point which was also canvassed in the preceding chapter of this book[86]).

I turn now to the second – and final – modern natural law theory considered in the present chapter: that of Professor John Finnis.

B. Finnis and Natural Law

i. *Finnis's Theory*

As already mentioned, I will be focusing on Professor John Finnis's treatise, *Natural Law and Natural Rights*.[87] It bears a close affinity to the work of Saint Thomas Aquinas,[88] although there are strands of Fuller[89] as well. In this latter respect, Finnis treats these strands as part of the *procedural* requirements of *the Rule of Law*.

[86] See ch 4 in this volume. See also Gross (n 79) 1227, where the learned author observes that '[o]ne need not go further than the history of human misery during the last century in the United States and Britain to see that the law served the maintenance of such misery while exhibiting a high degree of perfection of the conditions of internal morality'. See, to similar effect, Savarese (n 83) 257, where the learned author was of the view that Fuller's analysis of racial discrimination in South Africa (see the text to n 74, above) was 'strained'; indeed, the learned author was of the view that (ibid):

> Even absent historical examples, I am not convinced that a racial discrimination statute or any other basically brutal piece of legislation could not be constructed and administered so as to satisfy every precept of Professor Fuller's inner morality of law. We need something more than a procedural natural law, even granting its minimum substantive content. We need in full measure both substantive and procedural natural law or due process. We cannot content ourselves with focusing upon the procedural or inner morality alone; the substantive morality is equally if not more basic.

Reference might also be made to Nicholson (n 83) 312–313 and M Kramer, 'Scrupulousness Without Scruples: A Critique of Lon Fuller and His Defenders' (1998) 18 *OJLS* 235, 256.

However, it might also be queried whether such misery or discrimination might have been even worse if the conditions of Fuller's internal morality of law were not in fact observed (and *cf* also Savarese (n 83) 256, where the learned author observed thus: 'I believe [Fuller] has demonstrated as has no one before that a clear and valued minimum of substantive morality flows from procedural precepts of natural law and that therefore an emphasis on procedural guarantees can give us substantial benefits'; the observation just noted is consistent with the approach proffered above to the effect that there is nevertheless *a correlation as well as interaction* between procedural and substantive justice (*cf* also Summers, 'Professor Fuller on Morality and Law' (n 24) 25–26)).

[87] Finnis (n 5). Professor HLA Hart, in fact, commissioned this book for the Clarendon Law Series. See also generally the interesting background to the writing of the book by S Legarre, 'HLA Hart and the Making of the New Natural Law Theory' (2017) 8 *Jurisprudence* 82.

[88] See Pt II, above, entitled 'Classical Natural Law'.

[89] Just discussed above. For an interesting essay situating Finnis's theory in the context of other natural law theories subsequent to the publication of the former's book, see J Crowe, 'Natural Law Beyond Finnis' (2011) 2 *Jurisprudence* 293.

Finnis identifies certain basic forms of *human goods* (that are seven in number) which he argues 'can be secured only through the institutions of human law, *and* requirements of practical reasonableness that only those institutions can satisfy'.[90] Both the aforementioned elements also form, as it were, the foundational core of other concepts which Finnis analyses (for example, justice). Finnis elaborates, in this regard, as follows:[91]

> What are *principles of natural law*? The sense that the phrase 'natural law' has in this book can be indicated in the following … assertions … There is (i) a set of basic practical principles which indicate the basic forms of human flourishing as goods to be pursued and realized, and which are in one way or another used by everyone who considers what to do, however unsound his conclusions; and (ii) a set of basic methodological requirements of practical reasonableness (itself one of the basic forms of human flourishing) which distinguish sound from unsound practical thinking and which, when all brought to bear, provide the criteria for distinguishing between acts that (always or in particular circumstances) are reasonable-all-things-considered (and not merely relative-to-a-particular purpose) and acts that are unreasonable-all-things-considered, i.e. between ways of acting that are morally right or morally wrong – thus enabling one to formulate (iii) a set of general moral standards. … [T]hose principles [of natural law] justify the exercise of authority in community. They require, too, that that authority be exercised, in most circumstances, according to the manner conveniently labelled the Rule of Law, and with due respect for the human rights which embody the requirements of justice, and for the purpose of promoting a common good in which such respect for rights is a component. More particularly, the principles of natural law explain the obligatory force (in the fullest sense of 'obligation') of positive laws even when those laws cannot be deduced from those principles. And attention to the principles, in the context of these explanations of law and legal obligation, justifies regarding certain positive laws as radically defective, *precisely as laws*, for want of conformity to those principles. … [T]heories of natural law [are] theories of the rational foundations for moral judgment.

As an important preliminary point, Finnis recognises the problem posed by 'Hume's Guillotine' – that one cannot (logically) derive an 'ought' from an 'is' (a point that is dealt with in more detail in a previous chapter[92]). He avoids this problem by arguing that the basic forms of human goods and requirements of practical reasonableness, which he posits, are '*not derived or inferred* from *anything*'.[93] They are, instead, 'grasped'. In Finnis's own words:[94]

> Rather, by a simple act of *non-inferential* understanding one grasps that the object of the inclination which one experiences is an instance of a general form of good, for oneself (and others like one).

[90] Finnis (n 5) 3 (emphasis added).
[91] ibid 23–25 (emphasis in the original text).
[92] See ch 2 in this volume.
[93] Finnis (n 5) 34 (emphasis added).
[94] ibid (emphasis added).

Finnis argues that the basic forms of human goods are *self-evident*, and can be grasped by any reasonable human being as something *intrinsically* desirable to attain. He illustrates this by reference, for example, to the human good of *knowledge*. In this particular regard, he argues that knowledge is something good to have *and* that this proposition is supported by *practical reason* – in particular, the practical principle that can be formulated in various ways. One way is to state that 'Being well-informed and clear-headed is a good way to be.'[95] Alternatively, 'Muddle and ignorance are to be avoided.'[96] It can be immediately seen that the concept of *self-evidence* is very much in play. Indeed, in one rhetorical question, Finnis asks thus:[97]

> Is it not the case that knowledge is really a good, an aspect of authentic human flourishing, and that the principle which expresses its value formulates a real (intelligent) reason for action?

Finnis acknowledges that although the good of knowledge is, as has been just noted, self-evident and obvious, nevertheless, it *cannot* be *demonstrated*. But, then again, he argues that it *needs no demonstration* because (in his words)

> the value of truth becomes obvious only to one who has experienced the urge to question, who has grasped the connection between question and answer, who understands that knowledge is constituted by correct answers to particular questions, and who is aware of the possibility of further questions and of other questioners who like himself could enjoy the advantage of attaining correct answers.[98]

And at a later point in his book, Finnis asserts that a person who is well-informed is better off than the ignorant person, *whether we like it or not*. In yet another formulation that bears quoting, he states as follows:[99]

> I am contending only (i) that is one attends carefully and honestly to the relevant human possibilities one can understand, without reasoning from any other judgment, that the realization of those possibilities is, as such, good and desirable for the human person; and (ii) that one's understanding *needs no further justification*.

It will be seen, therefore, that the approach proffered by Finnis is based more on *experience* as opposed to demonstration. However, although there is a sense in which an argument based on experience connotes *subjectivity*, because (as Finnis argues) the forms of human goods are *self-evident*, they take on a kind of *objectivity*. Interestingly, because they are *also experienced*, they take on the quality of *practicality* as well. And lest it be argued that Finnis is asking us to rely merely on our feelings, he is at pains to point out that such self-evident human goods are *not* validated by feelings; on the contrary, these human goods (presumably coupled

[95] ibid 63.
[96] ibid.
[97] ibid 64.
[98] ibid 65.
[99] ibid 73 (emphasis added).

with the requirements of practical reasonableness) constitute the criteria by which we can in fact *discriminate between feelings* – thus discounting some or all of our feelings as irrational, unwarranted, misleading or delusive.[100]

Turning to the basic forms of human goods advocated by Finnis (which, as already mentioned, are seven in number), the first relates to *life*, for all human societies show a concern for the value of human life.

The second is *knowledge* which we have already considered above.[101]

The third is *play*.[102]

The fourth is *aesthetic experience*.[103]

The fifth is *sociability* (*friendship*).[104]

The sixth is *practical reasonableness* which appears to be the most important since it is *simultaneously* part of *the methodology* that is utilised in order to arrive at the seven basic forms of human goods.[105] Finnis himself defines 'practical reasonableness' as:[106]

> … the basic good of being able to bring one's own intelligence to bear effectively (in practical reasoning that issues in action) on the problems of choosing one's actions and lifestyle and shaping one's own character. Negatively, this involves that one has a measure of effective freedom; positively, it involves that one seeks to bring an intelligent and reasonable order into one's own actions and habits and practical attitudes.

It can be seen that, by its very nature and function, practical reasonableness is indispensable to, and an integral part of, the process of making sense of the world in general and the relevant facts and circumstances in particular. In terms of experience, each and every one of us utilises practical reasonableness to navigate our daily lives. Conversely, life (let alone basic flourishing) as we know it would not even begin to exist without such a human good. It is little surprise, then, that it is simultaneously one of the seven basic forms of human goods as well.

The seventh – and final – human good is that of *religion*[107] (which Finnis characterises as '*harmony with God*'[108]).

Insofar as the *other broad strand* in his book is concerned, viz, *the basic requirements of practical reasonableness*, Finnis provides guidance as to how one should go about determining whether a decision is practically reasonable. This is consistent with the view, already mentioned above, that practical reasonableness can be construed (as noted above[109]) as the *methodological* strand of his book – whilst (as also mentioned above) *simultaneously* constituting one of the human goods

[100] ibid 69.
[101] And see generally ibid ch 3 in this volume.
[102] ibid 87.
[103] ibid 87–88.
[104] ibid 88.
[105] ibid 88–89 as well as ibid ch 5 in this volume.
[106] ibid 88.
[107] ibid 89–90.
[108] ibid 410 (emphasis added).
[109] See the text to n 91, above.

(the sixth, to be precise). Receiving such guidance is of the first importance because (as Finnis points out[110]) practical reasonableness *shapes as well as guides our participation in the other basic goods*.

The *requirements* of *practical reasonableness* themselves comprise the following.

First, there is a rational plan of life.[111]

Second, there must be 'no leaving out of accounting, or arbitrary discounting or exaggeration, of any of the basic human values';[112] put simply, there must be no arbitrary preferences amongst values.[113]

Third, 'the basic goods are human goods and can in principle be pursued, realized, and participated in by *any* human being';[114] put simply, there must be *no arbitrary preferences amongst persons*.[115]

Fourth, there must be *detachment*.[116]

Fifth, there must be *commitment*.[117]

Sixth, there must be *efficiency within reason*.[118] It is important to note at this particular juncture that Finnis's reference here to 'efficiency' is *not* a reference to the doctrine of *utilitarianism*. In other words, he does *not* enforce efficiency in terms of consequentialism as a principle in itself. On the contrary, he *rejects* utilitarianism because it is 'senseless', for it assumes 'that man is made to flourish in only one way or for only one purpose',[119] and requires a common goal, or various goals must be at least reducible to some common factor in order that 'good(s)' could be measured as well as computed in the manner required by utilitarianism.[120] Hence, whilst efficiency is important to Finnis, it cannot – as is the case with utilitarianism – be the *sole* principle of practical thinking.

Seventh, there must be *respect for every basic value in every act*.[121] However, there may, as Finnis concedes, be problems of determining when a particular action actually contravenes this particular requirement.[122]

Eighth, there is the requirement of *the common good*.[123] Again (and consistently with the sixth requirement), the reference here to 'the common good' is not one that is allocated utilitarian garb but, instead, to 'a set of conditions which enables the members of a community to attain for themselves objectives, or to realize

[110] Finnis (n 5) 100.
[111] ibid 103–105 (citing and following the approach of Professor John Rawls's view in this particular regard in his seminal work in *A Theory of Justice* (Cambridge, Belknap Press of Harvard University Press, 1971)).
[112] ibid 105 (emphasis added).
[113] See generally ibid 105–106.
[114] ibid 106 (emphasis added).
[115] ibid 106–109.
[116] ibid 109–110.
[117] ibid.
[118] ibid 111–118.
[119] ibid 113.
[120] ibid.
[121] ibid 118–125.
[122] ibid 122.
[123] ibid 125.

reasonably for themselves the value(s), for the sake of which they have reason to collaborate with each other (positively and/or negatively) in a community'.[124] He proceeds (later, and quite pertinently) to add as follows:[125]

> Notice that this definition neither asserts nor entails that the members of a community must all have the same values or objectives (or set of values or objectives); it implies only that there be some set (or set of sets) of conditions which needs to obtain if each of the members is to attain his own objectives.

Insofar as the *content* of 'the common good' is concerned, this is dealt with in some detail by Finnis in three chapters. The first deals with *justice*.[126] The second concerns *rights*,[127] and the third relates to *authority*.[128] Insofar as *rights* are concerned, instead of pitting them (as is traditionally the case) against utilitarianism, Finnis adopts a rather interesting approach: he argues that rights are not subject to the common good simply because they are in fact *part of* the common good, although they may be subject to (or limited by) each other *and* by *other aspects* of the common good that may be subsumed under a very broad conception of human rights but that are more appropriately described by expressions such as 'public morality', 'public health', and 'public order'.[129] Insofar as *authority* is concerned, Finnis is of the view that authoritativeness derives from *the opportunity of advancing the common good*, which, in the situation of the authority of *rulers*, is based on 'the sheer fact of *effectiveness* that is presumptively (not indefeasibly) decisive'.[130]

Ninth, there is the requirement of *following one's conscience*, which Finnis interestingly states as a requirement which 'might be regarded as a *particular aspect* of the *seventh* requirement (that no basic good may be directly attacked in any act), *or* even as *a summary* of *all* the requirements'.[131] Finnis nevertheless argues that this particular requirement is also *distinctive* in itself in the sense that '[i]t is the requirement that one should not do what one judges or thinks or "feels"-all-in-all should not be done'.[132]

It is important to note that Finnis argues that the *product* of all of the above (nine) requirements is *morality*. In his view, those critics who advocate moral relativity focus too much on some of the basic forms of human goods and/or basic requirement(s) to the exclusion of others.[133] In his view, there is also the problem of what he terms 'unreasonable' inclinations and emotions, such as the bias of self-love.[134]

124 ibid 155.
125 ibid 156.
126 See ch 7, entitled 'Justice'. Reference may also be made to ch 12, entitled 'Unjust Laws'.
127 See ch 8, entitled 'Rights'.
128 See ch 9, entitled 'Authority'.
129 Finnis (n 5) 218.
130 ibid 247 (emphasis added). See also ibid 351.
131 ibid 125 (emphasis added).
132 ibid.
133 ibid 127.
134 ibid.

It is also worthy to note that Finnis *also* refers to the *law* itself.[135] In fact, he summarises a fairly lengthy discussion about the main features of a legal order in two slogans – first, that 'Law is a coercive order'[136] and, second, 'The law regulates its own creation'.[137] Insofar as the former is concerned, Finnis discusses *the criminal law* at some length, and argues that it not only provides recalcitrants with disincentives and law-abiding citizens with encouragement *but also* avoids injustice by preventing the criminal from escaping scot-free with *an unfair advantage*. Finally, the criminal law also has a *reformative* aspect which enables the reformed criminal to lead *a good life* in pursuing (in a reasonable manner) the *basic forms of human goods* we referred to earlier in the present chapter.[138]

Finnis also considers *the Rule of Law* and, as already alluded to above, his enunciation of its features bears (as already alluded to above) *a very striking similarity* to those proposed by Professor Fuller in formulating his inner morality of law (which we have considered earlier in this chapter).[139] As Finnis himself put it:[140]

> The fundamental point of the desiderata[141] is to secure to the subjects of authority the dignity of self-direction and freedom from certain forms of manipulation. *The Rule of Law is thus among the requirements of justice or fairness.*

What, then, about principles of *natural law*? This is indeed where Finnis's basic forms of human goods *and* the requirements of practical reasonableness come into play. For example, insofar as the law forbidding murder is concerned, this law is derived from the first basic form of human good (*life*) *in combination with* the seventh of the nine requirements of practical reasonableness (that there must be respect for every basic value in every act).[142] One might notice at once that this method of derivation of natural law has *not a little similarity* with that adopted by *Saint Thomas Aquinas*, although the *content* of both approaches is quite different,

[135] See ch 10, entitled 'Law'.

[136] Finnis (n 5) 270.

[137] ibid.

[138] ibid 261–264.

[139] See generally ibid 270–276. And Finnis states more specifically as follows (ibid 270–271):

> A legal system exemplifies the Rule of Law to the extent (it is a matter of degree in respect of each item of the list) that (i) its rules are prospective, not retroactive, and (ii) are not in any other way impossible to comply with; that (iii) its rules are promulgated, (iv) clear, and (v) coherent with one another; that (vi) its rules are sufficiently stable to allow people to be guided by their knowledge of the content of the rules; that (vii) the making of decrees and orders applicable to relatively limited situations is guided by rules that are promulgated, clear, stable, and relatively general; and that (viii) those people who have authority to make, administer, and apply the rules in an official capacity (a) are accountable for their compliance with rules applicable to their performance and (b) do actually administer the law consistently and in accordance with its tenor.

It can be readily seen that Finnis's concept of the Rule of Law bears close resemblance to Fuller's eight principles of legality that constitute his internal morality of law (as to which see the text to nn 36–60, above). See also SH Tan, 'Justification in Finnis' Natural Law Theory' [2000] *Singapore Journal of Legal Studies* 590, 593, n 10.

[140] Finnis (n 5) 273 (emphasis added).

[141] As to which, see n 139, above.

[142] Finnis (n 5) 281.

not least because (as already mentioned above) Finnis does *not* rely ultimately on any concept of God (which, of course, is (as we have seen earlier in the present chapter) *central* to *Aquinas's* concept of (classical) natural law).

There are *other* concepts discussed in the rest of the book as well, such as that relating to *obligation*.[143] An interesting point that emerges in this particular regard relates to Finnis's consideration of Professor Hart's concept of 'obligation' as formulated from an internal point of view.[144] In particular, Finnis argues that Hart does not take into account the fact that critical reactions to breaches of the law are *variable in both intensity and immediacy*, and that by not taking this fact into account, Hart is, in effect, reducing the 'directive' force of law to the 'coercive' force of law.[145]

This would be an appropriate juncture at which to turn to the *difficulties* with Finnis's theory.

ii. The Difficulties with Finnis's Theory

An obvious difficulty, perhaps, relates to Finnis's concept as well as use of 'self-evidence'. In particular, is Finnis's use of the argument from 'grasping' (as opposed to derivation and inference) persuasive? In this regard, the following attempted explanation by Finnis is relevant:[146]

> … in every field there is and must be, at some point or points, an end to derivation and inference. At that point or points we find ourselves in face of the self-evident, which makes possible all subsequent inferences in that field.

It is suggested that the most obvious point beyond which no further derivation and inference is possible (or, indeed, required) is the concept of 'God' (which Finnis in fact deals with in the final part of his book). However, we have noted the difficulties in the widespread acceptability of such a concept when discussing classical natural law above.[147] Indeed, Finnis himself also realises that, to some people at least, the use of the concept of 'God' may be too emotive; he opts, instead, for the concept of an 'uncaused cause'.[148] However, such an approach, with respect, does not really resolve the difficulties just noted. Indeed, the concept of an 'uncaused cause' may – to many persons – merely be an alternative way of referring to 'God'. More importantly, the same difficulties that accompanied an argument for the existence of God (which we considered briefly above[149]) would, it is suggested, apply with equal (if not more) force to an argument in favour of the concept of an 'uncaused cause'. However, absent the concept of either 'God' or an 'uncaused

[143] See ch 11, entitled 'Obligation'.
[144] As to which see ch 4 in this volume.
[145] Finnis (n 5) 313–314.
[146] ibid 70. See generally the powerful critique of Finnis's concept of 'self evidence' in Tan (n 139).
[147] See the text to nn 20–23.
[148] See generally Finnis (n 5) ch 13. See also Tan (n 139) 637–638.
[149] See the text to nn 20–23.

cause', we are back full circle to the basic issue relating to the source and justification for Finnis's natural law theory (focusing on the seven basic human goods). It is suggested, with respect, that such ambiguity arises from Finnis's attempt to chart a middle path, as it were, between those who endorse the concept of 'God' and those who do not. On balance, he clearly endorses the former – this is clear not only from his own personal beliefs[150] but also from the fact that he draws much from the work of Saint Thomas Aquinas as well as the Roman Catholic Church; indeed, in the Preface to his book, he states:[151]

> I do quite frequently refer to Thomas Aquinas, because on any view he occupies a uniquely strategic place in the history of natural law theorizing. Likewise, I refer occasionally to the Roman Catholic Church's pronouncements on natural law, because that body is perhaps unique in the modern world in claiming to be an authoritative exponent of natural law.

He then proceeds to qualify immediately what has just been said by observing thus:[152]

> But, while there is place for appeal to, and deference to, authority, that place is not in philosophical argument about the merits of theories or the right response to practical problems, and so is not in this book.

Hence, his arguments, he maintains, 'stand or fall by their own reasonableness or otherwise'.[153] However, in spite of these qualifications, it is suggested that Finnis cannot avoid the fact that, at bottom, he is – in substance – relying on God as the ultimate source of justification insofar as his theory of natural law is concerned and, as has just been argued, if he is not, then we are nevertheless back to 'square one', so to speak, in relation to the basic issue relating to source and justification for Finnis's natural law theory. Indeed, it is also important to note that Finnis's reference to the human good of '*religion*' is *necessarily* premised on a higher being (viz, God), and this much is in fact clear from the nature of his discussion of this

[150] Finnis is a Roman Catholic. And on the inevitability of a jurist's own conceptions and prejudices coupled, nevertheless, with the countervailing need 'to convert their own (and their culture's) practical "prejudices" into truly reasonable judgments about what is good and practically reasonable', see Finnis (n 5) 17.

[151] ibid vi. Indeed, there are numerous references to Aquinas throughout the book. See also V Bourke, 'Book Review of Natural Law and Natural Rights' (1981) 26 *American Journal of Jurisprudence* 243, 243, where the learned author observes that 'Finnis makes a valiant and largely successful effort to revise the Thomistic theory of natural law, in order to render it understandable and acceptable to readers working in the current of recent British ethico-legal discourse.' Reference may also be made to the attempted restoration of the material in Finnis's book to correspond with Aquinas's account of classical natural law in S Coyle, 'Natural Law Theory, "New" and Old' (2023) 68 *American Journal of Jurisprudence* 33 (not surprisingly, the learned author commences with issues relating, inter alia, to the existence of God and equally unsurprising is his finding that Finnis does also depart from Aquinas's doctrines (and see, in this last-mentioned regard, the text to n 152, below)). Reference may also be made to the comparative analysis between Finnis and Aquinas in Tan (n 139) 625–637.

[152] Finnis (n 5) vi.

[153] ibid.

human good itself.[154] It is also interesting to note the following (and, in my view, very perceptive) observations by a learned author:[155]

> Of the so-called basic goods Finnis lists, the only good which I think is literally indisputably basic is the good of knowledge (because any attempt to assert the contrary would be self-refuting on account of the fact that it would presumably have to be asserted *qua* true), which is why Finnis chooses to write an entire chapter on it as his illustrative example of a basic good …

Indeed, I would respectfully add that even the observations just quoted appear to cast the basic good of knowledge as a good based purely on *necessary function* (here, as an essential medium of communication as well as discourse) and that there might be some who would argue that a basic *good* ought to be *more* than one that simply performs such a minimal function.[156]

Turning more *specifically* to the forms of basic human goods he suggests, we have already touched upon those relating to knowledge and practical reasonableness.[157] The larger question that arises, however, is as to whether Finnis's list of seven basic forms of human goods is exhaustive. Somewhat surprisingly, perhaps, Finnis does acknowledge the possibility that his list is not exhaustive.[158] However, he does argue that although there could be other objectives as well as forms of good, his list is probably objective inasmuch as these so-called other forms of good 'will be found, on analysis, to be *ways or combinations of ways* of pursuing … and realizing … *one of the seven basic forms of good, or some combination of them*'.[159] Whilst a not unattractive argument, it is submitted that it is still not sufficiently persuasive and leaves the entire situation in a state of relative flux.

Finnis also argues – perhaps not surprisingly – that all the forms of basic human goods are *equally* fundamental.[160] In his words:[161]

> Each is fundamental. None is more fundamental than any of the others, for each can reasonably be focused upon, and each, when focused upon, claims a priority of value. Hence there is no objective priority of value amongst them.

[154] ibid 89–90. Reference may also be made to Tan (n 139) 637, n 176 and 637–638. But *cf* MC Murphy, 'Finnis on Nature, Reason, God' (2007) 13 *Legal Theory* 187, 195 where the learned author argues that '[t]he affirmation that religion is good is not a theistic fact; it does not presuppose God's existence (or, more accurately, that what is good is a relationship with God does not presuppose God's existence)', and that '[h]ence an atheist can consistently affirm that there is no God and that religion is a basic good'. With respect, however, such an approach does not really grapple with the *nature* of 'religion' as Finnis understands it (which, inter alia, *does* include the concept of *God*).

[155] MR Discher, 'Does Finnis Get Natural Rights for Everyone?' (1999) 80 *New Blackfriars* 19, 21.

[156] Though *cf* Tan (n 139) 602.

[157] The first and sixth of the basic human goods, respectively.

[158] Finnis (n 5) 90.

[159] ibid (emphasis added).

[160] See generally ibid 92–95.

[161] ibid 93.

He then proceeds to add thus:[162]

> Of course, each one of us can reasonably *choose* to treat one or some of the values as of more importance in *one's own* life. … Each of us has a subjective order of priority amongst the basic values; this ranking is no doubt partly shifting and partly stable, but is in any case essential if we are to act at all to some purpose. But one's reasons for choosing the particular ranking that one does choose are reasons that properly relate to one's temperament, upbringing, capacities, and opportunities, not to differences of rank of intrinsic value between the basic values.

Whilst the argument just considered (with respect to the relative importance of the forms of basic human goods amongst themselves) is a reasonable one, this *still* leaves us with the prior question (already touched upon) as to whether the list of the seven basic forms of human good is exhaustive. In this particular regard, Finnis actually proffered an *eighth* form of human good well *after* the book presently being considered had first been published – that of '*marriage*'.[163] Such an *addition* to the existing list does raise the question as to whether the *ultimate source* of the various basic forms of human good has an *objective* basis – or whether it is ultimately based, instead, on one's *subjective choice*.

It is also suggested that, compared to Fuller's internal morality of law, Finnis's theory of natural law is *much more theoretical as well as abstract*. This does not – I hasten to add – detract in any way from its immense scholarship as well as the thought his work provokes at the very fundamental level of human goods and values. Indeed, in my view, a strong case can be made out that Finnis's theory deals with many of the values that judges and courts embrace (whether consciously or subconsciously) in a more practical context. Nevertheless, it is still true that Finnis's theory is *not*, with respect, one that judges and courts engage in on an *explicit* level in the course of their work. To borrow a description from Fuller, the work of judges and courts is 'entirely terrestrial in origin and application'.[164] In contrast (and in Finnis's own words):[165]

> The principal concern of a theory of *natural law* is to explore the requirements of practical reasonableness in relation to the good of human beings who, because they live in community with one another, are confronted with problems of justice and rights, of authority, law, and obligation. And the principal jurisprudential concern of a theory of natural law is thus to identify the principles and limits of the Rule of Law …, and to trace the ways in which sound laws, in all their positivity and mutability, are to be derived (not, usually, deduced …) from unchanging principles – principles that have their force from their reasonableness, not from any originating acts or circumstances.

It is suggested that the principal task of *adjudication* is concerned not so much with natural law (whether as promulgated by Finnis or other authors such as

[162] ibid 93–94 (emphasis in the original text).
[163] ibid 447 (in the *Postscript* to the second edition of the book).
[164] Fuller (n 4) 96. See also n 64, above.
[165] Finnis (n 5) 351 (emphasis added).

Saint Thomas Aquinas) but, instead, with what Finnis himself deals with under the rubric of 'law'. Indeed, this is confirmed by Finnis himself when he observes that:[166]

> 'Natural law' – the set of principles of practical reasonableness in ordering human life and human community is *only analogically law* …

In this last-mentioned regard, the *Rule of Law* figures prominently in the context of adjudication. Indeed (and as we have seen), the focus on the Rule of Law is also the principal (*practical*) benefit that Fuller's internal morality of law brings in that particular context. However, it is also (at least *theoretically* possible) that – as one learned author perceptively observed – that '[t]he [legal] positivist … could be a natural law moral theorist, subscribing to every detail of Finnis's moral theory, while still remaining a positivist when it comes to legal theory'.[167] However, to the extent that this observation is premised upon a '*descriptive* theory', it would be subject to the critique which was considered in the preceding chapter.[168]

IV. Conclusion

It is suggested – in the context of adjudication – that the main benefit of natural law theory (whether classical or modern) is that it is a timely reminder of something so basic that we might be apt to take it for granted. And it is that there is a *moral* dimension to the law in general and the purpose as well as mission of adjudication in particular – the importance of *justice and fairness* as the *ultimate goal or aim* of adjudication. Looked at in this light, we must not become overly concerned with technical rules or even principles of law for their own sake. This is a point that may appear obvious, but it is also the case that we often (as just alluded to) take the most obvious for granted. In any event, it is a point that bears repeating.

However (and this is consistent with the reasons already set out in a previous chapter[169]), insofar as a *theory* of adjudication is concerned, whilst one must not neglect the moral dimension as just referred to in the preceding paragraph, it is (in my view at least) impossible to proffer a theory that takes into account *metaphysical* (as opposed to *epistemic*) objectivity. Hence, the main (*theoretical*)

[166] ibid 280 (emphasis added). See also the text to n 142, above. Reference may also be made to Tan (n 139) 593, where the learned author observes thus:

> On closer analysis, the issue of the test for law in the positivistic sense is not Finnis' chief concern. Finnis explains the 'Rule of Law' in terms of procedural requirements … He claims he propounds a theory of natural law that seeks to explain the very authority for law …

[167] See P Soper, 'Legal Theory and the Problem of Definition' (1983) 50 *University of Chicago Law Review* 1170, 1181.

[168] See ch 4 in this volume.

[169] See ch 3 in this volume.

benefit that arises from natural law theory is to be located in Fuller's internal morality of law, which (as we have seen) embodies most of the elements of what we understand today as comprising the *Rule of Law* (and which is also consistent with Finnis's own approach towards the same). Being if not wholly then at least primarily *procedural* in nature, it is also entirely consistent with the proposed theory of adjudication which I set out in the final chapter of this book.[170] This would be an appropriate juncture at which to turn to the next theory of adjudication that appears to locate itself between legal positivism on the one hand[171] and natural law on the other.[172] This is Professor Ronald Dworkin's theory of adjudication, which he developed over a number of years.[173]

[170] See ch 10 in this volume. However, it should be noted that whilst I have (like Fuller) endorsed a *procedural* approach towards the Rule of Law, there have been authors who have endorsed a *substantive* approach towards the same instead. With respect, the latter approach would encounter similar difficulties to those that accompany a *metaphysical* approach towards objectivity (as set out in detail in ch 3 in this volume). This is also recognised, eg, by P Craig, 'Formal and Substantive Conceptions of the Rule of Law: An Analytical Framework' [1997] *Public Law* 467, 487. Reference may also be made to BZ Tamanaha, 'The History and Elements of the Rule of Law' [2012] *Singapore Journal of Legal Studies* 232.

[171] And see ch 4 in this volume.

[172] Considered in the present chapter.

[173] See chs 6, 7 and 8 in this volume.

6

The Dworkinian Theory of Adjudication – The Basic Building Blocks

I. Introduction and Overview

It would be no exaggeration to state that the theory of adjudication set out by the late Professor Ronald Dworkin is perhaps one of the – if not the – most influential of such theories in the twentieth century (and arguably, the twenty-first as well). Professor Dworkin was in fact the successor to Professor HLA Hart's prestigious Chair of Jurisprudence at the University of Oxford. As we have seen in an earlier chapter,[1] Hart was himself an accomplished jurist of the very first rank. Interestingly (and perhaps somewhat ironically), Dworkin established his reputation as a jurist primarily through his critique of what he perceived to be deficiencies in Hart's account of the law. It might be apposite, even at this very early juncture of the present chapter, to note that, in essence, Dworkin viewed Hart's reliance on *rules* as being an inadequate account of how adjudication takes place because the latter had omitted to take into account *principles* (which Dworkin argued were *also part of the law*). Indeed, this distinction between rules on the one hand and principles on the other was first set out by Dworkin in 1963 in the *Journal of Philosophy*[2] and, most famously perhaps (in the expressly legal sphere), in an article published in the 1967 volume of the *University of Chicago Law Review*,[3] the latter of which was subsequently published as a chapter in his book, *Taking Rights Seriously*[4] (and references to this article hereafter will be to the latter[5]). It was later developed in some detail in Dworkin's inaugural lecture (which was, of course, delivered at Oxford University but was published in the pages of the *Harvard Law Review*[6]). This lecture (which contained what were to

[1] See ch 4 in this volume.
[2] See R Dworkin, 'Judicial Discretion' (1963) 60 *Journal of Philosophy* 624, especially 633–635.
[3] See R Dworkin, 'The Model of Rules' (1967) 35 *University of Chicago Law Review* 14.
[4] See R Dworkin, *Taking Rights Seriously*, rev edn (Cambridge, Harvard University Press, 1978).
[5] See Dworkin (n 4) ch 2, entitled 'The Model of Rules I'.
[6] See R Dworkin, 'Hard Cases' (1975) 88 *Harvard Law Review* 1057. This was published as ch 4 of Dworkin (n 4). All references to this article in the present chapter will be to this particular chapter.

be fundamental ideas of Dworkinian legal thought[7]) was to become the pivotal chapter in the book just mentioned, *Taking Rights Seriously*,[8] not least because it represented the first substantial enunciation of *Dworkin's own positive theory or programme*. However, as I point out (briefly) below, the aforementioned critique of Hart by Dworkin was, with respect, misconceived[9] – not least because Hart *did*, in fact, refer to *principles* in his seminal work, *The Concept of Law*.[10]

As just alluded to, Dworkin did not cease with merely his critique of Hart. Not surprisingly, he was led to postulate his *own* theory of adjudication as well, commencing (as I have just noted) with his inaugural lecture at Oxford. I observe, parenthetically, that owing to the nature of his discourse, he also proceeded to set out his views in the wider context of *political theory* as well. Whilst there is an interactive link between his theory of adjudication and his broader political theory, the focus of this chapter (consistently with the focus of this book generally) is on the former as opposed to the latter.

Returning to Dworkin's theory of adjudication, it may be said to be one that has, as its fundamental basis, the central idea that there is *always* an *objectively right* answer which judges should strive to locate; correlatively, judges do *not* have *unbridled* discretion to decide as they please *even if* they encounter a '*hard* case' (which, by definition, is one located in what Hart (as noted in the preceding chapter) had termed the 'penumbra' and where there is no established rule which covers the case in question (which (in turn) might be due to a number of possible reasons, for example, because an apparent rule contains relevant language that is too general or even unclear or (as I shall argue below) the fact situation is itself novel and is (for any number of possible reasons, including counsel's ingenuity in his or her litigation strategy) not covered by an existing rule)). Whilst an attractive theory of adjudication (that is also, as I shall argue, consistent with the *spirit* of adjudication in the *practical* sphere), what are its fundamental elements, and does the theory itself withstand critical scrutiny? This is an appropriate juncture at which to turn to Dworkin's theory of adjudication proper.

However, before proceeding to do so, it should be noted that the relevant literature on Dworkin's works in general and his theory of adjudication in particular is truly enormous. There are numerous books[11] and literally thousands of articles. Whilst I have endeavoured to read as widely as possible, given the nature of the

[7] Including the (further) distinction between principles and policies.

[8] 'Hard Cases' (which also constitutes the title of the chapter concerned), originally published in the *Harvard Law Review*, was published in ch 4 of this book (ie, Dworkin (n 4)). See also above, n 6.

[9] This argument was first made in A Phang, 'Jurisprudential Oaks from Mythical Acorns: The Har-Dworkin Debate Revisited' (1990) 3 *Ratio Juris* 385. See also the text to nn 17–18, below.

[10] See HLA Hart, *The Concept of Law* (Oxford, Clarendon Press, 1961). The third edition (which was published in 2012) contains a new *Introduction* by Professor Leslie Green.

[11] See, eg (and even this is but a sampling), S Guest, *Ronald Dworkin*, 3rd edn (Stanford, Stanford University Press, 2013) (probably the best single-volume overview of Dworkin's legal and political theories); S Hershovitz (gen ed), *Exploring Law's Empire: The Jurisprudence of Ronald Dworkin* (Oxford, Oxford University Press, 2008); A Ripstein (gen ed), *Ronald Dworkin* (Cambridge, Cambridge University Press, 2007); W Waluchow and S Sciaraffa, *The Legacy of Ronald Dworkin* (Oxford, Oxford

present book (which is to focus on theories of adjudication that have a bearing or focus on actual legal practice), I will concentrate on the relevant primary material (ie, Dworkin's own writings) as well as analyses that are *directly* relevant to it (particularly in the context of adjudication in the *practical* sphere). To this end, I will be adopting what is essentially a 'step-by-step' approach that entails examining, first, the basic building blocks, so to speak, of Dworkin's theory of adjudication and to consider (as well as critique) them at each stage before proceeding to the next. Not surprisingly, this approach is essentially chronological in nature. As we shall see, such an approach is also illuminating in at least one other respect inasmuch as it enables us to discern how Dworkin's theory of adjudication has grown steadily from a few seminal distinctions into a much broader *theory*. Indeed, the aforementioned (and, by their very nature, *specific*) distinctions *necessarily* led to the need for him to *commit* to a *broader and more general theory of adjudication*. And, as he developed as well as refined his more general theory of adjudication, we shall see that he has had to *shift* the overall nature as well as parameters of his theory simply because it became clear that it (or for that matter, *any* theory) could not (as I have been at pains to point out in an earlier chapter[12]) accommodate many of the difficulties associated with an approach that emphasised *metaphysical* (as opposed to *epistemic (or procedural)*) objectivity. In order to surmount these difficulties, Dworkin has relied, in the main, on the idea of 'essentially contested concepts', which was first mooted by Professor WB Gallie[13] (and which I have also dealt with in an earlier chapter[14]). This is a vitally important point which the reader should constantly bear in mind in the context of the present chapter, as well as chapters seven and eight.

What *is* clear is that Dworkin's theory of adjudication is (as we shall see) one that, in my view, *approximates most closely what actually takes place in the courts*. I will in fact deal with this theory in three separate chapters. The present chapter deals with the *basic building blocks* of Dworkin's theory, encompassed (not surprisingly) principally within his earlier work. In the following chapter, I deal with Dworkin's theory of adjudication proper. Finally, in the third chapter, I deal with the basic problems with Dworkin's theory of adjudication as well as possible practical solutions. Not surprisingly, therefore, these chapters comprise the lengthiest part of this book. This is not surprising in view of the fact that, as I have pointed out at the outset of the present paragraph, Dworkin's theory of adjudication approximates most closely, in my view, what actually takes place in the courts. Indeed, whilst many elements of his theory might (as we shall also see) be subject to critique, they are nevertheless useful in understanding the actual *practice* of

University Press, 2016); and LA Jacobs and M McManus, *Against Post-Liberal Courts and Justice – Rescuing Ronald Dworkin's Legacy* (Palgrave Macmillan, Switzerland, 2023).

[12] See ch 3 in this volume.

[13] See WB Gallie, 'Essentially Contested Concepts' (1955-1956) 56 *Proceedings of the Aristotelian Society* 167 (reprinted in ch 8 of WB Gallie, *Philosophy and the Historical Understanding* (New York, Schocken Books, 1968). References hereafter will be the original article.

[14] See ch 3 in this volume.

adjudication. Indeed, I shall also endeavour to illustrate this by reference to *actual decisions* in the final (ie, third) chapter dealing with his theory. Let us now turn to consider the first set of building blocks in Dworkin's theory of adjudication – the distinction between rules on the one hand and principles on the other.

II. The Basic Building Blocks (1) – The Distinction between Rules and Principles

A. The Distinction Stated

As already mentioned above, one of Dworkin's key critiques of Hart's theory of adjudication is that Hart, whilst endorsing a system of *rules*, was wrong inasmuch as he was of the view that the judge concerned would be able to exercise *unfettered* discretion to decide the case at hand once the system of rules had 'run out'.[15] Put simply, in Dworkin's view, the judge in the situation just mentioned had to *also* have regard to *principles*, which were *also part of* the law.

I pause at this juncture to return to a point to which I had alluded to in the briefest of terms above – that Hart *did*, in fact, refer to *principles* in a chapter of *The Concept of Law* (entitled 'Law and Morals'[16]).[17] Although Hart might not have described the concept of a principle in the precise language which Dworkin uses, Hart's concept of a 'principle' was, in fact, very similar to Dworkin's. This is not surprising since, *ex hypothesi*, Hart's concept of a 'principle' *had* to be *different* from his concept of a 'rule'. And it is also fair to say that Hart did not place as much emphasis on principles simply because he probably viewed them as being part of the broader fabric of *extra*-legal *morality* and, hence, the particular chapter in which he discussed them (as just noted above). Again, this is not surprising in view of the fact that Hart endorsed legal positivism (which holds that there is no *necessary* connection as such between law on the one hand and morality on the other).[18]

[15] See Dworkin (n 5) 17. For a good overview of the debate between Hart and Dworkin (albeit sympathetic towards Hart), see M Bayles, 'Hart vs. Dworkin' (1991) 10 *Law and Philosophy* 349. See also Scott J Shapiro, 'The "Hart-Dworkin" Debate: A Short Guide for the Perplexed' in ch 1 of Ripstein (n 11). But *quaere* whether this was a 'debate' in the truest sense: see, eg, F Schauer, '(Re)Taking Hart' (2006) 119 *Harvard Law Review* 852, 853, 869 and 875; Shapiro, above, 31; as well as N Stavropoulos, 'The Debate That Never Was' (2017) 130 *Harvard Law Review* 2082, especially 2085–2086 and 2092–2095. And for Dworkin's (posthumously published) response to Hart's (also posthumously published) *Postscript* to *The Concept of Law*, see R Dworkin, 'Hart's Posthumous Reply' (2017) 130 *Harvard Law Review* 2096. And, in the context of political philosophy, reference may be made to R Dworkin, 'Hart's Postscript and the Character of Political Philosophy' (2004) 24 *OJLS* 1.

[16] And published as ch 9 of *The Concept of Law*. See also above, n 10.

[17] And see generally Phang (n 9).

[18] And see ch 4 in this volume. Professor Neil MacCormick also notes that Hart did consider the concept of a 'principle' as well as that of a 'standard'. However, as he correctly notes (and not inconsistently with the main text above), '[t]he trouble is that Hart has not himself clarified what the

Returning to Dworkin's concept of principles, he defines a 'principle' as 'a standard that is to be observed, not because it will advance or secure an economic, political, or social situation deemed desirable, but because it is 'a requirement of justice or fairness or some other dimension of *morality*'.[19] It will be seen, even at this early stage in his writings, that Dworkin focuses – contrary to the approach adopted by legal positivists such as Hart – on *connecting* the law with *morality*. Indeed, if (as he argues), principles (like rules) are an integral *part* of *the law*, then the *morality* that principles embody (by definition) *also forms part of the law*.[20]

As an *illustration* of what constitutes a 'principle', Dworkin refers to 'the principle that no man may profit from his own wrong'.[21] However, he does acknowledge that, on occasion, that particular principle might not apply – for example, in the law of adverse possession.[22] Unlike a 'rule', a 'principle' does not apply in an all-or-nothing fashion;[23] as Dworkin puts it:[24]

> All that is meant, when we say that a particular principle is a principle of our law, is that the principle is one which officials must take into account, if it is relevant, as a consideration inclining in one direction or another.
>
> …
>
> Principles have a dimension that rules do not – the dimension of *weight or importance*.

At this particular juncture, it might be asked whether the process of *weighing* principles[25] *itself* results in the exercise by the judge of the very *discretion* which legal positivists such as Hart state happens when rules run out. Dworkin's response is that such discretion is a *constrained* one. This is a question which I will deal with when dealing below with the various difficulties in relation to Dworkin's distinction between rules on the one hand and principles on the other as well as (on a broader and more general level) his theory of adjudication proper.

assumed distinction [between 'rules' and 'principles' as well as between 'rules' and 'standards'] is': see N MacCormick, *HLA Hart*, 2nd edn (Stanford, Stanford University Press, 2008), 56. Reference may also be made to ibid 166 and 167 (where the learned author refers to Hart's underplaying or understating of standards other than 'rules').

[19] See Dworkin (n 5) 22 (emphasis added).

[20] See also R Dworkin, 'Jurisprudence' in ch 1 of Dworkin (n 4) 2–3, 5 and 7.

[21] Dworkin (n 5) 25.

[22] ibid.

[23] As Dworkin put it (ibid 24), 'Rules are applicable in an all-or-nothing fashion.' He proceeds to add thus (ibid):

> If the facts a rule stipulates are given, then either the rule is valid, in which case the answer it supplies must be accepted, or it is not, in which case it contributes nothing to the decision.

Though *cf* C Tapper, 'A Note on Principles' (1971) 34 *MLR* 628, 633–634.

[24] ibid 26 (emphasis added).

[25] See also Dworkin (n 4) ch 3, entitled 'The Model of Rules II', 78.

Let us turn now to the various *difficulties* that arise from Dworkin's distinction between rules on the one hand and principles on the other.

B. The Difficulties with the Distinction

The first – and most obvious – difficulty is whether or not it is always possible to distinguish between rules and principles. Indeed, Dworkin himself admits that '[i]t is not always clear from the form of a standard whether it is a rule or a principle'.[26] And his following observations bear noting:[27]

> 'A will is invalid unless signed by three witnesses' is not very different in form from 'A man may not profit from his own wrong', but one who knows something of American law knows that he must take the first as stating a rule and the second as stating a principle.

However, he then proceeds to admit that:[28]

> In many cases the distinction [between rules and principles] is difficult to make. … Sometimes a rule and a principle can play much the same role, and the difference between them is almost a matter of form alone.

That *both* rules *and* principles might themselves be subject to *exceptions*[29] only adds, in my view, to the difficulty.

In order to consider this particular issue more fully, it is best to consider concrete illustrations. And in this regard, I want to consider one that Dworkin himself raised (and which has already been alluded to above): the 'principle' that 'No person may profit from his or her own wrong.' And this is, in turn, best exemplified by the well-known case (which Dworkin himself refers to) of *Riggs v Palmer*[30] (in which the claimant, having murdered the testator, claimed the latter's

[26] Dworkin (n 5) 27.
[27] ibid.
[28] ibid.
[29] See, eg, ibid 24–25 (in relation to rules) and 25 (in relation to principles).
[30] *Riggs v Palmer* 115 NY 506, 22 NE 188 (1889) (a decision of the Court of Appeals of New York; see also below, n 36). There are also similar cases in England as well: see, eg, *In the Estate of Crippen* [1911] P 108 (considered in more recent times in *In re Callaway, Callaway v Treasury Solicitor* [1956] 3 WLR 257 and *Davitt v Titcumb* [1990] 2 WLR 168). Reference may also be made to the Supreme Court of Victoria decision of *Re Sangal, deceased, Perpetual Executors and Trustees Association of Australia Ltd v House* [1921] VLR 355. See also above, n 27. For a persuasive critique of Dworkin's characterisation of this particular case, see GC Christie, 'The Model of Principles' [1968] *Duke Law Journal* 649, where the learned author argues, inter alia, that there was in fact no pre-existing rule as such which would otherwise have permitted the claimant to make a successful claim under the testator's will (notwithstanding the fact that he had murdered the testator). This segues into that learned author's more general points (at 668) that '[o]ne cannot exhaustively state legal rules so that the statement of the rule includes the complete statement of its exceptions' and that 'the decision as to when a legal rule is or is not applicable is a very difficult one'. Indeed, he also refers (ibid) to a point that is made towards the end of the present paragraph – that 'one might say that Dworkin's principles are themselves closer to what most people would call rules' and that '[t]he sharp distinction between principles and rules that Dworkin draws is

property as stipulated in the testator's will). The court in this case held that this 'principle' prevented a successful claim. Whilst virtually nobody would object to such a principle (simply because a person seeking to profit from his or her own wrong would be indulging in what virtually everyone would consider morally heinous conduct), is it not possible to argue that such a 'principle' could be *equally well* characterised as a 'rule' instead? Put simply, it could simply be stated that there is a '*rule*' that any claimant who sought to profit from his or her wrong would be denied recovery. In summary, the line between a 'rule' and a 'principle' is not always clear and might even be blurred at best.

However, even if we accept that there is (more often than not at least) a clear distinction between rules and principles and that therefore when rules run out, judges are still constrained to decide according to principles (as Dworkin defines them), what would happen when *principles* run out? Perhaps, in fact, the answer to a *prior* question is necessary before we even attempt to answer the question just posed (which answer might simultaneously throw further light on the distinction itself) – what is *the precise nature* of (Dworkinian) *principles* to begin with?

One approach is to argue that principles *underlie* rules[31] – put simply, they constitute the *underlying rationale* that *justifies* the corresponding rules themselves (recall that, even on Dworkin's definition, a 'principle' is 'a requirement of *justice or fairness or some other dimension of morality*',[32] and this approach, in fact, now appears to be confirmed by Dworkin in his latest work). In my view, such an interpretation of the concept of principles does not really support Dworkin's view that a judge does not exercise *unfettered* discretion when rules run out. Put simply, if, indeed, principles underlie rules, then they can always be relied upon in order to develop *new* rules to deal with (in particular) hard cases. If so, however, would the judge concerned not then have *unfettered* discretion in deciding which principles are applicable in the development of such new rules?

simply not supported by the cases'. Reference may also be made to Tapper (n 23) especially 629–632. Though *cf* BN Cardozo, *The Nature of the Judicial Process* (New Haven, Yale University Press, 1921) 41 (where the comparison is not between rule and principle as such but, instead, between principle and 'another principle' that was 'of greater generality'). Reference may also be made to N Duxbury, *Patterns of American Jurisprudence* (Oxford, Clarendon Press, 1995) 219 (which supports the argument made at the end of the main text to this particular paragraph); in particular, the learned author poses the following questions (ibid): 'So was the refusal to sanction unjust enrichment a legal policy rather than a moral principle? What is the difference between a policy and a principle anyway?'.

[31] This appears to be at least hinted at by Dworkin himself: Dworkin (n 5) 27 ('A legal system may also prefer the rule supported by the more important principles.'). Indeed, Dworkin appears to be even more express when he states, at another point, as follows (see Dworkin (n 25) 77 (emphasis added)):

> Indeed, one of my reasons for drawing the distinction between rules and principles was just to show *how rules often represent a kind of compromise amongst competing principles* …, and that point may be lost or submerged if we speak too freely about rules conflicting with principles.

And insofar as this point appears to be also made in Dworkin's latest work, see the text to ch 7, n 350 in this volume.

[32] Dworkin (n 5) 22 (emphasis added). See also above, n 19.

Indeed, as we have already noted, Dworkin is of the view that since principles do not (unlike rules) apply in an all-or-nothing fashion, they have a dimension of *weight*, and hence, the very *weighing* of *principles* must, *ex hypothesi*, involve *the exercise of discretion*. If Dworkin's argument is (as it seems to be) that *principles themselves constrain the exercise of unfettered discretion*, that argument is, with respect, unpersuasive simply because it is *circular* inasmuch as it merely asserts what needs to be explained in the first place. Indeed, we are back full circle to the basic question posed in the preceding paragraph: what is the *precise nature* of (Dworkinian) *principles* to begin with? On a related note, at least one of the difficulties in arguing that principles themselves *constrain* the exercise of *unfettered* discretion relates to the *moral nature* of principles – a point which I shall address in a moment when I consider the issue relating to the *justification* of *principles*.

But what if, on the other hand, principles were considered as existing *in addition to* the existing rules (which does appear to be the approach that Dworkin was taking, at least in his earlier work[33])? Whilst this would support Dworkin's view that judges would take into account principles when rules run out, we encounter a question posed earlier: what if *principles* run out? At *that* point, judges would – logically speaking – be compelled to resort to the use of *unfettered* discretion to *create new* rules (*or principles*) simply because Dworkin's theory does not provide us with a *third* type of law (*apart from* rules and principles). Indeed, even if it did, we would then run into the problem that smacks of *infinite regress* (ie, rules, followed by principles, followed by (new) rules … in a process that is (theoretically at least) one that proceeds ad infinitum).

Even if we put to one side the difficulties set out in the preceding couple of paragraphs, there is, in my view, an equally (if not more) difficult problem: if, indeed, we accept that *principles* are also part of the law (whether as underpinning rules or as separate elements of the law in their own right), how do we *justify* them? It seems to me unhelpful if the response to the question just posed is that such principles are justified simply by the fact that they are standards of justice, fairness or some other dimension of morality simply because that would be merely repeating the very definition (which Dworkin gives) of principles, thus resulting in a wholly unsatisfactory *circularity* that does not help in answering the question itself. In fairness, it is not surprising that no satisfactory answer is forthcoming from Dworkin simply because the very ideas of justice, fairness and morality are themselves difficult to define in *universal* terms (especially in the context of the present time when arguments from subjectivity as well as relativity abound). Indeed, the issue just raised is not peculiar to Dworkinian theory but is

[33] Although *cf* above, nn 31 and 32 (especially in relation to his *latest* work). See also the *Appendix* to a later edition of *Taking Rights Seriously* (entitled 'A Reply to Critics') in Dworkin (n 4) 291–368, 344, where Dworkin states: 'I did not mean, in rejecting the idea that law is a system of rules, to replace that idea with the theory that law is a system of rules and principles. There is no such thing as "the law" as a collection of discrete propositions, each with its own canonical form.'

related to a much larger question that has perplexed philosophers and jurists literally since the dawn of philosophical knowledge as well as discourse. In fairness to Dworkin, however, he does point to the fact that principles operate independently of a judge's personal preferences and include standards such as the doctrine of 'legislative supremacy' as well as the doctrine of precedent.[34] In his view:[35]

> [I]f we were challenged to back up our claim that some principle is a principle of law, we would mention *any prior cases* in which that principle was cited, or figured in the argument. We would also mention *any statute* that seemed to exemplify that principle (even better if the principle was cited in the preamble of the statute, or in the committee reports or other legislative documents that accompanied it). Unless we could find some such *institutional support*, we would probably fail to make out our case, and the *more support* we found, the *more weight* we could claim for the principle.
>
> *Yet we could not devise any formula for testing how much and what kind of institutional support is necessary to make a principle a legal principle, still less to fix its weight at a particular order of magnitude.* We argue for a particular principle by grappling with a whole set of shifting, developing and interacting standards (themselves principles rather than rules) about institutional responsibility, statutory interpretation, the persuasive force of various sorts of precedent, the relation of all these to contemporary moral practices, and hosts of other such standards.

And, in a similar vein, Dworkin also observes thus:[36]

> [T]he great bulk of principles and policies judges cite are *controversial, at least as to weight; the weight of the principle that no man may profit from his own wrong*, for example, was *sufficiently controversial to provoke a dissent* in *Riggs v. Palmer. Second, a great many appeals to principle* are appeals to principle *that have not been the subject of any established judicial practice at all*; this is true of several of the examples I gave from the decision in the *Henningsen* case, which included principles that had not in fact been formulated before, in anything like the same fashion, like the principle that automobile manufacturers have a special responsibility to the public.

With respect, the above elaboration by Dworkin with regard to principles appears to be rather *vague and general.*

In fairness to Dworkin, though, he does in fact attempt to distinguish between *different senses* of the concept of *discretion*. He is perfectly comfortable with two senses of discretion. The first relates to 'standards that reasonable men can *interpret* in different ways, as a sergeant has discretion if he is told to take the five most experienced men on patrol'.[37] The second relates to a situation where a decision is 'final, in the sense that no higher author may review and set aside that decision, as when the decision whether a player is offside is left to the discretion of

[34] Dworkin (n 5) 37.
[35] ibid 40 (emphasis added).
[36] Dworkin (n 25) 65 (emphasis added). Insofar as the case of *Riggs v Palmer* is concerned, see also above, n 30.
[37] ibid 69 (emphasis added).

the lineman'.[38] It is, however, the *third* sense of discretion that Dworkin *does* take objection to:[39]

> Third, we may say that a man has discretion when some set of standards which impose duties upon him do not in fact purport to impose any duty as to a particular decision, as when a clause in a lease gives the tenant the option in his discretion to renew.

A significant question that arises is whether there is indeed any difference (in substance) between the first and third senses of discretion. Even at this early stage in his writing, Dworkin's focus is on a concept that figures prominently in his later writings – that of *interpretation*. It will suffice for present purposes to note that it might be possible for Dworkin's critics to argue that there can, *even* in the context of *interpretation*, be discretion that is exercised by the court concerned in the *third* sense (which, as we have just seen, Dworkin *objects* to). In other words, it might be asked why a court would not have *unfettered* discretion *even in* the context of interpretation. I will, in fact, deal with this particular issue (of interpretation) in more detail when evaluating Dworkin's *theory* of adjudication proper (and as set out in his *later* writings) below.

In my view, however, despite the various difficulties outlined above, Dworkin has nevertheless come as philosophically close as is possible to positing a coherent view not only of the adjudicative process but also of the very important prior (albeit utterly essential) issue of the objective nature of that process. He cannot be faulted for not being able to set out an even close to *perfect* theory, although he has, in my view, taken us as far as any jurist possibly can. That final gap cannot be filled by *theoretical* content as such, although, as I shall endeavour to demonstrate, *judges* in the *practical* sphere nevertheless *do* strive to – and, in fact, *do* – achieve *just and fair* outcomes in most of the cases that come before them. That it is not possible to encompass this in *theoretical* terms is due to the fact that the world in general is too complex and that fair and just outcomes are *necessarily* sought by judges and courts *in the context of the specific facts of the case concerned* (with *the possible factual matrices being, (with rare exceptions), both myriad as well as, in many cases, complex*).[40] Indeed (and given the myriad possibilities of

[38] ibid.

[39] ibid.

[40] A point made in an earlier chapter (see ch 3 in this volume) is important and is therefore worth reiterating in full once again: it should be noted that the 'facts' referred to here comprise *not only actual* 'facts' *but also relevant* 'facts', viz, facts which fall *within* the *factual parameters* that *constitute an integral part of* the *legal rule* itself. In this last-mentioned regard, it should be noted that part of the content of the *legal rule* itself would comprise the factual parameters just referred to. Hence, when we refer to the *application* of the law to the (*actual*) facts of a given case, we are referring only to those facts which are *relevant* inasmuch (as mentioned at the outset of the present note) as they fall *within* the *factual parameters* that are *part of* the *legal rule* itself. I should add that I am not here concerned with the actual jurisprudential nature of such (relevant) facts themselves – in particular, whether they are descriptive or normative in nature (see generally M Greenberg, 'How Facts Make Law' in ch 10 of S Hershovitz (n 11) and, by the same author, 'Hartian Positivism and Normative Facts: *How Facts Make Law II*' in ch 11 of the same book (the former chapter was originally published in (2004) 10 *Legal Theory* 157)). My own view is that as the relevant facts of a given case necessarily fall within the factual parameters that are

fact situations just mentioned), it is, in any event, impossible (in most cases at least) to predict the *outcome* of the case concerned until the *actual* facts have been *established*. It might, for example, well be the case that these facts fall *outside* the factual parameters that constitute an integral part of the relevant legal rule – and vice versa. *That* is why the *specific facts* are *crucial*. I elaborate upon these admittedly more general issues – *with actual illustrations from decided cases* – in (especially) chapter eight. At this juncture, let me turn to the *second* important set of distinctions, which forms an important building block in Dworkin's overall theory of adjudication.

Before proceeding to do so, however, perhaps I might venture at least a *tentative* view as to *how rules and principles (as defined by Dworkin) interact in the practical sphere of adjudication*. Put simply, courts and judges constantly strive to locate *as well as* apply *rules*, and, in the context of common law and equity at least, there is a constant openness to *ensuring that the rules are themselves consistent with not only logic and reason but are also themselves just and fair*. It is therefore suggested that *principles are part of the law, albeit not in the way Dworkin conceives them*. They do underlie rules, albeit (once again) *not* in the way *Dworkin* perceives it. *Principles*, in my view, constitute the *underlying spirit or rationale of justice and fairness* with regard to *the rules* concerned. In other words, principles are *inextricably connected with* rules in what should be viewed as an *integrated and interactive* process. *However*, the *actual doctrine of the law itself* (ie, what the courts traditionally refer to as 'the applicable law') comprises *rules only*. Looked

an integral part of the *legal* rule itself, whilst they are (on one view) *descriptive* in nature (particularly when viewed in isolation), when the legal rule concerned is *applied* to such facts, they also take on a *normative* nature as well (a view that is consistent with that advocated by Greenberg in the essays just cited (and see, in particular, Greenberg, 'How Facts Make Law', above, 254, where the learned author observes that 'value facts include facts about the *relevance* of descriptive facts' (emphasis added) as well as, by the same author, 'Hartian Positivism and Normative Facts: *How Facts Make Law II*', above (especially 267), where he discusses the concept of a 'legal fact', which he states 'is a true legal proposition – a fact about the content of law')). In his response to Greenberg, Dworkin himself, whilst agreeing with Greenberg's view that 'value facts are among the determinants of the content of the law', nevertheless distinguishes 'two forms of that claim' as follows, viz, '(1) value facts figure in the truth conditions of propositions of law; (2) value facts figure in the justification for any theory about the truth conditions of propositions of law' (see R Dworkin, 'Response' in Hershovitz (n 11) 291–311, 310) – stating that his 'arguments in *Law's Empire* [Dworkin (n 210)] are meant to support (2) as well as (1)' (ibid 311). In the context of the present discussion, my reference is more to (1) (instead of (2)), dealing with the actual adjudicative process as such.

Needless to say, this is an uniquely jurisprudential or conceptual issue which (based on my own practical experience as a judge at least) does not impact the process of adjudication in the *practical* context.

And, still in relation to the practical context, the process of fact-finding itself at first instance is no mean task. As Lord Bingham observed (see T Bingham, *The Business of Judging: Selected Essays and Speeches* (Oxford, Oxford University Press, 2000) 37):

> The judge must exercise judgment, not discretion, in finding the facts, and it is usually the most difficult and often the most exacting task which the civil trial judge has to undertake.

This was – as a trial judge – my own experience as well. Indeed, one might add that this difficult task applies equally to criminal trials as well. See also, on the importance of facts and fact-finding, KO See, *Fact-Finding and Reality: A Judicial Decision-Making Primer* (Singapore, Academy Publishing, 2022).

at in this light, it necessarily follows that – contrary to what Dworkin proposes – courts and judges *do make law* when an existing rule is modified *or* departed from *or* when the rules themselves run out. However, such law-making *must* take into account (as already mentioned) the need for the 'new' rule to be both consistent with logic and reason *as well as* to embody the ideal of justice and fairness (ie, the 'new' rule *must* be *consistent with principle in the manner I have just described*). Consistently, with such a view of rules and principles, we need not concern ourselves with the line between each since they are, on this view, not susceptible to comparison but, instead, *complement* each other (although it bears repeating that the *actual doctrine of the law itself* comprises *rules only*). In any event (and as we have already seen), the line between each (as Dworkin himself admits) is not always clear.

Let us now turn to the *second* set of Dworkinian 'building blocks' – the distinction between principle on the one hand and policy on the other.

III. The Basic Building Blocks (2) – The Distinction between Principle and Policy

A. In Theory

i. The Distinction Stated

We have just seen how important a role the idea of *principles* plays in Dworkinian legal theory. He has a *further* distinction that seeks to 'protect' this vital idea against theoretical erosion and/or confusion. In particular, Dworkin draws an *additional* distinction between principle on the one hand and *policy* on the other.

In essence, Dworkin argues that while principles (and, of course, rules) are part of the law that is considered as well as applied by *the courts*, *policy* on the other hand, can *only* be legitimately considered by *the legislature*. This is because judges are *not elected officials*[41] and therefore have *no* legal right or *locus standi* to deal with *policy* as such. Dworkin refers to a 'policy' as 'that kind of standard that sets out a *goal* to be reached, generally an improvement in some *economic, political, or social feature of the community*'.[42] Hence, policies – in *contrast* to principles – are *goal (instead of rights) based* and, in *those* circumstances, are best determined by *the legislature*. Looked at in this light, *utilitarianism* would be the paradigm philosophical model that best embodies as well as demonstrates the importance of policies.[43]

[41] It is true that some judges in the US are elected, but it is clear that in Singapore and other Commonwealth countries, judges are *not* elected officials.

[42] See Dworkin (n 5) 22 (emphasis added).

[43] See also generally Dworkin (n 6) 94–100.

I should pause here to note that when I was *lecturing* in jurisprudence and philosophy in law school, I was in fact quite *critical* of this particular distinction. Indeed, at a very *general or theoretical* level, it is, in fact, quite easy to level criticisms of this distinction. For example, one possible criticism is that it is difficult to distinguish principle from policy and that one person's policy might well be another's principle – and vice versa. It must be admitted that, viewed on a very general level, such a critique is not unpersuasive.

However, it was only when I actually heard cases whilst a judge that I discovered the *practical* utility of such a distinction (particularly in what Dworkin himself would term 'hard cases' (where there is no established rule which covers the case at hand)). The perennial distinction between 'law in the books' and 'law in action' never rang truer. And it is to the importance of the distinction between principle on the one hand and policy on the other in the *practical* sphere to which our attention must now turn. However, before proceeding to do so, I would like to deal briefly with some of the difficulties with the distinction at a *theoretical* level.

ii. The (Theoretical) Difficulties with the Distinction

It is easy to understand why, from a *theoretical* perspective, the line between principle and policy may be perceived to be problematic. It may well depend on how each is phrased as well as presented. Put simply, 'One person's principle may be another's policy – and vice versa.'

In fairness to Dworkin, however, he is clear that the 'policy' that he rejects insofar as the process of adjudication is concerned is one that is (in form and/or substance) *legislative* in nature. However, as we shall see, the concept of 'policy' is not a unidimensional one: As we shall see in the next section, there is a role for 'policy' as well in the adjudication process.

As already alluded to above, the real significance of the distinction between principle and policy can only be discerned in the *practical* context, and it is therefore to that sphere that our attention now turns.

B. In Practice

As mentioned, whilst I did in fact find Dworkin's distinction between principle and policy to be important as well as useful in practice (a point which I shall illustrate through concrete case law), I think that there is nevertheless still a place for 'policy' in the courts. As I shall explain in a moment, there are, in my view, *two* conceptions of the concept of 'policy' (and here, like Dworkin, I also draw from the concept of 'essentially contested concepts',[44] albeit in a slightly different manner) – the second of which is actually recognised expressly by the courts themselves.

[44] A concept first mooted by Professor WB Gallie: see Gallie (n 13).

The first conception of the concept of 'policy' is the one which Dworkin refers to – it represents policy in the context of the *legislative* sphere. Put simply, it concerns policy in the context of not merely law-making (here, in the form of legislation) but also takes into account *political considerations* as well. It is this last-mentioned element that renders this conception of 'policy' not only unsuitable for the *judicial* context but also renders it *illegitimate* for courts to consider it simply because judges are *not* elected officials (and therefore do not possess the mandate from the public to take such *extra*legal considerations into account in arriving at their respective decisions). If all this appears rather abstract, let me illustrate this from my own (judicial) experience.

In the Singapore Court of Appeal decision of *Lim Meng Suang v Attorney-General*,[45] the appellants filed applications to challenge the constitutionality of section 377A of the Penal Code[46] (which criminalised sex between consenting male adults). The Court held that that provision was not unconstitutional under Articles 9 and 12 of the Constitution of the Republic of Singapore.[47] For the purposes of the present section of this chapter, the following observations by the Court are directly apposite:[48]

> 7 Drawing such *a line in the legal sand* is imperative. If this is not done, the court will necessarily be sucked into and thereby descend into the *political* arena, which would in turn undermine (or even destroy) the very role which constitutes the *raison d'être* for the court's existence in the first place – namely, to furnish an *independent, neutral and objective* forum for deciding, on the basis of objective legal rules and principles, (*inter alia*) what rights parties have in a given situation. That the court's role as a neutral arbiter is utterly vital is underscored in a situation where (as is the case here) the arguments on either side of what is in substance a *legislative* divide are intensely controversial and the relevant empirical evidence is ambiguous at best. All that the court can – and must – be concerned with in these circumstances is whether any *fundamental rights* under *the Singapore Constitution* (such as those pursuant to Art 9 and Art 12) have indeed been violated.
>
> 8 In determining the constitutionality of a statute which is alleged to be inconsistent with Art 12 (or, for that matter, any other Article of the Singapore Constitution), the court's main concern is to be careful not to trespass into extra-legal territory which legitimately belongs only to the legislature. Looked at in this light, the many extra-legal arguments on the constitutionality of s 377A are *irrelevant* to the court's application of Art 12. We hasten to add that this does *not* mean that these arguments are *wholly* irrelevant in *all* contexts. They are appropriate to a *legislative* debate, but that is wholly beyond the remit of the court. The proponents of these arguments fail to see this because they overlook the vital distinction referred to above (at [6]) between legal principles and extra-legal

[45] *Lim Meng Suang v Attorney-General* [2015] 1 *Singapore Law Reports* 26.

[46] Chapter 224, 2008 Revised Edition of the Statutes of the Republic of Singapore.

[47] 1985 Rev Edn, 1999 Reprint; see now the Constitution of the Republic of Singapore (2020 Rev Edn). Art 9 relates to liberty of the person, whilst Art 12 relates to the equal protection of the law.

[48] [2015] 1 *Singapore Law Reports* 26, [7]–[8] (emphasis in the original text). See also the Singapore Court of Appeal decision of *Public Prosecutor v Lam Leng Hung* [2018] 1 *Singapore Law Reports* 659, especially [7]–[9] and [284].

> considerations. Hence, they proffer various extra-legal arguments as though those arguments are central to the court's task, when they serve only to muddy an already difficult legal path which the court is attempting its level best to negotiate. This is unfortunate, to say the least. Indeed, the difficulties are exacerbated by the fact that some of the extra-legal arguments might also have an overlay of emotional and/or other overtones, and, on this ground alone, are more suited (if at all) to a *legislative* (or even *philosophical*) – but *not* a *legal* – debate.

That the courts cannot be 'mini-legislatures' was such a fundamental point in this case that the Court was at pains to underscore this point at a number of further junctures in its judgment. This is evidenced, for example, by the following observations (which merit setting out in full):[49]

> 70 It should be noted that the threshold nature of the 'reasonable classification' test [pursuant to Art 12 of the Constitution of the Republic of Singapore] helps to *balance* the need to accord as much legislative leeway as possible to the legislature against the need to ensure that laws which are patently illogical and/or incoherent do not pass legal muster. In a related vein, this test simultaneously prevents the courts from becoming "mini-legislatures" (a point which is dealt with in more detail below, especially at [77]).
>
> …
>
> 77 It is important to commence our analysis in this regard by referring to a fundamental proposition that constitutes part of the wider concept of the separation of powers. Put simply, the courts are *separate and distinct from* the legislature. More specifically, whilst the courts do 'make' law, this is only permissible in the context of the interpretation of statutes and the development of the principles of common law and equity. It is *im*permissible for *the courts* to arrogate to themselves *legislative powers* – to become, in other words, '*mini-legislatures*'. This must necessarily be the case because the courts have no mandate whatsoever to create or amend laws in a manner which permits recourse to *extra-legal policy factors as well as considerations*. The jurisdiction as well as the power to do so lie exclusively within the sphere of *the legislature*. Indeed, the power of the legislature to enact and amend laws is governed by quite a different procedure. Hence, the duty of a court is to *interpret* statutes enacted by the legislature; it *cannot amend or modify statutes* based on its own personal preference or fiat as that would be an obvious (and unacceptable) usurpation of the *legislative* function.
>
> 78 The legislative powers which we have just discussed are different from the court's role in developing the law – a task which it frequently undertakes. As already alluded to above, the courts do indeed develop the principles of common law and equity. …
>
> …
>
> 82 Here, we come to the crux of the issue at hand. To permit the court the power – *over and above* its power of scrutinising legislation pursuant to *the 'reasonable classification' test* – to declare a statute inconsistent with Art 12(1) (and, therefore, unconstitutional

[49] [2015] 1 *Singapore Law Reports* 26, [70], [77]–[78], [82]–[85], [92], [93], [101], [154], [173] and [189] (emphasis in the original text). See also L Thio, 'Negotiating Particularisms, Excavating Principles and Delimiting Provinces – Justice Phang and Public Law' in Y Goh (gen ed), *Pursuing Justice and Justice Alone – The Heart and Humanity of Andrew Phang's Jurisprudence* (Singapore, Academy Publishing, 2022) 351–388 at 376–386.

under Art 4) because the ***object*** of that statute is *illegitimate would precisely be to confer on the court a licence to usurp the legislative function in the course of becoming (or at least acting like) a 'mini-legislature'.* Put another way, *only the legislature has the power to review its own legislation and amend legislation accordingly if it is of the view that this is necessary.* The *courts*, in contrast, have *no* such power – *nor ought they to have such power.*

83 Indeed, to argue, as the Appellants seemed to do, that the court has the duty to declare a statute unconstitutional if its object is 'illegitimate' *does not explain the legal basis upon which the court can find the object to be illegitimate in the first place.* If the argument is that the object of the statute is illegitimate because that object is unconstitutional, this would lead to a circularity which, *ex hypothesi*, lacks the requisite explanatory as well as normative power. The courts are called upon – and ought – to be 'bold spirits', *but* ***only*** *on* ***appropriate*** *occasions.* Put simply, they *cannot* claim to act as 'bold spirits' *when they are in fact acting outside their proper sphere of jurisdiction.* This point will become particularly important in the analysis below – especially in the face of the Appellants' calls to this court to update the law on s 377A based purely on *extra-legal arguments* which are *appropriate only* in the *legislative* sphere. *Put simply but clearly, to permit the court to effectively amend (as opposed to interpret) the law in this area would not only entail the court acting beyond its jurisdiction, but also permit the Appellants to obtain by the (judicial) backdoor what they ought to have sought to obtain by the (legislative) front door.*

84 That having been said, *an important qualification* is in order at this juncture. The important qualification is this: to the extent that there are *serious flaws* with regard to the *intelligibility* of the differentia embodied in a statute and/or a *clear disconnect* between that differentia and the purpose and object of the statute, the court will hold that the statute does not pass legal muster under Art 12(1). *This may be viewed, in substance at least, as introducing a limited element of illegitimacy which is embodied in the 'reasonable classification' test. However, it is vitally important to note that this element of illegitimacy is* ***not*** *an additional test over and above the 'reasonable classification' test; it is, instead, no more than an application of the 'reasonable classification' test.* The only *legal* test for the purposes of Art 12(1) is the 'reasonable classification' test, and it is important to note that in applying this test, the court would be applying a ***legal*** *test that is not based on extra-legal considerations, but rather, one that is clearly within its remit as a court of law (as opposed to acting as if it were a 'mini-legislature').*

85 Put simply, in determining the constitutionality of an impugned statute under Art 12(1), there are *no legal standards* which can guide the court in ascertaining whether the object of that statute is illegitimate. In the nature of things, any purported standards would be *extra-legal* in nature. This brings us back to the point just made – that *the legislature* is the appropriate forum to canvass the issue of whether or not the object of a particular statute is illegitimate because the extra-legal standards pertinent to such an issue would be quintessentially within the sphere of legislative review.

…

92 It can immediately be seen that Art 12(2) furnishes *specific legal criteria as to what constitutes discrimination and is therefore prohibited from a constitutional perspective.* In many ways, the approach adopted in Art 12(2) is more structured and principled compared to the approach under open-ended constitutional provisions in some

other jurisdictions that place the courts in the unenviable position of being (in effect) 'mini-legislatures' of sorts. …

93 Before proceeding to consider some other constitutional provisions in a comparative context, we ought to briefly address a further argument by Ms Barker [counsel for the Appellants in one of the appeals] based on the fact that Art 12(2) applies *only* to *citizens of Singapore*. She argued that in contrast, Art 12(1) was framed more broadly to apply to '*[a]ll* persons' [emphasis added], and hence (citing the paragraph of the 1966 Report quoted above at [87]), Art 12(1) ought to be given an *expansive* interpretation that goes *beyond* the 'reasonable classification' test so as to accord equal protection to all persons. *However*, that brings us back full circle to the difficulties outlined above (especially at [77]) to the effect that the courts would then become 'mini-legislatures'.

…

101 It can be seen that the provision just quoted in the preceding paragraph [*Ie*, the Fourteenth Amendment of the US Constitution] is open-ended inasmuch as *it does not contain any equivalent of Art 12(2)*. Not surprisingly, therefore, the US courts (in particular, the US Supreme Court) have taken the view that different grounds of discrimination will attract different levels of scrutiny, with the legal principles applicable to the different grounds to be enunciated and developed through *case law*. Had, in fact, the Fourteenth Amendment to the US Constitution contained a provision which was *equivalent to our Art 12(2)*, the position might have been quite different. We pause to observe, parenthetically, that an open-ended provision on the right to equality in a Constitution brings problems and difficulties of its own. How, for example, is the court to decide *which particular ground* of discrimination ought to come within the ambit of that provision? There is every danger that the court could end up acting like a 'mini-legislature'. Indeed, it might have *no choice* but to do so, except, perhaps, in the clearest instances (which would, *ex hypothesi*, have the endorsement of at least the majority of the population in that particular jurisdiction, although there would be very real and practical difficulties in the *court's* ability to ascertain the existence of such endorsement in the first place).

…

154 As already stated earlier in this judgment, there is *no separate or independent test of illegitimacy* (*vis-à-vis* the object of the impugned statute) for the purposes of ascertaining the constitutionality of that statute under Art 12. There is therefore no need for us to consider the issue of illegitimacy in relation to the facts and circumstances of the present appeals, given our finding (applying the 'reasonable classification' test to s 377A) that there is no illogicality or incoherence in the differentia embodied in that provision. It is important to reiterate that the courts cannot become 'mini-legislatures'. That would be an illegitimate use of their powers. Indeed, the present appeals illustrate precisely the dangers of adopting such an approach. To elaborate, we have already referred above (at [111]) to the intense controversy surrounding the debate on s 377A in the extra-legal sphere in general and during the October 2007 parliamentary debates mentioned in that same paragraph in particular. This controversy has been marked on both sides of a very stark (and often emotional) divide by a great number of *extra-legal* arguments which are clearly and wholly outside the remit of the courts, and which fall instead within the purview of the legislature.

…

> 173 Put simply, Art 9 and Art 12 would constitute a *legal* basis on which the Appellants can seek to vindicate their rights. The Appellants *cannot* ask the court to vindicate their rights based simply – and *without more* – on the argument that *they feel that the prevailing societal morality is wrong as it deprives them of their freedom*. This is *not* to state that such an argument cannot be made. But, a moment's reflection will reveal that in order to succeed in this argument, the Appellants will necessarily need to bring to bear a great number of *extra-legal arguments*, which, as we have already emphasised, are *uniquely* within the purview of *the legislature*. These extra-legal arguments include *empirical data in the form of*, inter alia, *surveys* (some of which were referred to by both the Appellants and the Respondent in the course of the present appeals) *which this court is not equipped to assess*. At this particular juncture, the vitally important distinction between the judicial function on the one hand and the legislative function on the other must be emphasised yet again. Put simply, the court *cannot and must not attempt to (still less actually) operate as a 'mini-legislature'* – lest the vital role of the court as an independent and neutral institution deciding objectively, on the basis of objective legal rules and principles, the rights which parties have in a particular situation (among other issues) be reduced to naught.
>
> …
>
> 189 The present appeals were argued by both Ms Barker as well as Mr Ravi with great passion on behalf of their respective clients. This is not surprising, especially when one takes into account the intensely controversial (and even emotional) nature of the arguments surrounding the nature and function of s 377A which have been canvassed by proponents on either side of the extra-legal divide. Indeed, many of the arguments tendered to this court, whilst valid (or, at least, plausible) in their own right, involved *extra-legal considerations and matters of social policy which were outside the remit of the court, and should, instead, have been canvassed in the legislative sphere*. It is entirely appropriate, at this juncture, to reiterate a point we have already made several times in the course of this judgment, not least because it is an extremely important and fundamental one: the court can only consider *legal* (as opposed to *extra-legal*) arguments. This ensures that it will not become a 'mini-legislature'. The court *cannot – and must not* – assume *legislative* functions which are necessarily beyond its remit. To do so would be to efface the very separation of powers which confers upon the court its *legitimacy* in the first place. If the court were to assume legislative functions, it would no longer be able to sit to assess the legality of statutes from an *objective* perspective. Worse still, it would necessarily be involved in expressing views on extra-legal issues which would – in the nature of things – be (or at least be perceived to be) *subjective* in nature. This would further erode the *legitimacy* of the court, which ought only to sit to administer the law in an *objective* manner.

I have set out extended extracts from the *Lim Meng Suang* case to underscore the strict adherence to the concept of the separation of powers by the Singapore courts and the fact that this point was felt to be so fundamental that it was reiterated so many times in this particular judgment. Indeed, the phrase 'mini-legislature' is utilised no fewer than *ten times* in the judgment itself.

A renewed constitutional challenge with respect to the same provision (ie, section 377A) was subsequently brought. Although the Singapore Court of Appeal in *Tan Seng Kee v Attorney-General*[50] adopted a somewhat different approach (arriving at the same result in the *Lim Meng Suang* case), the general approach that eschewed the courts becoming 'mini-legislatures' was nevertheless reiterated.[51] Significantly (particularly in relation to the point being presently made), it was indeed *the Legislature* that finally *repealed* section 377A.[52]

It should also be noted that the need for courts to avoid being (or even being perceived as being) 'mini-legislatures' is not unique to the Singapore context. In the House of Lords decision of *Duport Steels Ltd v Sirs*,[53] for example, Lord Diplock observed thus:[54]

> My Lords, at a time when more and more cases involve the application of legislation which gives effect to policies that are the subject of bitter public and parliamentary controversy, it cannot be too strongly emphasised that the British constitution, though largely unwritten, is firmly based upon the separation of powers; Parliament makes the laws, the judiciary interpret them. When Parliament legislates to remedy what the majority of its members at the time perceive to be a defect or a lacuna in the existing law (whether it be the written law enacted by existing statutes or the unwritten common law as it has been expounded by the judges in decided cases), the role of the judiciary is confined to ascertaining from the words that Parliament has approved as expressing its intention what that intention was, and to giving effect to it. Where the meaning of the statutory words is plain and unambiguous it is not for the judges to invent fancied ambiguities as an excuse for failing to give effect to its plain meaning because they themselves consider that the consequences of doing so would be inexpedient, or even unjust or immoral. In controversial matters such as are involved in industrial relations there is room for differences of opinion as to what is expedient, what is just and what is morally justifiable. Under our constitution it is Parliament's opinion on these matters that is paramount.
>
> …
>
> It endangers continued public confidence in the political impartiality of the judiciary, which is essential to the continuance of the rule of law, if judges, under the guise of interpretation, provide their own preferred amendments to statutes which experience of their operation has shown to have had consequences that members of the court before whom the matter comes consider to be injurious to the public interest.

In a similar vein, the other Law Lords expressed similar views. Lord Keith of Kinkel was of the view that:[55]

> The one public interest which courts of law are properly entitled to treat as their concern is the standing of and the degree of respect commanded by the judicial system.

[50] *Tan Seng Kee v Attorney-General* [2022] 1 *Singapore Law Reports* 1347.
[51] ibid, especially [156]–[158].
[52] See the Penal Code (Amendment) Act 2022 (No 39 of 2022).
[53] *Duport Steels Ltd v Sirs* [1980] 1 WLR 142.
[54] ibid 157.
[55] ibid 168.

> Involvement in political controversy, particularly in the legislatively governed field of industrial relations, is calculated to damage that interest. In the interpretation of statutes the courts must faithfully endeavour to give effect to the expressed intention of Parliament as gathered from the language used and the apparent policy of the enactment under consideration.

And Lord Scarman's very direct views left little to one's imagination:[56]

> My basic criticism of all three judgments in the Court of Appeal is that in their desire to do justice the court failed to do justice according to law. When one is considering law in the hands of the judges, law means the body of rules and guidelines within which society requires its judges to administer justice. Legal systems differ in the width of the discretionary power granted to judges: but in developed societies limits are invariably set, beyond which the judges may not go. Justice in such societies is not left to the unguided, even if experienced, sage sitting under the spreading oak tree.
>
> In our society the judges have in some aspects of their work a discretionary power to do justice so wide that they may be regarded as law-makers. The common law and equity, both of them in essence systems of private law, are fields where, subject to the increasing intrusion of statute law, society has been content to allow the judges to formulate and develop the law. The judges, even in this, their very own field of creative endeavour, have accepted, in the interests of certainty, the self-denying ordinance of 'stare decisis,' the doctrine of binding precedent: and no doubt this judicially imposed limitation on judicial law-making has helped to maintain confidence in the certainty and evenhandedness of the law.
>
> But in the field of statute law the judge must be obedient to the will of Parliament as expressed in its enactments. In this field Parliament makes, and un-makes, the law: the judge's duty is to interpret and to apply the law, not to change it to meet the judge's idea of what justice requires. Interpretation does, of course, imply in the interpreter a power of choice where differing constructions are possible. But our law requires the judge to choose the construction which in his judgment best meets the legislative purpose of the enactment. If the result be unjust but inevitable, the judge may say so and invite Parliament to reconsider its provision. But he must not deny the statute. Unpalatable statute law may not be disregarded or rejected, merely because it is unpalatable.
>
> …
>
> Great judges are in their different ways judicial activists. But the constitution's separation of powers, or more accurately functions, must be observed if judicial independence is not to be put at risk. For, if people and Parliament come to think that the judicial power is to be confined by nothing other than the judge's sense of what is right (or, as Selden put it, by the length of the Chancellor's foot), confidence in the judicial system will be replaced by fear of it becoming uncertain and arbitrary in its application. Society will then be ready for Parliament to cut the power of the judges. Their power to do justice will become more restricted by law than it need be, or is today.

[56] ibid. See also per Lord Edmund-Davies ibid 164–165. Reference may also be made to the observations by Lord Scarman in the (also) House of Lords decision of *Lim Poh Choo v Camden and Islington Area Health Authority* [1980] AC 174, 183.

A subsequent decision – also from the House of Lords – may be noted. This is the decision in *Regina (ProLife Alliance) v British Broadcasting Corporation*.[57] In that case, Lord Hoffmann observed as follows:[58]

> 75 My Lords, although the word 'deference' is now very popular in describing the relationship between the judicial and the other branches of government, I do not think that its overtones of servility, or perhaps gracious concession, are appropriate to describe what is happening.[59] In a society based upon the rule of law and the separation of powers, it is necessary to decide which branch of government has in any particular instance the decision-making power and what the legal limits of that power are. That is a question of law and must therefore be decided by the courts.
>
> 76 This means that the courts themselves often have to decide the limits of their own decision-making power. That is inevitable. But it does not mean that their allocation of decision-making power to the other branches of government is a matter of courtesy or deference. The principles upon which decision-making powers are allocated are principles of law. The courts are the independent branch of government and the legislature and executive are, directly and indirectly respectively, the elected branches of government. Independence makes the courts more suited to deciding some kinds of questions and being elected makes the legislature or executive more suited to deciding others. The allocation of these decision-making responsibilities is based upon recognised principles. The principle that the independence of the courts is necessary for a proper decision of disputed legal rights or claims of violation of human rights is a legal principle. It is reflected in article 6 of the Convention. On the other hand, the principle that majority approval is necessary for a proper decision on policy or allocation of resources is also a legal principle. Likewise, when a court decides that a decision is within the proper competence of the legislature or executive, it is not showing deference. It is deciding the law.

There is a *second* conception of the concept of 'policy' which I think Dworkin would *not* approve of. This is the concept of what I would term '*judicial public* policy', which has in fact been used in the development of *the common law*. Such a conception (of 'judicial public policy') *differs from* the 'legislative policy' which Dworkin clearly eschews. That having been said, I do not (as I have just mentioned) think that Dworkin would have approved of 'judicial public policy' either. His focus in the context of adjudication at common law has always been on 'principle' (as opposed to 'policy'). It is suggested, however, that that is, with respect, too narrow an approach to adopt. Put simply, it is important for the court – even in the context of the common law – to have regard occasionally, at least, to broader policy factors in order to arrive at a just and fair legal proposition that (in turn) would lead to a just and fair outcome in cases relating to a particular branch of the common law. Indeed, as a leading scholar in the field put it:[60]

[57] *Regina (ProLife Alliance) v British Broadcasting Corporation* [2004] 1 AC 185.

[58] ibid [75]–[76].

[59] See also ibid [144], per Lord Walker of Gestingthorpe.

[60] See J Morgan, 'Policy Reasoning in Tort Law: the Courts, the Law Commission and the Critics' (2009) 125 *LQR* 215, 215 (emphasis in the original text). Reference may also be made to the pathbreaking

> Policy reasoning has been a central, perhaps *the* central, characteristic of the judicial development of tort law.

In fairness to Dworkin, though, it appears clear that the *English courts* at least have avoided incorporating 'policy' expressly into the law. A clear example of this can be seen in their development of the concept of the duty of care in the law of negligence.[61]

In this last-mentioned regard, the seminal House of Lords decision in *Donoghue v Stevenson*[62] marked the birth of the modern tort of negligence in the English context. However, whilst the test of foreseeability established in this decision was sufficient to cover negligence that resulted in physical injury, situations involving pure economic loss posed (by their very nature) more difficult problems in relation to the formulation of a duty of care. It was in fact thought that Lord Wilberforce had, in the House of Lords in *Anns v Merton LBC*,[63] by laying down the famous two-stage test for ascertaining whether there was a duty of care, had settled the law in this latter regard as well. This test comprised, first, establishing the requisite degree of proximity between the parties concerned, followed, second, by establishing that no *policy* factors militated against a finding of a duty of care. However, this test was *rejected* by the House of Lords in the subsequent decision of *Murphy v Brentwood DC*.[64] Instead, a three-part approach was articulated by the House of Lords in *Caparo Industries Plc v Dickman*[65] (comprising foreseeability, proximity and the need for the imposition of a duty of care to be 'fair, just and reasonable'). Significantly, perhaps, the concept of 'policy', in its express form at least,[66] had been removed from the English law of negligence.

work by J Bell, *Policy Arguments in Judicial Decisions* (Oxford, Clarendon Press, 1983), especially 42–53 (in the context of the duty of care in the law of tort); interestingly, this work was based on the learned author's doctoral thesis which was supervised by none other than Professor Ronald Dworkin himself (ibid vi)! *Cf* also K Greenawalt, 'Book Reviews of *A Matter of Principle* and *Law's Empire*' (1987) 84 *Journal of Philosophy* 284, 290 (on the possibility of a 'pluralist account of legal interpretation' that takes into account consequences as well (as to which see also J Plunkett, 'Principle and Policy in Private Law Reasoning' [2016] *CLJ* 366)) and N Gur, 'Ronald Dworkin and the Curious Case of the Floodgates Argument' (2018) 31 *Canadian Journal of Law & Jurisprudence* 323, 335 (where it is observed, more specifically, that 'although the primary task of civil judges is to render principled decisions on the parties' entitlements according to the law, policy arguments sometimes do and should feature in their decisions' and that '[a]rguments of principle and arguments of policy both have essential roles to play in civil adjudication'). Reference may also be made to Y Muthu, 'Dworkin v Fish: Theoretical Premise of Awarding Damages for Psychiatric Illness in England and Australia' (2009) 95 *Archiv für Rechts- und Sozialphilosophie* 327, especially 347–350 (on the use of *policy* by the courts in the context of the issue of psychiatric illness in the law of negligence).

[61] In this part of the chapter, I draw liberally (and gratefully) from A Phang, 'Pure Economic Loss and Reproductive Negligence – The Singapore experience' (2017) 24 *Torts Law Journal* 95.

[62] *Donoghue v Stevenson* [1932] AC 562.

[63] *Anns v Merton LBC* [1978] AC 728.

[64] *Murphy v Brentwood DC* [1991] 1 AC 398.

[65] *Caparo Industries Plc v Dickman* [1990] 2 AC 605.

[66] But *cf* the reference to the requirement that the imposition of a duty of care be 'fair, just and reasonable' in the *Caparo* case (which has just been noted).

However, *despite* its rejection in England, the two-stage test in the *Anns* case found traction in one form or another in some other Commonwealth jurisdictions, most notably perhaps in Singapore.[67] It will suffice for the purposes of the present section of this chapter to note that the Singapore Court of Appeal, in *Spandeck Engineering (S) Pte Ltd v Defence Science & Technology Agency*,[68] held that a single test based on the *Anns* formulation should be used to determine the existence of a duty of care for all claims of negligence. A succinct statement of this particular test may be found in the penultimate paragraph of the judgment as follows:[69]

> A *single* test to determine the existence of a duty of care should be applied regardless of the nature of the damage caused (*ie*, pure economic loss or physical damage). It could be that a more restricted approach is preferable for cases of pure economic loss but this is to be done within the confines of a single test. This test is a two-stage test, comprising of, first, proximity and, second, policy considerations. These two stages are to be approached with reference to the facts of decided cases although the absence of such cases is not an absolute bar against a finding of duty. There is, of course, the threshold issue of factual foreseeability but since this is likely to be fulfilled in most cases, we do not see the need to include this as part of the *legal* test for a duty of care.

Under Singapore law, therefore, 'policy' *does* play an integral as well as important part in the formulation of a duty of care in the law of negligence. And (as already noted), the test in the *Spandeck* case comprises a universal test for ascertaining the existence of a duty of care in negligence, regardless of the situation concerned.[70] To reiterate, it is *quite different* from the corresponding *English* law. This is not to state that there were no legal wrinkles that needed to be ironed out with regard to such an approach. However, this is beyond the purview of the present chapter, and the interested reader is referred to the copious legal literature that exists in this particular regard (in large part due to the unusual nature of the *Spandeck* case).[71] What *is* important for present purposes is to note that where, as is the case

[67] For a detailed comparative study, see A Phang, CL Saw and G Chan, 'Of Precedent, Theory and Practice – The Case for A Return to Anns' [2006] *Singapore Journal of Legal Studies* 1.

[68] *Spandeck Engineering (S) Pte Ltd v Defence Science & Technology Agency* [2007] 4 *Singapore Law Reports (Reissue)* 100. This also constitutes a concrete example from the case law and see, in this regard, the point from practice raised in D Beyleveld and R Brownsword, 'Practice Made Perfect?' (1987) 50 *MLR* 662, 670.

[69] [2007] 4 *Singapore Law Reports (Reissue)* 100, [115] (emphasis in the original text).

[70] See, eg, the Singapore Court of Appeal decisions of *Ngiam Kong Seng v Lim Chiew Hock* [2008] 3 *Singapore Law Reports (Reissue)* 674 (relating to psychiatric harm) and *See Toh Siew Kee v Ho Ah Lam Ferrocement (Pte) Ltd* [2013] 3 *Singapore Law Reports* 284 (relating to occupiers' liability). For further discussion of the former decision, see GKY Chan, 'Three Proximities, Public Policy and the Discarded Page: The Singapore Approach' (2008) 16 *Tort Law Review* 127; Y Goh, 'Duty of Care in Psychiatric Harm Cases in Singapore' (2008) 124 *LQR* 539; Phang (n 61) 108–110; and GKY Chan, 'Justice Personified – Justice Phang and Tort Law' in Goh (n 49) 451–473 at 456–457; and for further discussion of the latter decision, see KY Low, 'Occupiers' Liability after *See Toh*: Change, Uncertainty and Complexity' [2013] *Singapore Journal of Legal Studies* 457; K Amirthalingam, 'Occupier's Liability and Negligence: Of Gordian Knots and Apron Strings' (2013) 25 *Singapore Academy of Law Journal* 580; and Phang (n 61) 110–113.

[71] See, eg, K Amirthalingam, 'Lord Atkin and the Philosopher's Stone: The Search for A Universal Test for Duty' [2007] *Singapore Journal of Legal Studies* 350; KW Kow, 'Spandeck Engineering Pte Ltd

with the legal (and normative) test for establishing a duty of care, the legal subject matter is inextricably linked to the extralegal (in this case, primarily policy) context, the legal test itself becomes (ironically, perhaps) more 'principled' when 'policy' is also incorporated within the test itself. However, it bears emphasising that such a conception of the concept of 'policy' (ie, 'judicial public policy') is *quite different from* a conception of 'policy' which is *legislative* in nature (and which is therefore *outside* the purview of the courts, lest (as already noted) they become 'mini-legislatures').

At the present juncture, however, it may be appropriate to contrast the approach adopted in the *Spandeck* case with Dworkin's own approach as encompassed within his treatment of a leading *English* decision on the test for the duty of care in negligence in the context of a claim for damages for alleged *psychiatric harm*.[72] This was the decision of the House of Lords in *McLoughlin v O'Brian*.[73] A couple of preliminary points should, however, be made at this juncture. First, this particular decision was current at the time Dworkin wrote on it, although, under English law at least, subsequent legal developments have not witnessed a radical alteration in the relevant law as such.[74] Second, this decision was (as we shall see) subsequently interpreted in the Singapore context, particularly in relation to the legal framework set out in the *Spandeck* case. It should also be noted that such 'judicial public policy' operates only as a restraining rather than an animating force.

With the aforementioned preliminary points in mind, a useful starting point would be to set out – in brief – the legal test for the duty of care in the *McLoughlin* case itself. It is suggested that the main general issue confronting the court in that

v DSTA: A Casenote' *The Mindef Legal Counsel*, October 2007, 8; ALR Joseph, 'Establishing a Duty of Care: Singapore's Single, Two-Stage Test' (2008) 20 *Singapore Academy of Law Journal* 251; CL Saw, 'Is Anns Alive and Well in Singapore?' (2008) 16 *Tort Law Review* 5; D Tan, 'The Salient Features of Proximity: Examining the *Spandeck* Formulation for Establishing A Duty of Care' [2010] *Singapore Journal of Legal Studies* 459; C Liew, 'Keeping it Spick and *Spandeck*: a Singaporean Approach to the Duty of Care' (2012) 20 *Torts Law Journal* 1; D Tan and Y Goh, 'The Promise of Universality – The *Spandeck* Formulation Half A Decade On' (2013) 25 *Singapore Academy of Law Journal* 510; J Tan, 'Proximity as Reasonable Expectations' [2019] *Singapore Journal of Legal Studies* 147; J Tan, 'Reconceiving Proximity in the Duty to Avoid Causing Pure Economic Loss – Should the Plaintiff have Protected Himself Through Contract?' (2021) 33 *Singapore Academy of Law Journal* 1083; and Chan, 'Justice Personified – Justice Phang and Tort Law' (n 70) 453–456.

[72] See R Dworkin, *Law's Empire* (Cambridge, Belknap Press, 1986) especially 23–29 and 238–250.

[73] *McLoughlin v O'Brian* [1983] AC 410.

[74] See, eg, the House of Lords decisions of *Alcock v Chief Constable of South Yorkshire Police* [1992] 1 AC 310 and *White v Chief Constable of South Yorkshire Police* [1999] 2 AC 455 and; as well as the more recent English Court of Appeal decision of *Paul v Royal Wolverhampton NHS Trust* [2023] QB 149 (affirmed by the UK Supreme Court in *Paul v Royal Wolverhampton NHS Trust* [2024] 2 WLR 417 (Lord Burrows dissenting)). Though *cf* the House of Lords decision of *Page v Smith* [1996] AC 155 (where it was held by the majority of the court that the requisite control mechanisms applied only in relation to secondary victims and did not apply where the plaintiff is the primary victim). It should be noted, however, that the Singapore Court of Appeal held, in *Ngiam Kong Seng v Lim Chiew Hock* [2008] 3 *Singapore Law Reports (Reissue)* 674, [83]–[95], that the approach of the majority in *Page v Smith*, as just stated, ought *not* to be followed.

case concerned the issue of *line-drawing*. Unlike a case of negligent conduct resulting in *physical* harm, the danger of *indeterminate liability* is very real in the context of negligent conduct resulting in *psychiatric* harm. In the *McLoughlin* case, the plaintiff's husband and three children were involved in a road accident. It was a tragic accident. Her youngest daughter was killed while her husband suffered bruising as well as shock, and her remaining two children were badly injured. The plaintiff was two miles away from the scene of the accident at the time it took place and was told, a couple of hours later, about it by a neighbour who took her to the hospital to see her family. The plaintiff brought an action against the defendants for damages for severe shock, depression, and a change of personality. The House of Lords, reversing the decisions of both the trial judge and the Court of Appeal, held in favour of the plaintiff. However, the reasons of the judges differed. Briefly put, Lord Wilberforce held that the relevant 'policy arguments' did not militate against recovery by the plaintiff. He also laid down 'three elements' that had to be considered in relation to such a claim; these elements were 'the class of persons whose claims should be recognised; the proximity of such persons to the accident; and the means by which the shock is caused'.[75] On the facts before him, the learned Law Lord held that the aforementioned elements had been satisfied. It appeared that Lord Edmund-Davies and Lord Russell of Killowen agreed with Lord Wilberforce.

However, Lord Bridge of Harwich adopted a different approach. In essence, he based his decision simply on the concept of *reasonable foreseeability*. This was a much broader ground than that relied upon by Lord Wilberforce. Lord Scarman agreed with Lord Bridge. It is also significant to note, though, that, in contrast to Lord Wilberforce's reference to 'policy', Lord Scarman referred more than once to 'principle' instead; the latter observed thus:[76]

> But whatever the court decides to do, it starts from a baseline of existing *principle* and seeks a solution consistent with or analogous to *a principle or principles* already recognised.
>
> The distinguishing feature of the common law is this judicial development and formation of *principle*. Policy considerations will have to be weighed: but the objective of the judges is the formulation of *principle*. And, if *principle* inexorably requires a decision which entails a degree of policy risk, the court's function is to adjudicate according to *principle, leaving policy curtailment to the judgment of Parliament*. Here lies the true role of the two law-making institutions in our constitution. By concentrating on *principle* the judges can keep the common law alive, flexible and consistent, and can *keep the legal system clear of policy problems* which neither they, nor the forensic process which it is their duty to operate, are equipped to resolve. If *principle* leads to results which are thought to be socially unacceptable, *Parliament* can legislate to draw a line or map out a new path.

[75] [1983] AC 410, 422.
[76] ibid 430 (emphasis added).

Not surprisingly, Dworkin refers to the quite different approaches adopted by the Law Lords as just (briefly) described.[77] It will come as no surprise to the reader that the approach from 'principle' is that which is favoured by Dworkin. It would appear, however, that the judgment of Lord Wilberforce (which referred to 'policy') is considered to be the leading one.[78] At this juncture, it is suggested that a mere *linguistic* analysis is, with respect, too superficial. Put simply, one has to have regard to the *substance* of the respective judgments – and *not* merely the *form* thereof. Let me elaborate.

First, whilst Lord Wilberforce's judgment refers to 'policy', a close perusal of it reveals that the learned Law Lord was concerned with 'policy' as only *a part* of his overall reasoning. In particular, his approach was wholly consistent with what he had set out in the *Anns* case (which, as we have seen, was adopted by the Singapore Court of Appeal in the *Spandeck* case). Indeed, it is suggested that this part of Lord Wilberforce's judgment corresponds to the second stage of the two-stage test set out in both the *Anns* case and the *Spandeck* case.[79]

As importantly, it should also be noted that the learned Law Lord set out legal criteria in the form of the 'three elements' referred to above.[80] Indeed, in the Singapore Court of Appeal decision of *Ngiam Kong Seng v Lim Chiew Hock*,[81] it was held, inter alia, that the 'three elements' were in fact *consistent with* the two-stage test in the *Spandeck* case; as the Court summarised:[82]

> In summary, a close analysis of the observations of Lord Wilberforce in *McLoughlin* … (in the context of his earlier enunciation of the two-stage test in *Anns* …) reveals that his statements of principle in both of these cases are consistent with what this court decided in *Spandeck* (which adopted a two-stage test, with (legal) foreseeability or proximity as the focus at the first stage and (broader) public policy as the focus at the second stage) to the extent that the three factors set out in *Part 3* of the learned law lord's judgment in *McLoughlin*[83] are an integral part of the *first* stage of the two-stage test in *Anns*, which formed the basis of the (likewise) two-stage test laid down in *Spandeck*.

A second point to note with regard to the decision in the *McLoughlin* case is that Lord Scarman's references to 'principle'[84] are by no means inconsistent with an approach that *integrates* both 'principle' *with* 'policy'. As we have seen, this was

[77] Dworkin (n 72) 27–29. Also not surprisingly, Dworkin made special mention of Lord Scarman's opinion which has just been quoted: ibid 28.

[78] See, eg, the House of Lords decision of *Alcock v Chief Constable of South Yorkshire Police* [1992] 1 AC 310, 395–396 and 397–398 (per Lord Keith of Kinkel) 402–405 (per Lord Ackner) 413–415 (per Lord Oliver of Aylmerton) 419–424 (per Lord Jauncey of Tullichettle) and 424 (per Lord Lowry).

[79] Above, nn 63 and 69.

[80] See above, n 75.

[81] *Ngiam Kong Seng v Lim Chiew Hock* [2008] 3 *Singapore Law Reports (Reissue)* 674 (see also above, n 75).

[82] ibid [57]. And see the general analysis of court ibid [36]–[57].

[83] These are the 'three elements' in Lord Wilberforce's judgment referred to earlier at n 75, above.

[84] See above, n 76.

indeed the approach adopted by the Singapore Court of Appeal in the *Spandeck* case – with the first of the two-stage test having regard to the former (viz, 'principle' (in particular, in relation to the concept of 'proximity')) and the second stage having regard to the latter (viz, 'policy').

I should point out at this juncture that Dworkin does deal with the *McLoughlin* case from the perspective of his (later) theory of 'law as integrity'.[85] Without meaning to run ahead of the story, so to speak, it is suggested, with respect, that Dworkin's account is a little too abstract and general. This is perhaps not surprising because he has to set the theoretical stage in order to demonstrate why his theory of adjudication is the best interpretation on offer. Indeed, he sets out six possible interpretations in relation to the resolution of the *McLoughlin* case and arrives at the conclusion that the two best interpretations are the final two (viz, interpretations (5) and (6)).[86] Interpretation (5) states that '[p]eople have a moral right to compensation for emotional or physical injury that is the consequence of careless conduct, but only if that injury was reasonably foreseeable by the person who acted carelessly',[87] whilst interpretation (6) states that '[p]eople have a moral right to compensation for reasonably foreseeable injury but not in circumstances when recognizing such a right would impose massive and destructive financial burdens on people who have been careless out of proportion to their moral fault'.[88] It is suggested that both these interpretations are still at a very high level of abstraction and generality and that Dworkin's own analysis of both demonstrates this.[89] In contrast, the actual reasoning and decision in the *McLoughlin* case itself in the House of Lords demonstrates how the actual process of adjudication takes place on the ground, so to speak. This is especially evident in Lord Wilberforce's judgment (which has been considered briefly above).

Finally (and turning to a wholly separate point), it should be noted that, in exceptional legal situations, the concept of public policy is in fact *central* to the actual content of the law itself. This is quintessentially the case in relation to the doctrine of illegality and public policy (in the law of contract and tort, and even the law of trusts[90]) as well as the doctrine of restraint of trade in the law of contract.[91]

[85] Dworkin (n 72) 238–250. And see generally chapter 7 in this volume.

[86] See generally ibid 240–250.

[87] ibid 241.

[88] ibid.

[89] ibid 245–250.

[90] In this last-mentioned respect, see the recent Singapore General Division of the High Court decision of *Devin Jethanand Bhojwani v Jethanand Harkishindas Bhojwani* [2024] SGHC 310, especially [72]–[75].

[91] As to which see Bell (n 60) ch VI. But *cf* R Stevens, *Torts and Rights* (Oxford, Oxford University Press, 2007), which (as the title itself suggests) adopts a 'rights model' instead (and see, especially, ibid ch 14, entitled 'Policy'.

IV. An 'Interlude' – The Importance of Objectivity in the Law

I need not spend too much time on this prior – yet vitally important – issue as I have dealt in some detail with the issue of objectivity in a previous chapter.[92] Suffice it to reiterate that Dworkin reminds us that it is *logically incoherent* to argue that the law (or anything else for that matter) is riddled with subjectivity, and his defence of objectivity is theoretically robust. To recapitulate, even an argument that the law is subjective must, if it is to persuade us that it has *universal* application, *necessarily* contain *an objective claim* (ie, *that the argument itself is an objective one that is of universal application*). There is no escape from such inexorable as well as inevitable logic. However, I would add that such an argument (from subjectivity), whilst *necessarily* objective in nature, is an extremely *disempowering* one, as it is but a shell or counterfeit of a true normative compass that can help and guide us (here, through the legal system). Perhaps even more importantly, acceptance of such an argument would lead to a loss of legitimacy of the law in the eyes of the public.

It is interesting to note that Dworkin deals expressly with this issue (ie, the importance of objectivity in the law) only in his *middle to later* writings onwards.[93] As I shall point out below, this is not surprising because the natural trajectory of Dworkin's theory of adjudication had hitherto taken a course that ultimately required him to address this particular issue in more express terms – particularly in relation to the use of the concept of 'essentially contested concepts'.[94] However, of this, more later. Let us now turn to Dworkin's *theory* of adjudication proper – which is the focus of the next chapter.

[92] See ch 3 in this volume.
[93] See, eg, relevant parts of the following chapter (ch 7) in this volume.
[94] See also above, n 13.

7

The Dworkinian Theory of Adjudication – The Labours of Hercules

I. Introduction

In the preceding chapter, we considered the basic building blocks of Dworkin's theory of adjudication.[1] We are now ready – in the present chapter – to fully unveil Dworkin's theory proper. And in the following chapter,[2] we will consider the basic problems as well as possible practical solutions relating to this particular theory. Let us turn now to consider Dworkin's theory of adjudication. Before proceeding to do so, however, it should be noted that this theory was developed over many years and over a number of essays as well as books. In order to obtain as complete as well as an accurate and properly nuanced picture of the theory, the present chapter will trace Dworkin's theory of adjudication right from its very beginnings in his book, *Taking Rights Seriously*,[3] through to his final book (published almost three and a half decades later) in *Justice for Hedgehogs*.[4] It will not surprise the reader to learn that Dworkin also modified his theory of adjudication over the years, which therefore also necessitates a detailed rendition of his theory. All this has contributed to the relative length of the present chapter. That having been said, Dworkin's theory of adjudication is an extremely interesting as well as thought-provoking one – and one well worth the reader's attention and thought.

II. Dworkin's Theory of Adjudication – The Labours of Hercules

A. The Theory

i. The 'Early' Theory

As we have seen, Dworkin's earlier writings began with a critique of (principally) Hart's theory of adjudication that centred on rules. Dworkin developed the idea

[1] See ch 6 in this volume.
[2] See ch 8 in this volume.
[3] See R Dworkin, *Taking Rights Seriously*, rev edn (Cambridge, Harvard University Press, 1978).
[4] See R Dworkin, *Justice for Hedgehogs* (Cambridge, Belknap Press, 2011).

of a principle that (like rules) was also part of the law. However, he distinguished principles from policies (the latter being within the province of the Legislature and not the courts). As Dworkin thus developed various 'pieces' of his theory, it was only a matter of time before he would develop a more holistic and systematic *theory* of adjudication. Indeed, such a development was the logical theoretical extension as Dworkin moved from critique to construction. An early hint at such a theory of adjudication can be found as early as the third chapter of *Taking Rights Seriously*,[5] where he refers to the fact that 'a principle is a principle of law if it figures in *the soundest theory of law* that can be provided as a justification for the explicit substantive and institutional rules of the jurisdiction in question'.[6] Whether or not one theory is superior to another depends, in Dworkin's view, on various arguments of moral and political theory.[7]

As noted at the outset of the previous chapter, the first substantial enunciation of Dworkin's own *theory* of adjudication is to be found in his chapter in *Taking Rights Seriously* entitled 'Hard Cases'.[8] In my respectful view, this is probably the *most important* of all of Dworkin's writings on adjudication, as all the foundational building blocks as well as the consequent structure of his theory of adjudication are to be found within this particular chapter. I will therefore spend a little more time and space on it.

As might be surmised from the pains that he took to distinguish principle from policy, it is not surprising that Dworkin's theory of adjudication as set out in this chapter is unabashedly *rights*-based (as opposed to utilitarianism[9] (which, *ex hypothesi*, operates on the basis of *policy*)). As he put it right at the outset of 'Hard Cases', the focus is on which party has 'a *right* to win' and that '[i]t remains the judge's duty, even in hard cases, to discover what the *rights* of the parties are, not to invent new rights retrospectively'.[10] Not surprisingly, therefore, Dworkin describes his proposed theory of adjudication as 'the *rights* thesis'.[11] In his view, this thesis holds that 'judicial decisions enforce existing political rights'.[12]

Turning to the particulars of his rights thesis, Dworkin first defines 'a hard case' as one 'when no settled rule dictates a decision either way'.[13] At this point he notes that the court concerned can have recourse to 'either policy or principle'.[14] In order to illustrate the point, Dworkin refers to the English Court of Appeal

[5] See Dworkin (n 3) ch 3, entitled 'The Model of Rules II'.
[6] ibid 66 (emphasis added).
[7] ibid 67–68.
[8] See R Dworkin, 'Hard Cases' (1975) 88 *Harvard Law Review* 1057. This was published as ch 4 of Dworkin (n 3). All references to this article in the present chapter will be to this particular chapter. And see, to like effect, N Stavropoulos, 'The Debate That Never Was' (2017) 130 *Harvard Law Review* 2082, 2082, n 3.
[9] See generally Dworkin (n 8) 94–100. See also the text to nn 41–43 at ch 6 in this volume.
[10] Dworkin (n 8) 81 (emphasis added).
[11] ibid 82 (emphasis added).
[12] ibid 87.
[13] ibid 83.
[14] ibid.

decision of *Spartan Steel & Alloys Ltd v Martin & Co*,[15] which concerned the vexed issue of liability for pure economic loss in the context of tortious negligence. I have in fact touched on the Singapore position (as now embodied in the *Spandeck* case) in the previous chapter. It will suffice for present purposes to note that Dworkin characterises the *Spartan Steel* case as having been decided on the grounds of *policy*. Not surprisingly, he takes issue with such an approach, arguing that hard cases such as the aforementioned case should be decided, instead, on grounds of *principle*. Indeed, he provided two reasons as to why judges should *not* exercise discretion in the strong sense and create new law that is not based on principle. The first is that judges are *un*elected officials and, unlike legislators, do not have the mandate to make law (which lies in the sphere of *policy*).[16] Second, 'if a judge makes new law and applies it retroactively in the case before him, then the losing party will be punished, not because he violated some duty he had, but rather a new duty created after the event'.[17] In his view, judges are ill-equipped to engage in *policy* decisions; this is in contradistinction to legislators who have been furnished the mandate to balance the different interests that are involved in arriving at a policy decision.[18]

Dworkin's theory of adjudication focuses, therefore, only on arguments of *principle*; as he puts it:[19]

> Arguments of *principle* are arguments intended to establish *an individual right*; arguments of *policy* are arguments intended to establish a *collective goal*.

Put simply, Dworkin's *rights thesis* 'relies, first, on a general distinction between individual rights and social goals'.[20] Second, '[t]he thesis provides … a theory of *the role of precedent and institutional history* in the decision of hard cases'.[21] In this regard, the judge concerned *must* consider relevant precedents, *regardless* of his view of them – this is, as Dworkin puts it, required by 'the *doctrine of articulate consistency*'.[22] Third, 'judges must sometimes make judgments of political morality in order to decide what the legal rights of litigants are'.[23]

Not surprisingly, Dworkin's rights thesis concerns *institutional* rights (here, in the context of adjudication, *legal* rights[24]) as opposed to *background* rights.[25]

[15] *Spartan Steel & Alloys Ltd v Martin & Co* [1973] 1 QB 27.
[16] Dworkin (n 8) 84.
[17] ibid.
[18] ibid 85. But *cf* R Stevens, *Torts and Rights* (Oxford, Oxford University Press, 2007), which (as the title itself suggests) adopts a 'rights model' instead (and see, especially, ibid ch 14, entitled 'Policy'.
[19] ibid 90 (emphasis added).
[20] ibid 89.
[21] ibid (emphasis added).
[22] ibid (emphasis added).
[23] ibid 90.
[24] ibid 101.
[25] In his view (ibid 93 (emphasis added)):

> Any adequate theory will distinguish, for example, between *background* rights, which are rights that provide a justification for political decisions by society in *the abstract*, and *institutional* rights, that provide a justification for a decision by *some particular and specified political institution*.

He also distinguishes between *abstract* rights on the one hand and *concrete* rights on the other. In his view, '[a]n abstract right is a general political aim the statement of which does not indicate how that general aim is to be weighed or compromised in particular circumstances against other political aims'.[26] On the other hand, '[c]oncrete rights ... are political aims that are more precisely defined so as to express more definitely the weight they have against other political aims on particular occasions'.[27]

However, the rules that ensure that institutional rights are given effect to might run out. At this stage, we are approaching the nub of the rights thesis. It is also at this particular juncture that Dworkin refers *expressly* to the fact that when rules (or, non-legally speaking, conventions) run out, judges will not be faced with a situation where they are free to utilise strong (and unbridled) discretion to create or invent new rules but will, rather, be faced with the more general or abstract situation in which the judge concerned will have to deal with 'a *'concept'* that admits of *'different conceptions'*; that is, ... a *contested* concept'.[28] Not surprisingly, Dworkin cites, in this particular regard, Professor Gallie's work on 'essentially contested concepts'.[29] He then proceeds to argue that '[o]nce an autonomous institution is established, such that participants have institutional rights under distinct rules belonging to that institution, then hard cases may arise that must, in the nature of the case, be supposed *to have an answer*'.[30] And, in the institution of *the law*, courts will – not surprisingly – enforce *legal* rights on the basis that *there is, in fact, a correct or right answer to the legal issue(s) at hand.*

At this particular juncture, Dworkin is ready to *unveil* his *rights thesis*.[31] It will be useful to recapitulate that Dworkin has hitherto laid the groundwork for his rights thesis in the form of the argument that judges should only decide on grounds of *principle* (and not policy) and that, in doing so, they are enforcing *institutional (specifically, legal) rights* of the party who deserves to prevail in the case at hand. In arriving at their respective decisions, judges will have regard to relevant precedents pursuant to the doctrine of 'articulate consistency'. From a *systemic* perspective, constructing the *rights thesis* based on the aforementioned building blocks will require, in Dworkin's view, 'a lawyer of superhuman skill, learning, patience and acumen' whom Dworkin calls '*Hercules*'.[32] And Hercules will construct as well as develop the *rights thesis* in three main areas.

[26] ibid.
[27] ibid.
[28] ibid 103 (emphasis in italics in the original text; emphasis added in quoted italics).
[29] See WB Gallie, 'Essentially Contested Concepts' (1955-1956) 56 *Proceedings of the Aristotelian Society* 167 (reprinted in ch 8 of WB Gallie, *Philosophy and the Historical Understanding* (New York, Schocken Books, 1968). References hereafter will be the original article. cited in Dworkin (n 8) 103, n 1. See also Dworkin (n 8) 105. As an interesting aside, I had difficulties locating Professor Gallie's essay many decades ago simply because the year in the citation in the aforementioned note was transposed (ie, 1965 instead of 1956)!
[30] Dworkin (n 8) 104 (emphasis added).
[31] And see generally ibid 105–118.
[32] ibid 105 (emphasis added).

The first area relates to *legislation*. In this context, the judge must have regard to 'the "intention" or "purpose" of a particular statute or statutory clause'.[33] Second, he or she must have regard to 'the concept of principles that "underlie" or are "embedded in" the positive rules of law'.[34]

The second area relates to *the Constitution*. In this particular regard, Hercules 'must … ask just what scheme of principles has been settled'; '[h]e must construct, that is, a constitutional theory; since he is Hercules we may suppose that he can develop a full political theory that justifies the constitution as a whole' and that '[i]t must be a scheme that fits the particular rules of this constitution, of course'.[35] That Hercules will be faced with alternative constitutional theories is inevitable, and in constructing his own theory, he must refer to both 'political philosophy and institutional detail'.[36] Interestingly, Dworkin refers once again to the idea of 'essentially contested concepts'.[37] As already alluded to above, this particular idea plays a *crucial* role in Dworkin's theory, and the reader should bear it in mind until I return to it below.

The third area relates to *statutes*. Hercules's task in this regard is to construct 'a special political theory that justifies [the] statute, in light of the legislature's more general responsibilities, better than any alternative theory'.[38] More specifically (and in the context of statutory interpretation), the 'calculations judges make about the purposes of statutes are calculations about political rights'.[39] Once again, however, Dworkin is careful to emphasise that such 'calculations' are not merely created or invented by the judge concerned:[40]

> It would be inaccurate, first, to say that Hercules supplemented what the legislature did in enacting the statute, or that he tried to determine what it would have done if it had been aware of the problem presented by the case. The act of a legislature is not, as these descriptions suggest, an event whose force we can in some way measure so as to say it has run out at a particular point; it is rather an event whose content is *contested* in the way in which the content of an agreement to play a game is *contested*. Hercules constructs his political theory as an argument about what the legislature has, on this occasion, done. The contrary argument, that it did not actually do what he said, is not a realistic piece of common sense, but a competitive claim about the true content of that *contested* concept.

Notice, once again, the use of the idea of 'essentially contested concepts' by Dworkin in order to evade the charge that judges are creating or inventing new rules. Once again, I shall have occasion to return to this *fundamental* idea that Dworkin so heavily relies upon. It is also interesting that Dworkin emphasises 'how great a

[33] ibid.
[34] ibid.
[35] ibid 106.
[36] ibid 107.
[37] ibid. See also ch 5 of Dworkin (n 3), entitled 'Constitutional Cases', 134 and 147–148.
[38] Dworkin (n 8) 108.
[39] ibid 109.
[40] ibid (emphasis added).

role *the canonical terms of the actual statute* play' and that '[t]hey provide a limit to what must otherwise be, in the nature of the case, unlimited'.[41]

The fourth (and final) area – and the one that is *particularly relevant* in the context of the present book – relates to *the common law*. Consistently with the doctrine of 'articulate consistency' which he had already set out as a basic building block earlier in the chapter, Dworkin deals first with *precedent*. Unlike, however, statutes, which (as we have just seen) contain a canonical form of words, the precedents that form part of the overall case law are quite different. In particular, they will vary in content, and depending on the content, precedents will contain either 'enactment force' or 'gravitational force'[42] – the former being different from the latter inasmuch as the precedents concerned contain (by analogy with statutes) a canonical form of the rule (and hence, perhaps, why the descriptive term 'enactment' is used) and which therefore only governs future cases that fall within the ambit of the exact words contained within that canonical form. Nevertheless, as the judge will (unlike the case with statutes) interpret such precedents in accordance with *only* arguments of *principle* (and not policy),[43] to the extent that the canonical form of the rule is not justified by arguments of principle, it would, presumably, only have (broader) 'gravitational force'. Such 'gravitational force' is, in fact, important and 'is part of the practice that Hercules' general theory of precedent must capture'.[44] Indeed, '[t]he gravitational force of a precedent may be explained by appeal, not to the wisdom of enforcing enactments,[45] but to *the fairness of treating like cases alike*'.[46] It should, however, be noted that to the extent that a precedent is justified *only* by arguments of *policy*, its precedential value would (perhaps not surprisingly) be *limited* to only its '*enactment* force' (ie, only 'to further cases captured by some particular words of the opinion').[47] In other words, a precedent possesses '*gravitational* force' only to the extent that it is justified by arguments of *principle*.[48]

Dworkin then proceeds to draw all the abovementioned threads together into what may be considered to be a *nascent* version of his *theory* of *adjudication*. Not surprisingly, the architect of this theory is Hercules who constructs what

[41] ibid (emphasis added).

[42] ibid 111.

[43] ibid 111, n 1.

[44] ibid.

[45] And *cf* the interpretation of statutes as well as the 'enactment force' of precedent, both of which have been briefly discussed above.

[46] Dworkin (n 8) 113 (emphasis added). See also D Pannick, 'A Note on Dworkin and Precedent' (1980) 43 *MLR* 36. And *cf* TRS Allan, 'Principle, Practice, and Precedent: Vindicating Justice, According to Law' [2018] *CLJ* 269. Reference may also be made to S Hershovitz, 'Integrity and Stare Decisis' in ch 5 of S Hershovitz (gen ed), *Exploring Law's Empire: The Jurisprudence of Ronald Dworkin* (Oxford, Oxford University Press, 2008). On the doctrine of precedent generally, see R Cross and JW Harris, *Precedent in English Law*, 4th edn (Oxford, Clarendon Press, 1991) as well as N Duxbury, *The Nature and Authority of Precedent* (Cambridge, Cambridge University Press, 2008) and, by the same author, *The Intricacies of* Dicta *and Dissent* (Cambridge, Cambridge University Press, 2021).

[47] Dworkin (n 8) 113.

[48] ibid 115.

Dworkin terms '[t]he *seamless web*' of the law.[49] It is best described by Dworkin himself thus (in a description so crucial that it merits quotation *in extenso*):[50]

> Hercules must now develop his concept of principles that underlie the common law by *assigning* to *each* of the relevant precedents *some scheme of principle* that justifies the decision of that precedent. He will now discover a further important difference between this concept and the concept of statutory purpose that he used in statutory interpretation. In the case of statutes, he found it necessary to choose some theory about the purpose of the particular statute in question, looking to other acts of the legislature only insofar as these might help to select between theories that fit the statute about equally well. But if [in the case of the *common law*] *the gravitational force of precedent* rests on the idea that fairness requires *the consistent enforcement of rights, then Hercules must discover 'principles' that 'fit', not only the particular precedent to which some litigation directs his attention, but 'all other' judicial decisions within his general jurisdiction 'and', indeed, statutes as well, so far as these must be seen to be generated by 'principle' rather than policy.* He does not satisfy his duty to show that his decision is consistent with established principles, and therefore fair, if the principles he cites as established are themselves inconsistent with other decisions that his court also proposes to uphold.
>
> …
>
> *The law may not be 'a seamless web'; but the plaintiff is 'entitled' to ask 'Hercules to treat it as if it were'.*
>
> *'You will now see why I called our judge Hercules. He must construct a scheme of abstract and concrete principles that provides a coherent justification for all common law precedents and, so far as these are to be justified on principle, constitutional and statutory provisions as well'.* We may grasp the *'magnitude'* of this enterprise by distinguishing, within the vast material of legal decisions that Hercules must justify, *'a vertical and a horizonal ordering'.* The *'vertical' ordering* is provided by distinguishing layers of authority; that is, layers at which official decisions might be taken to be controlling over decisions made at lower levels. … The *'horizontal' ordering* simply requires that principles taken to justify a decision at one level must also be consistent with the justification offered for other decisions at that level.
>
> …
>
> [A]nd though he will, of course, *reflect his own intellectual and philosophical convictions* in making that judgment, that is *a very different matter from supposing that those convictions have some independent force in his argument just because they are his.*

Having set out a *theory* of adjudication as constructed by Hercules, Dworkin also posits a theory of *mistakes* for, as he acknowledges, even Hercules 'will be unable,

[49] ibid (emphasis added).

[50] ibid 116–118 (emphasis added in italics and quoted italics). See, in particular, the reference to Hercules treating the law as if it were a seamless web and thus acting as if there is a single right answer despite the fact that, in practice, the identification of that answer in an uncontestable fashion is (more often than not) not possible. This reference is consistent with the *attitudinal* approach advocated in the present book (as to which see below, ch 10 in this volume).

even with his superb imagination, to find any set of principles that reconciles all standing statutes and precedents'.[51] Indeed, as Dworkin himself observes:[52]

> This is hardly surprising: the legislators and judges of the past did not all have Hercules' ability or insight, nor were they men and women who were all of the same mind and opinion.

Whilst Hercules must develop 'some theory of institutional mistakes', Dworkin is at pains to point out that 'he cannot make impudent use of this device'.[53] This is wholly understandable lest the institutional theory of mistakes completely 'swallows up' the 'seamless web' of the law that constitutes Hercules's theory of adjudication. To this end, Dworkin states that Hercules's theory of institutional mistakes comprises two parts.

The first part comprises two sets of distinctions:[54]

> He will first distinguish between the specific authority of any institutional event, which is its power as an institutional act to effect just the specific institutional consequences it describes, and its gravitational force. If he classifies some event as a mistake, then he does not deny its specific authority but he does deny its gravitational force, and he cannot consistently appeal to that force in other arguments. He will also distinguish between embedded and corrigible mistakes; embedded mistakes are those whose specific authority is fixed so that it survives their loss of gravitational force; corrigible mistakes are those whose specific authority depends on gravitational force in such a way that it cannot survive this loss.
>
> The constitutional level of his theory will determine which mistakes are embedded.

The second part of Dworkin's theory of institutional mistakes is as follows (possessing, inter alia, a forward-looking perspective):[55]

> If Hercules discovers that some previous decision, whether a statute or a judicial decision, is now widely regretted within the pertinent branch of the profession, that fact in itself distinguishes that decision as vulnerable. He must remember, second, that the argument from fairness that demands consistency is not the only argument from fairness to which government in general, or judges in particular, must respond. If he believes, quite apart from any argument of consistency, that a particular statute or decision was wrong because unfair, within the community's own concept of fairness, then that belief is sufficient to distinguish the decision, and make it vulnerable. Of course, he must apply the guidelines with a sense of the vertical structure of his overall justification, so that decisions at a lower level are more vulnerable than decisions at a higher.
>
> Hercules will therefore apply at least two maxims in the second part of his theory of mistakes. If he can show, by arguments of history or by appeal to some sense of the legal community, that a particular principle, though it once had sufficient appeal

[51] ibid 119.
[52] ibid.
[53] ibid 121.
[54] ibid.
[55] ibid 122–123.

> to persuade a legislature or court to a legal decision, has now so little force that it is unlikely to generate any further such decisions, then the argument from fairness that supports that principle is undercut. If he can show by arguments of political morality that such a principle, apart from its popularity, is unjust, then the argument from fairness that supports the principle is overridden. Hercules will be delighted to find that these discriminations are familiar in the practice of other judges. The jurisprudential importance of his career does not lie in the novelty, but just in the familiarity, of the theory of hard cases that he has now created.

It should also be noted that the final chapter in *Taking Rights Seriously* considers the possibility of a 'tie judgment', which Dworkin considers to be rare, if not impossible.[56]

Having set out Dworkin's (admittedly nascent) theory of adjudication, there is one remaining – and significant – issue which Dworkin himself deals with in some detail. This is not surprising, as it is a very important as well as powerful difficulty. Put simply, given the fact that, notwithstanding his superhuman abilities, Hercules still has his own intellectual and philosophical convictions,[57] how does he transcend those convictions lest he be accused of introducing *his own personal bias* into his theory of adjudication? As Dworkin puts it, '[t]he objection charges Hercules with relying upon his own convictions in matters of political morality'.[58] However, he argues that a judge 'must … rely upon the substance of his own judgment at some point, in order to make any judgment at all'.[59] Dworkin then distinguishes between two types of judgment. The first is when a judge 'relies upon the naked fact that he holds a particular political view as itself a justification for his decision'.[60] The second is when a judge relies 'upon his own belief in the different sense of relying upon *the truth or soundness of that belief*'.[61] Dworkin argues that only the *first* type of judgment is *objectionable*. However, the second type of judgment is *not* objectionable because the judge concerned 'does not count the fact that he himself happens to favor a particular conception of religious liberty, for example, as providing an argument in favor of a decision that advances that conception'.[62] Put simply, Dworkin draws a distinction between a situation where a judge incorporates his or her own preferences as part of his or her decision and a situation where this does not in fact happen.[63] So, for example, if Hercules arrives

[56] See generally ch 13 of Dworkin (n 3), entitled 'Can Rights be Controversial?'.

[57] Dworkin (n 8) 118 (and reproduced in the last para of the quotation at n 50, above).

[58] ibid 123.

[59] ibid 124.

[60] ibid.

[61] ibid (emphasis added).

[62] ibid.

[63] This is, in fact (albeit subject to the important caveat that follows), an early version of the distinction between 'personal preferences' on the one hand (this is the first type of judgment) and 'external preferences' on the other (the second type of judgment). Not surprisingly, this particular distinction figures most prominently in Dworkin's *political theory* (as compared to his theory of *adjudication*). And see, at this very early stage in Dworkin's writings, ch 9 of Dworkin (n 3), entitled 'Reverse Discrimination', especially 234–235 as well as ch 12 of Dworkin (n 3), entitled 'What Rights Do We Have?', especially 272–278 (where the aforementioned distinction constitutes an integral part of Dworkin's general and fundamental principle of political theory centring on that of *equal*

at a decision that is at odds with popular morality in relation to a particular issue, '[h]e does not, in this case, enforce his own convictions against the community's' but 'rather judges that the community's morality is inconsistent on this issue'.[64] In summary:[65]

> Hercules' theory of adjudication at no point provides for any choice between his own political convictions and those he takes to be the political convictions of the community

concern and respect). It would, however, appear that in the context of Dworkin's *political theory* (as opposed to his theory of *adjudication*), the distinction operates somewhat *differently* (perhaps owing to the *different contexts*) inasmuch as an individual *is* permitted to invoke his or her *personal* preferences but *cannot impose that* preference on *others* (by way of *external* preferences) in the context of (Dworkinian) *political theory*. Put simply, Dworkin (despite being an advocate for *rights* as opposed to *utilitarianism* (because the latter relies on *policy* instead of principle)) might well be prepared to countenance a form of utilitarianism that *only* takes into account *personal* preferences and which correspondingly *excludes* from account *external* preferences. Whether, however, one can effectively distinguish personal preferences from external preferences in *practice* may well be problematic (and see the concession by Dworkin himself in 'Reverse Discrimination', above, 236), but as this book in general and this chapter in particular deals with *adjudication*, the various elements as well as problems relating to Dworkinian *political theory* need *not* concern us here. For subsequent work from Dworkin in the sphere of political theory centring specifically on the general right to equal concern and respect, see, eg, the following chapters in R Dworkin, *A Matter of Principle* (Cambridge, Harvard University Press, 1985) ch 2 (entitled 'The Forum of Principle'); ch 8 (entitled 'Liberalism'); ch 9 (entitled 'Why Liberals Should Care About Equality'); and ch 17 (entitled 'Do We Have A Right to Pornography?'). And for an early academic engagement with Dworkin's political theory, see JH Ely, 'Professor Dworkin's External/Personal Preference Distinction' [1983] *Duke Law Journal* 959. Reference may also be made to the following work by Dworkin: R Dworkin, *Sovereign Virtue: The Theory and Practice of Equality* (Cambridge, Harvard University Press, 2000).

And for an excellent overview of Dworkin's broader political theory (that includes the general right to equal concern and respect just referred to), see S Guest, *Ronald Dworkin*, 3rd edn (Stanford, Stanford University Press, 2013) ch 8, entitled 'Treating People as Equals'; ch 9, entitled 'Justice for Hedgehogs'; ch 10, entitled 'Equality of What?'; and ch 11, entitled 'The Basis of Liberalism'.

Dworkin also dealt with other major topics such as religion (see Dworkin (n 4) and R Dworkin, *Religion Without God* (Cambridge, Harvard University Press, 2013)) as well as abortion and euthanasia (see R Dworkin, *Life's Dominion: An Argument about Abortion, Euthanasia, and Individual Freedom* (New York, Knopf, 1993)). And see also Guest (n 63) ch 12, entitled 'Religion and the Beginning and End of Life' for an excellent overview of these topics. It might be observed at this juncture that Dworkin was not a natural lawyer as such. Indeed, Dworkin's theory has been called 'the third theory of law because it contrasts both with legal positivism and with the doctrine of natural law, and is in some ways intermediate between the two': see J Mackie, 'The Third Theory of Law' (1977) 7 *Philosophy & Public Affairs* 3, 3. It might also be observed that Dworkin eschews the concept of God in *Religion Without God* although, with respect, he has not engaged fully with, inter alia, the detailed arguments contained in support of the Christian faith (including, albeit not limited to, Christian theology and apologetics): see, eg, SL Carter, 'Dworkin versus Tillich' (2014) 29 *Journal of Law and Religion* 510; R Domingo, 'The Dworkinian Religion of Value' (2014) 29 *Journal of Law and Religion* 526; TP Jackson, 'The Relevance of God: A Reply to Ronald Dworkin' (2014) 29 *Journal of Law and Religion* 535; SD Smith, 'Is God Irrelevant?' (2014) 94 *Boston University Law Review* 1339; and CC Ungureanu, 'Dworkin's Last Word: *Religion Without God*' (2014) 38 *Journal for the Study of Religions and Ideologies* 220. This is perhaps not surprising, for, as a learned writer has perceptively observed, Dworkin's views on religion in *Religion Without God* is a form of *ethical liberalism*: see LC McClain, 'Can *Religion Without God* Lead to Religious Liberty Without Conflict?' (2014) 94 *Boston University Law Review* 1273, especially 1288–1298 (Dworkin refers, in fact, to the concept of 'religious atheism' as well as to the responsibility or 'living well': see *Religion Without God*, 5 and 10, respectively). See also generally ch 5 in this volume.

[64] Dworkin (n 8) 126.

[65] ibid (emphasis added).

> at large. On the contrary, his theory identifies *a particular conception of community morality* as decisive of legal issues; that conception holds that community morality is *the political morality presupposed by the laws and institutions of the community*. He must, of course, rely on his own judgment as to what the principles of that morality are, but this form of reliance is the second form[66] we distinguished, which at some level is inevitable.

Hence, Dworkin argues, when 'reflective citizens' hold different views, 'it is wrong to suppose that [they] are simply setting their personal convictions against the convictions of others'. In his view, '[t]hey too are *contesting different conceptions of a concept they suppose they hold in common*; they are debating which of different theories of that concept best explains the settled or clear cases that fix the concept'.[67] And likewise, '[w]hen Hercules relies upon *his own conception* …, in the second sense[68] of reliance we distinguished, he is still relying on his own sense of what *the community's morality* provides'.[69]

Dworkin concludes this extremely important chapter by bringing the reader back to the *terra firma* of practical adjudicative reality. His is, it is suggested, a call for *humility*. For example, Dworkin acknowledges the injustice that occurs when judges make *mistakes*. He nevertheless states:[70]

> But of course, though we, as social critics, know that mistakes will be made, we do not know when because we are not Hercules either. We must commend techniques of adjudication that might be expected to *reduce* the number of mistakes overall based on some judgment of the relative capacities of men and women who might occupy different roles.

And he concludes the chapter thus:[71]

> Hercules' technique encourages a judge to make his own judgments about institutional rights. The argument from judicial fallibility might be thought to suggest *two alternatives*. The *first* argues that since judges are fallible they should make no effort at all to determine the institutional rights of the parties before them, but should decide hard cases only on grounds of policy, or not at all. But that is *perverse*; it argues that because judges will often, by misadventure, produce unjust decisions they should make no effort to produce just ones. The *second* alternative argues that since judges are fallible they should submit questions of institutional right raised by hard cases to someone else. But to whom? There is no reason to credit any other particular group with better facilities of moral argument; or, if there is, then it is the process of selecting judges, not the techniques of judging that they are asked to use, that must be changed. So this form of skepticism does not in itself argue against Hercules' technique of adjudication, though of course it serves as a useful reminder to any judge that he might well be wrong in his political judgments, and that he should therefore decide hard cases *with humility*.

[66] See above, n 61.
[67] Dworkin (n 8) 128 (emphasis added).
[68] See above, n 151.
[69] Dworkin (n 8) 129 (emphasis added) – and not on his own *personal* (and biased) preferences.
[70] ibid 130 (emphasis added).
[71] ibid (emphasis added).

It should also be noted that in an *Appendix* to a later edition of *Taking Rights Seriously*, entitled 'A Reply To Critics',[72] Dworkin does make the important point that his rights thesis 'was meant to be both descriptive *and* normative'[73] (and which is a point I shall return to later). As he put it:[74]

> If I thought that my thesis was a banner for revolution, I would hardly argue that judges characteristically do what it recommends. I was at pains to stress that I meant to offer not a programme of reform, but a *better characterization* of what we all know judges do.

I would like to resist the temptation to critique Dworkin's theory of adjudication at this particular point simply because, as already mentioned, this is but a *nascent* version of his theory. Not surprisingly, it is still a little vague and general and requires more detailed development – even leaving to one side the various difficulties that are to be found in the basic building blocks in his theory (for example, the distinction between rules and principles and that between principle and policy (which were considered in an earlier part of this chapter)). In particular, Dworkin's heavy reliance upon the doctrine of precedent (by way of his doctrine of 'articulate consistency'), whilst an important point, does not really deal with how Hercules considers the *content* of the various legal rules and principles themselves. And his theory of institutional mistakes does not really provide us with specific illustrations as to how such a theory would work in practice. Finally, whilst Dworkin attempts to draw a distinction between a judge's personal preferences (which contain elements of personal bias) and external preferences (that are objective because they are based on principle and may even run *against* that judge's personal preferences), he does not, with respect, elaborate on how that might work in *practice*. Indeed, the skeptic might just dismiss such a distinction out of hand, although, in fairness to Dworkin, I can attest to the fact, as a practising judge, that what Dworkin argues *is*, in fact, practised by judges deciding actual cases in the real world. However, this is a matter of *practice* as opposed to theory and is something that I elaborate upon in the final chapter of this book, where I proffer a new theory of adjudication.[75]

To return to Dworkin's *theory* of adjudication in the form of his rights thesis, he does in fact proceed – in his later writings – to *elaborate upon as well as refine* it. For example, he recognises in his later writings that the doctrine of precedent alone deals with only one aspect of adjudication proper (that of '*fit*'[76]) and therefore proceeds to develop another aspect (that deals with *content* (or, as he puts it, '*substance*')). Indeed, these two aspects – as we shall see in a moment – fall under the rubric of a concept that will become a dominant (perhaps even fundamental)

[72] See the *Appendix* to a later edition of *Taking Rights Seriously* (entitled 'A Reply to Critics') in Dworkin (n 3) 291–368.
[73] ibid 312 (emphasis added).
[74] ibid (emphasis added).
[75] See ch 10 in this volume.
[76] Which is in fact the precise word he uses even at this early stage of his writings: see, eg, above, n 35.

part of his theory of adjudication: *interpretation*. And it is therefore to his later writings that our attention now turns. However, before proceeding to do so, I note that Dworkin does, in fact, familiarise us (albeit briefly) with the concepts of 'fit' and 'substance', which, as just mentioned, he would develop more fully in his later writings; he does this in the aforementioned *Appendix* to *Taking Rights Seriously*,[77] in which he attempts to respond to his then critics. Although he claims to have referred to both these concepts in *Hard Cases*,[78] it is suggested that the reference is *not very explicit*. In the circumstances, his clarification in the *Appendix* is to be welcomed and is also a *prelude* of sorts to fuller development in his later writings; to this end, it is important to quote the relevant portion of the *Appendix* in full, as follows:[79]

> In *Hard Cases*,[80] I offered an account of what it means to say that a principle is 'embedded in' or 'implicit in' or may be 'inferred by analogy from' a set of earlier decisions. I said that a principle bears that relationship to earlier decisions, or other legal material, if the principle figures in what I called the best *justification* of that material. That makes it, of course, a matter of judgment, about which *lawyers may and will disagree*, whether a particular principle is indeed 'inferable' from past material. One *justification may be better than another* (I also said) in *'two different dimensions'*: it may prove a *better 'fit'*, in the sense that it requires less of the material to be taken to be 'mistakes', '*or*' it may prove *'a morally more compelling justification'*, because it comes closer to capturing sound political morality. If a theory containing one principle is better on *the dimension of 'fit'*, *'but'* a theory containing a *contrary* principle is *better* on *the dimension of 'morality'*, *then* the jurisprudential question is raised as to *'which dimension'* is *more important* in *determining* institutional rights in cases of that sort. One answer to that jurisprudential question (stated in a crude and simple form) would be this: No theory can count as an adequate justification of institutional history *'unless'* it *provides a good 'fit' with that history*; it must not expose more than a low threshold of decisions, particularly recent decisions, as mistakes; *but if 'two or more' theories 'each provide an adequate fit'*, on that test, *then* the theory among these that is *'morally the strongest' provides 'the best justification'*, even though it exposes more decisions as mistakes than another.

It will be seen that Dworkin does not – in the quotation just set out above – use the actual term 'substance', although, in *substance*, the reference to 'a morally more compelling justification' clearly impacts the *moral content* (ie, 'substance') of the relevant decision. This raises further issues as to whether or not – unlike the dimension of 'fit' which relates to precedent – engagement with the *moral* content of a particular decision might *undermine* the *objective* nature of the decision itself. Before, however, considering such issues, it would be preferable (as already mentioned) to consider Dworkin's later writings first before considering his entire theory of adjudication in a *holistic* manner.

[77] Dworkin (n 72).
[78] Dworkin (n 8), and discussed extensively in this part of the present chapter.
[79] Dworkin (n 72) 340 (emphasis added in italics and quoted italics).
[80] Dworkin (n 8).

ii. The 'Later' Theory

a. A Matter of Principle

As already mentioned, Dworkin began developing the ideas first set out in *Taking Rights Seriously*[81] in his subsequent work – in particular (and in the first instance), in three essays which were subsequently published in *A Matter of Principle*.[82]

The first essay, entitled 'Is There Really No Right Answer in Hard Cases?',[83] actually deals (as the title of the essay itself suggests) with the more fundamental issue that was briefly described in the final part of the preceding chapter, which relates to *the importance of objectivity* in the law. In this particular chapter, Dworkin reiterates the arguments he had already made in his earlier work (and which I shall therefore not revisit, save to reiterate the importance of the proposition to the effect that it does not necessarily follow that just because it may be uncertain and controversial what the right answer is in a given case, there is therefore no right answer to the legal issue(s) in that case). Put simply, uncertainty and indeterminacy are not the same thing. In the former regard, Dworkin rejects what he calls 'the demonstrability thesis' (which 'states that if a proposition cannot be demonstrated to be true, after all the hard facts that might be relevant to its truth are either known or stipulated, then it cannot be true'[84]). In his view, it is perfectly acceptable for reasonable lawyers to disagree as to what the right answer is.[85] As I understand his argument, such uncertainty is *not* to be equated with the fact that there is *no* right answer (viz, that there is indeterminacy as to what the right answer is). In this essay, Dworkin also refers, once again, to the *second* dimension of 'substance' – which he expressly terms as 'the dimension of *political morality*'.[86] Not surprisingly, '[t]he availability of this second dimension makes it even less likely that any particular case will have no right answer',[87] although, once again, reasonable lawyers might disagree as to what the right answer is. Dworkin does, however, admit of the *possibility* (and no more, it seems to me) of 'a tie'[88] (and, hence, no definitive right answer), although this would be 'extremely rare'.[89] Indeed, this, in my view at least, accords with *practical reality* because courts *always* arrive at decisions which, *ex hypothesi*, must decide in favour of one party over the other (instead of holding that there is 'a tie', in which case the decision can, again *ex hypothesi*, be in favour of *neither*).[90]

[81] Dworkin (n 3).

[82] See Dworkin (n 63). These essays are to be found in Part II of this book (entitled 'Law as Interpretation'). The significance of the title of this Part will be evident in the discussion that follows.

[83] See Dworkin, *A Matter of Principle* (n 63) ch 5, entitled 'Is There Really No Right Answer in Hard Cases?'.

[84] ibid 137.

[85] ibid, especially 137–138. See also ibid 142.

[86] ibid 143 (emphasis added).

[87] ibid.

[88] ibid 144.

[89] ibid.

[90] See, to like effect, ibid.

In the second essay, entitled 'How Law is Like Literature',[91] Dworkin *compares* (as the title of the essay itself suggests) law with *literature*.[92] In particular, he argues, first, that law is distinct from personal or partisan politics.[93] He then proceeds to argue for what he terms the '*aesthetic hypothesis*', which he describes as 'an *interpretation* of a piece of literature that attempts to show which way of reading the text reveals it to be the *best* work of art'.[94] Put simply, law is a matter of *interpretation*.[95] To run perhaps a little ahead of the story, so to speak, interpretation, in Dworkin's view, is *quite different from* Hart's legal positivism, which is not only 'wholly descriptive' but also treats 'propositions of law' as 'pieces of *history*'.[96] Looked at in this light, by focusing (only) on the historical record, as it were, legal positivism is (only) *backward*-looking. Interpretation is *also quite different* from the skeptical theory, which holds that judges (only) *invent* new law. In *contrast* to both Dworkin's 'aesthetic hypothesis' *and* to legal positivism, such an approach is (only) *forward*-looking. Most importantly, Dworkin views his theory (of interpretation) as being *both* backward-looking *and* forward-looking.[97]

In order to accomplish as well as fulfil this task of interpretation, 'the *text* provides one severe constraint'.[98] In this particular regard, Dworkin argues that one cannot discount or do away with a large part of the text by arguing that such text is either irrelevant or accidental.[99] This is understandable and corresponds to Dworkin's concept of a 'mistake' as discussed in his earlier work.[100] Indeed, if, in fact, the judge (or, in the context of literature, the artist) treats the greater part of (here) the law as a 'mistake', then the entire enterprise of law must (even from the perspective of common sense) become an exercise in futility.

[91] See Dworkin, *A Matter of Principle* (n 63) ch 6, entitled 'How Law is Like Literature'.

[92] This point is already alluded to in the earlier essay just considered: see Dworkin (n 83) 141–142. See also Dworkin (n 91) 148, where he states that '[l]awyers would do well to study literary and other forms of artistic interpretation'.

[93] ibid (this is in contrast to the conception of law by the Critical Legal Scholars, discussed in ch 9 in this volume).

[94] Dworkin (n 91) 149 (emphasis added).

[95] Dworkin in fact commences this essay by stating that he is arguing 'that legal practice is *an exercise in interpretation* not only when lawyers interpret particular documents or statutes but generally': ibid 146 (emphasis added). And see the title of the Part in which this essay appears (entitled 'Law as Interpretation' (see also above, n 82)). As to whether or not Dworkin has committed the logical mistake of deriving a theory of law (here an interpretive theory of law) from a metasemantic theory of meaning, see the contrasting views, on the one hand, of MS Green, 'Dworkin's Fallacy, Or What the Philosophy of Language Can't Teach Us About the Law' (2003) 89 *Virginia Law Review* 1897 as well as, by the same author, 'Does Dworkin Commit Dworkin's Fallacy?: A Reply to *Justice in Robes*' (2008) 28 *OJLS* 33 and, on the other, T Bustamante and TL Decat, 'Semantic theories and interpretation: a critique of Michael S Green's "Dworkin's Fallacy"' in ch 12 of T Gizbert-Studnicki, F Poggi and I Skoczeń (gen eds), *Interpretivism and the Limits of Law* (Cheltenham, Edward Elgar Publishing Limited, 2022).

[96] Dworkin (n 91) 147 (emphasis added).

[97] See also ibid. See also the text to nn 121 and 217, below.

[98] ibid 150 (emphasis added).

[99] ibid.

[100] See the text to nn 51–55, above.

The difficulty, however, with such an (interpretive) approach is that there may be a number of *different* theories of interpretation – of which Dworkin's is but one (and here he (perhaps playfully) distinguishes between Hart J (who flies, as it were, the legal positivist's flag[101]) on the one hand and Hercules J (who flies the Dworkinian flag[102]) on the other). It will be recalled that Dworkin attempted to argue in his earlier work that *his* theory of adjudication distinguished between the strong and weak senses of discretion and that this distinction should be linked together with the concept of institutional constraints. The latter constraints ensure that the discretion exercised by the judge is *guided*, although Dworkin himself admits that judges must *necessarily* have *some* discretion (ie, discretion in the *weak* sense) inasmuch as *some* sort of *choice must necessarily* be made by the judge concerned. Such a choice is nevertheless *constrained* by various *institutional* factors. In other words, what Hercules J is doing is, in effect, exercising a *choice* of a particular *conception* of the (*general*) concept of law[103] in arriving at *his* particular theory of adjudication.

Insofar as the specific content of his theory of adjudication is concerned, Dworkin harnesses the ideas in his earlier writings and places them in the context of *literary interpretation* (hence the title of the essay, 'How Law is Like Literature'). Not surprisingly, a central concern of this essay is to address Hart's view that judges and courts can exercise unbridled discretion once rules run out. As just alluded to, however, Dworkin admits that there can be *different* theories of adjudication (as exemplified, for example, between that held by Hart J on the one hand and by Hercules J on the other). According to Dworkin, these different theories are merely competing *conceptions* of the *concept* of *interpretation* – put simply, they are *candidates* vying for the 'title' of being the *best theory of interpretation in the context of the 'law'*.[104] The reader will readily discern that Dworkin is relying once again on Professor Gallie's idea of 'essentially contested concepts'.[105] As we have already seen in an earlier chapter,[106] whilst this particular idea is not very satisfactory from a *theoretical* perspective, it is *practically* useful. To elaborate on this last-mentioned point in the context of Dworkin's theory of adjudication, the upshot of Dworkin's approach is – consistently with the idea of 'essentially contested concepts' – that there *is* an *objectively best theory of adjudication, although it is not possible to demonstrate it as such.*[107] Put simply, there are *various candidates*, so to speak, that

[101] And is clearly a reference to the preeminent legal positivist, Professor HLA Hart (and see generally ch 4 in this volume).
[102] And see the very title of this chapter, entitled 'The Dworkinian Theory of Adjudication – The Labours of *Hercules*' (emphasis added).
[103] Adopting the approach centred on the idea of 'essentially contested concepts' as first advanced by Professor Gallie: see Gallie (n 29).
[104] Dworkin (n 91) 152–153 and 163.
[105] Gallie (n 29).
[106] See ch 3 in this volume.
[107] Dworkin (n 91) 153.

would vie for the 'honour' of being the objectively best theory of adjudication (this would include Dworkin's and Hart's theories of adjudication, amongst others) *and* that they are all *viable* candidates in their own right. The reader will immediately discern the *theoretical* weakness of such an approach because *no one theory (here, of adjudication) can lay claim, as it were, to an immediate and decisive 'victory'* – hence, whilst there is a 'right' or 'best' theory of adjudication, it is nevertheless *controversial* as to which it is. That having been said, Dworkin has nonetheless advanced our (theoretical) understanding insofar as he is arguing that there *is*, *objectively speaking, a best theory of adjudication*, although (to reiterate a point just made) it is *controversial* as to *which specific theory* is indeed *the best*.[108] In other words, it does *not* follow that, just because it is *uncertain* as to which theory of adjudication is the best, it is therefore *indeterminate* as to whether there is indeed a best theory.

I pause at this juncture to note that whilst the reader might be dissatisfied with Dworkin's approach inasmuch as it does not tell us *which specific* theory is *the* best (and, correlatively, why he is arguing that *his* theory is indeed *the* best), the *practicality* of such an approach cannot be gainsaid. As I observed in an earlier chapter,[109] although positing a *perfect* theory is an impossible task, we cannot (for that reason alone) throw up our hands in despair. Reason and logic alone lead us to the conclusion that *objectivity* is *an integral part* of our very discourse. Put simply (and to reiterate the important point made at the end of the preceding paragraph), just because the answer as to which theory of adjudication is clearly and objectively the correct one is *uncertain*, this does *not* mean that there is *no* (*objectively* speaking) *best* theory of adjudication.

As already alluded to above, Dworkin elaborates upon the aforementioned process by comparing law and *literature*. It will be recalled that his focus is on what he has termed the 'aesthetic hypothesis' (which involves *interpreting* the text concerned in such a way as would show the text concerned to be the *best* work of art on the whole). In this regard, Dworkin first considers the process of *interpretation* by reference to the theory whereby one attempts to ascertain the '*author's intention*' only to *reject* it as a viable *theory* of interpretation.[110] In his view, this particular concept (of 'author's intention) introduces a huge element of *subjectivity* that would (in the legal context) approximate the *strong* sense of *discretion* which Dworkin had (as we have seen) already *rejected* and which in fact constituted the basis upon which he had *critiqued Hart's* theory of adjudication in the first place. Indeed, Dworkin argues that *the author himself or herself* might consider a *different* theory as constituting (*objectively* speaking) *an even better* approach than the one

[108] And in this regard, Dworkin rejects once again the 'demonstrability thesis': ibid 153 (see also the text to n 84, above).

[109] See ch 3 in this volume.

[110] See generally Dworkin (n 91) 154–158.

that *he or she* had in mind when writing the book (or, in the case of a judge, the judgment).[111] In this regard, he notes that:[112]

> An author is capable of detaching what he has written from his earlier intentions and beliefs, of treating it as an object in itself. He is capable of reaching fresh conclusions about his work grounded in aesthetic judgments: that his book is both more coherent and a better analysis of more important themes read in a somewhat different way from what he thought when he was writing it.

In this context, Dworkin quotes the author John Fowles,[113] the latter of whom states:[114]

> Only one reason is shared by all of us [novelists]: *we wish to create worlds as real as, but other than, the world that is.* Or was. That is why we cannot plan … We also know that a genuinely created world must be independent of its creator.

It is significant, in my view, that the novel by Fowles which Dworkin focuses upon[115] is itself a work of *postmodern* historical fiction. That even an author with such free rein such as Fowles[116] holds a view that supports Dworkin's theory is of no mean importance.

However, Dworkin does not discount (entirely at least) 'author's intention' as a viable theory of interpretation – consistent with his adoption of the idea of 'essentially contested concepts', he accepts 'author's intention' as one competing *conception* of the *concept* of *interpretation* (albeit (and not surprisingly) a weak one in his view!).[117]

Insofar as *his* own theory of (*legal*) interpretation is concerned, Dworkin (consistently with adopting and adapting the approach from *literary interpretation*) proffers what he terms the '*chain of law*', which is very akin to the 'chain *novel*' in the context of literature.[118] According to him, each novelist (for 'novelist', read 'judge'), *except the first*,[119] has *dual* responsibilities – of both *interpreting* what has gone on before *and creating* a 'new chapter' in the 'chain of law', thereby *advancing* the overall enterprise in some small way whilst *adding to* the pool of *principles* that the *next* judge has to interpret.[120] And it is this particular process that constitutes the 'chain of law' that is continued into the future. As already alluded

[111] ibid 156.
[112] ibid 157.
[113] Author, amongst a number of famous novels, of *The French Lieutenant's Woman* (Boston, Little, Brown, 1969), which is in fact the novel Dworkin focuses on in this particular essay.
[114] Fowles (n 113) 105–106 (emphasis added by Dworkin).
[115] See above, n 113.
[116] Whose postmodernist stance provided him with the most extensive creative licence.
[117] Dworkin (n 91) 155.
[118] See generally ibid 158–162.
[119] For obvious reasons as, *ex hypothesi*, there would be nothing for him to interpret at the commencement of the process itself.
[120] Dworkin (n 91) 158 and 407.

to above, this process also embodies elements of *both* legal positivism on the one hand (backward-looking) and pragmatism (forward-looking) on the other.[121]

It is also important to note that Dworkin elaborates on *two dimensions* of *interpretation* (which had also been made earlier in *Taking Rights Seriously*[122]).[123] The first dimension is the *formal* dimension, which examines how far the interpretation considered fits and integrates the text completed thus far (this corresponds to the dimension of '*fit*' referred to in his earlier work[124]). Thus, in the case where there are a few different theories (or, perhaps more accurately, *conceptions*[125]) of interpretation, the judge has to ascertain which one best *fits* the text (allowing, of course, for some (albeit not all or a greater proportion) of the text to be disregarded as a mistake[126]). As already noted earlier in this chapter, the dimension of fit will involve concepts such as the doctrine of precedent, and this is noted once again by Dworkin in the present essay.[127] It should also be noted that he also observes (correctly, in my view) that '*easy* cases' (as opposed to 'hard cases') will enable the judge concerned to arrive at his or her decision based solely on this first dimension (of 'fit') as it is likely that 'the particular judge's theory of fit' will (in such 'easy' cases) be likely 'to produce a unique interpretation' that will enable that judge to decide the case concerned.[128] It may, however, well be the case that *more than one* of the possible theories fits the text equally well inasmuch as each is a *plausible* interpretation of the existing legal practice (which is likely, as just mentioned, to be the situation with 'hard' cases). It is at this point that Dworkin states that we have to make the final decision or choice based on a *second* dimension, which is *substantive* (as opposed to formal) in character (and which corresponds to the dimension of '*substance*' or '*moral content*' referred to in his earlier work[129]). However, before proceeding to consider this second dimension of Dworkin's theory of adjudication, it should be noted that a learned author has argued that Dworkin's (first) dimension of 'fit' is *not normative* and that there is therefore 'no important difference between this aspect of Dworkin's theory and the view of the legal positivist who extracts legal principles from legal sources'.[130] Whilst this is a very interesting argument, at least three points may be usefully noted. First, the dimension of 'fit' is only one of *two* dimensions of Dworkin's theory of adjudication. Second

[121] See, further, ibid 162 and 164. See also the text to n 97, above and n 217, below. However, as a learned author perceptively points out, 'law and literature have different goals and pressures' and that while a literary critic seeks 'multiplicity of meaning', a judge seeks, instead, 'one coherent reading': see M Sadowski, '"Language is Not Life!": The Chain Enterprise, Interpretive Communities, and the Dworkin/Fish Debate' (2001) 33 *Connecticut Law Review* 1099, 1107.

[122] Specifically in ch 4: see Dworkin (n 8) as well as (especially) in the *Appendix* (Dworkin (n 72)); see also the text to nn 76–80, above.

[123] See generally Dworkin (n 91) 160–162.

[124] See the text to nn 35 and 76, above.

[125] And see Gallie (n 29).

[126] Which was also to be found in his earlier work: see the text to nn 51–55 and 99–100, above.

[127] Dworkin (n 91) 161.

[128] ibid.

[129] See the text to nn 76–79, above.

[130] See CL Ten, 'The Soundest Theory of Law' (1979) 88 *Mind* 522, 532.

(and as a closely related point), it appears to be the case that Dworkin intended both dimensions to operate in an *integrated* manner with one another (and, perhaps just as importantly, that the dimension of 'fit' has (unlike legal positivism) *normative* qualities as well). In this regard, Dworkin's observations on the distinction between these two dimensions might also be usefully noted:[131]

> I intend the distinction not as a phenomenological report but *an analytic device* to help understand the logic of interpretation and the different ways in which an interpretation may be challenged. In any case it is important not to misunderstand the distinction by supposing, as some commentators have, that the test of fit is only a mechanical test of consistency. On the contrary, the two dimensions of fit and value represent different aspects of *a single overall judgment of political morality, and how we apply the two tests and bring them together in a final assessment of interpretive success at the doctrinal stage will reflect our judgment at the prior jurisprudential stage.*

Third, however, might it be argued that if an 'easy case' satisfied the dimension of 'fit' and there was therefore no need to have recourse to that of 'substance', the view just espoused (that there would be 'no important difference' between the dimension of 'fit' and the legal positivist approach) would hold good? I do not think that Dworkin would have difficulties with such an argument – save that, unlike legal positivists such as Hart, he would probably argue that cases which satisfy wholly the dimension of 'fit' would not be merely *descriptive* in nature but that they would have *already satisfied* the dimension of 'substance' (being based, for example, on an underlying *principle*). Put simply, what might look like a similarity between Dworkin and the legal positivist turns out, in the final analysis, to have *a completely different source as well as outlook altogether.*

Turning now to the *second* dimension of Dworkin's theory of adjudication, this particular dimension considers the *soundness* of the view about which particular theory interpretation (amongst several competing theories of interpretation) makes a novel (in literature) or a judgment (in law) good. Presumably, Dworkin's judge, Hercules J, will choose the theory of interpretation that, in his view (and taken together with the various institutional constraints) is the *soundest*. Insofar as the sphere of *literature* is concerned, Dworkin argues that the *criterion* that should be utilised is that of *artistic merit*. Insofar, however, as *the law* is concerned, the relevant *criterion*, in his view, is one pertaining to *political merit or morality* since, in Dworkin's view, law is *a political enterprise*.[132] Hercules J's *object*, therefore, is *to create a single, unified novel (or, more correctly, judgment)* and *not* a series of independent short stories (or, more correctly, legal precedents); put simply (and translated into the *legal* sphere), the judgment that Hercules J authors in respect of a particular case should *not* stick out like a proverbial 'sore thumb' in light of the prior existing legal precedents as well as relevant institutional history.

[131] See R Dworkin, *Justice in Robes* (Cambridge, Belknap Press, 2006) 15 (emphasis added).
[132] Dworkin (n 91) 161.

Dworkin concedes (as we have already seen at many junctures in his writings) that there will be *different* views at the level of *political morality*. In this regard, he characterises such controversy and disagreement as an 'internal question' which relates to 'politics *in rather than* the politics *of* interpretation'.[133] Nevertheless, that does not mean that there is no right answer in the case concerned.

To summarise, under the common law, each judge is *like a novelist in a 'chain novel'*; in Dworkin's words:[134]

> Each judge must regard himself, in deciding the new case before him, as a part in a complex chain enterprise of which these innumerable decisions, structures, conventions, and practices are the history; it is his job to continue that history into the future through what he does on the day. He *must* interpret what has gone before because he has a responsibility to advance the enterprise in hand rather than strike out in some new direction on his own.[135] So he must determine, according to his judgment[136] what the earlier decisions come to, what the point or theme of the practice so far, taken as a whole, really is.

Again, according to Dworkin:[137]

> A judge's duty is to interpret the legal history he finds, not to invent a better history.

I turn now to consider what is, in my view at least, the *centrepiece* of Dworkin's work in the context of *adjudication*. However, before proceeding to do so, I deal – in the briefest of terms – with Dworkin's final essay on law as interpretation in *A Matter of Principle*: it is entitled 'On Interpretation and Objectivity'.[138] This particular chapter is important inasmuch as its content is a precursor of sorts to the more detailed treatment in Dworkin's next book: in particular, this essay focuses on the issue of *objectivity* and draws in this regard the important distinction between 'internal skepticism' on the one hand and 'external skepticism' on the other.[139] Put simply, Dworkin endorses the former but rejects the latter. The former (viz, 'internal skepticism') relates to disagreements *within* the enterprise (here, of law), but where the individuals concerned nevertheless believe that there is a right theory or a right answer to a particular legal problem, as the case may be. In contrast, the latter (viz, 'external skepticism') rejects the proposition that there is a right theory or answer and that interpretation is a free-for-all. I will not revisit arguments that reject the concept of 'external skepticism', save to reiterate that I am in full agreement with Dworkin on this particular score.

[133] ibid 165 (emphasis added).
[134] ibid 159 (emphasis in the original text).
[135] Which, presumably, is what Hart's judge, Herbert J, does.
[136] Utilising the *weak* sense of discretion that he first formulated in Dworkin (n 3) ch 2, entitled 'The Model of Rules I'; see also the text to nn 37–39 in ch 6 in this volume.
[137] Dworkin (n 91) 160.
[138] See Dworkin, *A Matter of Principle* (n 63) ch 7, entitled 'On Interpretation and Objectivity'.
[139] See, especially, ibid 175–177.

b. Law's Empire

Dworkin's first real attempt to pull the threads, so to speak, together in order to construct a holistic as well as coherent *book-length* theory of adjudication is, however, to be found in *Law's Empire*[140] (and published just a year after *A Matter of Principle*[141]). Indeed, Dworkin himself states as much right at the outset of this particular book:[142]

> This book sets out *in full-length form* an answer I have been developing piecemeal, in fits and starts, for several years: that legal reasoning is an exercise in constructive interpretation, that our law consists in the best justification of our legal practices as a whole, that it consists in the narrative story that makes of these practices the best they can be.

It is interesting, in my view, that Dworkin does also (again, right at the outset of *Law's Empire*) debunk[143] the 'demonstrability thesis'[144] to the effect that a right answer must be demonstrable; to reiterate a point which Dworkin has repeatedly emphasised in his writings, there can, in logic and principle, be a right answer although reasonable individuals may disagree as to what the right answer is.[145] In addition, this particular book *expressly* places his theory within the context of other legal theories (and not just legal positivism). As a result, there is much in *Law's Empire* that clarifies as well as elucidates his earlier work.[146]

In *Law's Empire*, Dworkin develops the ideas in the essay we have already considered – 'How Law is Like Literature'[147] – in particular, the concept of *interpretation*. As he clearly states: 'Law is an interpretive concept'.[148] As just mentioned, he also seeks to locate his theory of interpretation in the context of the other major legal theories. Unlike, however, his theory, Dworkin argues that

[140] See R Dworkin, *Law's Empire* (Cambridge, Belknap Press, 1986). See also Guest (n 63) 20 as well as BB Levenbook, 'The Sustained Dworkin' (1986) 53 *University of Chicago Law Review* 1108, 1108; D Beyleveld and R Brownsword, 'Practice Made Perfect?' (1987) 50 *MLR* 662, 662; K Greenawalt, 'Book Reviews of *A Matter of Principle* and *Law's Empire*' (1987) 84 *Journal of Philosophy* 284, 286; AC Hutchinson, 'Indiana Dworkin and Law's Empire' (1987) 96 *Yale Law Journal* 637, 638; and LA Jacobs and M McManus, *Against Post-Liberal Courts and Justice – Rescuing Ronald Dworkin's Legacy* (Palgrave Macmillan, Switzerland, 2023) ch 2, entitled 'Ronald Dworkin's Legacy', 11.

[141] Dworkin (n 63).

[142] Dworkin (n 140) vii (emphasis added). Somewhat frustratingly for the reader, perhaps, he states that he had 'made no effort to discover how far this book alters or replaces positions I defended in earlier work' (ibid viii). However, as we shall see, there has been no change – in substance at least – in Dworkin's *basic or fundamental ideas as well as concepts*. See also P Soper, 'Dworkin's Domain' (1987) 100 *Harvard Law Review* 1166, 1166–1167, where the learned author observes that '[t]he substance of Dworkin's theory has changed little over the last twenty years, although the metaphors are different'.

[143] Dworkin (n 140) viii–ix.

[144] See the text to n 84, above.

[145] As I have also (repeatedly) emphasised, this is based on Professor Gallie's idea of 'essentially contested concepts' (see Gallie (n 29)).

[146] See also above, n 142.

[147] Dworkin (n 91).

[148] Dworkin (n 140) 87 and 410 (indeed, this point is so important that it is reiterated once again almost at the end of this book).

there are other theories that suffer from what he terms the 'semantic sting'[149] (which, in his view, paralyses any form of substantive theoretical discourse or debate since judges and lawyers, according to these other theories, follow only *linguistic criteria* for judging propositions of law). In these (other) semantic theories, judges and lawyers share a rough consensus about the linguistic criteria and differ only as to the actual details of the application of those criteria[150] – a paradigm example of which, in Dworkin's view, is legal positivism.[151] Legal positivism essentially treats propositions of law as 'factual' in nature.[152] In this regard, legal positivism focuses on what Dworkin terms 'the *grounds* of law' (as opposed to 'the *force* of law')[153] – the latter relating to 'the relative power of any true proposition of law to *justify*[154] coercion in different sorts of exceptional circumstance'.[155] Somewhat idiosyncratically perhaps, Dworkin is of the view that '[p]olitical philosophers consider problems about the force of law, and academic lawyers and specialists in jurisprudence study issues about its grounds'.[156] What *is* clear, however, is that 'the grounds of law' relate more to the *second* dimension of 'substance' in Dworkin's theory of interpretation. This is not surprising because, as we have already seen, this second dimension centres on the issue of political morality.[157]

In contrast, *interpretation* – again, in Dworkin's view – is 'not conversational but *constructive*'.[158] It is 'essentially concerned with purpose not cause' and that it is 'a matter of imposing purpose on an object or practice in order to make of it the best possible example of the form or genre to which it is taken to belong'.[159] The process of interpretation also involves generally (whether, for example, in relation to law or literature) the *two dimensions* of *fit*[160] and *substance*[161] (which we have already considered above). It is also interesting to note that – perhaps for the very first time – Dworkin refers *expressly* to the distinction between concept and conceptions[162] (which, as I have already argued, is *a central pillar* of his theory and which can be traced back to the idea of 'essentially contested concepts' first mooted by Professor WB Gallie[163]). Curiously, though, apart from the citation in

[149] See generally ibid 45–46.
[150] ibid 33.
[151] See generally ibid 33–35 and 37–43.
[152] ibid 109.
[153] ibid 110 (emphasis in the original text).
[154] And, hence, imports a *normative as well as evaluative* perspective which legal positivism eschews.
[155] Dworkin (n 140) 110 (emphasis added).
[156] ibid 111.
[157] See also the text to nn 23, 79, 86, 132 and 133, above.
[158] Dworkin (n 140) 52 (emphasis in the original text).
[159] ibid. See also ibid 53 and 62.
[160] ibid 67.
[161] ibid 67–68.
[162] ibid 70–72 and 90–96 (the latter refers to 'Concepts and Conceptions of *Law*') (emphasis added). And see also (in this latter regard) ibid 108 and 112.
[163] Gallie (n 29).

'Hard Cases',[164] Dworkin does *not* appear to have cited Gallie specifically as such in *Law's Empire*.[165]

Dworkin also elaborates in more detail on the important distinction between 'internal skepticism' and 'external skepticism'[166] which he first considered (as noted at the end of the previous section of this chapter) in *A Matter of Principle*.[167] As also noted earlier, 'internal skepticism' operates on the premise that, despite the existence of differently held views, it is nevertheless the case that 'one view *is* right'[168] – that is to say that there *is* a right or correct answer in relation to the situation at hand. In contrast, 'external skepticism' is 'disengaged'[169] and whilst an external skeptic may in fact hold an opinion on a given issue, he or she does not believe that there is objective truth and, hence, a right or correct answer to that particular issue. Not surprisingly, whilst he endorses 'internal skepticism', Dworkin rejects 'external skepticism' out of hand; in his view:[170]

> My advice is straightforward: this preliminary dance of skepticism is silly and wasteful; it neither adds to nor subtracts from the business at hand. The only skepticism worth anything is skepticism of the internal kind, and this must be earned by arguments of the same contested character as the arguments it opposes, not claimed in advance by some pretense at hard-hitting empirical metaphysics.

Let us turn now to Dworkin's consideration of the various theories of adjudication.

The *first* theory[171] (which Dworkin disagrees with) is what he terms '*conventionalism*'.[172] Under conventionalism, the judge is required to look at past decisions (or legal conventions) *only*. In Dworkin's words, conventionalism 'makes law depend on distinct social conventions it designates as legal conventions; in particular on conventions about which institutions should have power to make law and how'.[173] There is in fact no 'law' outside legal conventions: in other words,

[164] See above, n 29.

[165] Indeed, an author actually attributes the distinction to Dworkin instead of Gallie: see MS Sohal, 'Legal Practice and the Case Against Theory: Dworkin versus Fish' [2000] *UCL Jurisprudence Review* 234, 236.

[166] See generally Dworkin (n 140) 78–86.

[167] Dworkin (n 138).

[168] Dworkin (n 140) 78 (emphasis in the original text).

[169] ibid 80.

[170] ibid 86. The external skeptics nevertheless appear to be rather entrenched in their views: see, eg, J Allan, 'Legal Interpretation and the Separation of Law and Morality: A Moral Sceptic's Attack on Dworkin' (1997) 26 *Anglo-American Law Review* 405 and, by the same author, 'Truth's Empire – A Reply to Ronald Dworkin's "Objectivity and Truth: You'd Better Believe It"' (2001) 26 *Australian Journal of Legal Philosophy* 61. With respect, though, the learned author has not fully engaged with Dworkin's distinction between uncertainty on the one hand and indeterminacy on the other. And although he does refer to Dworkin's reliance on Gallie's idea of 'essentially contested concepts' in the former article (at 422–425), he finds (without much, if any, elaboration) that reliance unpersuasive.

[171] All three theories that follow are introduced preliminarily by Dworkin in ch 3, entitled 'Jurisprudence Revisited': see Dworkin (n 140) 94–96.

[172] See generally ibid, ch 4, entitled 'Conventionalism'.

[173] ibid 114.

conventionalism 'insists … that [judges] must treat as law what convention stipulates is law'.[174]

In Dworkin's view, there are in fact two basic features in conventionalism. The first (as just seen) is that law is dependent on conventions, and the second is that '[l]aw by convention is *never complete*'.[175] Because of this (and because judges ought not to be seen as making or inventing law), the court at this point (ie, when legal conventions run out) must exercise *discretion* in the *strong* sense, relying upon *extra*legal standards to arrive at a decision.[176] Dworkin does consider whether one possible solution in such a situation is to *extend* the scope and ambit of such conventions so that there is no need to rely upon *extra*legal standards. He is of the view that such an attempted extension can take one of two forms.[177] First, it can be effected *implicitly*.[178] In Dworkin's view, such an *implicit* extension is really a form of *interpretation*; indeed, he terms this '*soft* conventionalism', which he views as being 'a very abstract, underdeveloped form' of the theory that *he* endorses – 'law as integrity'.[179]

A second form of extension of the scope and ambit of conventions is by way of *express or explicit* extension.[180] In Dworkin's view, this is, by definition, *not* possible since, *ex hypothesi*, the relevant or material legal conventions have run out and, therefore, further elaboration along this line is virtually impossible, and recourse to *extra*legal standards is necessary. Dworkin terms conventionalism that only permits such express extension as '*strict* conventionalism'. And this is the form of conventionalism that is advocated by proponents of conventionalism generally.[181]

The reader would have discerned by now that *Hart's legal positivism* would be classified under the rubric of conventionalism (in particular, 'strict conventionalism'). Not surprisingly, therefore, Dworkin's assessment of conventionalism – consistent with his assessment of Hart's theory thus far – is an *adverse* one. In particular, in assessing conventionalism in accordance with the two dimensions of 'fit' and 'substance', he finds that it fails on both these counts. First, conventionalism fails the dimension of 'fit' because it generates *no* consistency in *principle* – only in *strategy* (which is, of course, akin to *policy*) and is thus characterised by *expedience* (instead of principle).[182] Put simply, pursuant to conventionalism, individuals do *not* have established legal *rights*. In *contrast*, Dworkin's theory of 'law as integrity' *does* suppose that individuals have legal rights[183] – as Dworkin

[174] ibid 116.
[175] ibid 115 (emphasis added).
[176] ibid 117. See also ibid 119 and 128–129.
[177] See generally ibid 124–130.
[178] ibid 124.
[179] ibid 127–128. And on the concept of 'law as integrity', see the text to nn 198–237, below.
[180] Dworkin (n 140) 124.
[181] See also ibid 128.
[182] See generally ibid 130–135.
[183] ibid 134.

puts it, 'rights that follow from past decisions of political institutions and [which] therefore licence or legitimise coercion', and 'that go beyond the explicit extension of political practices conceived as conventions'.[184] Put simply (and in contrast to conventionalism), 'law as integrity' 'supposes that people are entitled to a *coherent and principled* extension of past political decision *even when* judges profoundly disagree about what this means'.[185]

Conventionalism also fails the dimension of 'substance' insofar as the justification of its practice is concerned.[186] Put simply, Dworkin argues that when judges *legislate* under conventionalism (since they have run out of conventions and cannot expressly extend them), there is *surprise* generated, thus 'exploding' the myth that conventionalism protects expectations. In contrast, pursuant to Dworkin's theory of 'law as integrity', judges in reality pay more attention to sources of law (focusing not on *extra*legal legislation but, instead, on principles). In fairness to conventionalism, however, Dworkin does acknowledge that when judges legislate under this theory, they do not fly off the handle, so to speak, inasmuch as they would still be concerned with past legal doctrine, albeit only in an *evidential* sense; such past doctrine would not (unlike 'law as integrity') be important for its own sake.[187]

The *second* theory (which Dworkin also disagrees with) is what he terms '*legal pragmatism*'[188] (hereafter referred to as 'pragmatism'). The general idea, insofar as this particular theory is concerned, is relatively easy to grasp. It consists basically of a *skeptical* attitude towards the law,[189] justifying it on the basis of *justice or efficiency*; put simply, *policy* is 'all'. Another important point to note is that pragmatism (again, unlike 'law as integrity') *denies* that individuals ever have genuine *non*strategic legal *rights*, although it may sometimes act *as if* individuals had legal rights[190] (Dworkin terms these (ersatz) rights 'as-if rights'[191]) in the interests of efficiency (and, of course, as a matter of strategy). Dworkin negatively refers to such an approach as purveying a 'noble-lie'.[192]

Surprisingly, though, Dworkin does not claim that pragmatism is equivalent to *American Realism*,[193] although it is suggested that pragmatism certainly appears to be very similar to it. That having been said, given the policy-orientation of pragmatism, the doctrine of *utilitarianism* could also be said to fall within the rubric of pragmatism.

[184] ibid.
[185] ibid 134 (emphasis added).
[186] See generally ibid 139–147.
[187] ibid 132. For a spirited defence of legal positivism in the context of Dworkin's critique of conventionalism, see K Kress, 'The Interpretive Turn' (1987) 97 *Ethics* 834.
[188] See generally Dworkin (n 140) 147–150 as well as ch 5, entitled 'Pragmatism and Personification', especially 151–164.
[189] ibid 151.
[190] ibid 152.
[191] ibid 154.
[192] ibid 159.
[193] ibid 153. American Realism is discussed in ch 9 in this volume.

Comparing conventionalism on the one hand and pragmatism on the other, Dworkin's *relative* preference is for the latter (as opposed to the former).[194] This is not surprising in view of the fact that conventionalism fails on both the dimensions of 'fit' and 'substance'.[195] Nevertheless, pragmatism has its drawbacks as well (although it possesses the flexibility (albeit only in the form of strategy, not principle) that is missing in conventionalism[196]). Insofar as the dimension of 'fit' is concerned, there is, Dworkin argues, a kind of 'deception' by the judges who subscribe to pragmatism, especially where the reference to 'as-if rights' (just noted) is concerned. Dworkin does, however, admit that the second dimension of 'substance' (in relation to political justification) might be acceptable if it is powerful enough. However, because pragmatism does not take legal rights seriously and therefore has no respect for (and makes no attempt to) secure consistency in *principle* as an enterprise that is important for its own sake, it is a theory which Dworkin clearly rejects.[197]

The *third* theory (which I have already alluded to above) is *Dworkin's* preferred theory, and he therefore recommends it to us – '*law as integrity*'. Before proceeding to unveil, as it were, this theory, Dworkin introduces us first to an important preliminary concept – that of *personification* (of the community or state). He defends this particular concept right at the outset, stating that it is not metaphysical in nature in the sense that it is an esoteric summation of individuals but, rather, has to do with the community as a whole and as a *distinct moral agent* – with officials acting as agents for the community in ensuring, for example, impartiality amongst its members. This results in the concept or idea of *group responsibility*.[198] As we shall see, this concept of *personification* is important in order for Dworkin to work out the full implications of his theory of 'law as integrity'. In this last-mentioned regard, Dworkin devotes five chapters to various aspects of his theory. In the first of these chapters, he deals with the concept of integrity itself, which, on a closer reading, would reveal that it has (in effect) to do with *legislation*.[199] And in the second, Dworkin deals with *adjudication*.[200] It should also be noted that both these aforementioned chapters deal with the underlying basic concepts that ought to be utilised as tools of analysis. It is only in the subsequent two chapters that *specific illustrations* from the common law and statute law, respectively, are considered by Dworkin[201] – both these chapters thus demonstrate the basic concepts in the preceding two chapters[202] 'in motion'

[194] 'Pragmatism tells a more promising story.': Dworkin (n 140) 157.
[195] ibid 150. See also the text to nn 182–187, above.
[196] ibid.
[197] See, especially, ibid 160.
[198] See generally ibid 167–175.
[199] Dworkin (n 140) ch 6, entitled 'Integrity'.
[200] ibid, ch 7, entitled 'Integrity in Law'.
[201] ibid, ch 8, entitled 'The Common Law' and ch 9, entitled 'Statutes'.
[202] ibid.

or 'in action', so to speak. Finally, the fifth chapter deals with constitutional law.[203] Indeed, this last-mentioned chapter is in fact the penultimate chapter in *Law's Empire*, which concludes in the final chapter of the book with a brief review as well as a peek into the future.[204]

As the present book deals with the topic of adjudication, I will consider only briefly Dworkin's views on the legislative process in *Law's Empire*. Put simply, he is of the view that the legislative process takes into account two (ofttimes competing) concepts – that of 'justice' and 'fairness', respectively. These two concepts compete to the extent that the former is viewed *procedurally* only and is not concerned as such with *substantive outcomes* (which is represented by the concept of 'fairness'); put simply, the former is represented by the slogan, 'justice as fairness', whereas the latter is represented by the slogan, 'fairness as justice'. Dworkin, however, argues for a *third* ideal, which he terms '*integrity*',[205] which may *sometimes* come into *conflict* with the concepts of both 'justice' and 'fairness'.[206]

And it is the concept of 'integrity' that Dworkin argues ought to guide legislators. This, in his view, is justified by the concept of community or personification (to which we have already referred above).[207] In his view, it is only by pursuing such an approach that the *legitimacy (or moral authority)* of the law can be maintained.[208] Pursuant to the concept of community, there is reciprocity[209] in a general sense in which individuals in that community share rights and responsibilities, provided that four conditions are satisfied: (i) that people regard that group's obligations as *special*; (ii) that people must accept that responsibilities within that community are *personal*; (iii) that responsibilities must flow from a more general responsibility of *concern* for the well-being of others in the community; and (iv) that members of the community must show not only concern but also *equal* concern for all members.[210]

Of the three possible models of community, only the third meets all four requirements just mentioned.[211] The first model of community is one that is a de facto accident of history and geography – a community, in other words, that has come into existence as a matter of *circumstance*, and to which *none* of the four conditions applies.

The second model of community is what Dworkin terms the 'rule-book' model, which correlates to the concept of *conventionalism* discussed above (and to which the third condition is *not* satisfied).

[203] ibid, ch 10, entitled 'The Constitution'.
[204] ibid, ch 11, entitled 'Law Beyond Law'.
[205] 'Integrity is our Neptune.': ibid 183. *Contra* what Dworkin terms a 'checkerboard strategy': see generally ibid 179–182.
[206] ibid 188. See also ibid 263 and 404.
[207] See also ibid.
[208] See, especially, ibid 190–192.
[209] ibid 198.
[210] See generally ibid 199–201.
[211] See generally ibid 208–216.

The third model of community (which Dworkin considers the *best*) is what he terms *the model of principle* (in which *all four* conditions are satisfied). Such a model transforms a bare political society into a true fraternal mode of association. And, perhaps most importantly, it provides the best explanation of political legitimacy in general and the legitimacy of the legal system in particular.

Although integrity requires coherence with fundamental principle, Dworkin admits that, in the realm of *legislation*, legislators can *also* take account of the *general interest* as well and can thus also have regard to matters of *policy*. In other words, *integrity* in *legislation* does *not* require *strict* consistency, although he argues that there ought, *as far as is possible*, also be fidelity to *principle*.[212]

I turn now to focus on *adjudication*. The relevant chapter[213] builds on the main ideas and concepts that had already been canvassed in his earlier essay considered above, 'How Law is Like Literature'.[214] These include concepts such as the chain of law,[215] as well as the two dimensions of fit and substantive political justification (the latter dimension having regard to 'substance').[216] In this particular chapter, Dworkin clarifies – once again[217] – the extremely important point that, insofar as 'law as integrity' is concerned, such a concept is both backward- *and* forward-looking. In other words, law as integrity is *unlike* either conventionalism or pragmatism, inasmuch as conventionalism *only* looks backwards (at factual reports in the process of finding the law), whilst pragmatism *only* looks forward in an *instrumental* fashion (and *invents* law).[218]

Dworkin also states that law as integrity is *interpretive* – a point that he had already emphasised in his earlier work. In this particular chapter, however, he speaks about a *single* author – *the community personified* (thus bringing into play a concept that we have already referred to above). It is also important to note that Dworkin views the enterprise of *legal* interpretation from (not surprisingly) an *internal* perspective in general and (wherever possible) from the perspective of the *specific branch* of the law concerned in particular.[219]

Next (and this is a rather important point), Dworkin appears to have *abandoned* the distinction which he drew in his earliest work between easy cases

[212] See generally ibid 219–224.

[213] ibid, ch 7, entitled 'Integrity in Law' (see also above, n 200).

[214] Dworkin (n 91).

[215] Dworkin (n 140) 229–232.

[216] See, eg, ibid 228, 230–231, 235, 237, 239, 246–247, 248, 257, 265, 283–288 and 410–411. As already noted earlier in this chapter in relation to Dworkin's earlier writings, the judge must have recourse to the second dimension (of substance) if *more than one interpretation 'fits'* the bulk of the text: see, especially, ibid 230–231. It should, however, also be noted that (quite correctly, in my view) Dworkin does not insist on a strict dichotomy or divide between these two dimensions: see, eg, ibid 231.

[217] See also the text to nn 97 and 121, above.

[218] See also Dworkin (n 140) 226–227 and 234.

[219] See, in this latter respect, his concept of 'compartmentalization' that (in turn) shapes that of 'local priority' which is given to that particular area of the law: ibid 252–253. See also (in relation to the concept of 'local priority') ibid 405.

on the one hand and hard cases on the other. For example, he observes as follows:[220]

> Law as integrity explains and justifies easy cases as well as hard ones; it also shows why they are easy. … So easy cases are, for law as integrity, only special cases of hard ones, …

And later, when discussing the interpretation of statutes, Dworkin states as follows:[221]

> Hercules does not need one method for hard cases and another for easy ones. His method is equally at work in easy cases, but since the answers to the questions it puts are then obvious, or at least seem to be so, we are not aware that any theory is at work at all.

Put simply, Dworkin's arguments now take on *a much more general* flavour.

Finally (and importantly), Dworkin deals in *a more express manner* with the (in my view, quite powerful) objection that Hercules nevertheless exercises his discretion *in the final analysis*.[222] He argues, first, that the existence of (as well as consequent variety of, or difference in[223]) background convictions of political morality are *inevitable*. For example, the critic's own assertion that Hercules is playing politics is part of *the critic's own* political values. Second (and this is a point that we have in fact already canvassed at various points in the present chapter), Hercules's method is the best method of ascertaining what is the correct answer in a given case. In this regard, Dworkin argues that there *is* such a thing as 'one right answer', although there may be different conceptions or justifications (relying, once again, on Professor Gallie's idea of 'essentially contested concepts'[224]). The argument that this approach is too subjective is, in Dworkin's view, misconceived. In particular, he argues that insofar as the argument just mentioned has to do with what he terms 'external skepticism', it is fallacious.[225]

Elaborating, Dworkin states that external skepticism basically holds that *nothing* can be objective and there can therefore be no real argument, only various differing opinions. He argues that this is too extreme a view, although he would accept what he terms 'internal skepticism' which holds that although there is an ascertainable and correct answer, there can in fact be various differing arguments about which is the correct answer. I pause at this juncture to note that Dworkin's responses via the distinction between internal skepticism and external skepticism are not new and are something I have touched upon briefly in an

[220] Dworkin (n 140) 266.
[221] Dworkin (n 140) ch 9, entitled 'Statutes', 354.
[222] See generally, and in particular, ibid 260–266.
[223] 'Judges will have different ideas of fairness …': ibid 250. See, to like effect, ibid 256.
[224] Gallie (n 29). However, some writers have perceived Dworkin to have 'retreated' from his 'one right answer thesis' (see, eg, GC Christie, 'Dworkin's "Empire"' [1987] *Duke Law Journal* 157, 184). In fairness, I think that Dworkin has *modified* this thesis in order to make it more realistic and, as just mentioned, this is achieved by reliance on Professor Gallie's idea of 'essentially contested concepts'.
[225] See generally Dworkin (n 140) 266–275.

earlier part of this chapter.[226] I would also add that, although this is not expressly stated by Dworkin himself, *we have to assume some datum measure of good faith on the part of Hercules – or, indeed, any other judge for that matter*. It should also be noted that Hercules is a kind of 'ideal type' as no judge would – in reality – have the same ability as well as acumen as Hercules.[227]

As already mentioned, Dworkin also provides us with *illustrative accounts* of the concept of integrity at work in the spheres of the common law,[228] statute law,[229] and the constitution,[230] respectively.

Insofar as the interpretation of statutes is concerned, Dworkin states that the basic question is this: which reading of the act or statute (or provision thereof) concerned shows the political history including and surrounding it in a better light? As already noted above, the significant difference between the interpretation of statutes on the one hand and interpretation under the common law on the other is that when Hercules is interpreting a statute, he would *also* take into account matters of *policy* when deciding which *rights* the statute concerned should be deemed to have created, whereas when Hercules is deciding in the common law context, he can *only* have regard to arguments of *principle*.

It should also be noted that just as (according to Dworkin) 'author's intention' under the common law must be assiduously avoided, so also must the very similar concept of 'speaker's meaning' (in the context of statutory interpretation). In other words, interpretation in the statutory context is not a matter of ascertaining the mental state of the legislator(s) – which is, of course, *practically* very difficult (at the very least) for obvious reasons.[231] What are important, in Dworkin's view, are the legislators' *own political convictions*.[232] Hence, the judge concerned ought to interpret the record of *the legislature itself*. Two sub-points, so to speak, need to be noted at this point. First, there is no problem in interpreting the record of *the legislature* itself simply because of the concept of *personification*, which we noted earlier in the present chapter. Second, the 'record' refers here to the record of institutions and practices as well as of individuals, although Dworkin points out that insofar as legislative history proper is concerned, this is likely to be *less* relevant *over time* simply because of *changed circumstances*; and, at this particular point, Hercules's method is a real *advantage* over 'speaker's meaning' theory, the

[226] See the text to nn 139 and 166–170, above. And see more generally ch 3 in this volume.

[227] Dworkin (n 140) 265.

[228] ibid, ch 8, entitled 'The Common Law' (see also above, n 201). Integrity is contrasted, in the main, with economic and (related) utilitarian arguments. This is something which Dworkin focused on in his earlier writings as well (as noted earlier in the present chapter). Not surprisingly, therefore, he argues that law as integrity prefers and egalitarian approach instead: see generally ibid 295–312. It is suggested that Dworkin's arguments have considerably more traction insofar as *private* law is concerned (for example, his case law illustrations in the context of the law of negligence) simply because, generally speaking at least, the *rights* of *individuals* are involved.

[229] ibid, ch 9, entitled 'Statutes' (see also above, n 201).

[230] ibid, ch 10, entitled 'The Constitution' (see also above, n 203).

[231] ibid 324.

[232] ibid 328–333.

latter of which tends to 'freeze' the legislative intention at the moment when the statute was first enacted (with no recourse being permitted in relation to later developments).[233]

Insofar as interpretation of the *constitution* is concerned, Dworkin argues – in a similar manner – against what he terms the 'framer's intent' (which is similar to both 'author's intention' under the common law and to 'speaker's meaning' with regard to statutes).[234] And he argues, in particular, against the twin processes that are the constitutional counterparts of conventionalism and pragmatism under the common law – what he terms 'passivism' and 'activism', respectively.[235] Put simply, passivism appeals to conventionalism and, when the situation is felt to be 'desperate', to skepticism as well. Activism, on the other hand, is, according to Dworkin, 'a virulent form of legal pragmatism',[236] viz, pure fiat. Not surprisingly, Dworkin observes thus:[237]

> Hercules is not a historicist, but neither is his the buccaneer style sometimes lampooned under the epithet 'natural law'. He does not think that the Constitution is only what the best theory of abstract justice and fairness would produce by way of ideal theory. He is guided instead by a sense of constitutional *integrity*; he believes that the American Constitution consists in *the best available interpretation* of American constitutional text and practice as a whole, and his judgment about which *interpretation* is *best* is sensitive to the great complexity of *political virtues* bearing on that issue.
>
> His arguments embrace popular conviction and national tradition whenever these are pertinent to the sovereign question, which reading of constitutional history shows that history overall in its best light. For the same reason and toward the same end, they draw on his own convictions about justice and fairness and the right relation between them. *He is not a passivist because he rejects the rigid idea that judges must defer to elected officials, no matter what part of the constitutional scheme is in question.*
>
> …
>
> *He is not an 'activist' either.* He will refuse to substitute his judgment for that of the legislature *when he believes the issue in play is primarily one of policy rather than principle*, when the argument is about the best strategies for achieving the overall collective interest through goals like prosperity or the eradication of poverty or the right balance between economy and conservation.

In the final chapter of *Law's Empire*,[238] Dworkin (quite cleverly, in my view) attempts to pre-empt any argument to the effect that Hercules has already effected a perfect job. In his view, such a perception is, in his view, 'too crude'.[239] There are, for example, certain institutional constraints (such as the doctrine of binding

[233] See generally ibid 333–354.
[234] Which Dworkin characterises as 'historicism': see generally ibid 359–369.
[235] See generally ibid 369–379.
[236] ibid 378.
[237] ibid 397–398 (emphasis added).
[238] Dworkin (n 140) ch 11, entitled 'Law Beyond Law' (see also above, n 204).
[239] ibid 400.

precedent) that may themselves hamper the concept of integrity in its second (and more substantive) dimension. Hence, in Dworkin's view, the process is never fool-proof or perfect. Furthermore, insofar as the first dimension of fit is concerned, there may in fact be problems there as well, inasmuch as there may be more than one interpretation that 'fits' the legal text concerned.

In Dworkin's view, there are in fact *two kinds* of 'integrity' in the final analysis. The first is '*inclusive* integrity', which is the *concrete* law for the *judge* to administer as well as work out.[240] At this point, *all* the various variables are present, and there can therefore be no 'perfect' result as such.

The second is '*pure* integrity', which is based *solely* on principles of *justice* and is *not* tied to *specific* institutions within the community itself.[241]

In Dworkin's view:[242]

> Present law gropes towards pure law when modes of decision appear that seem to satisfy fairness and process and bring law closer to its own ambition; lawyers declare optimism about this process when they say that law works itself pure.

In the context of *the present book*, it is *extremely significant* that, in his concluding observations in *Law's Empire*, Dworkin not only underscores (yet again) the element of controversy in the actual adjudicative process but also reminds us (as I am also at pains to emphasise, particularly in the final chapter of this book[243]) that that process is also one that *must* embody the *fundamental spirit* of the adjudicative enterprise itself – in particular, the datum requirement of *good faith in judging*. As Dworkin observes:[244]

> Integrity does not enforce itself: *judgment is required*. That judgment is not structured by different dimensions of interpretation and different aspects of these. We noticed how convictions about fit contest with and constrain judgments of substance, and how convictions about fairness and justice and procedural due process contest with one another. *The interpretive judgment must notice and take account of these several dimensions; if it does not, it is incompetent or in bad faith, ordinary politics in disguise.* But it must also meld these dimensions into an overall opinion: about which interpretation, all things considered, makes the community's legal record the best it can be from the point of view of political morality. So legal judgments are *pervasively contestable*.[245]
>
> ...
>
> Law as integrity ... provides both a better fit with and a better justification of our legal practice as a whole.

[240] ibid 405, 406 and 410.
[241] ibid 405–407.
[242] ibid 407. See also BN Cardozo, *The Nature of the Judicial Process* (New Haven, Yale University Press, 1921) 179.
[243] See ch 10 in this volume.
[244] Dworkin (n 140) 410–411 (emphasis added).
[245] This particular sentence resonates with Gallie's idea of 'essentially contested concepts' (Gallie (n 29)), although he is not cited expressly by Dworkin (a point noted earlier in the present chapter).

> …
>
> We should accept integrity as a virtue of ordinary politics because we should try to conceive our political community as an association of principle; we should aim at this because, among other reasons, that conception of community[246] offers an attractive basis for claims of political legitimacy in a community of free and independent people who disagree about political morality and wisdom.

As already emphasised throughout the present chapter, Dworkin is all too aware that his theory of adjudication (of law as integrity) is not a knockdown theory. Indeed, on the penultimate page of *Law's Empire*, he concedes thus:[247]

> Have I said what law is? The best reply is: up to a point. I have not devised an algorithm for the courtroom. No electronic magician could design from my arguments a computer program that would supply a verdict everyone would accept once the facts of the case and the text of all past statutes and judicial decisions were put at the computer's disposal. But I have not drawn the conclusion many readers thinks sensible. *I have not said that there is never one right answer, only different ways, to decide a hard case.*
>
> …
>
> For every route Hercules took from that general conception to a particular verdict, another lawyer or judge who began in the same conception would find a different route and end in a different place, as several of the judges in our sample of cases [in this book] did. He would end differently because he would take leave of Hercules, following his own lights, at some branching point sooner or later in the argument.
>
> The question how far I have succeeded in showing what law is is therefore a distinct question for each reader.

Having acknowledged the *reality* of adjudication, it is worth quoting (in its entirety) Dworkin's *closing words* to *Law's Empire* because it acknowledges as well as underscores – *yet again* – the *central thesis* of this book: the datum requirement of *good faith in judging*. Much of that thesis (as is also evident in Dworkin's words) is *attitudinal*, although I shall also endeavour to demonstrate that there are *substantive* implications as well as consequences or results as well. As just mentioned, this will be the task of the final chapter of this book.[248] For the present, however, this is what Dworkin has to say (and which is *wholly consistent with* that final chapter itself):[249]

> What is law? Now I offer a different kind of answer. Law is not exhausted by any catalogue of rules or principles, each with its own dominion over some discrete theater of behavior. Nor by any roster of officials and their powers each over part of our lives. *Law's empire* is *defined by attitude*, not territory or power or process. We studied that

[246] *Cf*, once again, Gallie's idea of 'essentially contested concepts' (Gallie (n 29)).
[247] Dworkin (n 140) 412 (emphasis added).
[248] See ch 10 in this volume (see also above, n 243).
[249] Dworkin (n 140) 413 (emphasis added). See also Guest (n 63) 99 (emphasis added), where the learned author observes thus: 'It is helpful to think of Dworkin's theory of law as concerned fundamentally with *a cast of mind*, that of the argumentative lawyer.' See also ibid 21.

> *attitude* mainly in appellate courts, where it is dressed for inspection, but it must be pervasive in our ordinary lives if it is to serve us well even in court. It is an interpretive, self-reflective *attitude* addressed to politics in the broadest sense. It is a protestant *attitude* that makes each citizen responsible for imagining what his society's public commitments to *principle* are, and what these commitments require in new circumstances. The protestant character of law is confirmed, and the creative role of private decisions acknowledged, by the backward-looking, judgmental nature of judicial decisions, and also by the regulative assumption that though judges must have the last word, their word is not for that reason the best word. Law's *attitude* is constructive: it aims, in the *interpretive spirit*, to lay *principle* over practice to show the best route to a better future, keeping the *right faith* with the past. It is, finally, a fraternal *attitude*, an expression of how we are united in community though divided in project, interest and conviction. That is, anyway, what law is for us: for the people we want to be and the community we aim to have.

Notice that the word 'attitude' appears *six times* in the above quotation. The emphasis – over half a dozen times – on the *spirit* of the adjudicative enterprise (the word 'spirit', incidentally, appears once in the quotation) is, as I have already mentioned, *wholly consistent with* the basic thesis of *good faith judging* which I advance in this book (in particular, in the final chapter[250]). As also noted above, I should nevertheless hasten to add that the present book is *not only* about 'attitude'. However, the *spirit* of '*attitude*' in the form of *good faith judging* is a *central pillar* of it.

For the present (and more modest as well as specific) purposes of this chapter (which focuses on Dworkin's writings), it is appropriate to consider his final extended work in relation to his theory of adjudication,[251] and it is to that book that our attention now turns.

c. Justice for Hedgehogs

Introduction

In the conclusion to his (much earlier) essay entitled 'How Law is Like Literature',[252] Dworkin – quite intriguingly – concludes that essay by observing thus:[253]

> I only report my sense that politics, art, and law are united, somehow, in philosophy.

This concept in fact forms the premise of what could be considered his final magnum opus – *Justice for Hedgehogs*.[254] This book goes *far beyond* adjudication: it is,

[250] See ch 10 in this volume (see also above, nn 243 and 248).

[251] There was, in fact, one more volume prior to that final work which, however, comprised a collection of essays that reprised many of the issues as well as themes already considered in his earlier work: see Dworkin (n 131).

[252] Dworkin (n 91).

[253] ibid 166.

[254] See Dworkin (n 4).

put simply, a *book-length summation* of Dworkin's work across *every* field he has traversed (including law, political theory, philosophy, literature, science, psychiatry, psychology and art). The central ('hedgehogian') thread is *philosophy* in general and 'the unity of value' in particular.[255] The title of the book itself is, of course, based on that world-famous essay on Leo Tolstoy's view of history by Professor Isaiah Berlin, who (in turn) drew his inspiration (and title of his essay) from a line from the fragments of the Greek poet Archilochus, which states: 'The fox knows many things, but the hedgehog knows one big thing.'[256]

For the purposes of the present chapter, however, we need only refer to those parts of *Justice for Hedgehogs* that relate to Dworkin's theory of *adjudication*. It will be seen that his views in this book are consistent (and even, I would suggest, in perfect alignment) with many of his ideas stated in his earlier books (viz, *Taking Rights Seriously*, *A Matter of Principle* and *Law's Empire*). However, before proceeding to consider them, it would be appropriate – particularly in view of the title of the book itself – to consider Dworkin's concept of the *hedgehog*. It is in fact related to the issue of *theoretical frameworks*, which I dealt with in an earlier chapter.[257] As we shall see, I respectfully differ from Dworkin in this particular regard. For the reasons set out in the next section of this chapter, I argue that we should be *neither* hedgehogs *nor* foxes – but *eagles* instead.

Neither Hedgehogs nor Foxes, but Eagles instead

As just mentioned, I would respectfully *differ from* Dworkin inasmuch as I think that a lawyer or judge should be *neither a hedgehog nor a fox*. These two extremes do not capture the *balance* that is required in the actual *practice* of adjudication. The lawyer and (especially) the judge should, in my view, be *an eagle* instead. Let me elaborate.

A hedgehog is guided by an overriding or overarching framework (in the case of Dworkin, this is philosophy). In contrast, a fox is concerned with specifics. With respect, the former risks staying at too high a level of abstraction. This is particularly undesirable when dealing with *actual* cases where the *relevant facts* are an integral part of the entire (and indivisible) canvas of the case concerned (indeed,

[255] ibid ch 1, entitled 'Baedeker'. 'Baedeker' refers to 'any of the various travel guidebooks published by the firm founded by the German Karl *Baedeker* (d. 1859)': see *The Concise Oxford Dictionary* (Oxford, Clarendon Press, 1990) 80. Indeed, in this particular chapter, Dworkin summarises the various themes in the book itself. And by way of an advance summary prior to the actual publication of the book itself, see R Dworkin, 'Keynote Address: *Justice for Hedgehogs*' (2010) 90 *Boston University Law Review* 469. Reference may also be made to Guest (n 63) ch 9, entitled 'Justice for Hedgehogs' as well as J Raz, 'A Hedgehog's Unity of Value' in ch 1 of W Waluchow and S Sciaraffa (eds), *The Legacy of Ronald Dworkin* (Oxford, Oxford University Press, 2016). And, as one learned author observed of the title of this book, '[p]erhaps *Values for Hedgehogs* might have been more appropriate': see S Steel, 'Book Review of *Justice for Hedgehogs*' (2012) 128 *LQR* 167, 169. In a similar vein, it has also been observed by yet another learned author thus: 'Truth in advertising first: despite the title, this isn't centrally a book about justice. It's a book about the realm of value – *all* of that realm.': see D Herzog, 'Cute Prickly Critter with Presbyopia' (2012) 110 *Michigan Law Review* 953, 953 (emphasis in the original text).

[256] See I Berlin, *The Hedgehog and the Fox – An Essay on Tolstoy's View of History*, 2nd edn (London, W&N Essentials, 2013) 1. See also Dworkin (n 255) 1–2.

[257] See ch 3 in this volume.

this is the situation even when the case is being heard on appeal).[258] Whilst a hedgehog has the advantage of being able to avoid missing the wood for the trees, he or she might nevertheless miss the trees that are relevant to the resolution of a case (whether it relates to one or more *specific* rules or principles of law and/or (as is more common where the applicable law is well-settled) findings of fact).

In *contrast*, a fox who is *overly* preoccupied with the *specifics* (whether of law and/or fact) risks missing the larger picture – unlike the hedgehog, he or she might indeed miss the wood for the trees.

The perspectives of *both* the hedgehog *and* the fox are of *equal* importance. The *general or overall* perspective pertaining to the legal as well as factual 'terrain' of a particular case (ie, the perspective of the *hedgehog*) is important in assisting the court in knowing which direction it ought to take and to avoid 'wandering off' into unnecessary as well as unhelpful 'alleyways' or 'side streets', so to speak. The existence of *an overall framework* assists the court in *channelling its efforts and energy in the correct direction*.

On the other hand, the *specific* perspective pertaining to the *actual legal as well as factual conditions on 'the ground'*, so to speak (ie, the perspective of the *fox*), is *equally* important in ensuring that the court deals with *the case itself*, and *avoids* being mired in *abstractions* that are more appropriately within the province of *the jurist* (who, *ex hypothesi*) does *not* need to concern himself or herself with *specific* facts as well as the accompanying decision of *actual cases*. They are concerned with what I had, in an earlier chapter,[259] termed *metaphysical* theories (which, by their very nature, are controversial and would be 'pitted against' each other). In short, the jurist is the quintessential 'hedgehog'. *However*, if a court focuses only (or mainly) on the specifics without having an appropriate *general* view of the legal and factual 'terrain' which the dispute between the parties occupies, he or she may mischaracterise (or even misunderstand) the case itself. Hence, for example, I often ask counsel for the parties relatively early on at the hearing what their 'case theory' is. This assists the court in ascertaining what the *general or overall* perspective is. However, I also often ask counsel for the parties what *specific* law and/or facts *support* their 'case theory'.

If, however, one is to be *neither* a hedgehog *nor* a fox, what is one to be? In point of fact, lawyers and judges are performing the functions of *both*, whether they realise it or not. However, unless we have no alternative to inventing an entirely new (and necessarily mythical) creature that has the characteristics of both a hedgehog and a fox, we should look for an answer that is closer to home, so to speak, and therefore both useful as well as relatable.

[258] The main difference being that appellate courts are extremely reluctant (for good reason as it did not observe and process the relevant evidence at trial) to overturn findings of fact at first instance on appeal. In order for them to do so, the findings of fact must (as the traditional rubric goes) be against the weight of the evidence (in extreme cases, the findings of fact might even be held to be perverse (although this is, in my experience at least, rarely the situation)).

[259] See ch 3 in this volume.

My answer is simple: be an *eagle*. An eagle soars high above the ground[260] and, with its *perfect eyesight*, is able to take in the entire – and *general* – terrain. But that is not all that it accomplishes. After all, an eagle needs to find food as well. And so it also *swoops down* once it has surveyed (again with its perfect eyesight) the *specific (and relevant) aspects on the ground (in particular, its prey).*

I liken the task of the lawyer and (especially) the judge to that of the eagle. *Both* the general perspective (of the hedgehog) *and* the specific perspective (of the fox) are important. It is also useful to note that these perspectives are *not* to be applied in a *mechanistic* fashion. Indeed, given the complexity of life generally and legal practice as well as adjudication in particular, these perspectives are likely to *interact* in actual practice. When a particular perspective is to be deployed, so to speak, it depends very much on the manner in which the actual case proceeds. Looked at in this light, the following observations by a famous historian are apposite:[261]

> There is something about the advancing movement of historical scholarship that induces this periodic absorption of creative minds in technical problem –solving – *an alternating dipping and soaring motion of the mind as it drops down to scrutinize puzzling, tangled details, then struggles, not always successfully, to rise again to view the landscape whole. Perhaps that is the way historical understanding must grow.* But, whether or not that is so, large areas of history, including some of the most intensively cultivated, have become shapeless, and scholarship is heavily concentrated on unconnected technical problems. Narratives that once gave meaning to the details have been undermined and discredited with the advance of technical scholarship, and no new narrative structures have been constructed to replace the old.

There is much wisdom in the words just quoted, and although they apply to historical scholarship, it is submitted that they apply equally to the process of adjudication. Professor Bailyn has, perhaps, captured a more realistic picture, so to speak, in the words just quoted. We aspire to be 'eagles', but we are also constrained by our own limitations. In the circumstances, we can only do the best we can with whatever materials we have. The lesson, however, is both clear as it is valuable: we must not lose the wood for the trees and must tend to the trees when it is necessary in order that the wood not be depleted or even lost. We do this by what I have termed an '*interactive*' process[262] – a point to which I have also just alluded to above. It is admittedly, rather 'hazy', but it furnishes us with a *balanced* perspective of both overall structure as well as the specific details within that structure. Only then, I believe, will courts and judges be able to arrive at a just and fair result in the case at hand. This is, of course, easier said than done. However, it is precisely in the 'doing' that the justice that we aspire towards is, in fact, attained.

I now turn to the substantive aspects of *Justice for Hedgehogs* that bear directly on the issue of adjudication.

[260] Often with the aid of the prevailing air currents.

[261] See B Bailyn, 'The Challenge of Modern Historiography' (1982) 87 *American Historical Review* 1, 7 (emphasis added).

[262] See generally ABL Phang, *The Development of Singapore Law – Historical and Socio-Legal Perspectives* (Singapore, Butterworths, 1990) 8–13.

Objectivity and Truth

Dworkin's views on objectivity and truth in *Justice for Hedgehogs* mirrors – in substance at least – his earlier views on the same. They are contained in Part One of the book,[263] and are contained in, essentially, four (related) chapters.[264]

Dworkin's main distinction is one that has already been considered in some detail above – that between external skepticism on the one hand and internal skepticism on the other.[265] In *Justice for Hedgehogs*, he also describes the former as 'Archimedian skepticism'.[266] It is also analysed in a separate chapter,[267] as is internal skepticism.[268]

As already alluded to earlier in this chapter, Dworkin refutes 'external skepticism'. In his view, '[a]ny theory about what makes a moral conviction true or what are good reasons for accepting it must be itself a moral theory and therefore must include a moral premise or presupposition'.[269] Indeed, 'moral skeptcism is itself a moral position' and that '[i]f it is true, then external skepticism defeats itself'.[270] Indeed, Dworkin skilfully and persuasively demonstrates that external skepticism *cannot help but* take *a moral stand or position*, no matter how cleverly it attempts (by way of language) to assert otherwise.[271] As he very perceptively puts it:[272]

> The message … seems clear. When you make a statement about what moral responsibilities people have, you are declaring how things stand – morally speaking. There is no way out of or around the independence of value.

[263] Entitled 'Independence'. This is a reference to 'the independence of value': Dworkin (n 4) 44. See also below, n 272.

[264] See Dworkin (n 4) ch 2, entitled 'Truth in Morals'; ch 3, entitled 'External Skepticism'; ch 4, entitled 'Morals and Causes'; and ch 5, entitled 'Internal Skepticism'. For ease as well as simplicity of reference, I will refer to the relevant pagination in *Justice for Hedgehogs* itself. See also generally Guest (n 63) ch 7, entitled 'Objectivity in Law and Morality'.

[265] See generally the text to nn 139, 166–170 and 225–226, above. See also Dworkin (n 4) 30–32. Reference may also be made to Guest (n 63) 132–139.

[266] Which is described as 'skepticism that denies any basis for itself in morality or ethics': see Dworkin (n 4) 25; see also ibid 31, 82 and 86. In contrast, 'internal skepticism' 'claims to reach moral conclusions from more general assumptions that are themselves moral in character and subject matter' and 'is a first-order, substantive moral judgment': ibid 30 and 31. And insofar as the former (external skepticism) is concerned, 'Archimedes calculated he could lift the Earth if he were sufficiently *external* to it and had both a long pole and a fulcrum': see Guest (n 63) 133 (emphasis added).

[267] Dworkin (n 4) ch 3, entitled 'External Skepticism'. See also above, n 264. Dworkin sub-divides 'external skeptics' into 'error skeptics' and 'status skeptics', respectively, with the former being more extreme as they 'hold that all moral judgments are false', whereas the latter do not, unlike the former, hold the view that morality is a 'misconceived enterprise' but, instead, are of the view that it is 'a misunderstood enterprise': ibid 32. Looked at in this light, 'internal skeptics' are '*partial* error skeptics': ibid 33 (emphasis added).

[268] Dworkin (n 4) ch 5, entitled 'Internal Skepticism'. See also above, n 264.

[269] ibid 38.

[270] ibid 40.

[271] See generally ibid 42–44. And this applies, logically, to all forms of 'external skepticism' (briefly set out at n 267, above). Put simply, no external skeptic can escape the clear fact that he or she is taking a *moral* stand or position, *regardless* of the content (and even inventiveness) of the stand or position taken. Hence, even Professor John Rawls's ingenious device of the 'original position' (which Dworkin describes as 'constructivism') cannot disengage itself from a background moral theory: see generally ibid 63–66.

[272] ibid 44. See also Guest (n 63) 1–2.

As we have already seen (also earlier in this chapter and, indeed, in an earlier one[273]), Dworkin's analysis and arguments are in fact rooted in clear *logic*, if nothing else. Put simply, external skeptics engage in self-contradiction if they desire us to take *their* arguments seriously (which, in turn, entails the accompanying claim that those arguments themselves have *moral value* (and are therefore *universalisable*)). Dworkin also argues – correctly, in my view – that recourse to various forms of 'causal' argument is a 'red herring'.[274]

Of importance, too, is a distinction which was also present in Dworkin's earlier writings and that we have also touched upon in both this chapter and an earlier one:[275] that between indeterminacy on the one hand and uncertainty on the other.[276] I wholly agree with Dworkin that the former ought not to be conflated with the latter. And insofar as the latter is concerned, we must (in Dworkin's view) do the best that we can:[277]

> Absolute confidence or clarity is the privilege of fools and fanatics. The rest of us must do the best we can: we must choose among all the substantive views on offer by asking which strikes us, after reflection and due thought, as more plausible than the others. And if none does, we must then settle for the true default view, which is not indeterminacy but uncertainty.

At this point, it would be appropriate to set out Dworkin's views in *Justice for Hedgehogs* with regard to the key concept in his theory of adjudication – that of *interpretation*.

Law, Adjudication and Interpretation

As we have seen, Dworkin's theory of adjudication is inextricably connected with his vision of law and the process of interpretation. This is evident in all of his writings, culminating in his first book-length treatment of law and adjudication in *Law's Empire*.[278] As already alluded to above, such treatment is consistent with his views in *Justice for Hedgehogs*. To that extent, I can be brief. To this end, an excellent starting point is Dworkin's own summary of *the law* in the very first chapter of *Justice for Hedgehogs*.[279] In his words:[280]

> I describe a conception of law that takes it to be not a rival system of rules that might conflict with morality but *as itself a branch of morality*. It is necessary, to make that suggestion plausible, to emphasize what might be called *procedural justice*, the morality

[273] See ch 3 in this volume.

[274] See generally Dworkin (n 4) ch 4, entitled 'Morals and Causes'. In this chapter, Dworkin discusses the 'causal impact hypothesis' and the 'causal dependence hypothesis'. Without delving into the intricacies of each, it is nevertheless significant to note that a focus on cause relates to the 'explanation' of a moral conviction as a matter of *fact*, whereas the *justification* of a moral conviction is what is crucial (and which is *normative* in nature (see also ch 2 in this volume)): ibid 79–80.

[275] See ch 3 in this volume.

[276] See generally Dworkin (n 4) 90–96.

[277] ibid 95–96.

[278] Dworkin (n 140).

[279] Dworkin (n 255). This is a summary of ch 19, entitled 'Law'.

[280] ibid 5 (emphasis added).

> of fair governance as well as just outcome. It is also necessary to understand morality in general as having a tree structure: law is a branch of political morality, which is itself a branch of a more general personal morality, which is in turn a branch of a yet more general theory of what it is to live well. … I mean to submit each of the political concepts I describe to the test of conviction.

I have highlighted the reference to 'procedural justice' in the above quotation because, as I have already shown[281] (and will, indeed, endeavour to show[282]), the best way forward is really *procedural* in nature, although both the procedural and substantive do *interact* with each other.

However, as we have also already noted in the present chapter, Dworkin admits that there may indeed be rival theories of adjudication. This is because there may be genuine disagreements as to what a concept means even though that concept is agreed upon and therefore held in common. As he puts it in the same (first) chapter:[283]

> We must ask: When do people *share a concept* so that their agreements and disagreements are *genuine*? We *share* some *concepts because we agree*, except in cases we all regard as borderline, *about what criteria to use in identifying examples.*

Indeed, Dworkin refers to such concepts as '*interpretive* concepts'.[284] And they are '[shared] … because we share social practices and experiences in which these concepts figure'.[285] He proceeds to observe that '[w]e take the concepts to describe values, but we disagree, sometimes to a marked degree, about what these values are and how they should be expressed'.[286] Importantly, he then adds thus:[287]

> We disagree because we '*interpret*' the practices we '*share*' rather '*differently*': we hold somewhat different theories about '*which values best justify*' what we accept as central or paradigm features of that practice. That structure makes our conceptual disagreements … '*genuine*'. It also makes them *value* disagreements rather than disagreements of fact or disagreements about dictionary or standard meanings.

And insofar as the concept of *interpretation* is concerned, Dworkin states that:[288]

> I suggest a *value-based* general theory. Interpreters have critical responsibilities, and the best interpretation of a law or a poem or an epoch is the interpretation that *best realizes* those responsibilities on that occasion.

These observations by Dworkin in the very first chapter of *Justice for Hedgehogs* are valuable in a number of ways.

First, there is value in what is *not* expressly stated. Let me elaborate. I have, in fact, already alluded to this point in earlier parts of the present chapter of this

[281] See ch 3 in this volume.
[282] See ch 10 in this volume.
[283] Dworkin (n 255) 6 (emphasis added).
[284] ibid (emphasis in the original text).
[285] ibid.
[286] ibid.
[287] ibid 6–7 (emphasis in italics in the original text; emphasis added in quoted italics).
[288] ibid 7 (emphasis added).

book. It is that Professor WB Gallie's idea of 'essentially contested concepts'[289] is *absolutely crucial* to Dworkin's entire argument. Indeed, his references to shared *concepts* and the accompanying (albeit *rival*) *conceptions* of the respective concept track directly Gallie's own argument in his seminal essay.[290] However, apart from a reference to Gallie's essay in his very earliest work,[291] there does not appear to be any (at least express) reference to that work thereafter (including *Justice for Hedgehogs*). Yet, Gallie's idea of 'essentially contested concepts' is *foundational* to Dworkin's fundamental premise that there *can* be *a right answer* even in the midst of *rival theories* because the advocates of these rival theories themselves (by *sharing in and agreeing with the concept concerned and by advocating their own theory as the answer) must necessarily be working on the premise that there is a right answer* (which they claim is what *they* are advocating). The reader will also have noticed that all this is also closely related to as well as inextricably connected with Dworkin's concept of objectivity and truth, which we looked at briefly in the preceding section of this chapter.

Second (and as a closely related point), the advocates of rival theories are therefore not – as Dworkin observes – being involved in an incoherent enterprise. On the contrary (and this is Dworkin's unique contribution to our understanding in this sphere), they are involved in *the enterprise of interpretation*. What we, the readers, are faced with are *rival* interpretations – each of which endeavours or attempts to persuade us by (and again, as Dworkin observes) *the inherent power within those arguments* themselves.

Third (and, again, as a closely related point), this is what I suggest – viewed admittedly at a *very general level – actually takes place in a court of law, in the actual process of adjudication itself*. What *remains* to be seen is whether the various *elements* in the Dworkinian theory of adjudication *also* reflect what actually takes place in *practice*. This last-mentioned issue will be the subject of chapter eight of this book as I evaluate these various elements by reference to *actual decided cases* as well.

To turn to Dworkin's views in relation to *interpretation* in *Justice for Hedgehogs* proper, it is important to reiterate that they are *entirely consistent with* the views he proffered in his earlier writings. What is interesting is Dworkin's elaboration in the present book of the more *general philosophical underpinnings* of the concept of interpretation itself.[292]

[289] Gallie (n 29).

[290] ibid.

[291] See above, n 29. Professor Guest acknowledges the importance of Professor Gallie's idea of 'essentially contested concepts' but, with respect, does not confer on it the prominence it truly deserves in Dworkin's theory of adjudication (see Guest (n 63) 73–74; reference may also be made to ibid 77–78 and 87). Curiously the same error resulting in the transposition of the year in the citation of Professor Gallie's essay which Dworkin made is also replicated by Professor Guest (see ibid 255, n 17 as well as above, n 29).

[292] See generally Part Two, entitled 'Interpretation', comprising ch 6, entitled 'Moral Responsibility'; ch 7, entitled 'Interpretation in General'; and ch 8, entitled 'Conceptual Interpretation'. For ease of reference, specific references hereafter will be to the actual pages in the book itself.

First, Dworkin endorses 'Hume's Guillotine', which I dealt with in an earlier chapter[293] and which holds that one cannot derive a normative proposition from a purely factual premise.[294] This is not surprising, as it is entirely consistent with Dworkin's view that *justificatory* reasons must be proffered in support of each theory (here, of adjudication).[295] However, it is then also likely the case that competing moral propositions will result in controversy – which then underscores, yet again, the importance of deploying Professor Gallie's idea of 'essentially contested concepts'[296] (which, as we have seen, is precisely what Dworkin does[297]).

Second (and following from the preceding point), Dworkin does indeed acknowledge that there will be no knock-down arguments in the sphere of moral argument. Indeed, in his view, '[m]oral responsibility is *never complete: we are constantly reinterpreting our concepts as we use them*'.[298] And as he candidly puts it, 'I cannot *demonstrate* to him [the person holding a contrary moral argument] that my opinions are true and his false'.[299] And that is why Dworkin states that one must have 'acted *responsibly* in reaching [one's] opinions'.[300] And, in his view, 'the *nerve of responsibility* is *integrity* and … the epistemology of a morally *responsible* person is *interpretive*'.[301] Indeed, the requirement of *responsibility* is so important as a prerequisite to interpretation that Dworkin devotes a whole chapter to it.[302] What is also interesting is that he appears to focus (at least at this particular juncture) on the issue of 'fit'[303] – a dimension in his earlier writings that we have referred to earlier in this chapter. Most importantly to the present author, though, is not only Dworkin's acknowledgment that there are no knock-down arguments in the context of moral argument but also the fact that his argument is more *methodological* (as opposed to *metaphysical*) in nature; in his words:[304]

[293] See ch 2 in this volume. See also Guest (n 63) vii, where the learned author states thus: 'In particular, I hope readers will appreciate the significance in *Justice for Hedgehogs* of his clear endorsement of the Humean principle separating the empirical world from that of value. In a way, all else, especially concerning law, follows.' See also, by the same author, 'The Unity and Objectivity of Value' (2011) 25 *Ethics & International Affairs* 463, 469 as well as 'Unity and Sense in Ronald Dworkin's Theory of Law' [2013] *Law of Ukraine Legal Journal* 273, 274. Reference may also be made to WB Allen, 'Book Review of *Justice for Hedgehogs*' (2012) 1 *American Political Thought* 337, 338 and 339.

[294] Dworkin (n 4) 99. See also ibid 122.

[295] As Dworkin puts it, 'When a value judgment is true, there must be a *reason* why it is true. It can't be *just* true.': ibid 114 (emphasis in the original text).

[296] Gallie (n 29).

[297] See, eg, the text to nn 28–29, 104–108, 162–164 and 224, above as well as the text to nn 13–14 in the previous chapter (ch 6) in this volume.

[298] Dworkin (n 4) 119 (emphasis added).

[299] ibid 100 (emphasis in the original text). In a similar vein, Dworkin observes that the interpretive project 'seems impossible wholly to succeed': ibid 101.

[300] ibid 100 (emphasis added).

[301] ibid 101 (emphasis added).

[302] See ch 6, entitled 'Moral Responsibility'. See also n 292, above.

[303] Dworkin (n 4) 120–121.

[304] ibid 121 (emphasis added).

> I intend no kind of relativism. I do not suggest that a moral opinion is true only for those who think it true. *I mean to describe method, not metaphysics: how you must proceed* if truth is your agenda. Two people who both reason *responsibly and find conviction* in what they believe will reach different conclusions about what is right and wrong. But they will share the belief that there is a getting it right and a getting it wrong about what is right and wrong. … [T]here is *no political safe harbor in the neighborhood.* We must each believe what we *responsibly* believe. We are all out on some limb, even if it is not the same limb.

It is important to keep our present focus by noting, once again, that this point centres on the need for *responsibility*. However, Dworkin's reference to '*method, not metaphysics*' in the above quotation is, in my view, of *the highest significance* insofar as the thesis in the present book is concerned, as I argue (particularly in the final chapter[305]) that the main focus should be on judging in good faith via objective procedure (as opposed to a substantive metaphysical theory), although that focus on procedure (including method) does impact (and is, in turn, impacted by) substance (including substantively just outcomes) in what (for want of a better term) is an interactional process. I have strayed somewhat from this particular point (of the need for responsibility) simply because Dworkin has – *whether intentionally or unwittingly* – espoused a view that is indeed *consistent with the thesis in the present book.*

Third, Dworkin makes the perhaps obvious but nevertheless vital point that 'there is no such thing as interpreting in general, that is, interpreting in the abstract rather than in some particular genre'.[306] Indeed, interpretation is – and must be – *contextual.*

Fourth, he reiterates a point that has already been made in his earlier writings (and which is nevertheless of fundamental importance not only to his theory but also to mine[307]) – that there is a clear (and critical) difference between uncertainty on the one hand and indeterminacy on the other.[308] Dworkin accepts the former, albeit not the latter. In my view, this is a realistic approach, which Dworkin captures in the following words:[309]

> A successful theory of interpretation must achieve a tenuous balance. It must account for the sense and possibility of truth in interpretation, but it must also account for the ineffability of that truth and the familiar, irresolvable clash of opinion about where it lies.

[305] See ch 10 in this volume. *Cf* also Allan (n 46) 285 (albeit with a narrower focus on the specific principles of natural justice).

[306] Dworkin (n 4) 124.

[307] See, especially, ch 10 in this volume.

[308] Dworkin (n 4) 127. See also ibid 118 and 148. See, further, ibid 156 (emphasis added) ('Still, for all that, we are left only with uncertainty, not nihilism. … So – yet again – everything depends in the end what you actually and responsibly think. Not because your thinking makes it right, but because, in thinking it right, you think it *right*.').

[309] ibid 130.

Fifth, as Dworkin puts it, '[w]e can interpret as we do only because there are *practices or traditions of interpretation* we can join'.[310] In a similar vein, he observes that '[w]e share an interpretive concept when our collective behavior in using that concept is best explained by taking its correct use to depend on the best justification of the role it plays for us'.[311] Correlatively, this results (in turn) in interpretive schools; as Dworkin puts it, '[a]n interpretive school is a shared interpretation of the point of the larger practice a group of interpreters take themselves to have joined'.[312]

Sixth, the abovementioned practices are '*truth*-seeking' and therefore entail *responsibility*[313] on the part of all concerned.[314] As Dworkin puts it, 'We can seek truth about morality only by pursuing coherence endorsed by conviction.'[315]

Seventh, there are different types of interpretation – collaborative, explanatory, and conceptual interpretation, respectively.[316] For example (and germane for the purposes of the present book), '[l]aw is … *collaborative*: a judge takes himself to aim at the same goal – justice – as the statesmen who made the laws he interprets' and that '[e]ven when he sees his role as entirely subordinate to theirs, the subordination is, in his view, itself justified by the overall goal of justice he *shares* with them'.[317] On the other hand, explanatory interpretation does not presuppose collaboration, whilst in conceptual interpretation, 'the interpreter seeks the meaning of a concept, like justice or truth, that has been created and recreated not by single authors but the community whose concept it is, a community that includes the interpreter as a creator as well'.[318] Not surprisingly, conceptual interpretation in this last-mentioned manner is also important in the context of Dworkin's theory of adjudication, as we witnessed particularly in his discourse in *Law's Empire*, as discussed briefly earlier in the present chapter.[319] Indeed, the concept of conceptual interpretation generally has been assigned an entire separate chapter by Dworkin himself.[320]

Eighth, there are *different ways* in which interpretations *interact*.[321] Each interpretation could be *independent*. Alternatively, interpretations could *complement* each other. Finally, interpretations could *compete* with each other. As Dworkin perceptively points out, the discipline of law especially demonstrates the last-mentioned category; as he puts it, we should '[c]ompare the deep conflicts among

[310] ibid (emphasis added).
[311] ibid 158.
[312] ibid 141.
[313] See the second point, above.
[314] Dworkin (n 4) 131 (emphasis added).
[315] ibid 120.
[316] See generally ibid 134–139.
[317] ibid 136 (emphasis added).
[318] ibid.
[319] See, eg, the text to n 198, above.
[320] See ch 8, entitled 'Conceptual Interpretation'. See also above, n 292.
[321] See generally Dworkin (n 4) 139–144.

schools of interpretation in law'.[322] However, as with reality generally, there may be *overlaps* even within a particular discipline. Hence, for example, insofar as the discipline of law is concerned, explanatory interpretation and even complementary interpretation could exist despite the appearance of competitive interpretation.[323]

Ninth, Dworkin refers to a point closely related to the second point in response to authors such as Stanley Fish[324] who adopt what is essentially external skepticism. As we have already noted earlier in the present chapter, Dworkin rejects external skepticism although he is prepared to accept internal skepticism.[325] However, it is clear, in his view, that the search is, in the final analysis, for the truth (see the fourth point above) and an objectively correct answer (and not, as external skeptics would have us 'believe', that everything is relative and each answer has as much status as the other). Indeed, as he pointedly as well as perceptively puts it, 'a judge who sends someone to jail on an interpretation of the law he believes no better than, but only different from, rival interpretations *should be jailed himself*!'[326]

[322] ibid 142. See also generally ibid 142–144.

[323] Dworkin utilises the example of the Critical Legal Studies movement to illustrate this particular point: see ibid 143–144. See also J Waldron, 'Did Dworkin Ever Answer the Crits?' in ch 7 of Hershovitz (n 46).

[324] Not surprisingly, Professor Fish adopts a postmodernist and deconstructionist approach towards the law. Whilst he does adopt the concept of an 'interpretive community', the actual process of interpretation itself is freewheeling. However (and this is consistent with Dworkin's critique of external skepticism), if we accept Fish's concept of external skepticism, then, as one learned author observes (see L Kaplan, 'Without Foundation: Stanley Fish and the Legal Academy' (1991) 16 *Law and Social Inquiry* 593, 612):

> Perhaps the most biting criticism of Fish is that if we take him on his own word, what he has to preach about continuing or transforming practice is irrelevant; we will do what we believe, we can do nothing else.

I would also observe that Fish's endorsement of an 'interpretive community' (and, hence, the introduction of some measure of (objective) consensus) appears to stand in contradiction to his endorsement of subjective views within that community. Put simply, as a learned author puts it, Fish appears to '[want] it both ways' (see Sadowski (n 121) 1125 (who also notes (at 1126) that Fish 'never clearly defines what he means by interpretive community, how its members are identified, and how an interpretive community derives any power'). One explanation is that Fish is arguing for objective consensus in relation to (*only*) the *forms* of legal argumentation. If so, however, this would be looking at mere form – as opposed to (*subjective*) substance. Again, put simply, the bottom-line of Fish's approach would be that 'anything goes' with regard to interpretation (which brings us back, full circle, to external skepticism (and the arguments (including Dworkin's arguments) against it)).

For Fish's critique of Dworkin, reference may be made to S Fish, 'Working on the Chain Gang: Interpretation in Law and Literature' (1982) 60 *Texas Law Review* 551 and, by the same author, 'Wrong Again' (1983) 62 *Texas Law Review* 299 as well as 'Still Wrong After All These Years' (1987) 6 *Law and Philosophy* 401. It might be apposite to point out that Dworkin does not take issue with Fish with regard to the *fact* of disagreement amongst judges on a given legal issue (which is reiterated once again by Fish in 'Fish v. Fiss' (1984) 5 *Mississippi College Law Review* 1). Dworkin's point, however, is that there is nevertheless a correct answer to that legal issue and that it is not (as Fish argues) all a subjective legal free-for-all (relying, in my view, heavily on Professor Gallie's idea of 'essentially contested concepts' (see Gallie (n 29)). See also generally T Bustamante and M Martin, *New Essays on the Fish-Dworkin Debate* (Oxford, Hart Publishing, 2023).

[325] See generally Dworkin (n 4) 145–147.

[326] ibid 151 (emphasis added).

Tenth, Dworkin reiterates a point made in his earlier writings in relation to the author's intention in the context of legal as well as literary interpretation:[327]

> Legal interpretation is not dominated by the actual mental states of legislators and other officials because the best understanding of the purpose of interpreting statutes and other legal data makes irrelevant most of what those officials actually think or intend. The role of an author's intention is controversial in the interpretation of literature, and the importance that critics attach to that intention fluctuates, because it is controversial among critics how far the value of a work of art depends on an author's inspiration and its realization in the work.

Eleventh, Dworkin is of the view that interpretation is 'dramatically different' from science[328] inasmuch as insofar as the former is concerned, '*justifying* purpose is at the heart of success'.[329] In contrast, science, in his view, operates as a fact without us having to justify how something in its context operates.[330] On the other hand, 'literary critics or constitutional lawyers whose values are strikingly different in some pertinent respect are likely to disagree across a very broad area of interpretive convictions'.[331] With respect, whilst I agree with Dworkin that there is almost always controversy in interpretation that requires (in turn) justification, he takes too sanguine a view of science. As the field of quantum mechanics, for example, has demonstrated, there is much more uncertainty in science than he assumes, and, looked at in that light, perhaps justification is also required (in some scientific fields at least) in order to enable us to even understand (in an even basic manner) the very *nature* of that particular topic itself. That having been said, this does not detract in any way from the need – as Dworkin argues – for justification in the context of interpretation.

Following up on one aspect of the seventh point above (viz, conceptual interpretation), Dworkin has considered it so important as to devote an entire chapter in *Justice for Hedgehogs* to it – conceptual interpretation.[332] In particular, he is concerned with moral reasoning; as Dworkin puts it:[333]

> Moral reasoning is interpretation, but it is not collaborative or explanator interpretation. It belongs to the third type I distinguished in the last chapter:[334] conceptual interpretation.

Conceptual interpretation itself is complex. Dworkin points, for example, to the fact that 'moral concepts have different degrees of thickness, and each has different degrees in different contexts'.[335] What *is* clear, however, is that there will almost

[327] ibid 149–150.
[328] See generally ibid 152–156.
[329] ibid 153 (emphasis added).
[330] See ibid 155, where Dworkin refers to the 'linearity of science'. See also ibid 122.
[331] ibid 155.
[332] See ch 8, entitled (not surprisingly) 'Conceptual Interpretation'. See also above, nn 292 and 320.
[333] Dworkin (n 4) 157.
[334] Viz, ch 7, entitled 'Interpretation in General'. See also above, n 292.
[335] Dworkin (n 4) 182.

invariably be different views – particularly when we look at the different theories 'in action', so to speak (see, especially, the second point above). Indeed, this is evident as Dworkin masterfully examines how Plato and Aristotle constructed their respective moral and political theories.[336] The analysis is succinct yet nuanced. Most importantly, however, Dworkin utilises the word '*conception*' (or its plural form '*conceptions*') a total of *ten times* within just *five* pages of *Justice for Hedgehogs*. This demonstrates, once again, *the vital importance of Professor Gallie's idea of 'essentially contested concepts'*[337] *in Dworkinian theory*.

In a specific chapter dedicated to the law,[338] Dworkin shows how his 'jurisprudential views … take their place within the integrated scheme of value this book[339] attempts'.[340] His task, as he tells us, is '*not* to summarize my jurisprudential views' although he has 'written more about law than other parts of political morality'.[341] What this means is that the details – as well as critique – of his theory of adjudication in his earlier writings (culminating in *Law's Empire*), which have been described earlier in this chapter remain and need not be elaborated upon. Indeed, it is suggested that the eleven points just referred to in relation to interpretation in *general* are *wholly consistent* with the details of his theory of adjudication in his earlier writings.

In this particular chapter of *Justice for Hedgehogs*, Dworkin concentrates, instead, on what he terms 'the hottest of the chestnuts burning lawyers' fingers for centuries'[342] – 'What is the relation between law and morals?'[343] To this end, he compares and contrasts 'legal positivism' on the one hand and 'interpretivism' on the other.[344] As we have already seen in an earlier chapter,[345] legal positivism posits a separation between law on the one hand and morality on the other. Put simply, it holds that there is no *necessary* connection as such between law and morality. In *contrast*, interpretivism (which Dworkin advocates) 'denies that law and morals are wholly independent systems' and 'argues that law includes not only the specific rules enacted in accordance with the community's accepted practices but also the *principles* that provide the best *moral justification* for *those* enacted *rules*'.[346] Importantly, Dworkin proceeds to observe thus:[347]

> The law *then also includes* the rules that *follow from* those *justifying principles*, even though those further rules were never enacted. Interpretivism, in other words, treats

[336] See generally ibid 184–188.
[337] Gallie (n 29).
[338] Ch 19, entitled (simply) 'Law'.
[339] Viz, *Justice for Hedgehogs* (and see Dworkin (n 4)).
[340] Dworkin (n 4) 400.
[341] ibid (emphasis added).
[342] ibid.
[343] ibid.
[344] ibid 401.
[345] See, especially, ch 4 in this volume.
[346] Dworkin (n 4) 402 (emphasis added).
[347] ibid (emphasis added).

> legal reasoning as I have argued in this book we must treat all interpretive reasoning. *It treats the concept of law as an interpretive concept.*

Even more importantly, Dworkin states that '[a]ctually there are *several concepts* of law'.[348] As he puts it, '[p]ositivism and interpretivism are both theories about the correct use of the doctrinal concept'.[349]

It is important, in my view, to pause at this somewhat critical juncture to make two points.

The first is that in this latest book, Dworkin appears to confirm that principles *underlie* rules (see, in particular, the references above to principles *justifying* rules). The reader will recall that this was an issue that I had raised in an earlier chapter in relation to Dworkin's earliest writings.[350] Indeed, if principles underlie rules, then the point I made earlier in that chapter[351] to the effect that if judges can rely upon principles to develop *new* rules to deal with (in particular) hard cases, would they not then have *unfettered* discretion in deciding which principles are applicable in the development of such new rules? In this regard, one must bear in mind the fact that principles – unlike rules – do (in the Dworkinian theory of adjudication) have a dimension of *weight*. Recall also the point I made earlier that it cannot simply be argued without more that the principles themselves constrain the exercise of unfettered discretion because such an argument would – without more – be *circular* in nature.

The second is a point that I have referred to throughout the present chapter. It is, in my view, of the first importance and relates to Dworkin's (critical and fundamental) reliance on Professor Gallie's idea of 'essentially contested concepts'.[352] Hence, legal positivism and interpretivism are different *conceptions* of the *concept* of law.[353]

Dworkin *also* raises what *he claims* is essentially *an entirely new perspective* on the aforementioned debate as to whether or not there is a *necessary* connection between law and morality. Indeed, he states that it was only when he wrote *Justice for Hedgehogs* that he discovered this new perspective.[354] In essence, the traditional debate that asks whether there is a *necessary* connection between law and morality is a *flawed* one. Dworkin terms this debate 'the two-systems picture'[355] of the problem itself. He describes this particular model as a 'dead-end' one.[356] In his view, Dworkin views such a model as having 'created an important distinction

[348] ibid (emphasis added).
[349] ibid.
[350] See the text to nn 31–32 in ch 6 in this volume.
[351] ibid Part II.B.
[352] Gallie (n 29).
[353] See also Dworkin (n 4) 405 (referring to the construction of 'a conception of law' as well as the inevitability of controversy when it is considered as against other theories; and on a further reference to controversy, see ibid 406 as well as the text to nn 364–367, below).
[354] ibid 402.
[355] ibid.
[356] ibid 409. See also ibid 411.

between process and substance: between procedures through which the law is created and the content of the law that is created'.[357]

Instead, he proposes 'a one-system picture'[358] in which 'we now treat law *as a part of political morality*'.[359] As he elaborates:[360]

> A theory of law treats legal rights, but it is nevertheless a political theory because it seeks a normative answer to a normative political question: Under what conditions do people acquire genuine rights and duties that are enforceable on demand in the way described?

Unlike the 'two-systems picture', Dworkin views his 'one-system picture' as one that *integrates* law and (political) morality. There is, presumably, no longer a distinction between process and substance because the judge in question will be concerned with *both* process *and* substance. In my view, this corresponds with and can be correlated with the two dimensions which Dworkin advocates in relation to his theory of adjudication in his earlier writings. As we have seen earlier in this chapter, these two dimensions concern 'fit' and 'substance', respectively.

Consistent with his idea of interpretation in general and his theory of interpretivism in particular, Dworkin acknowledges that both legal positivism and interpretivism are 'rival normative political theories'.[361] And he observes that each had historical analogues as well that corresponded to the *contrast* between *rights* on the one hand and *utilitarianism* on the other; as he succinctly put it:[362]

> Once, in Coke's time, the idea that individuals have rights as trumps over the collective good – natural rights – was very widely accepted. In the nineteenth century a different political morality was dominant. Jeremy Bentham declared natural rights nonsense on stilts, and lawyers of that opinion created the idea of absolute parliamentary sovereignty. Now the wheel is turning again: utilitarianism is giving way once again to a recognition of individual rights, now called human rights, and parliamentary sovereignty is no longer evidently just. The status of Parliament as lawgiver, among the most fundamental of legal issues, has once again become a deep question of political morality. *Law is effectively integrated with morality: lawyers and judges are working political philosophers of a democratic state.*

What, then, are we to make of Dworkin's latest views? It is respectfully suggested that there is no real difference in *substance* between the 'two-systems picture' (which Dworkin rejects) and the 'one-system picture' (which he endorses). They focus on the *same* problem and differ only to the extent to which they endorse different *theories* as to how that problem is to be resolved. Put simply, whether we adopt the 'two-systems picture' or the 'one-system picture', the fundamental

[357] ibid 413.
[358] ibid 405.
[359] ibid (emphasis added).
[360] ibid 406.
[361] ibid 407.
[362] ibid 414 (emphasis added).

issue is still that which was posed by the former: whether or not there is a *necessary* connection between law and morality. Legal positivism proffers a negative response and therefore naturally adopts the 'two-systems picture' since law and morality are, in its view, *separate*. Dworkin disagrees as he adopts an integrated and holistic view of the issue and *does* view law as *necessarily* connected with morality (in particular, political morality).[363] Put simply, the 'two-systems picture' and the 'one-system picture' are merely *two sides of the same coin*. It is, at bottom, simply a question of *perspective*.

The more important issue, in my view, is that of *content*. Put simply once again, *which* theory is *more persuasive*? Is it legal positivism? Or is it interpretivism? Looked at in this light, Dworkin is careful – in *both* his earlier writings *and* in *Justice for Hedgehogs* – in acknowledging that there is *no knockdown argument* in favour of *either*. As he already admits (and we have seen[364]), they are '*rival* normative political theories'.[365] This being the case, it is, as Dworkin would in fact be at pains to emphasise, an issue of *interpretation*. And that brings (in turn) into play Professor Gallie's idea of 'essentially contested concepts'.[366] Both legal positivism and interpretivism are *(rival) conceptions* of the *concept* of *law*.[367] Looked at in this light, the reader will have to choose which he or she prefers, based on the arguments that each rival conception proffers. All this (as I have already suggested) is *entirely consistent with Dworkin's earlier writings*. Indeed, in *Justice for Hedgehogs*, Dworkin returns – *full circle*, as it were – to where he began in *Taking Rights Seriously*.[368] As we have seen, he states as much when contrasting the theory of rights (which he endorses) with that of utilitarianism (which he rejects[369]).[370] And as we have also seen, the earliest iteration of his theory of adjudication was termed 'the *rights* thesis'.[371] Looked at in this light, all the various arguments (in particular, critique) concerning Dworkin's theory made earlier in this chapter and (in fairness) the (especially practical) benefits as well as applications thereof *continue to hold good*. However, before we conclude the present part, it might be appropriate to consider – if only in the briefest of fashions – Dworkin's own concluding chapter to *Justice for Hedgehogs*. It is appropriately characterised as an epilogue.[372]

In *Justice for Hedgehogs*, Dworkin is concerned with *the independence of value*. This is one of the central threads that underlies all the various disciplines to which he devoted his academic life (including law and political theory), and

[363] See above, nn 359 and 362.

[364] See above, n 361.

[365] Dworkin (n 4) 407 (emphasis added). See also above, n 361.

[366] Gallie (n 29).

[367] See also the text to nn 352 and 353, above.

[368] Dworkin (n 3).

[369] And which, not surprisingly, legal positivists such as Professor Hart *endorse*: see, eg, HLA Hart, *Essays on Bentham – Jurisprudence and Political Theory* (Oxford, Oxford University Press, 1982).

[370] See the text to n 362, above.

[371] See the text to nn 11–12, above.

[372] See Dworkin (n 4), entitled 'Epilogue: Dignity Indivisible', 417–423.

this includes the view that, *despite the variety of different views, there is objective truth and, hence, a right answer in the context of morality*. And its consequences, in Dworkin's view, are clear:[373]

> [T]here must be a right answer about the best thing to do, even if that answer is only that nothing is. That is not a trick: it is a way of reminding yourself that skepticism is not a default. Any conviction that nothing matters must be as much the target of your suspicion and doubt – and misplaced hope for external validation – as any more positive conviction. If you do think that nothing matters, remember that that is also a conclusion that other people, who think as hard and long as you, do not accept. There is no escape from the isolation of believing what others do not. Skepticism or nihilism is certainly no escape.

And as he puts it:[374]

> Why shouldn't you simply believe what you then believe? Really *believe* it? … if you have been responsible, you have no reason, pending further reflection, not to believe – fully believe – what you believe.

As we have also seen, uncertainty as to which is the right answer does not entail throwing up our hands in despair because uncertainty is *not* the same as indeterminacy.[375] Indeed, as Dworkin observes, 'uncertainty too, as we saw, assumes that there is truth to be had'.[376]

In *addition* to *independence* of value, Dworkin is also concerned with the '*unity* of value'.[377] This goes to the *content* of 'a much more inclusive *theory of ethics and morality*'.[378] And this entails *living well*; in Dworkin's words, '[s]omeone lives well when he senses and pursues a good life for himself *and* does so *with dignity*: with respect for the importance of other peoples lives and for their ethical responsibility as well as his own'.[379] However, he is careful to note that '[t]he two ethical ideals – living well and having a good life – are different'.[380] For example, therefore, 'people who live and die in great poverty can nevertheless live well'.[381] Nevertheless, as Dworkin correctly points out, 'we must each do what we can to make our own life as good as it could have been' and that '[y]ou live badly if you do not try hard enough to make your life good'.[382] In this regard we must 'take personal *responsibility*' for the choices we make.[383] We must also '*reflect* on what

[373] ibid 418.
[374] ibid 419 (emphasis in the original text).
[375] See also the text to nn 84–85, 275–277 and 307–309, above.
[376] Dworkin (n 4) 419.
[377] ibid (emphasis added).
[378] ibid (emphasis added).
[379] ibid (emphasis added).
[380] ibid.
[381] ibid 420.
[382] ibid.
[383] ibid (emphasis added).

living well means' for us in our respective situations.[384] It is only by doing so that we give ourselves 'more *dignity*'.[385] Dworkin also states that when we 'come to consider what life would be good for [ourselves], [we] must distinguish between two aspects of [our] situation: the parameters that affect the answer – [our] culture, background, talents, tastes, and allegiances – and the limitations that make it difficult or impossible for [us] to lead the life – or any of the lives – that those parameters pick out as good'.[386] In this regard, 'disease and physical handicaps count as limitations, not parameters' as 'they do not help to define what lives would be good for [us] but may rather doom [us] to a bad one'.[387] On the other hand, '[our] material resources and economic, social, and political opportunities may, however, be either parameters or limitations'.[388] What is clear, though (in Dworkin's view), is that the teaching that 'the most important metric of a good life is wealth and the luxury and power it brings' is 'a malign and apparently persuasive lie'.[389] I could not agree more.[390] As Dworkin himself very correctly observes, 'many people lead contented lives without wealth'.[391] Perhaps I can, in fact, do no better than to quote – in extenso – the closing (as well as characteristically eloquent) words by Dworkin in *Justice for Hedgehogs* before concluding this particular chapter proper:[392]

> Nothing better illustrates the tragedy of an unexamined life: there are no winners in this macabre dance of greed and delusion. No respectable or even intelligible theory of value supposes that making and spending money has any value or importance in itself and almost everything people buy with that money lacks any importance as well. The ridiculous dream of a princely life is kept alive by ethical sleepwalkers. And they in turn keep injustice alive because their self-contempt breeds a politics of contempt for others. *Dignity is indivisible.*
>
> But remember, finally, the truth as well as its corruption. The *justice* we have imagined begins in what seems an unchallengeable proposition: that government must treat those under its dominion *with equal concern and respect. That justice does not threaten – it expands – our liberty*. It does not trade freedom for equality or the other way around. It does not cripple enterprise for the sake of cheats. It favors neither big nor small government but only just government. *It is drawn from dignity and aims at dignity. It makes it easier and more likely for each of us to live a good life well. Remember, too, that the stakes are more than mortal. Without dignity our lives are only blinks of duration. But if we manage to lead a good life well, we create something more. We write a subscript to our mortality. We make our lives tiny diamonds in the cosmic sands.*

[384] ibid (emphasis added).
[385] ibid (emphasis added).
[386] ibid 421.
[387] ibid.
[388] ibid.
[389] ibid 422.
[390] See A Phang, 'Address by Justice Andrew Phang' in 'Valedictory Reference in Honour of Justice Andrew Phang' (2023) 3 *Singapore Law Journal* 37, 38–41.
[391] Dworkin (n 4) 422.
[392] ibid 422–423 (emphasis added).

Again, I could not agree with Dworkin more. As I have ventured to suggest in similar terms elsewhere:[393]

> Books, articles and judgments will become outdated with time. You can leave behind material wealth but you cannot take it with you. However, the life you have touched (even if the person concerned does not thank you expressly) is part of *a living legacy*. Whilst you might not be able to measure success in this context in conventional terms, I believe that if you have touched even one life for the better, that is more precious than all the material accolades the world has to offer (and it is very likely that you would in fact have touched far more lives than that). This is not to downplay the achievements of those who are materially successful but if you happen to fall within this category, wear your honours lightly and use your talents and resources to enrich the lives of others. Above all, never neglect your family – value them and love them – for they are irreplaceable to you as you are to them.

Having set out Dworkin's *theory* of adjudication in some detail (ranging from his earliest writings to his latest, *Justice for Hedgehogs*), it would now be appropriate to deal with not only the basic problems with his theory but also (and in fairness to Dworkin) with the practical solutions (with accompanying and concrete case law illustrations). These are, in fact, the tasks of the next chapter.

[393] Phang (n 390) 41 (emphasis in the original text).

8

The Dworkinian Theory of Adjudication – Basic Problems and Practical Solutions

I. Introduction

The present chapter concludes our survey of the Dworkinian theory of adjudication. Having set out Dworkin's theory in the previous chapter,[1] we now turn to the basic problems with that theory as well as consider some practical solutions to those problems. In this last-mentioned regard, it will come as no surprise to the reader that I draw on various case law illustrations. This is not new, as I did in fact draw on such illustrations when dealing with the various elements of Dworkin's theory – what I termed 'the basic building blocks' – in the chapter before last.[2] It is also important to emphasise at this juncture that the reference to the relevant case law (in particular, to their interaction with the relevant theoretical concepts) is precisely one of the main aims of the present book.

II. The Basic Problems with Dworkin's Theory of Adjudication

The basic problem with Dworkin's theory of adjudication may be stated simply. It will be recalled that Dworkin argues – pursuant to his 'one right answer' thesis – that there is one uniquely right or correct answer to every legal question, although (in *practice*) *controversy* may exist as to what *precisely* the correct answer is (relying, essentially, on the concept of 'essentially contested concepts').

Whilst one might agree – purely as a matter of logic, if nothing else – that there ought indeed be a uniquely right or correct answer to a given legal question, Dworkin's theory itself fails to furnish us with a *theory* that tells us how judges go about locating the uniquely right or correct answer, and it is no answer, with

[1] See ch 7 in this volume.
[2] See ch 6 in this volume.

respect, to state that the perfect judge, Hercules, would be able to do so simply because such a judge *does not exist in real life*. Indeed, as we have already seen, Dworkin himself is not prepared to state that even Hercules has already effected a perfect job.[3] This shortcoming in Dworkin's theory of adjudication is not surprising because, *in real life*, different judges might (and often do) approach the same legal question differently – a point which (as we have also seen) Dworkin is quick to acknowledge (relying, in the main, on Professor Gallie's idea of 'essentially contested concepts'[4]). If so, are we then effectively left in the jurisprudential lurch inasmuch as we are back to 'square one', so to speak, with no coherent (let alone useful) theory of adjudication?

It is suggested that to give up the jurisprudential ghost at this juncture is to throw out the jurisprudential baby together with the bathwater. I would suggest that Dworkin's theory of adjudication, whilst imperfect, is a pre-requisite to – and sets the jurisprudential stage for – judges and courts seeking *in good faith and using their best efforts to locate the just and fair decision in the case at hand*. There is, in fact, more than a hint of such an approach by Dworkin himself when he argues that 'the law must work itself pure'.[5]

At this juncture, I trust that the reader would have realised that Dworkin's theory of adjudication has hit a jurisprudential brick wall, so to speak, precisely because of the problem of theoretical frameworks that we considered in an earlier chapter of this book.[6] Put briefly, it is impossible for any given *theoretical* framework to be perfect inasmuch as it would be able to capture – as well as apply to – *every (or even most) factual scenario simply because the latter are too myriad and varied to begin with.*[7] *However*, it does *not necessarily* follow that Dworkin's theory of adjudication is therefore not useful *at all*. As just alluded to in the preceding paragraph, it must, nevertheless, be *supplemented and complemented* on *a practical level* (ie, *the level of actual judging)* by the correct *attitudinal approach*. A caveat at this juncture is in order: this does *not* mean that the decision arrived at by the judge and court concerned will *always* be just and fair. However, my own experience has demonstrated that the decisions arrived at will – at the very least – be reasonable and (in the main) defensible as being just and fair. At this point, we need to descend into the *particular facts* of *cases* – in order to illustrate what I have been attempting to convey (particularly in the present paragraph).

[3] See the text to n 239 in the previous chapter (ch 7) in this volume. See also the text to ibid n 277.

[4] See WB Gallie, 'Essentially Contested Concepts' (1955-1956) 56 *Proceedings of the Aristotelian Society* 167 (reprinted in ch 8 of WB Gallie, *Philosophy and the Historical Understanding* (New York, Schocken Books, 1968). References hereafter will be the original article.

[5] See n 242 in the previous chapter (ch 7) in this volume. *Contra* JM Balkin, 'Taking Ideology Seriously: Ronald Dworkin and the CLS Critique' (1987) 55 *UMKC Law Review* 392 (not surprisingly, in endorsing the approach of the Critical Legal Studies Movement, there is an emphasis on judges' ideological bias (see also ch 9 in this volume)).

[6] See ch 3 in this volume.

[7] See also the text to n 40 in ch 6 in this volume.

III. The Practical Solutions

A. Introduction

As I have been at pains more than once to point out, judges and courts *do* indeed believe that there is a uniquely right or correct answer to every legal question (even in hard cases), and that they *do*, in fact, strive to arrive at just and fair decisions. I will attempt to illustrate this via consideration of a number of case law illustrations.

B. Hard Cases in Practice

A paradigm example of a 'hard case' which I had personal experience in was the Singapore Court of Appeal decision of *ACB v Thomson Medical Pte Ltd*.[8] I am sure that Professor Dworkin himself would classify it as a 'hard case'. It related to the issue of reproductive negligence for which there was no real legal precedent in the Commonwealth that was directly on point, although (as we shall see) there were some alternative (and existing) legal routes that, however, turned out to be cul-de-sacs that meant that there was (in substance and practice) no real legal precedent that enabled the court to arrive at a just and fair result based on the relevant facts. It was thus a novel case in every sense of the word. Not surprisingly, therefore, it was subsequently the subject of much local as well as international commentary[9]

[8] *ACB v Thomson Medical Pte Ltd* [2017] 1 *Singapore Law Reports* 918.

[9] See, eg, D Lee, 'IVF Mix-up Case: Claim allowed for loss of "genetic affinity"' (25 March 2017) ionsg.blogspot.sg/2017/03/ivf-mix-up-case-claim-allowed-for-loss.html?m=1 (accessed 6 February 2023); H Hakkim and KHT Ho, 'Genetic affinity as a novel remedy for wrongful fertilisation – a case of assessing the incalculable?' (9 April 2017) www.singaporelawblog.sg/blog/article/182 (accessed 6 February 2023); C Purshouse, 'Autonomy, Affinity and the Assessment of Damages: *ACB v Thomson Medical Pte Ltd* [2017] SGCA 20 and *Shaw v Kovak* [2017] EWCA Civ 1028' (2017) 26 *Medical Law Review* 675; TE Chan and PR Prabakaran, 'Biomedical Law and Ethics' (2017) 18 *Singapore Academy of Law Annual Review of Singapore Cases* 100, 100–106; K Amirthalingam, 'Reproductive Negligence: Unwanted Child or Unwanted Parenthood?' (2018) 134 *LQR* 15; T Foxton, 'Inaccurate Conception: *ACB v Thomson Medical*' (2018) 81 *MLR* 337; J English and MJ Hafeez-Baig, 'Recovery of Upkeep Costs, Claims for Loss of Autonomy and Loss of Genetic Affinity: Fertile Ground for Development?' (2018) 41 *Melbourne University Law Review* 1360; T Tomlinson, 'Negligent Disruption of Genetic Planning: Carving Out A New Tort Theory to Address Novel Questions of Liability in An Era of Reproductive Innovation' (2018) 87 *Fordham Law Review Online* 113; T Keren-Paz, 'Gender Injustice in Compensating Injury to Autonomy in English and Singaporean Negligence Law' (2019) 27 *Feminist Legal Studies* 33; CM Lam, 'Damages for Wrongful Fertilisation: Reliance on Policy Considerations' (2019) 24 *Deakin Law Review* 139; and VL Rapaso, 'Wrongful Genetic Connection: Neither Blood of my Blood, nor Flesh of my Flesh' (2020) 23 *Medicine, Health Care and Philosophy* 309. Reference may also be made to GKY Chan, 'Justice Personified – Justice Phang and Tort Law' in Y Goh (gen ed), *Pursuing Justice and Justice Alone – The Heart and Humanity of Andrew Phang's Jurisprudence* (Singapore, Academy Publishing, 2022) 451–473 at 465–468 and J Morgan, *Great Debates in Tort Law* (Oxford, Hart Publishing, 2022) 211 and 217. Reference may also be made to my papers (from which I also gratefully (and liberally) draw for the purposes of this section of the present chapter): see A Phang, 'Pure Economic Loss and Reproductive Negligence – The Singapore experience' (2017)

and was also reported in two international law reports.[10] Indeed, such attention would otherwise have been extremely rare in the context of a Singapore case.

I was part of the *coram* in that case and delivered judgment on behalf of the court. I hasten to add that although only a single judgment was delivered on behalf of the court, all the judges (as would be expected) extended their respective inputs. The *coram* in this case also consisted of five judges (instead of the traditional three). Five-judge panels in the Singapore Court of Appeal are rare and are only empanelled by the Chief Justice for very important cases. As we shall see, this was obviously one of them.

In order to understand why I focus on this case and, in particular, why I consider it to be a 'hard case', it might be apposite to note that this particular decision was one of the hardest which my colleagues and I have ever had to deal with. Indeed, the court in the *Thomson Medical* case said so in the third-to-last paragraph of the judgment, as follows: 'This has been a difficult case, possibly one of the most difficult to have come before the court thus far.'[11] Why was this so? In order to answer this question, we need to set out the facts as well as legal issues.

The Appellant and her husband sought to conceive a child through in-vitro fertilisation ('IVF'). The Appellant underwent IVF treatment and delivered a daughter, who was referred to in the judgment as 'Baby P'. After the birth of Baby P, it was discovered that a terrible mistake had been made: the Appellant's ovum had been fertilised using sperm from an unknown third party instead of sperm from the Appellant's husband. She sued the Respondents, the private hospital that had provided the IVF treatment and other related parties, in tort and contract and sought damages for, among other things, the expenses she would incur in raising Baby P, or 'upkeep costs' for short. The Respondents conceded liability but argued that the Appellant should not be allowed to recover upkeep costs. They argued that the child was a blessing, and that there was something distasteful, if not morally offensive, in treating the birth of a normal, healthy child as a matter for compensation. The trial judge agreed and in the penultimate paragraph of his judgment added, '[w]ere the [Appellant] to succeed in her upkeep claim, whether in tort or in contract every cent spent in the upbringing of Baby P will remind her that it was money from compensation for a mistake. Baby P should not ever have to grow up thinking that her very existence was a mistake.'[12]

Initially, the sole issue which was placed before the court was simply whether the upkeep claim was legally sustainable. However, this generated no small

24 *Torts Law Journal* 95 and, by the same author, 'The Importance of Comparative Common Law – A View from Singapore' [2023] *Journal of Business Law* 538.

[10] See [2017] 4 *Law Reports of the Commonwealth* 187 and [2018] *Medical Law Reports* 55.

[11] [2017] 1 *Singapore Law Reports* 918, [210].

[12] [2015] 2 *Singapore Law Reports* 218, [16]. See also M Fordham, 'An IVF Baby and a Catastrophic Error – Actions for Wrongful Conception and Wrongful Birth Revisited in Singapore' [2015] *Singapore Journal of Legal Studies* 232 and RJJ Wong, 'Upkeep claims for wrongful birth, wrongful conception or wrongful fertilisation? IVF mix-up in the Singapore High Court: ACB v Thomson Medical Pte Ltd [2015] SGHC 9' (2015) 23 *Tort Law Review* 172.

measure of concern for the court. As the court observed from the outset of the case, the claim for upkeep was, as a statement of the consequences of parenthood (and, consequently, as a statement about the situation in which the Appellant found herself in), wholly inadequate. In the words of the court, it had 'the effect of selecting – out of the myriad of legally, morally, and socially significant obligations that attended the institution of parenthood – only the financial costs of raising a child'.[13] This was, the court noted, not a problem confined only to the case but one which afflicted the case-law in the area more generally. For this reason, the court invited the parties to present further submissions on two additional issues: first, a possible claim for 'loss of autonomy' and/or second, whether an award of punitive damages could be made.

Constraints of space preclude an extended discussion in this chapter, although the interested reader is referred to both my papers for a more extended discussion.[14] It will suffice for present purposes to note that had the court been able to decide on the upkeep claim or either or both of the two additional issues referred to at the end of the preceding paragraph, the case itself could (arguably at least) have ceased to be a 'hard case' inasmuch as the court would have been able to arrive at a decision by reference to *established law*. However, the court was *unable* to do so. Let me elaborate.

The court first considered the issue of upkeep costs (which, it will be recalled, was the primary claim). Such a claim had no clear Commonwealth precedent, with courts in various jurisdictions adopting directly opposed positions.[15] The court in the *Thomson Medical* case *rejected* the upkeep claim. In brief, it was of the view that such a claim arose from the parental relationship between the Appellant and Baby P. However, it observed, '[t]he duty to maintain one's child is a duty which lies at the very heart of parenthood, and thus the expenses which are incurred towards the discharge of this estate are not capable of characterisation as a loss'.[16] The court clarified that this was not a factual claim about the felt reality of parenthood, which could on occasion feel like a chore, but a normative claim about the paradigm of family relationships as it existed in the law. The costs of providing for a child are not independent of the parental responsibility to care for one's children but part and parcel of it.[17] That being the case, the court turned the matter on its head and asked: '[t]he challenge, for those who would allow claims for the costs of upkeep, is to find a principled justification as to why the pecuniary consequences of the birth of, an unplanned child should sound

[13] [2017] 1 *Singapore Law Reports* 918, [18].

[14] Cited at n 9, above.

[15] Contrast, eg, the House of Lords decision of *McFarland v Tayside Health Board* [2000] 2 AC 59 and the decision of the High Court of Australia (by a bare majority of 4–3) in *Cattanach v Melchior* (2003) 199 ALR 131.

[16] [2017] 1 *Singapore Law Reports* 918, [90].

[17] This obligation – in the Singapore context – is enshrined in s 68 of the Women's Charter 1961 (2020 Rev Edn).

in damages but the non-pecuniary costs should not.'[18] It did not think that any satisfactory answer could be given because there was none to be had. Explaining, the court said:[19]

> … The financial cost of raising a child lies beyond the compass of the law in the same way that the effort expended by the Appellant in all other aspects of raising Baby P – for instance, the hours of lost sleep spent putting her to bed; the sorrow and worry endured during a bout of illness; or the simple act of blowing on a spoonful of hot soup before feeding it to her – falls outside the domain of the law. These, and a million other sacrifices, both big and small, that parents make unthinkingly for their children during the course of their lifetime, are – to use the words of Viscount Simon LC in the House of Lords decision of *Benham v Gambling* [1941] AC 157 … at 168 – '*incapable* of being measured in coin of the realm' [emphasis added]. …

Concluding, the court held that the obligations of parenthood were 'fundamental, indivisible, and incapable of sounding in damages'.[20] It was therefore not open for the Appellant to argue, on the one hand, that she was Baby P's parent and yet contend, on the other hand, that the responsibility of maintaining Baby P was not something which she should bear. Parenthood, the court said, 'comprises an indivisible bundle of rights and obligations which cannot be peeled away and hived off *à la carte*'.[21] It clarified that in denying the upkeep claim, it was in no way relying on the doctrine of *novus actus interveniens*, which carried with it the imputation that the Appellant's decision to keep Baby P was 'wholly unreasonable'.[22] Rather, the court stated that it was focusing on the *nature* of the damage which had been suffered and explained why it was *not* a 'loss' of a form which the court could recognise as being legally actionable.

Furthermore, the court held that the recognition of the upkeep claim would raise the spectre of a conflict of interest between the parents' private interests in the litigation and their duties vis-à-vis their children. As the court noted,

> In order to establish a case for the recovery of upkeep costs, parents would have to come to court to prove that their children represent a net *loss* to them. The very nature of such an exercise encourages the exaggeration of any infirmities and the diminution of benefits as might exist in their children, in order that the account may be as favourable to the parents as possible. This is conduct which is fundamentally at odds with the overarching duty that parents have to provide, care for, and love their children.[23]

This provided an additional reason for the court in the *Thomson Medical* case to *reject* the upkeep claim. *However*, as the court candidly acknowledged, the outcome which had been reached was not wholly satisfactory, for it had the effect

[18] [2017] 1 *Singapore Law Reports* 918, [92].
[19] ibid [91].
[20] ibid [93].
[21] ibid.
[22] ibid [94].
[23] ibid [95] (emphasis in the original text).

of leaving the Appellant with a relatively modest sum in compensation for what, by any account, was a grievous wrong. It was for this reason – that somehow justice and fairness had not been achieved in the decision at hand – that the court then proceeded to consider the additional two issues referred to briefly above, viz, whether there could be a possible claim for 'loss of autonomy' and/or whether an award of punitive damages could be made in favour of the Appellant. Before considering – in brief – these latter two issues, it should be pointed out that, in Dworkinian terms, the court in the *Thomson Medical* case had rejected the upkeep claim based on what was correct on *principle* (and based on *specific arguments* which I have outlined in brief above). It is also germane to note that there had been *no definitive precedent in the Commonwealth* and, a fortiori, in Singapore. In other words, no established rule governed the fact situation in the *Thomson Medical* case. As already alluded to above, the court in this case then proceeded to consider two other (*established*) rules to ascertain whether either or both of them might be able to provide an answer in this 'hard case'.

Once again, constraints of space preclude a detailed elaboration of the court's reasoning in respect of both these issues. To summarise, the court, first, *rejected* the possible claim for 'loss of autonomy',[24] whilst acknowledging that the concept of autonomy was nevertheless relevant, albeit only as an important background consideration or principle that underlay the development of the law, even if it could not (in and of itself) be the subject of legal protection.

Insofar as the issue as to whether an award of punitive damages could be made in favour of the Appellant, the court in the *Thomson Medical* case had first to decide on the preliminary issue as to whether the decision of the House of Lords in *Rookes v Barnard*,[25] which confined the award of punitive damages in tort to three categories of cases (the 'Categories Test'), should continue to be followed in Singapore. After an extensive review of the relevant authorities, it concluded that it ought *not*.[26] The court held that punitive damages ought, instead, to be awarded where the totality of the defendant's conduct was so outrageous as to warrant punishment, deterrence and condemnation.[27] On the facts of the *Thomson Medical* case itself, however, the court held that the facts were too scant to support a finding of outrageous conduct.

[24] The court furnished three reasons for this: the 'conceptual objection', the 'coherence objection' and the 'over-inclusiveness objection', respectively: see generally ibid, [115]–[125]. Though *cf* D Nolan, 'Negligence and Autonomy' [2022] *Singapore Journal of Legal Studies* 356 and S Fulham-McQuinlan, 'Infringement of Autonomy as Damage in Medical Negligence' (2023) 139 *LQR* 126.

[25] *Rookes v Barnard* [1964] AC 1129.

[26] For a summary of the specific reasons, see Phang (n 9).

[27] The court clarified that the use of the expression 'outrageous' did not 'entail that the imposition of a punitive award is contingent on public distaste or any sort of emotional response. Rather, it sets out a reasoned normative standard that requires the court to consider whether the defendant's conduct is so reprehensible that a normal compensatory award is insufficient and something more is required. This involves an exercise of reasoned judgment of the sort that courts perform on a regular basis': see [2017] 1 *Singapore Law Reports* 918, [205].

The upshot of the above findings was that, whilst it was clear (as already alluded to above) that the Appellant ought (in the context of a just and fair decision) to have been awarded a substantial quantum of damages, this was *not* possible based on *the existing law*.

An important point should be made at this juncture in the context of the present book in general and Dworkin's theory of adjudication in particular. First, a 'hard case' can arise not only when the *existing* rules 'run out' (per Dworkin) but also where the *facts* are such as to prevent (as was the case here) the court from arriving at a just and fair result. In this latter sense, it could be argued that, in *substance* at least, the *existing* rules had indeed 'run out'. This is the important *general* point, with the *specific consequence* in the context of *the present case* being that the Appellant was left with no *just and fair* remedy as such. It is suggested that such a situation would *also* represent a '*hard case*', although, strictly as well as literally speaking, the existing *rules* as such had not 'run out'. How, then, did the court decide this 'hard case'?

A strict *legal positivist* approach would (according to Dworkin at least) result in the court being free to *create new law*. In contrast, Dworkin would argue that the court ought to arrive at a just and fair result (and remedy) by having resort to *principles* embedded in the *existing* law.

The court in the *Thomson Medical* case did in fact arrive at what it considered to be a just and fair result by creating a *new* category of damages for *loss of genetic affinity*. This was perhaps why this case was considered to be so *novel* by authors as well as law reporters from other jurisdictions.[28]

It would appear, therefore, that the court in the *Thomson Medical* case had adopted a *legal positivist* approach by *creating new law* – a *new* head of damages for *loss of genetic affinity*.

It is suggested, however, that whilst Dworkin's theory of how 'hard cases' ought to be decided appeared to be ignored, his theory (relating to the importance of *principles*) was *still relevant*. Put simply, whilst the *legal positivist* approach appeared to be the *preferable* one that was embodied in the decision in the *Thomson Medical* case, it was *not* a 'pure' legal positivist approach as such; there were *strands* of *Dworkinian* theoretical influence as well. In order to make good this point, it is necessary, in my view, to examine *the precise reasoning* of the court in the *Thomson Medical* case that enabled it to arrive at the creation of a new head of damages for loss of genetic affinity.

It will be recalled that the court in the *Thomson Medical* case opined that the concept of autonomy, whilst not an independent legal principle in and of itself, was nevertheless an important background consideration. In particular, the court was of the view that what was needed in the context of the facts of that case was a more complex and substantive account of autonomy that took into account 'existing family building practices, kinship arrangements, and the

[28] See above, nn 9 and 10, respectively.

socially-constituted value of genetic relatedness'.[29] At this particular juncture, it is apposite to quote *in extenso* from the judgment of the court in the *Thomson Medical* case, as follows:[30]

> 127 We begin with this. The Appellant's desire to have a child of *her own, with her Husband*, is a desire that is a basic human impulse, and its loss is keenly and deeply felt, even if it is difficult to put into words. Her desire (and therefore her loss), as explained by Fred Norton in an excellent article, was for 'genetic affinity' (see Fred Norton, 'Assisted Reproduction and the Frustration of Genetic Affinity: Interest, Injury, and Damages' (1999) 74 NYU L Rev 793 ('*Genetic Affinity*')). One prominent bioethicist put it the following way (see Leon R Kass, *Life, Liberty and the Defense of Dignity: The Challenge for Bioethics* (Encounter Books, 2002) at pp 96–97):
>
>> … the desire to have a child of one's own is a couple's desire to embody, out of the conjugal union of their separate bodies, a child who is flesh of their separate flesh made one. This archaic language may sound quaint, but … this is precisely what is being celebrated by most people who rejoice at the birth of Louise Brown [the first baby born via IVF], whether they would articulate it this way or not. Mr. and Mrs. Brown, by the birth of their daughter, embody themselves in another, and thus fulfil this aspect of their separate sexual natures and of their married life together. …
>
> 128 To say, as [counsel for the Respondents did], that the issue here is merely one about '"incorrect" / "undesired" genetic mix or skin tone' (which we categorically state to be language that we abjure), is to completely miss the point. As Norton goes on to explain, the desire for genetic affinity is complex and multi-faceted. It is, at its core, a desire for identity bounded in consanguinity. The ordinary human experience is that parents and children are bound by ties of blood and share physical traits. This fact of biological experience – heredity – carries deep socio-cultural significance. For many, the emotional bond between parent and child is forged in part through a sense of common ancestry and a recognition of commonalities in appearance, temperament, and physical appearance. For yet others, genetic continuity and biological lineage is deeply important to religious and cultural belonging (see Dov Fox, 'Reproductive Negligence' (2017) 117 Colum L Rev 149 ("*Reproductive Negligence*") at 179). This interest in affinity does not exist only at the bilateral level (between parent and child), but also multilaterally – it affects the parents' relationship with their extended relations; the child's relationship with his/her siblings; as well as the family's relationship with the wider community of which they are a part.
>
> 129 It is 'affinity' – which Norton uses as a convenient shorthand for all those ties which are partly a result of genetic relatedness and partly a result of the social significance which it carries – which distinguishes familial ties from ties of friendship. Put simply, families cannot be thought of as just another social group such as a football club or a running club. This difference lies at the root of why the obligations of parenthood and the relationship between parents and children are so special and socially

[29] [2017] 1 *Singapore Law Reports* 918, [126]. A couple of authors, however, go further and argue that the recognition of loss of genetic affinity in the case was very difficult to distinguish from an award for loss of autonomy: see English and Hafeez-Baig (n 9) 1379–1381.

[30] [2017] 1 *Singapore Law Reports* 918, [127]–[129] (emphasis in the original text).

> fundamental: obligations of kinship are inherited and not voluntarily assumed. Now, all this is not to lay out a prescriptive definition of what family should be or, worse, to denigrate adoption, which is a precious and valuable thing, but to explain that persons who *consciously choose* to undergo IVF do so because of a deep desire to experience, as far as it is possible, the ordinary experience and incidents of parenthood. And when, as in the present case, a person has been denied this experience due to the negligence of others then she has lost something of profound significance and has suffered a serious wrong.

The court explained that to say that the Appellant had suffered financial losses as a result of having to care for the child – which was the gist of the upkeep claim – 'severely misconstrues' the nature of the harm suffered. It was also not enough to say that she had suffered a loss of decisional autonomy – that is to say, an ability to make plans for her life – for her loss went deeper than that. She had lost the chance to have a child with whom both she and her husband would be genetically related and, consequently, a family structure which comported with her aspirations. This was a positive good which she had been denied.

If 'affinity' is the positive aspect of genetic relatedness, then its obverse is chauvinism, in its many and varied forms. In her affidavit the Appellant explained, in aching detail, the consequences of the mistake to her life and that of her family: the sideways glances, the quizzical looks, and the impolitic questions. At this point, I should explain that the Appellant was a Chinese Singaporean woman; her husband was a Caucasian male; and the donor whose sperm was mistakenly used was ethnically Indian. I, like the court in *Thomson Medical*, hasten to add that I draw attention to the race of the parties involved not because of any personal approval of these outmoded attitudes towards race and ethnicity, but because of a recognition of 'the complex role that physical resemblance, race, and cultural and ethnic identity have had and continue to have on our individual well-being', as they so evidently did have on the Appellant's.[31] This, as the court noted, was the social reality that had to be confronted, even if it was not to be endorsed, and the Appellant would be ill-served by a judicial refusal to fully engage with these issues.[32] Even without the additional patina of race and ethnicity, the Appellant's loss would have been significant and profound; but with the overlay of race (and the attendant social complexities which it brings), the Appellant's loss took on an additional dimension.

Summarising, the court explained that the loss suffered by the Appellant was the product of a 'complex amalgam of biological, social, ethical, and historical

[31] ibid [134].

[32] ibid [134] and [135]. By sheer coincidence, the second oral hearing for this matter took place shortly before the Constitution of the Republic of Singapore (Amendment) Bill (No 28 of 2016) was tabled. The key proposal in the Bill was the introduction of a scheme to safeguard minority representation in the Presidency. The Bill, which was itself based on a report prepared by a Constitutional Commission which released its report in August 2016, triggered a national debate about the role of race in contemporary Singapore society.

factors'. Many of these, the court said, had to 'do with certain aspects of human relationships and personhood that are fundamental parts of the human condition, such as the role of genetic relatedness, physical resemblance, race, culture, and the importance of familial relations'. Some of these, the court said, were rightly cherished, while others were 'perhaps regrettable features of the society which we inhabit'.[33] For all these reasons, the court held that the Appellant's interest in 'genetic affinity' was one which the law ought to recognise and protect.

In the closing paragraph of this section of the judgment, the court noted that there was an important difference between the Appellant's case and so-called cases of 'wrongful conception', which typically dominated the literature.[34] In cases of wrongful conception, a child born following a failed sterilisation would be related to both parents, who would have a normal addition to their family. There is no loss of 'affinity' in the sense described in the judgment. The court clarified that this was not to say that plaintiffs in wrongful conception and wrongful birth cases had not suffered a disruption to their reproductive plans, for they clearly had. However, the types of harm which resulted from that disruption were qualitatively different. The court therefore reserved for another day the question of whether plaintiffs in those types of cases may bring a claim such as that which was allowed in this particular case.[35]

It should also be noted that the *quantification* of damages for loss of affinity was also an issue that was fraught with difficulty. However, as it is one that is not,

[33] ibid [135].

[34] The expression 'wrongful conception' was taken from S Todd, 'Wrongful Conception, Wrongful Birth and Wrongful Life' (2005) 27 *Sydney Law Review* 525. As the court explained in [2017] 1 *Singapore Law Reports*. 918, [29(c)], wrongful conception claims are brought by the parents for the failure of a healthcare professional to perform a sterilisation operation properly or to properly advise on the efficacy of the procedure (eg, by advising the parents that the procedure was successful when it was not). The essence of such a claim is that the parents never planned to have children – hence, it is the 'conception' that is unwanted – and, concomitantly, never planned to undertake the commitments of parenthood. However, the present case was quite different. The premise of the Appellant's case was not that she did not want to conceive. Rather, it was quite the opposite – the Appellant actively desired to have a child and was fully willing to bear the costs of raising one, although she *only planned* to have a child that was conceived using *her husband's sperm* (see [2017] 1 *Singapore Law Reports* 918, [27]). Thus presented, the essence of the Appellant's claim (and those brought by others similarly situated) was that she never planned to have *this child* (that is to say, the child who was born as a result of the use of the wrong genetic material) but instead planned for and desired to have a child with whom they would share genetic kinship (see [2017] 1 *Singapore Law Reports* 918, [34]).

[35] [2017] 1 *Singapore Law Reports* 918, [136]. There were also a couple of other (albeit somewhat different) points on which the court did not express a concluded view. In particular, there might be two possible exceptions where the outcome of a claim for upkeep costs might differ depending on whether it was framed in contract or in tort: (a) where there was a contractual warranty guaranteeing a particular outcome – that is, that a child containing the genetic material of both parents would be born – or (b) a clause providing for damages in the event of a situation such as the present. The latter would require the court to resolve the tension between two sets of competing principles: the general enforceability of bargains on the one hand and the policy considerations against the award of upkeep on the other. On the question of how such a balance was to be struck, the court expressed no concluded view and left the question to be decided on another occasion should the issue arise (at [105]).

strictly speaking, directly relevant to the present section of this book,[36] the interested reader is referred to a summary as well as analysis by the present author elsewhere.[37]

I have set out the court's reasoning on the *new* head of damages for *loss of genetic affinity* in some detail in order to demonstrate that while consistent with the *spirit* of Dworkin's theory of adjudication in relation to the *good faith* search for a just and fair decision *in a novel situation* based on, most importantly, *principle*, the approach adopted in the *Thomson Medical* case nevertheless *did create new law*. As also noted earlier in this chapter, the court in this case also identified it as a 'hard case' in a manner that was *somewhat different* from what Dworkin had contemplated. *However*, to the extent that the court in this case developed the law *incrementally and consistently with (as well as from) existing legal rules*, it cannot be said that it had created new law in the *broad* sense which legal positivists are said to do in 'hard cases' (at least according to Dworkin); in particular, the court in the *Thomson Medical* case did *not* have resort to *extra*legal considerations, *except* to the extent that they *aided* it in formulating a new *(legal)* head of damages (viz, damages for *loss of genetic affinity*). So the reader will see that the approach in the *Thomson Medical* case was in fact consistent with *both* legal positivism *and* Dworkinian theory (or, more accurately, with *specific aspects* of *both* theories). All this also illustrates a *central theme* of the present book – that *no single theory* can capture accurately the *actual process of adjudication*, but that many *aspects* of many of such theories *do* capture various *aspects* of what transpires during the *actual* process of adjudication itself. Indeed, this last-mentioned reference to *aspects* of *theories of adjudication* has also been illustrated in an earlier chapter when I considered Dworkin's distinction between principle and policy (in particular, that the courts cannot be 'mini-legislatures') and the concept of '*judicial public* policy' – all as they operated in the context of the *actual practice of adjudication* itself.[38]

In the next section of the present chapter of this book, I deal with a related issue – in particular, *the complexity of adjudication in real life* and the fact that, in any given case, there might be *two equally persuasive answers* insofar as a just and fair outcome is concerned. Before proceeding to do so, however, I deal with a possible objection to the effect that the sample I considered in considering the issue of 'hard cases' in practice is too small – focusing as it does only on the *Thomson Medical* case. This point is well taken. However, I suspect that even if I had considered many other (actual) 'hard cases', it would not have made much *qualitative* difference. As also mentioned at the outset of this section of the present chapter, having had personal experience in the *Thomson Medical* case itself, I can

[36] Although it might be argued that, being inextricably connected with the issue of damages for loss of genetic affinity, it, too, is a novel issue.

[37] Phang (n 9) 560–561.

[38] See the text to nn 45–52 and 61–71, respectively in ch 6 in this volume.

testify personally to the fact that it was a truly 'hard case'. It bears repeating what the court in that case stated (this time in full):[39]

> This has been a difficult case, possibly one of the most difficult to come before this court thus far. However, not once have we wavered in our conviction as to the truth of the following principle, which has already been emphasised right at the outset of this judgment: ***the life of every person carries with it its own inestimable value and dignity and the worth of a person can neither be enlarged nor its importance abridged by any pronouncement of this court – nothing we have said should (or, indeed, could) be taken as a reflection of this court's view of the worth of Baby P. That is not the issue before this court nor can it ever be.*** The question in this appeal was the proper legal response to what is, by any account, a tragic set of facts. …

Finally, it should be noted that *Dworkin himself* also refers to *representative cases* in supporting as well as illustrating his theory of adjudication.

C. The Complexity of Adjudication in Real Life

A 'pure' application of Dworkin's theory of adjudication would result in the court concerned arriving at the correct legal rule or principle that would (in turn) apply to the facts of the case before it. *However*, this is not always the case in adjudication in *real life*. There may, for example, be situations where there are *equally* persuasive rules or principles which may be *at odds* with each other. How, then, is the court to choose? It might be argued that the court should choose the rule or principle that provides it with the just and fair result. However, what if *both* rules or principles embody *justice and fairness (albeit of a different kind)*? That this *is* indeed possible in the *practical* sphere can be seen in the Singapore Court of Appeal decision of *RDC Concrete Pte Ltd v Sato Kogyo (S) Pte Ltd.*[40] Significantly, this particular decision related not to some distant and esoteric legal doctrine but, instead, to a very vital as well as practically relevant issue in the law of contract – the law relating to discharge by breach of contract and the specific legal issue as to when an innocent party would be justified in terminating a contract in the event of a breach of contract by the other party.

In order to understand fully the more general jurisprudential point referred to in the preceding paragraph, it is important to set out the relevant legal background. To this end, there are two *quite distinct (and conceptually inconsistent)*

[39] [2017] 1 *Singapore Law Reports* 918, [210] (emphasis in the original text). See also the text to n 367 in ch 7 in this volume.

[40] *RDC Concrete Pte Ltd v Sato Kogyo (S) Pte Ltd* [2007] 4 *Singapore Law Reports* 413; and also reported at (2008) 115 *Construction Law Reports* 154. See also JW Carter, 'Intermediate Terms Arrive in Australia and Singapore' (2008) 24 *Journal of Contract Law* 226 and Y Goh, 'Towards a Consistent Approach in Breach and Termination of Contract at Common Law: RDC Concrete Pte Ltd v Sato Kogyo (S) Pte Ltd' (2008) 24 *Journal of Contract Law* 251. See also CGS Tan, 'Nesting the Taxonomy in the Remedial: A Re-examination of Promissory Terms' (2011) 62 *Northern Ireland Legal Quarterly* 321 (which also discusses the *RDC Concrete* case in some detail).

approaches towards ascertaining when an innocent party would be justified in terminating a contract in the event of a breach of contract by the other party.

The *first* is termed the 'condition-warranty approach',[41] whilst the second is termed the '*Hongkong Fir* approach'.[42] As already mentioned above, both these approaches are distinct and conceptually inconsistent with each other. To elaborate, the 'condition-warranty approach' focuses on *the nature of the term* breached (permitting termination if the term concerned is considered sufficiently important to be a 'condition'), whereas the '*Hongkong Fir* approach' focuses on *the nature and consequences* of the breach (permitting termination if the innocent party is deprived of substantially the whole benefit of the contract that it was intended that that party should have). These two tests, whilst conceptually distinct, *might* lead to the same result, although this is *not necessarily* the case and *depends upon the particular factual matrix concerned.* A *perfect* integration of both approaches is therefore not possible. Faced with those circumstances, the Singapore Court of Appeal in the *RDC Concrete* case nevertheless attempted to integrate both of the abovementioned approaches, although, given the conceptually inconsistent bases, a *perfect* integration of these approaches was *not* possible. Before (for the sake of completeness) setting out the approach adopted in the *RDC Concrete* case, it is of the first importance – insofar as the present section of this chapter in the book is concerned – to elaborate on the jurisprudential implications of each of the above approaches, particularly in *Dworkinian* terms. To run slightly ahead of the story, so to speak, it is suggested that *neither* the 'condition-warranty approach' *nor* the '*Hongkong Fir* approach' was superior to the other insofar as *a just and fair result or outcome* was concerned.

Looked at from the perspective of *justice and fairness* in *giving effect to the agreement between the parties* was concerned, the *principle* embodied in the 'condition-warranty approach' was *eminently justified.* And this was a fortiori the case, given that this was a situation relating to the breach of *a contract or agreement* between the parties.

On the other hand, looked at from the perspective of justice and fairness in ensuring (pursuant to the '*Hongkong Fir* approach') that a breach of contract that resulted only in very minor or trivial consequences did not penalise unduly the party in breach (by permitting the other party to thenceforth discharge itself completely from the contract), the *principle* embodied in the '*Hongkong Fir* approach' was *also* eminently justified.

Put simply, what was at work in *each* of the above two approaches was *a different conception of the concept of 'justice'* (here in the context of the *same* situation pertaining to a breach of contract). It is suggested that viewed from the perspective of *principle*, *neither* was *obviously* superior to the other. In other words, what

[41] See per Bowen LJ (as he then was) in the English Court of Appeal decision of *Bentsen v Taylor, Sons & Co* [1893] 2 QB 274, 281.

[42] Named after the seminal English Court of Appeal decision of *Hongkong Fir Shipping Co Ltd v Kawasaki Kisen Kaisha Ltd* [1962] 2 QB 26.

the court in the *RDC Concrete* case was faced with were *two equally persuasive (yet opposed) principles of justice* as embodied in the two respective approaches described briefly above. Again, put simply, it is therefore possible to argue that there could be *Dworkinian principles* that can – and *do* – *conflict* with each other. It is admitted, however, that there are at least a couple of ways in which Dworkin might deal with such an argument.

The first is to argue that the two approaches set out above relate to conflicting *rules* (and not principles). However, as I have already pointed out in an earlier chapter, the line between rules on the one hand and principles on the other is not always a clear and distinct one.[43] As I have also suggested, it is possible, in any event, to argue that principles *underlie* rules.[44] Indeed, the reader would have discerned that the manner in which both approaches conflict is one that is focused on their respective ideas (or *conceptions*) of justice and fairness (in this regard, recall that Dworkin refers to a 'principle' as being 'a standard that is to be observed, not because it will advance or secure an economic, political, or social situation deemed desirable, but because it is *a requirement of justice or fairness or some other dimension of morality*').[45]

A second way in which Dworkin might deal with the argument that 'principles' can (and do) conflict with each other is to argue that he accepts (as we have already seen earlier in this chapter) that it *can* be controversial as to what the right answer is. Indeed, his (essential) reliance on Professor Gallie's idea of 'essentially contested concepts'[46] is in fact also embodied in my reference (above) to *different conceptions of the concept of 'justice'*. If so, it would appear that at least part of Dworkin's theory of adjudication describes perhaps most accurately amongst all the various theories of adjudication on offer what *actually* takes place *in practice* – including the *RDC Concrete* case. What is equally clear, however, is that insofar as Dworkin posits a substantive – and metaphysical – theory (in the form of law as integrity), this is not one that accurately depicts what actually transpires in practice: save, perhaps, for the more general proposition that courts generally adopt a good faith *approach* towards adjudication, seeking the most principled law (together with an equally principled application thereof) in order to arrive at a just and fair decision in the case at hand. However, the concept of 'principle' I have just referred to is not identical to that utilised by Dworkin (and as I explained in more detail earlier in chapter six[47]). It is, consistent with what I have proffered in an earlier chapter,[48]

[43] See the text to nn 27–39 in ch 6 in this volume.

[44] See the text to ibid nn 31–32. And see also what are apparently Dworkin's latest views on this particular issue: see the text to nn 350–351, above.

[45] See R Dworkin, 'The Model of Rules I' in ch 2 of *Taking Rights Seriously*, rev edn (Cambridge, Harvard University Press, 1978) 22 (emphasis added) (this particular essay was originally published as R Dworkin, 'The Model of Rules' (1967) 35 *University of Chicago Law Review* 14). See also the text to n 19 in ch 6 in this volume.

[46] Gallie (n 4).

[47] See the text between nn 39 and 41 in ch 6 in this volume.

[48] See ch 3 in this volume.

more of a *procedural* approach, although (as I was also at pains to emphasise in both that chapter and in the final chapter of this book[49]) procedure and substance cannot be neatly distinguished and, indeed, often *interact* with each other.

To return by way of a denouement to the *RDC Concrete* case, the court accorded *priority* to the 'condition-warranty approach' over the '*Hongkong Fir* approach', although, *unlike* the traditional (binary) approach, it also gave a role to the latter approach as well.[50] In particular, the court attempted an 'imperfect' integration of sorts, and summarised it in *diagrammatic* form, as follows:[51]

SITUATIONS ENTITLING AN INNOCENT PARTY TO TERMINATE THE CONTRACT AT COMMON LAW

SITUATION	CIRCUMSTANCES IN WHICH TERMINATION IS LEGALLY JUSTIFIED	RELATIONSHIP TO OTHER SITUATIONS
I *Express* Reference to the Right to Terminate **and** What will Entitle the Innocent Party to Terminate the Contract		
(1)	The contractual term breached clearly states that, in the event of certain event or events occurring, the innocent party is entitled to terminate the contract.	None – it operates *independently of all other* situations. In other words — Situations (2), (3)(a) and (3)(b) (*ie*, all the situations in II, below) are *not* relevant.
II *No* Express Reference to the Right to Terminate **and** What will Entitle the Innocent Party to Terminate the Contract		
(2)	Party in breach ***renounces*** the contract by clearly conveying to the innocent party that it ***will not perform*** *its contractual obligations* ***at all***. ***Quaere*** whether the innocent party can terminate the contract if the party in breach *deliberately* chooses to perform its part of the contract in a manner that amounts to a *substantial breach.*	None – it operates *independently* of *all other* situations. In other words — Situation (1) is *not* relevant. Situations (3)(a) and (3)(b) are *not* relevant.

(continued)

[49] See ch 10 in this volume.

[50] For a more detailed analysis (including how *history* resulted in the two (conflicting) approaches, see A Phang and Y Goh, 'Encounters with History, Theory and Doctrine – Some Reflections on Discharge by Breach of Contract' in ch 12 of S Degeling, J Edelman and J Goudkamp (gen eds), *Contract in Commercial Law* (Australia, Thomson Reuters, 2016).

[51] [2007] 4 *Singapore Law Reports (Reissue)* 413, [113].

(Continued)

SITUATION	CIRCUMSTANCES IN WHICH TERMINATION IS LEGALLY JUSTIFIED	RELATIONSHIP TO OTHER SITUATIONS
(3)(a)	**'Condition-Warranty Approach'** – Party in breach has breached a ***condition*** of the contract (as opposed to a *warranty*).	Should be applied ***before*** the '*Hongkong Fir* Approach' in Situation (3)(b). Situation (1) is *not* relevant. Situation (2) is *not* relevant.
(3)(b)	'*Hongkong Fir* Approach' – Party in breach which has committed a breach, the **consequences** of which will **deprive the innocent party of substantially the whole benefit** which it was intended that the innocent party should obtain from the contract.	Should be applied only ***after*** the 'Condition-Warranty Approach' in Situation (3)(a) *and* if the term breached is *not* found to be a *condition.* Situation (1) is *not* relevant. Situation (2) is *not* relevant.

For the reader who works better with language and words, the Singapore Court of Appeal subsequently provided, in *Man Financial (S) Pte Ltd v Wong Bark Chuan David*,[52] a similar summary in *non*-diagrammatic form, as follows:[53]

> 153 As stated in *RDC Concrete*, there are four situations which entitle the innocent party (here, the appellant) to elect to treat the contract as discharged as a result of the other party's (here, the respondent's) breach.
>
> 154 The *first* ('Situation 1') is where the contractual term in question clearly and unambiguously states that, should an event or certain events occur, the innocent party would be entitled to terminate the contract (see *RDC Concrete* at [91]).
>
> 155 The *second* ('Situation 2') is where the party in breach of contract ("the guilty party"), by its words or conduct, simply *renounces* the contract inasmuch as it clearly conveys to the innocent party that it will not perform its contractual obligations at all (see *RDC Concrete* at [93]).
>
> 156 The *third* ('Situation 3(a)') is where the term breached (here, Clause C.1) is a *condition*[54] of the contract. Under what has been termed the 'condition-warranty approach', the innocent party is entitled to terminate the contract if the term which is breached is a condition (as opposed to a warranty): see *RDC Concrete* at [97]. The focus

[52] *Man Financial (S) Pte Ltd v Wong Bark Chuan David* [2008] 1 *Singapore Law Reports (Reissue)* 663.

[53] ibid [153]–[158] (emphasis in the original text). Reference may also be made to the further (albeit very specific) refinement in the Singapore Court of Appeal decision of *Sports Connection Pte Ltd v Deuter Sports GmbH* [2009] 3 *Singapore Law Reports (Reissue)* 883, [57].

[54] The court in the *Man Financial* case also considered a number of (non-exhaustive) factors that could be applied in ascertaining whether or not a term was a 'condition' pursuant to the 'condition-warranty approach': see generally [2008] 1 *Singapore Law Reports (Reissue)* 663, [160]–[174].

here, unlike that in the next situation discussed below, is not so much on the (actual) consequences of the breach, but, rather, on the *nature of the term* breached.

157 The *fourth* ('Situation 3(b)') is where the breach of a term deprives the innocent party of substantially the whole benefit which it was intended to obtain from the contract (see *RDC Concrete* at [99]). (This approach is also commonly termed the '*Hongkong Fir* approach' after the leading English Court of Appeal decision of *Hongkong Fir Shipping Co Ltd v Kawasaki Kisen Kaisha Ltd* [1962] 2 QB 26; see especially *id* at 70.) The focus here, unlike that in Situation 3(a), is not so much on the nature of the term breached, but, rather, on the *nature and consequences of the breach.*

158 Because of the different perspectives adopted in Situation 3(a) and Situation 3(b), respectively (as briefly noted above), which differences might, depending on the precise factual matrix, yield different results when applied to the fact situation, this court in *RDC Concrete* concluded that, as between both the aforementioned situations, the approach in Situation 3(a) should be *applied first*, as follows (*id* at [112]):

> If the term is a *condition*, then the innocent party would be entitled to terminate the contract. *However*, if the term is a *warranty* (instead of a condition), then the court should nevertheless proceed to apply the approach in Situation 3(b) (*viz*, the *Hongkong Fir* approach). [emphasis in original]

It should also be noted that the court in the *RDC Concrete* case adopted an approach that was (arguably at least) *unique* in the context of the law relating to discharge by breach in *the Commonwealth*. It is suggested that this, too, is itself an illustration that courts (contrary to Dworkin's theory of adjudication) can – and *do* – *make new law*. Again, however, it is equally important to note that this is nevertheless effected in a *principled* manner in order to lay down a legal proposition that will aid the court concerned in achieving a just and fair result in the case at hand.

We turn next to situations where the local court has to decide on an issue of law for which there is a divergence of precedents in other jurisdictions.

D. Divergence of Precedents in Other Jurisdictions

In this section of the present chapter, I focus on the situation where the local court has to decide on an issue of law in the face of divergent precedents in other jurisdictions. In this regard (and not surprisingly perhaps), I will focus on Singapore decisions.[55] Such a situation is not something which Dworkin's theory of adjudication appears to deal with. As noted in the preceding section, Dworkin might argue that the divergent precedents merely embody different conceptions of the concept of 'justice'.[56]

[55] It should also be noted that Singapore, being a relatively 'young' jurisdiction, is more likely to encounter such a situation.

[56] Drawing once again from Professor Gallie's idea of 'essentially contested concepts': see Gallie (n 4).

In actual practice, the focus (in the Singapore courts at least) is on two (related) levels: first, which of the (competing) rules is most persuasive at the level of logic and reason and, second, which of the same would be best suited to the Singapore context.[57] Dworkin might argue that such an approach is not inconsistent with his theory of adjudication, particularly in relation to the two dimensions of 'fit' and 'substance'. I would respectfully agree. Although it is suggested that the approach adopted by the Singapore courts is not, at first blush, the same as Dworkin's theory of adjudication, they are not (in substance at least) diametrically opposed to each other. Indeed, an argument may be made that the local court's attempt to choose which (or none of) the relevant divergent precedents is an exercise (in Dworkinian terms) in the ascertainment of 'fit' in the first instance and that its assessment in relation to the coherence of the logic and reason and/or the appropriateness of the precedent in question to Singapore is (at least roughly speaking) an ascertainment that parallels Dworkin's second dimension of 'substance'.

What *is* of the first importance is the fact that Singapore courts[58] approach a situation where there is a divergence of precedents or relevant authorities in a *principled* manner. And at the *most fundamental* level, this entails being perceived as *not* (in the case of Singapore[59]) being slavishly bound to English law. However, the approach must be a *balanced (and, hence, principled) one* inasmuch as English law should not (in contrast) be rejected simply because it in fact emanates from another jurisdiction. At this juncture, some brief historical context is necessary. Singapore was a British colony, and (not surprisingly) English law was received (commencing with the Second Charter of Justice of 1826[60]). Unfortunately (but again not surprisingly), the Singapore law during the colonial period[61] was a mere 'carbon copy' of the English common law.[62] Fortunately, this is no longer the case, and there have, during more recent times, been significant developments in Singapore law.[63] A detailed rendition of these developments is beyond the scope of the present book.[64] A few (brief) examples will suffice.

[57] See generally Phang, 'The Importance of Comparative Common Law' (n 9).

[58] And it is assumed courts in other jurisdictions as well.

[59] Which received English law, having been a former British colony. And see the brief historical background, below.

[60] Or, more accurately, Letters Patent establishing the Court of Judicature at Prince of Wales' Island, Singapore, and Malacca dated 27 November 1826, and made under the authority of Act 6 Geo. 4, c. 85. The First Charter of Justice applied to Penang. Singapore was, of course, founded by the British only in 1819. And see generally ABL Phang, *From Foundation to Legacy: The Second Charter of Justice* (Singapore, Academy Publishing, 2006).

[61] Singapore was founded as a British colony by Sir Thomas Stamford Raffles in 1819. It achieved internal self-government in 1959 before becoming part of the Federation of Malaysia in 1963. Singapore became a fully independent nation on 9 August 1965.

[62] See generally ch 2 of ABL Phang, *The Development of Singapore Law – Historical and Socio-Legal Perspectives* (Singapore, Butterworths, 1990).

[63] The groundwork for this was laid by the second Chief Justice of modern Singapore, Chief Justice Yong Pung How: see generally A Phang (gen ed), *Pioneer, Polymath and Mentor – The Life and Legacy of Yong Pung How* (Singapore, Academy Publishing, 2024).

[64] For further details, see generally A Phang, Y Goh and J Soh, 'The Development of Singapore Law: A Bicentennial Retrospective' (2020) 32 *Singapore Academy of Law Journal* 805, 827–874.

Singapore courts have encountered situations where the established English law itself has changed. In many instances, the Singapore courts have in fact held that the *existing* English law is *to be preferred in principle* to the (new) English law. Examples include the law relating to the duty of care in negligence,[65] the law relating to remoteness of damage in contract law,[66] the law of contractual illegality,[67] as well as the penalty rule.[68]

[65] See the discussion of the *Spandeck* case in the text at nn 52–62 in ch 6 in this volume (and the accompanying legal literature referred to).

[66] See the Singapore Court of Appeal decision of *MFM Restaurants Pte Ltd v Fish & Co Restaurants Pte Ltd* [2011] 1 *Singapore Law Reports* 150, endorsing the test laid down by Alderson B in the celebrated English decision of *Hadley v Baxendale* (1854) 9 Exch 341, and rejecting the apparently new legal criterion introduced by the majority of the House of Lords in *Transfield Shipping Inc v Mercator Shipping Inc (The Achilleas)* [2009] 1 AC 61. For a comment on the *MFM Restaurants* case, see, eg, Y Goh, 'Explaining Contractual Remoteness in Singapore' [2011] *Journal of Business Law* 282. See further S Sabapathy, '*The Achilleas*: Struggling to Stay Afloat' [2013] *Singapore Journal of Legal Studies* 384.

[67] See the Singapore Court of Appeal decision of *Ochroid Trading Ltd v Chua Siok Lui* [2018] 1 *Singapore Law Reports* 363, which endorsed the *existing* English law and *declined* to follow the approach of the majority of the UK Supreme Court in *Patel v Mirza* [2017] AC 467. For commentary on the former decision, see A Loke, 'Disagreement over the Illegality Defence' (2018) 35 *Journal of Contract Law* 169 and G Virgo, 'Jones Day Professorship of Commercial Law Lecture 2019 – "The State of Illegality"' (2019) 31 *Singapore Academy of Law Journal* 747.

In order to *fully* appreciate the *significance* of the *Ochroid Trading* case in *not* following *Patel v Mirza* (the highest appellate court in England and Wales), it should be pointed out that *Patel v Mirza* is obviously a seminal one in the context of the English law of contractual illegality, and which has therefore been the subject of much academic commentary: see, eg, J Goudkamp, 'The End of an Era? Illegality in Private Law in the Supreme Court' (2017) 133 *LQR* 14; JC Fisher, 'The Latest Word on Illegality' [2016] *LMCLQ* 483; N Strauss, 'The Diminishing Power of the Defendant: Illegality after *Patel v Mirza*' [2016] *Restitution Law Review* 145; E Murphy, 'The *Ex Turpi Causa* Defence in Claims against Professionals' (2016) 32 *Professional Negligence* 241; A Burrows, 'A New Dawn for the Law of Illegality' (2 June 2017) ssrn.com/abstract=2979425 (accessed 20 August 2024) (see now ch 2 of S Green and A Bogg (gen eds), *Illegality after Patel v Mirza* (Oxford, Hart Publishing, 2018)); Lord Grabiner QC, Master of Clare College, '*Patel v Mirza* [2016] UKSC 42 – Illegality and Restitution Explained by the Supreme Court', The Second Distinguished Law Lecture, Queen's College, Cambridge (19 October 2016) www.law.cam.ac.uk/press/events/2016/10/queens-distinguished-lecture-law-patel-v-mirza-illegality-and-restitution (accessed 20 August 2024); MP Furmston, 'Recent Developments in Illegal Contracts' in ch 11 of Rob Merkin and James Devenney (gen eds), *Essays in Memory of Jill Poole – Coherence, Modernisation and Integration in Contract, Commercial and Corporate Laws* (Oxford, Informa Law, 2018); Y Goh, 'The 35th Singapore Law Review Annual Lecture: The Effect of Illegality on Private Law Claims' (2024) 41 *Singapore Law Review* 1; and G Virgo, 'The Illegality Revolution' in ch 14 of S Worthington, A Robertson and G Virgo (gen eds), *Revolution and Evolution in Private Law* (Oxford, Hart Publishing, 2018) as well as (by the same author), 'Jones Day Professorship of Commercial Law Lecture 2019 – "The State of Illegality"', above. Indeed, Goudkamp went so far as to observe that '*Patel v Mirza* … is a pivotal moment in English private law': see Goudkamp, above, 14. See also the very recent collection of essays in *Illegality after Patel v Mirza*, above as well as A Phang, 'The Intractable Problems of Illegality and Public Policy in the Law of Contract – A Comparative Perspective' in ch 12 of *Essays in Memory of Jill Poole – Coherence, Modernisation and Integration in Contract, Commercial and Corporate Laws*, above.

[68] See the Singapore Court of Appeal decision of *Denka Advantech Pte Ltd v Seraya Energy Pte Ltd* [2021] 1 *Singapore Law Reports* 631 (also reported in [2021] BLR 340), which endorsed the existing English law as laid down by Lord Dunedin in the House of Lords decision of *Dunlop Pneumatic Tyre Co Ltd v New Garage & Motor Co Ltd* [1915] AC 79, and declining to follow the approach adopted by the UK Supreme Court in *El Makdessi v Cavendish Square Holding BV* [2016] AC 1172. See also R Halson, 'Liquidated Damages and Penalties – A Review of the Cavendish Decision by the Singapore Court of Appeal' (2021) 137 *LQR* 375 and A Phang, 'Penalty Clauses and Restraint of Trade – A View from

The Singapore Court of Appeal, in *Foo Jong Peng v Phua Kiah Mai*[69] as well as *Sembcorp Marine Ltd v PPL Holdings Pte Ltd*,[70] also declined to follow the approach proffered by Lord Hoffmann in the Privy Council decision of *Attorney General of Belize v Belize Telecom Ltd*[71] insofar as the learned judge sought to recast implication as interpretation (relegating the 'business efficacy' and 'officious bystander' tests to a less than central role in the context of 'terms implied in fact'). Once again, a detailed discussion is beyond the remit of this book, and the reader is referred to the relevant literature cited above.[72] The significant point to note is that the UK Supreme Court has, in *Marks and Spencer plc v BNP Paribas Securities Services Trust Co (Jersey) Ltd*,[73] seemingly *disagreed with* Lord Hoffmann's view in the *Belize* case (citing, inter alia, both the aforementioned Singapore Court of Appeal decisions). Indeed, the *Marks and Spencer* case is one of the rare occasions when the highest appellate court in England and Wales has endorsed Singapore decisions in a context in which the English courts themselves seldom refer to foreign decisions – and this is, hence, a significant landmark in the development of Singapore law.

We have also witnessed in previous sections in this chapter that the Singapore courts have also charted their *own* course in certain areas of the law. In this regard, the *Thomson Medical* case (where a *new* head of damages for loss of genetic affinity was created)[74] and the *RDC Concrete* case (with regard to the test for ascertaining when an innocent party could treat itself as discharged in the context of a breach of contract)[75] are significant examples.[76]

Singapore' [2022] *Journal of Business Law* 208. Reference may also be made to the Singapore Court of Appeal decision of *Ethoz Capital Ltd v Im8ex Pte Ltd* [2023] 1 *Singapore Law Reports* 922.

[69] *Foo Jong Peng v Phua Kiah Mai* [2012] 4 *Singapore Law Reports* 1267.

[70] *Sembcorp Marine Ltd v PPL Holdings Pte Ltd* [2013] 4 *Singapore Law Reports* 193.

[71] *Attorney General of Belize v Belize Telecom Ltd* [2009] 1 WLR 1988 (on appeal from the Court of Appeal of Belize). Reference may also be made to the following essay by Lord Hoffmann, 'Language and Lawyers' (2018) 134 *LQR* 553. Indeed, the literature itself on the *Belize* case is copious: see, eg, K Low and K Loi, 'The Many "Tests" for Terms Implied in Fact' (2009) 125 *LQR* 561; PS Davies, 'Recent Developments in the Law of Implied Terms' [2010] *LMCLQ* 140; J McCaughran, 'Implied Terms: The Journey of the Man on the Clapham Omnibus' [2011] *CLJ* 607; JW Carter, 'The Implication of Contractual Terms: Problems with *Belize Telecom*' (2013) 27(3) *Commercial Law Quarterly* 3; W Courtney and JW Carter, 'Implied Terms: What *Is* the Role of Construction?' (2014) 31 *Journal of Contract Law* 151; R Hooley, 'Implied Terms after *Belize Telecom*' [2014] *CLJ* 315; A Phang, 'The Challenge of Principled Gap-Filling: A Study of Implied Terms in a Comparative Context' [2014] *Journal of Business Law* 263; D McLauchlan, 'Construction and Implication: In Defence of *Belize Telecom*' [2014] *LMCLQ* 203; as well as JW Carter and W Courtney, '*Belize Telecom*: A Reply to Professor McLauchlan' [2015] *LMCLQ* 245. An excellent summary of *Belize* and subsequent developments is to be found in R Austen-Banker, *Implied Terms in English Contract Law*, 3rd edn (Cheltenham, Elgar Commercial Law and Practice, 2023) paras 7.54–7.69.

[72] Above, n 71. Reference may also be made to A Phang and Y Goh, 'Contract Law in Commonwealth Countries: Uniformity or Divergence?' (2019) 31 *Singapore Academy of Law Journal* 170, 179–187.

[73] *Marks and Spencer plc v BNP Paribas Securities Services Trust Co (Jersey) Ltd* [2016] AC 742.

[74] Discussed above, nn 11–39.

[75] Discussed above, nn 40–54.

[76] *Cf* also the developing law of unjust enrichment in the Singapore context (indeed, the *general* law of unjust enrichment is *itself* a developing area of the private law of obligations). Reference may, in this regard, be made to the Singapore Court of Appeal decision of *Esben Finance Ltd v Wong*

It will be seen – from even the above brief illustrations – that courts are constantly involved in ascertaining what (in their view) the best legal rules and principles are. This entails – in turn – that *choices* be made, particularly when the court is faced with *divergent* precedents from other jurisdictions.[77] Such choices, as we have seen, are made in a variety of ways. Nevertheless, what *is* clear is that they are made in accordance with *principle*. As already alluded to above, this is entirely consistent with Dworkin's theory of adjudication. However, a close comparison of his theory with what actually takes place in practice also demonstrates that Dworkin's theory of adjudication *cannot* be utilised as *an overarching metaphysical theory* as such in *guiding* the courts in making their respective decisions. From a much more *general* perspective, however, Dworkin's theory of adjudication does describe (with a fair amount of accuracy) what courts *strive to do* and, to that extent, is (in the present author's view at least) the most persuasive of all the theories considered in the present book.[78]

IV. Conclusion

I have spent much time and space on Dworkin's theory of adjudication because it is, in my view, the most important and useful amongst the various theories of adjudication (at common law) considered in the present book. That this is so is also demonstrated by the numerous case law illustrations.[79]

In this concluding part of the chapter, only a brief recapitulation is possible. Dworkin's theory of adjudication is valuable in a number of ways.

First, it leads us away from technical, legalistic and/or arid jurisprudence – in particular, the relatively conservative approach of legal positivism, which focuses

Hou-Lianq Neil [2022] 1 *Singapore Law Reports* 136 (noted in HW Tang, 'Limitation Period for Unjust Enrichment Claims, at the Claimant's Expense, Lack of Consent, Illegality, and Vindication of Property Rights: *Esben Finance Ltd and Others v Wong Hou-Lianq Neil*' (2022) 33 *King's Law Journal* 345 as well as R Leow and T Liau, 'A Pyrrhic Victory for Unjust Enrichment in Singapore? – *Esben Finance Ltd v Wong Hou-Lianq Neil*' (2023) 86 *MLR* 518). Reference may also be made to HW Tang, 'The Indefatigable Explorer, Guide and Mapmaker – Justice Phang and Law of Restitution' in Y Goh (gen ed), *Pursuing Justice and Justice Alone – The Heart and Humanity of Andrew Phang's Jurisprudence* (Singapore, Academy Publishing, 2022) 391–419 at 403–415.

[77] It is of course entirely possible that the court might be faced with divergent precedents *within* its own jurisdiction. The approach it ought to adopt, though, should, in *principle*, be the *same*.

[78] See also the text between nn 39 and 41 in ch 6 in this volume.

[79] See, eg, the *Lim Meng Suang* case, the *Spandeck* case, the *Thomson Medical* case and the *RDC Concrete* case – all of which have been discussed above. On a somewhat unrelated note, perhaps the *practical* value of Dworkin's theory of adjudication is due (in part at least) to the fact that he was in actual practice for some four years at a leading New York law firm (see S Guest, *Ronald Dworkin*, 3rd edn (Stanford, Stanford University Press, 2013) 12; see also, for Guest's own view of the practical nature of Dworkin's theory ibid 23). However, Hart also practised as a barrister at the Chancery Bar for some eight years (see N MacCormick, *HLA Hart*, 2nd edn (Stanford, Stanford University Press, 2008) 5). It might nevertheless be observed that Hart's jurisprudential focus was not so much (as was Dworkin's) on a theory of *adjudication* as such but more on a theory concerning the legal *system* (and see MacCormick, above, 212).

merely on the descriptive as constituting the normative. Indeed, the weakness of this particular approach has been discussed in an earlier chapter of this book.[80]

Second (and as a closely related point), Dworkin's theory is, instead, more in tune with the *reality* of what takes place in actual adjudication. In particular, it reminds us that there is *more* to the law than just the doctrinal rules. It posits that *principles* are also a part of the law. It further reminds us of the dangers of introducing *policies* into common law reasoning – at least insofar as such policies reflect content that is more appropriately within the sphere of *the legislature*. Put another way, it reminds the courts that they cannot – and ought not to – become 'mini-legislatures'.[81] At the same time, though, I respectfully differed from Dworkin inasmuch as I suggested that courts *can* utilise – and, in fact, have utilised – 'policy' where necessary in order to develop *the common law*.[82]

Third, Dworkin is at pains to emphasise the reality of *objectivity* in the law and, hence, the result that there *is* a right answer to every legal problem or issue. In particular, he consistently reminds us that uncertainty (as to what the right answer is) is *not* the same as indeterminacy (which entails there being no right answer at all). As I have already noted in the present chapter, I am wholly in agreement with his approach – if nothing else, because an appeal to naked subjectivity (what Dworkin, as we have seen, terms 'external skepticism') involves self-contradiction as well as disempowerment. It is also useful to note that Dworkin does permit 'internal skepticism', which addresses the situation of uncertainty, particularly in the face of two or more viable (albeit competing) theories of adjudication. However, at this specific juncture, Dworkin nevertheless encounters the inevitable difficulty which the legal positivists were eager to (and did) avoid – the objection that, *in the final analysis*, the *choice that is ultimately made as to which theory of adjudication is preferable (as purportedly being the objectively true or right theory) must necessarily be a subjective one – especially in light of the fact that Dworkin himself views law as an aspect of political morality*.[83] More specifically, pursuant to his 'rights thesis, Dworkin – as we have seen – proposes two dimensions: that of 'fit' and 'substance', respectively, both of which culminate in Dworkin's umbrella concept of *interpretation* (which takes the form of *law as integrity*). It is primarily in relation to the second dimension (that of 'substance') that Dworkin's theory of adjudication is perhaps most susceptible to the objection from subjectivity, as it involves assessment of the *moral* content of the theory (and, as we have seen, when the dimension of 'fit' yields two equally persuasive theories[84]).

Whilst it is true that Dworkin can invoke – yet again – the distinction between uncertainty and indeterminacy, it is suggested that he would nevertheless need a

[80] See ch 4 in this volume.
[81] See the text to nn 44–59 in ch 6 in this volume.
[82] See ibid the text to nn 60–91.
[83] See the text to nn 359, 362 and 363 in ch 7 in this volume.
[84] See ibid the text between nn 128 and 129.

theoretical framework upon which the aforementioned distinction could rest. And it is suggested further that this theoretical framework is to be found in Professor Gallie's idea of 'essentially contested concepts'.[85] Indeed (and as I have argued), this particular idea is *vital and critical* to *Dworkin's* theory of adjudication, without which I would even venture to suggest might lead to the total collapse of his theory itself (not unlike, for those readers familiar with it, the game of Jenga[86]). As I have also noted in the previous chapter, although Dworkin does cite this idea expressly in his earliest work,[87] this does not appear to be the case in his later work. Nevertheless, as with life in general and the law in particular, the focus is on *substance* (as opposed to mere form). Looked at in this light, Dworkin does refer to Professor Gallie's idea of 'essentially contested concepts' *repeatedly* throughout all his writings. That this is the case can be seen from just the (*numerous*) references provided in the present chapter alone.[88] *However*, Professor Gallie's idea of 'essentially contested concepts' is no panacea or magic bullet.[89] This is especially the case if one seeks to proffer a theory of adjudication that is *metaphysical* in nature.[90] In the present book, however, I posit a new theory of adjudication that is more *procedural* in nature whilst attempting to avoid falling into the extreme of neglecting *substance* altogether. It will not do to fall prey either to the Scylla of procedure or the Charybdis of substance. Indeed, this is not what transpires in *actual* adjudication, where there is a constant process of the court seeking to *mediate the tension between (and achieve a balance) of both procedure and substance*. As I have alluded to earlier in this book,[91] the process (in both theory and action) is one of *interaction*. Indeed, procedure cannot be divorced entirely from substance. By the same token, neither can substance be divorced from procedure. Both interact in a manner that is integral, holistic and even (to adopt a biological term) symbiotic in nature. What this means is that whilst – as this book does[92] – there is a focus on procedure, this interactive process ensures that substance is simultaneously impacted *as well*. All this enables the court concerned to arrive at a just and fair result in the case at hand. In this regard (and given the importance of the point

[85] Gallie (n 4).

[86] The following description is from www.target.com/p/classic-jenga-game/-/A-11199378 (accessed 4 September 2024): 'Want a game experience that combines friends, skill, suspense, laughter, and a little luck? Carefully pull a Jenga block out of the tower and place it on top. It's easy at first, but as more blocks get pulled, the Jenga tower starts to get unsteady. Players will be on the edge of their seats just trying to keep the tower from tumbling. The classic Jenga game is quick to set up, and can be played just about anytime, almost anywhere. It's a great game for parties, family game night, and the rules are simple enough for the whole family to play.'

[87] See the text to n 29 in ch 7 in this volume.

[88] See the text to nn 13–14 in ch 6 in this volume; the text to nn 29–30, 104–108, 162–164, 224, 289–291, 296–297, 337, 352–353, and 366–367 in ch 7 in this volume; as well as the text to nn 4, 46, 56 and 85, above.

[89] See also the discussion at ch 3 in this volume.

[90] See also generally ibid.

[91] See ch 2 in this volume.

[92] See ch 10 in this volume.

presently being made), it bears quoting, once again, what I had already quoted in an earlier chapter.[93] In particular, as I observed in a judicial capacity:[94]

> 4 It is axiomatic that every party ought to have its day in court. This is the very embodiment of *procedural* justice. The appellation 'procedural' is important. Procedural justice is just one aspect of the holistic ideal and concept of justice itself. In the final analysis, the achievement of a substantively just result or decision is the desideratum. It is more than that, however. It is not merely an ideal. It must be a practical outcome – at least as far as the court can aid in its attainment.
>
> 5 However, the court must be extremely wary of falling into the flawed approach to the effect that 'the ends justify the means'. This ought never to be the case. The obsession with achieving a substantively fair and just outcome does not justify the utilisation of any and every means to achieve that objective. There must be fairness in the *procedure or manner* in which the final outcome is achieved.
>
> 6 Indeed, if the procedure is unjust, that will itself taint the outcome.
>
> 7 On the other hand, a just and fair procedure does *not*, in and of itself, ensure a just outcome. In other words, procedural fairness is a necessary but not sufficient condition for a fair and just result.
>
> 8 The quest for justice, therefore, entails a continuous need to balance the procedural with the substantive. More than that, it is a continuous attempt to ensure that both are *integrated*, as far as that is humanly possible. Both *interact* with each other. One cannot survive without the other. There must, therefore, be – as far as is possible – a fair and just procedure that leads to a fair and just result. This is not merely abstract theorising. It is the *very basis* of what the courts do – and ought to do. When in doubt, the courts would do well to keep these bedrock principles in mind. This is especially significant because, in many ways, this is how, I believe, laypersons perceive the administration of justice to be. The legitimacy of the law in their eyes must never be compromised. On the contrary, it should, as far as is possible, be enhanced.
>
> 9 It is true, however, that in the sphere of practical reality, there is often a *tension* between the need for procedural justice on the one hand and substantive justice on the other. The task of the court is to attempt, as I have pointed out in the preceding paragraph, to *resolve* this tension. There is a *further* task: it is to actually attempt, simultaneously, to *integrate* these two conceptions of justice in order that justice in its fullest orb may shine forth.

One of the main elements in the new theory I propose involves *judging in good faith*. This is in fact wholly consistent with Dworkin's theory of adjudication.[95] As (if not more) importantly, it appears that Dworkin himself has adopted – in his latest work[96] – a *procedural* approach as well.[97] If this is indeed a correct

[93] See ch 2 in this volume and, in particular, the text to n 26 of that particular chapter.
[94] *United Overseas Bank Ltd v Ng Huat Foundations Pte Ltd* [2005] 2 *Singapore Law Reports (Reissue)* 425, [4]–[9] (emphasis in the original text).
[95] See the text to nn 243–250, above.
[96] See R Dworkin, *Justice for Hedgehogs* (Cambridge, Belknap Press, 2011).
[97] See the text to nn 304–305.

'interpretation' of Dworkin's approach, then there would be little – if any – difference between Dworkin's theory of adjudication on the one hand and my proposed theory of adjudication on the other.[98]

There nevertheless remains at least one respect in which I respectfully differ from Dworkin. Unlike Dworkin (and as I have suggested in this chapter), judges *do* make law in 'hard cases'.[99] However, they do so in a *principled* manner.[100] It is important to note that this is not the same as Dworkin's use of the concept of a 'principle'. As just alluded to in the preceding paragraph, such an approach is more *procedural* in nature, although I have been at pains to emphasise that procedure cannot be divorced from substance and that both *interact* with each other.[101] Because of its importance, it bears reiterating exactly what I had stated earlier in this chapter. In particular, courts and judges constantly strive to locate *as well as* apply *rules*, and, in the context of common law and equity at least, there is a constant openness to ensuring that the rules are themselves consistent with *not only logic and reason but are also themselves just and fair*. It is therefore suggested that *principles* are part of the law, albeit *not* in the way Dworkin conceives them. They do *underlie* rules, *albeit (once again) not in the way Dworkin perceives it. Principles* constitute the *underlying spirit or rationale of justice and fairness with regard to the rules concerned*. In other words, *principles* are *inextricably connected with* rules in what should be viewed as an *integrated and interactive* process. *However*, the *actual doctrine of the law itself* (ie, what the courts traditionally refer to as 'the applicable law') comprises *rules only*. Looked at in this light, it *necessarily* follows that – *contrary* to what Dworkin proposes – courts and judges *do make law* when an existing rule is modified *or* departed from *or* when the rules themselves run out. However, such law-making *must* take into account (as already mentioned) the need for the 'new' rule to be both consistent with logic and reason *as well as* to embody the ideal of justice and fairness (ie, the 'new' rule *must* be *consistent with principle)*. Consistent with such a view of rules and principles, we need *not* concern ourselves with the line between each since they are, on this view, not susceptible to comparison but, instead, *complement* each other (although it bears repeating that the *actual doctrine of the law itself* comprises *rules only)*. In any event (and as we have already seen), the line between each (as Dworkin himself admits) is not always clear.

At this particular juncture of the book, we are perhaps ready to embark on setting out the theory of adjudication proposed in *this* book. However, there is one remaining task. There have been numerous *skeptical* theories that must be dealt with simply because they deny that *any* theory of adjudication is viable to begin with. This is the task of the next chapter – to which our attention must now turn.

[98] As to which, see ch 10 in this volume.

[99] Reference may also be made to the now classic essay by Lord Reid, 'The Judge as Law Maker' (1972) 22 *Journal of the Society of Public Teachers of Law (NS)* 22.

[100] For significant illustrations in this chapter, see the discussions of the *Thomson Medical* case and the *RDC Concrete* cases, as to which see the text to nn 11–39 and 40–54, respectively.

[101] See, eg, the text to nn 93–94, above.

9

Against Adjudication – Skeptical[1] Theories and their Implications

I. Introduction

The present chapter considers theories that are, in substance and effect, negative in nature. They are, in short, skeptical theories and share the common view that it is futile to attempt to set out an objective theory of law in general and of adjudication in particular.

I will deal – albeit briefly (but not simplistically) – with three main theories – two of which are American in origin,[2] with the third being European in its source. To elaborate, the former two theories are American Realism and the Critical Legal Studies Movement, respectively.[3] The third – and final – theory focuses on Marxian theory.

By way of a very brief overview of the genesis of the first two theories (viz, American Realism and the Critical Legal Studies Movement), we need to note that the former was a response to *formalism* which, in its heyday, proffered the assurance that the law was settled and certain and that all one needed was to ascertain and apply the rules of law in question.[4] There followed what has been termed the 'revolt against formalism'[5] in virtually all aspects of the social

[1] I have used the US variant of the word as most of the theories considered in this chapter hail from that country.

[2] The classic work on American legal theory generally is probably N Duxbury, *Patterns of American Jurisprudence* (Oxford, Oxford University Press, 1995) Rather curiously, perhaps, Duxbury is English and is presently based at the University of London. However, as Professor Robert Gordon has very aptly observed, in his perceptive review of Duxbury's book, '[h]is has been a baptism by total immersion. I doubt that any American, not to mention any other foreign scholar, has ever read so widely and deeply in the literature of the American legal academy – texts, treatises, and law review articles by the ton, in the thousands.': see RW Gordon, 'American Law Through English Eyes: A Century of Nightmares and Noble Dreams' (1996) *Georgia Law Review* 84, 2215, 2215.

[3] I draw liberally (albeit not exclusively) throughout this chapter – insofar as these two theories are concerned – from A Phang, 'American Jurisprudence Through Christian Eyes – Beyond the Nightmare and the Noble Dream' (2004) 81 *University of Detroit Mercy Law Review* 867.

[4] See generally Duxbury (n 2) ch 1, entitled 'The Challenge of Formalism'.

[5] A phrase coined by Morton White: see M White, *Social Thought in America: The Revolt Against Formalism* (New York, Viking Press, 1949). But *cf* Duxbury (n 4). And *cf* (in turn) W Twining, *Karl Llewellyn and the Realist Movement*, 2nd edn (Cambridge, Cambridge University Press, 2012) 376.

sciences, including the law.[6] In the law itself, *American Realism* led the battle but (as we shall see) ultimately declined and fizzled out, not least because (again, as we shall see) it failed to develop a satisfactory theory. The 'hope' held out by formalism was nevertheless effectively shattered by American Realism, but the latter, by failing to provide any viable alternative, engendered 'despair' instead.[7] The *legal process school*[8] and (much later) the *law and economics movement*[9] sought to redress the situation by recourse to allegedly objective or neutral principles.[10] Not wholly unjustifiably, perhaps, the legal thought of the late Professor Lon Fuller[11] and Professor Ronald Dworkin[12] might also be mentioned: at least insofar as they also purport to rekindle as well as recover the hope of an objective view of the law. However, that 'hope' was again undermined considerably by the *Critical Legal Studies Movement*,[13] which (save, as we shall see later in the present chapter, for the work of Professor Roberto Mangabeira Unger[14]) offers (consistently with its postmodern stance) no real alternative to the 'black hole' of nihilism. We are back, once again, to 'despair' in a roller-coaster ride that has lasted well over a century, all told.

On a more general level, it should be emphasised (as, in fact, noted at the outset of the present chapter) that implicit within both American Realism and the Critical Legal Studies Movement is a rejection of objective standards. Much of the Critical Legal Studies Movement goes much further and explicitly rejects objective standards altogether, consistently with the postmodernist approach

[6] See generally EA Purcell, Jr, *The Crisis of Democratic Theory – Scientific Naturalism & The Problem of Value* (Lexington, University Press of Kentucky, 1973); *cf* MJ Horwitz, *The Transformation of American Law, 1870–1960: The Crisis of Legal Orthodoxy* (Oxford, Oxford University Press, 1992).

[7] For a general account of American Realism, see Duxbury (n 2) ch 2, entitled 'The Evolution of a Mood'. See also L Kalman, *Legal Realism at Yale, 1927–1960* (Chapel Hill, University of North Carolina Press, 1986); JH Schlegel, *American Legal Realism and Empirical Social Science* (Chapel Hill, University of North Carolina Press, 1995); Horwitz (n 6); and Twining (n 5). Reference may also be made to JH Schlegel, 'American Legal Realism and Empirical Social Science: From the Yale Experience' (1979) 28 *Buffalo Law Review* 459 and, by the same author, 'American Realism and Empirical Social Science: The Singular Case of Underhill Moore' (1980) 29 *Buffalo Law Review* 195 (with the material from both these articles being incorporated as part of the learned author's book cited in the earlier part of this note).

[8] See generally Duxbury (n 2) ch 4, entitled 'Finding Faith in Reason'.

[9] ibid, ch 5, entitled 'Economics in Law'.

[10] Insofar as the former movement was concerned, see HM Hart Jr and AM Sacks, *The Legal Process: Basic Problems in the Making and Application of Law* (New York, Foundation Press, 1994 (prepared from the tentative edition by the authors, 1958)) as well as H Wechsler, 'Toward Neutral Principles of Constitutional Law' (1959) 73 *Harvard Law Review* 1.

[11] See, in particular, LL Fuller, *The Morality of Law* (New Haven, Yale University Press, 1963). The revised edition was published in 1969. I consider Fuller's work in ch 5 in this volume.

[12] See, eg, R Dworkin, *Taking Rights Seriously*, rev edn (Cambridge, Harvard University Press, 1978); R Dworkin, *A Matter of Principle* (Cambridge, Harvard University Press, 1985); R Dworkin, *Law's Empire* (Cambridge, Belknap Press, 1986); and R Dworkin, *Justice for Hedgehogs* (Cambridge, Belknap Press, 2011). I consider Dworkin's work in chs 6, 7 and 8 in this volume.

[13] See generally AC Hutchinson and PJ Monahan, 'Law, Politics, and the Critical Legal Scholars: The Unfolding Drama of American Legal Thought' (1984) 36 *Stanford Law Review* 199 and M Kelman, *A Guide to Critical Legal Studies* (Cambridge, Harvard University Press, 1987).

[14] See the text to nn 73–78, below.

which it endorses. That having been said, American Realism (as we shall see) also almost explicitly adopted a similar approach – primarily because of its preoccupation with particulars as opposed to universals, even though it did not *expressly* reject the concept of objective standards as such. Indeed, even Langdellian legal formalism, as well as the legal process school and the law and economics movement, at least implicitly argued in favour of a certain measure of subjectivity, at least insofar as the extralegal context is concerned; the objectivity endorsed by these theories is, in other words, only a *qualified* one that is embedded only within the specific criteria set out in the individual theories themselves.

Finally, insofar as the third theory (viz, the Marxian Theory of Law) is concerned, it has – as we shall see – little (if any) to do with the law as such and is focused, instead, on political economy instead.

With this brief overview, let us now turn to the first theory – American Realism.

II. American Realism[15]

A. The Theory

American Realism has been traditionally divided into two branches – Fact Skepticism and Rule Skepticism, respectively.[16] Both branches eschewed the idea that legal doctrine – in and of itself – led to legal certainty.

The so-called 'Fact Skeptics' in the movement[17] pointed to the uncertainty in the factual realm – not least because of the adversarial system.[18] Indeed, at this

[15] For an excellent and representative collection of readings (and superb introductions to each main topic) on American Realism, see WW Fisher III, MJ Horwitz and TA Reed (gen eds), *American Legal Realism* (New York, Oxford University Press, 1993). And *cf* H Dagan, *Reconstructing Legal Realism & Rethinking Private Law Theory* (Oxford, Oxford University Press, 2013) which is, however (and with respect), overly theoretical and (as the title of the book suggests) reconstructive in nature, and does not really deal with the specific (and very real) difficulties that are considered later in this chapter.

[16] See generally, WE Rumble Jr, 'American Legal Realism and the Reduction of Uncertainty' (1964) 13 *Journal of Public Law* 45 for an excellent overview.

[17] In particular, Jerome Frank: see, eg, *Law and the Modern Mind* (New York, Brentano's, Inc, 1930) as well as *Courts on Trial: Myth and Reality in American Justice* (Princeton, Princeton University Press, 1949). The relevant factors include both institutional as well as psychological factors: see, eg, SN Verdun-Jones, 'The Jurisprudence of Jerome N. Frank – A Study in American Realism' (1974) 7 *Sydney Law Review* 180, 203–206. See also J Paul, *The Legal Realism of Jerome N. Frank – A Study of Fact-Skepticism and the Judicial Process* (The Hague, Martinus Nijhoff, 1959). *Cf* also BN Cardozo, *The Nature of the Judicial Process* (New Haven, Yale University Press, 1921) 129 (whom, however, Frank thought nevertheless concentrated too much, as a 'Rule Skeptic', on the legal rules). It should also be noted that Frank thought that the 'Rule Skeptics' (discussed briefly below) were mistaken in their approach as they focused on legal rules applied in the *appellate* context instead of the work of the *trial courts* where *facts* were of the first importance (see J Frank, 'Cardozo and the Upper-Court Myth' (1948) 13 *Law and Contemporary Problems* 369).

[18] See Rumble (n 16) 47.

juncture, it is apposite, in my view, to canvass a point that I have also already dealt with briefly in other chapters of this book:[19] that the facts of cases are myriad and that it is therefore difficult (even impossible) to predict the *outcome* in most cases (even assuming that the factual parameters constituting an integral part of the legal rule itself are clearly delineated). The American Realists dealt with a closely connected issue – that the *ascertainment* of the *actual* facts in any given case is itself *unpredictable*. As a sitting (especially trial) judge, I can confirm that that is indeed the case. As has just been noted, the adversarial system contributes to such difficulty.[20] Ascertaining the evidence of witnesses is a closely related difficulty as well.[21] However, it is suggested that the difficulties with the unpredictability of the *facts* of a given case do not *necessarily* detract from the *importance* of *legal doctrine*. What it *does* suggest, however, is that it would be difficult – if not impossible – to posit a comprehensive *theoretical framework* that would be able to take into account (let alone predict) the *results* of cases.[22] This brings us to the second branch of the movement that argues, however, *against* the point that has just been made.

The so-called 'Rule Skeptics' view even *legal* rules as being *unpredictable*.[23] However, the view that legal rules are 'but delightful word jousts' that are 'not dependable guides to the workings of the judicial process'[24] is, with respect, too skeptical a view to take. Whilst American Realists are correct in pointing to the possible (especially subconscious) biases of judges[25] (and that, for example, the discipline of psychology is therefore important[26]), it is suggested that the rather skeptical view adopted by the 'Rule Skeptics' throws out the legal baby together with the bathwater. As I suggest later in this chapter and (especially) in the final chapter of the present book,[27] the way forward is not to give up on legal rules but to adopt the approach of 'good faith judging' instead. Indeed, I would add that there is nothing wrong with the legal rules per se and that any unpredictability

[19] See, eg, chs 3 and 6 in this volume.

[20] In the US and other jurisdictions, trial by *jury* contributes to this difficulty as well (see, eg, Rumble (n 16) 48–51). It should be noted that Singapore never had trial by jury in the civil context and that trial by jury for criminal cases has been abolished (see A Phang, 'Jury Trial in Singapore and Malaysia: The Unmaking of A Legal Institution' (1983) 25 *Malaya Law Review* 50).

[21] See also generally KO See, *Fact-Finding and Reality: A Judicial Decision-Making Primer* (Singapore, Academy of Publishing, 2022).

[22] And see generally ch 3 in this volume.

[23] See, eg, Rumble (n 16) 51, where the learned author observes as follows: 'But for most of the legal realists, the more important objective was the reduction of rule-uncertainty, the uncertainty which stems from an inability to predict the rules which courts will use to classify the facts of particular cases.' Reference may also be made to the following article by the same author: see WE Rumble, 'Rule-Skepticism and the Role of the Judge: A Study of American Legal Realism' (1966) 15 *Journal of Public Law* 251.

[24] See Rumble (n 16) 52.

[25] ibid 51–53.

[26] ibid 53. Psychology also played a major part in Jerome Frank's works (as to which see n 17, above).

[27] See ch 10 in this volume.

arises from the *application* of those legal rules to the *facts* of a given case – a point noted, in fact, in the preceding paragraph (in relation to the 'Fact Skeptics').

Indeed, both branches of American Realism just referred to had – arguably at least – their source in the influence of that great judge and jurist, Oliver Wendell Holmes, Jr. Virtually everyone, for example, is acquainted with his famous words from *The Common Law*:[28]

> *The life of the law has not been logic: it has been experience.* The felt necessities of the time, the prevalent moral and political theories, intuitions of public policy, avowed or unconscious, even the prejudices which judges share with their fellow-men, have had a good deal more to do than the syllogism in determining the rules by which men should be governed.

Indeed, Holmes was never enamoured of legal rules per se; as he put it:[29]

> The *prophecies* of what the courts will do *in fact*, and nothing more pretentious, are what I mean by the law.

Despite the traditional classification of American Realism into the two branches as briefly described above, the movement itself is not easy to describe. Indeed, even its origins are less than clear, although it has traditionally been traced to the 1930s in general and the exchange between those legal giants, Karl Llewellyn and Roscoe Pound in particular.[30] As a leading commentator has put it, American Realism was not so much a jurisprudential movement as such but was, rather, a mood.[31] That having been said, apart from its critique of legal formalism, it did

[28] See OW Holmes, *The Common Law* (Boston, Little, Brown and Company, 1881) 1 (emphasis added).

[29] See OW Holmes, 'The Path of the Law' (1997) 110 *Harvard Law Review* 991, 994 (emphasis added). See also Rumble (n 16) 73 as well as Horwitz (n 6) ch 4, entitled 'The Place of Justice Holmes in American Legal Thought'. Indeed, Holmes has been described as 'the most important and influential legal thinker America has had': Horwitz (n 6) 109.

[30] See generally KN Llewellyn, 'A Realistic Jurisprudence – The Next Step' (1930) 30 *Columbia Law Review* 431 and, by the same author, 'Some Realism About Realism – Responding to Dean Pound' (1931) 44 *Harvard Law Review* 1222 as well as R Pound, 'The Call for a Realist Jurisprudence' (1931) 44 *Harvard Law Review* 697. And as a leading commentator has observed, '[n]othing has so shaped – and distorted – our picture of Legal Realism as the famous exchange over Realism between Karl Llewellyn and Roscoe Pound in 1930-1931': see Horwitz (n 6) 170. For fascinating and insightful background, see NEH Hull, 'Some Realism About the Llewellyn-Pound Exchange Over Realism: The Newly Uncovered Private Correspondence, 1927-1931 [1987] *Wisconsin Law Review* 921 and, by the same author, 'Reconstructing the Origins of Realistic Jurisprudence: A Prequel to the Llewellyn-Pound Exchange over Legal Realism' [1989] *Duke Law Journal* 1302 as well as *Roscoe Pound and Karl Llewellyn – Searching for an American Jurisprudence* (Chicago, University of Chicago Press, 1997) (this last-mentioned book contains material in the learned author's two articles which have just been cited). Reference may also be made to Twining (n 5), especially ch 5, entitled 'The Realist Controversy, 1930-I'.

[31] See generally Duxbury (n 7). See also Llewellyn, 'Some Realism About Realism – Responding to Dean Pound' (n 30) 1233: 'There is no school of realists.' Reference may also be made (to like effect) to Twining (n 5), where the learned observed that '[t]he realist movement should viewed, in first instance, not as a school of jurisprudence but as an historical phenomenon'. See also Horwitz (n 6) 169, where the learned author was of the view that American Realism 'expressed more an intellectual mood than a clear body of tenets, more a set of sometimes contradictory tendencies than a rigorous set of methodologies or propositions about legal theory'.

endeavour (at least through the efforts of some of its protagonists) to explore the *practical* nature of the law in a *scientific* manner. This was in keeping with its focus on the 'law in *action*' (as opposed to the static legal rules themselves). This meant – in turn – the need (as Llewellyn put it) to effect an at least 'temporary' *divorce* of the 'is' from the 'ought' for the purpose of an *empirical* study of the law as it operated in society.[32] This brings us back – in part at least – to the discipline of psychology (briefly alluded to above). There needed – in short – to be a *scientific* approach towards the 'law in action'.[33] Whilst laudable, the efforts at empirical inquiry turned out, in the final analysis, to be (unfortunately and with respect) damp squibs.[34]

B. The Difficulties

Dealing with the difficulties with American Realism is an enormous task; I will therefore focus only on what seem to me to be *two* extremely major weaknesses – first, its reliance upon the more general (and extralegal) concept of scientific naturalism (and, consequently, the inability to formulate an appropriate *normative programme*) and, second, the fact that such a skeptical approach towards the law in general and (consequently) adjudication in particular will engender a *disempowering effect* on judges and lawyers as well as *a loss of legitimacy* of the law in the eyes of *the public.*

Insofar as the former (viz, scientific naturalism) is concerned, it is suggested that this is in fact *a pivotal concept* that applies across the various disciplines (including the law) – and, hence, its specific consideration in this part of the present chapter. Indeed, it is clear that both scientific naturalism and (more specifically) American Realism are concerned with both the 'law in action' as well as accompanying *scientific and empirical inquiry.*[35]

I will specifically canvass the more specific implications of scientific naturalism in a manner that has not, to the best of my knowledge, been adopted before in at least explicitly legal tomes. Most of the existing works correctly point to the fact that American Realism fizzled out and was unable to provide normative

[32] See Llewellyn, 'Some Realism About Realism – Responding to Dean Pound' (n 30) 1236. But *cf* HE Yntema, 'American Legal Realism in Retrospect' (1960) 14 *Vanderbilt Law Review* 317, 324–325. Reference may also be made to Horwitz (n 6) 5, where the learned author interestingly observes that 'Llewellyn's positivism – his wish to sharply separate law and morals, as well as facts and values – was hardly typical of Realism'.

[33] See, eg, SN Verdun-Jones, 'Cook, Oliphant and Yntema: The Scientific Wing of American Legal Realism' (1979) 5 *Dalhousie Law Journal* 3 and, by the same author, 'Cook, Oliphant and Yntema: The Scientific Wing of American Legal Realism (Part II)' (1979) 5 *Dalhousie Law Journal* 249, as well as Rumble (n 16) 64–73 and the works by Schlegel cited at n 7, above.

[34] See the works by Schlegel cited at n 7, above as well as Yntema (n 32) 329. Though *cf* the views of Twining at n 60, below.

[35] See, in relation to the latter (viz, American Realism) the text to nn 32–34, above.

guidance.[36] I attempt to go one step further and argue that, by its very embrace of scientific naturalism, *no normative programme or theory was possible*. Purcell[37] does in fact describe the datum problem in contrasting scientific naturalism with rational absolutism. However, I would like to unpack the implications in a far more explicit fashion.

Returning to the effect of scientific naturalism in general and on American Realism in particular, Professor Purcell succinctly defined 'scientific naturalism' as follows:[38]

> Absolute rational principles did not govern or explain the universe. No *a priori* truths existed, and metaphysics was merely a cover for human ignorance and superstition. Only concrete, scientific investigations could yield true knowledge … and that knowledge was empirical, particular, and experimentally verifiable.

The definition just quoted is instructive. According to scientific naturalism, absolute values did not exist. One notes, further, the overwhelming bias against anything that is not in material or physical form. Intangible ideas, such as values, are dismissed out of hand because they are (according to this concept) somehow not scientifically verifiable. Yet another important aspect of scientific naturalism to note is its focus on *the particular*; indeed, since absolute values (which are necessarily universal in nature) are taboo, there is no alternative but to look to the particular (factual) circumstances for guidance through empirical verification. As we shall see soon, however, these premises which underpin scientific naturalism are, with respect, fatally flawed. It will suffice for the moment to emphasise that the recourse to scientific naturalism is one that is based purely upon the rational and the material, the transcendent having been abandoned altogether.

Bearing in mind the working definition of scientific naturalism just referred to,[39] we need to deal with the specific weakness in each of the assumptions underlying it. The first is that absolute values do not exist. As I have already argued in an earlier chapter, this is an untenable assumption.[40] Indeed, the very argument to the effect that absolute values do not exist is *itself* a proposition containing an absolute which, if true, would render it suspect! A related point might be raised: the reference in the working definition just referred to in the quotation above is to 'absolute *rational* principles',[41] and, in this regard, some clarification may be in order. 'Absolute principles' are consistent with rationality; however, it does *not* follow that the *only* conception of 'absolute principles' is one that is premised *wholly* on *rationality*. Indeed, the ordinary conception of 'absolute principles' entails the idea of *intangible* values that may be justified by rational argument, albeit only on

[36] See, eg, Duxbury (n 7). See also Horwitz (n 6).
[37] See Purcell (n 6).
[38] ibid 3 (citing the views of the Swedish American physiologist Anton Julius Carlson).
[39] See above, n 38.
[40] See ch 3 in this volume.
[41] See above, n 38 (emphasis added).

probabilities, since the very nature of rational argument itself precludes an argument from absolute certainty.

This brings us, in fact, to the next assumption of scientific naturalism – that anything that is not in physical or material form and/or that cannot be empirically or scientifically verified is mere superstition. Many difficulties surround such an assumption: not least the conclusion (necessarily entailed by such an argument) that moral *values* cannot exist because they are, *ex hypothesi*, intangible and hence not generally susceptible of scientific or empirical investigation – not, at least, in the manner and to the extent embodied in (as well as required by) the concept of scientific naturalism itself. Indeed, even where, for example, sociological studies could be conducted, no (even close to absolute) proof can be forthcoming, if nothing else, because of David Hume's famous (and powerful) argument to the effect that one cannot derive an 'ought' from an 'is'. This is in fact what has been termed the 'Humean Guillotine'.[42]

More important, however, is the fact that the argument that everything depends solely on scientific and empirical investigation as well as verification is wholly contrary to human experience and intuition. But lest the reader be under the impression that I am appealing to mere feelings and emotionalism, I should hasten to add that the very argument from scientific and empirical investigation is *itself premised upon an intangible value system* which requires *as much (if not more) faith* to believe in than the belief in (intangible) moral values themselves. More to the point, the argument presently critiqued is heavily dependent upon *Darwinian evolutionary theory*.[43] Indeed, the Darwinian theory of natural selection is coterminous with scientific naturalism in a number of ways. First, it purports to focus not on universal and absolute values as such but, rather, on particular facts instead. Second – and this is a closely related point – it is based on the idea that everything there is came about not by design but, on the contrary, by *chance*.

This book is not the venue to embark on a discussion of both the merits and the demerits of scientific naturalism. It suffices for present purposes to state that its foundations in Darwinian evolutionary theory are – at best – controversial. More importantly, perhaps, *values* such as justice and fairness are not – as every judge and lawyer will tell you (and which has already been emphasised above) – susceptible to precise *scientific* analysis. As already mentioned, this is not to state that such values are inconsistent with reason and logic. Quite the contrary. However, the fact remains that one must – as the scientific naturalists would have us – go further by dismissing out of hand any values that are not *empirically verifiable*. Indeed, it is

[42] And discussed in this book at ch 2 in this volume. See also M Black, 'The Gap Between "Is" and "Should"' (1964) 73 *The Philosophical Review* 165, 166 (where the phrase 'Humean Guillotine' appears to have been coined). Reference may also be made to M Black, 'The "Factual" and the "Normative"' in K Kuypers (ed), *Human Sciences and the Problem of Values* (The Hague, Martinus Nijhoff, 1972) 56.

[43] See Purcell (n 6) 5–6.

suggested (and as we shall see) that it was precisely because of this (with respect, obsessive) preoccupation with empirical *fact* that resulted in American Realism being unable to posit a *normative* theory. And this, in turn, caused American Realism to ultimately *fizzle as well as peter out*. Let me elaborate.

Although scientific naturalism offered the promise of a viable *normative* alternative, its *very nature closes off* this option *right at the outset*. As we have already seen, by focusing on only the material sphere, it eschews the possibility of moral values, which are, *ex hypothesi*, intangible. I want now to elaborate on a point that was only alluded to above: that by necessarily focusing also on the realm of (here, scientific) *facts*, scientific naturalism traps itself within the straitjacket of both the descriptive (or realm of the 'is') and of the particular. This is the other extreme, in other words, of the continuum which separates the universal (normative theory) from the particular (descriptive facts). The universal and the particular must be integrated.[44] Scientific naturalism, however, disqualifies itself, as it were, from such integration right from the outset. It is no wonder, then, that American Realism, which was based upon scientific naturalism, fizzled out: primarily because it was unable to furnish a cogent *normative* theory or, indeed, any theory at all. That this fizzling or petering out took place precisely because American Realism was unable to provide a cogent *normative* alternative is well-documented in the relevant literature.[45] For example, Professor Horwitz is highly critical of the 'social science methodology' which Llewellyn employed (principally through his temporary divorce of the 'is' from the 'ought'[46]).[47] And as he pertinently observed:[48]

> In the absence of any autonomous method for objectively determining values, secularly inclined social reformers *turned to society to generate values*. They maintained that what was wrong with Classical Legal Thought was not that it was based on bad values – for who could presume to defend the objectivity of any system of values? – but that it was simply out of touch with social reality. *Social reality – the Is – became the source of the Ought. Description was privileged over prescription. Value was to be discovered from social fact. The turn to positivist social science was thus an attempt to evade the value question by substituting expertise and professionalism as the central forms of legitimation.*

Professor Horwitz's account is consistent with my suggestion above that scientific naturalism – in and of itself – could not furnish an appropriate *normative* framework. Horwitz argues that American Realism turned to *society* instead in order 'to

[44] See also ch 3 in this volume.

[45] See, eg, the works cited at n 6, above.

[46] As to which, see above, n 32.

[47] See Horwitz (n 6) 210. As already mentioned, such methodology relied heavily on the concept of scientific naturalism.

[48] ibid 211 (emphasis added). Professor Horwitz also cites (correctly and perceptively, in my view) Professor Lon Fuller's views in support: see LL Fuller, 'American Legal Realism' (1934) 82 *University of Pennsylvania Law Review* 429, 461.

generate values'.[49] Not surprisingly, this did not provide a solution either simply because of the 'Humean guillotine' to the effect that one cannot logically derive an 'ought' from an 'is'.[50]

I turn now to the *second* major difficulty with American Realism. This particular difficulty stems in fact – and is closely related to – the first. It relates to problems on two (related) fronts and perspectives. From the *internal* perspective of the principal protagonists in the legal system (viz, the judges and the lawyers), the skeptical approach which characterises American Realism would, I suggest, serve to undermine what I propose in this book as 'good faith judging'[51] at best and might even lead to a feeling of disempowerment at worst. The second – and related – perspective is an *external* one in relation to the view of *the public* insofar as the standing of the legal system is concerned. If, indeed, the public accepts the characterisation of the legal system by American Realism, this would lead to *a loss of legitimacy* of the same in the eyes of the public. Conversely, a legal system that would command the respect of the public is one that is perceived as being objectively just and fair.

Drawing from my own experience and observations as a judge, it is clear that the skeptical approach proffered by American Realism is clearly *not* an accurate depiction of what actually occurs in the practical context of actual adjudication. I will elaborate on this in the next – and final – chapter of the present book.[52] It will suffice for present purposes to note – indeed, underscore – the fact that judges (following their Oath of Office) *strive to arrive at just and fair decisions based on the relevant facts in each and every case they hear. And they do so in the sincere belief – indeed, conviction – that there is an objective right answer to the case at hand. And this is real and not a self-deception. Still less is there a skeptical or cynical manipulation of the facts to arrive at a subjective result that the judge concerned personally prefers. And it is precisely such an attitude as well as process that results in the law in general and its adjudicative process in particular having the respect and legitimacy it has in the eyes of the public.* All this may appear simple. However, as I shall endeavour to demonstrate in the next – and final – chapter of this book,[53] it is by no means simplistic. *It comprises many of the best as well as practical elements of many of the theories considered in the preceding chapters of the present book.* Indeed, it even comprises one of the main insights of *American Realism itself* – to which our attention now turns.

[49] Horwitz (n 6) 211. See also Duxbury (n 2) 158, who refers to 'a catalogue of missed opportunities' that suggested 'that legal realists generally lost their nerve when faced with the implications of their own jurisprudential constructions'.

[50] See the text to n 42, above. Professor Horwitz argues that the result was the focus on *process* instead: see generally Horwitz (n 6) ch 9, entitled 'Post-War Legal Thought 1945–1960'. See also the text to nn 8–12, above. But *cf* Duxbury (n 8); indeed, the learned author argues that '[t]he process tradition in fact evolved alongside realism rather than in reaction to it': ibid 298.

[51] See ch 10 in this volume.

[52] ibid.

[53] ibid.

C. The Positive Insights and Legacy

The main – as well as enduring – insight of American Realism, in my view, was to underscore the fact that the *facts* of cases (or perhaps, more correctly, judicial findings as to the *facts* of cases) were of fundamental importance in determining the outcome in any given case. This might appear to be an obvious point, but it is often the obvious points, hiding in plain sight as it were, that are most overlooked. Indeed, this is particularly so (ironically) in relation to legal *theory*. In this last-mentioned regard, even a cursory review of the relevant legal literature will demonstrate how rarefied the discussion is. It is interesting, however, to note at this juncture that this insight of American Realism was *simultaneously (and perhaps ironically)* also its *weakness* inasmuch as it was taken to the extreme by scientific naturalism (as noted in the preceding part of this chapter).

However, as a trial – then an appellate – judge, I can attest to the importance of the facts of cases. As, for example, Jerome Frank aptly points out, facts are especially important at the trial stage.[54] They are nevertheless also important at the appellate stage as well. Put simply, a court does not decide a case in a factual vacuum. Indeed, even at the appellate level (for example, insofar as the Singapore Court of Appeal is concerned), whilst the court does take the opportunity to clarify important (especially novel) points of law as a court of last resort, the focus is always on the result between the parties, for this is the raison d'être of any given hearing. It might not surprise the reader in the least to learn that parties are interested only in the final result – whether they have won or lost the case concerned.[55] After all, these are more often than not laypersons who have spent enormous sums of money in the process of litigating their respective cases.

More importantly, as just alluded to, the court itself cannot decide a case (which, *ex hypothesi*, it must) without close attention to the actual facts of the case at hand. This is what I think that famous aphorism by Holmes to which we have already referred (that 'The life of the law has not been logic: it has been experience'[56]) means. This is not, however, to state that the law is unimportant. However, it is impossible for a court to decide a case by *merely* looking at *the law*. And, on occasion, the recognition of *essential facts* can make a crucial difference – even at the appellate level. Let me provide you with an illustration of this last-mentioned point.

In the Singapore Court of Appeal decision of *Ang Sin Hock v Khoo Eng Lim*,[57] the trial court had held, amongst other things, that the claim in contract by the Appellant had been time-barred under the provisions of the Singapore

[54] See above, n 17.

[55] Indeed, on many occasions, I am told that the person collecting the judgment of the court on behalf of the party concerned (or, as is sometimes the case, the actual party itself) will turn immediately to the very last page of the judgment where the decision or verdict of the court is to be found.

[56] See above, n 28.

[57] *Ang Sin Hock v Khoo Eng Lim* [2010] 3 *Singapore Law Reports* 179.

Limitation Act.[58] This was indeed the situation. However, the appellate court looked at what it considered *crucial facts* that had *not* been considered by the trial court. It could do this because no new findings of fact needed to be made. It then proceeded to hold that the letter from the Respondent to the Appellant on 12 April 2000, in which he promised to make payment by 18 April 2000, was a fresh contract for which the Appellant had given good consideration in the form of forbearance to sue. The Respondent's failure to pay the Appellant on 18 April 2000 constituted a breach of *that new (collateral) contract*, which entitled the Appellant to damages which would put him in the same position as if the contract had been performed. The limitation period of six years under the Limitation Act with regard to this particular contract commenced from the time the contract was breached (here, 18 April 2000). Given that the writ was issued on 17 April 2006, the Appellant's claim based on this fresh contract was commenced within the limitation period, and there was therefore no issue of a time bar. The appeal was therefore allowed on this basis.

However, this insight provided by American Realism missed, with respect, an important *normative* point. That the facts of cases are important (and will almost invariably differ from case to case) does *not necessarily* entail the conclusion that *the law* (which constitutes the *normative guides* for the court) *is uncertain*. Indeed, the stance adopted by (at least extreme forms of) American Realism that the law is uncertain because the facts are all-important and vary from case to case is *itself* a *normative* guide of sorts. Unfortunately, too, such a stance is – on both theoretical and practical levels – apt to engender a skepticism which is disempowering for courts, lawyers and litigants alike. Put simply (and harking back to the relevant discussion in chapter two of this book), the so-called *normative* approach of American Realism *conflates* the prescriptive and the descriptive. What is required, on the other hand, are *prescriptive (or normative)* rules and principles of *law*, which will then *guide* the court in arriving at a fair and just decision after applying those rules and principles of *law* to the *relevant facts* of the case.

It might be reasonably asked what an *alternative theory* might then look like – given that the entire process (of applying the law to the facts) is such a *dynamic* process. Put simply once again, how can a (normative) *theory* be posited in light of the nature of such a process? This is what I seek to do in the next chapter when I posit a new (and alternative) theory of adjudication that seeks to take into account the *dynamic* nature of adjudication itself. What *is* clear, however, is that when – as I suggest was indeed the case with American Realism – the resultant normative theory or framework is one that is (in substance at least) rooted in *the descriptive facts*, it cannot, with respect, serve as a *theoretical* framework that is *necessarily universal* in nature (or at least application). Perhaps that explains – as

[58] Cap 163, 1996 Rev Edn; now the Limitation Act 1959 (2020 Rev Edn) (the provisions of which were similar to the equivalent provisions of the UK Limitation Act).

Horwitz appears to suggest[59] – why American Realism never really took off and (on the contrary) fizzled out despite its enormous initial promise.

At this juncture, it should nevertheless be noted that there is a *second* insight as well as legacy which American Realism has left us with – that the study of law must take into account the wider society which it serves lest the court lose touch with the society that the law ultimately serves. This might be easier said than done in *practice*, but we ignore this simple (yet paradoxically profound) point at our peril.[60]

III. The Critical Legal Studies Movement[61]

A. The Theory

The Critical Legal Studies Movement is in fact a relatively recent jurisprudential movement (commencing only around the mid-1970s or so). It is best characterised by the statement that 'law is politics'. Put simply, the Critical Legal Studies Movement has two closely related facets. The first is very similar to the stance adopted by American Realism – the rejection of legal formalism (again, traditionally characterised by legal positivism). The second is the emphasis, instead, on politics and ideology (consistent with the statement referred to at the outset of the present paragraph). It should be noted that the concept of 'politics' referred to by this jurisprudential movement is quite different from that embraced, for example, by jurists such as Professor Ronald Dworkin.[62] In particular, it refers to ad hoc as well as expedient decisions based on ideological leanings and the resultant extra-legal policy decisions made. In many ways, such an approach is the very *antithesis* of the objective as well as principled decision-making process in the context of *adjudication*.

Not surprisingly, therefore, the Critical Legal Studies Movement explicitly rejects objective standards altogether, consistently with the postmodernist approach which it endorses.

[59] See the text to nn 46–50, above.

[60] And see Twining (n 5) 383, where the learned author observed that 'the main achievement of the movement was to concretize sociological jurisprudence'; he also observed (ibid 386–387) that '[o]ne of the main lessons to be drawn from the story of the realist movement is that it is easy to ignore or to underestimate the difficulties, theoretical and practical, of sustained interdisciplinary work'. And in the *Afterword* to the second edition of that same book (entitled 'Framing Llewellyn'), Twining opined (ibid 443) that 'the central message of realism is that understanding law involves studying both the law in books and the law in action'. And, as Horwitz put it, '[a]ll realists shared one basic premise – that the law had come to be out of touch with reality': see Horwitz (n 6) 187.

[61] And see generally Hutchinson and Monahan (n 13) as well as Kelman (n 13) and Duxbury (n 2) ch 6, entitled 'Uses of Critique'.

[62] As to which see chs 6, 7 and 8 in this volume.

As Hutchinson and Monahan put it in their perceptive article, the Critical Legal Studies Movement is literally a reaction against *everything*.[63] Despite, therefore, sharing the basic leftist critique levelled by Marxian theory against liberal legal theory, the Critical Legal Studies Movement must perforce also reject Marxian legal theory because it (Marxian theory) does posit, at bottom, a unique theory (which is based on historical materialism and which, through the process of class struggle, will result in a classless society where law and the state will wither away[64]).[65] Not surprisingly, given its basic orientation, the Critical Legal Studies Movement also strongly critiques liberal legal theory, which (unlike Marxian legal theory) is at the other end of the spectrum. Liberal legal theory (which would include, for example, the works of Dworkin[66] and Rawls[67]) also posits one unique path, which is of course dependent on the particular theory proffered. More importantly, each of these liberal legal theories argues that there are *objective* ways of looking at as well as resolving legal theory and issues. The Critical Legal Studies Movement, as we have already seen, of course totally dismisses the very concept of objectivity to begin with – its deconstructive cast is an absolute and devastating one.

On a more specific level, one main theme which that the Critical Legal Studies Movement grapples with – what Professor Duncan Kennedy has referred to as 'the fundamental contradiction'[68] – might be usefully noted. Simply put, this is the tension between individualism on the one hand and (conflicting) community demands on the other. Where, of course, there is a coincidence between the two, no conflict arises. However, conflict is more often likely than not. Indeed, 'the fundamental contradiction' is, in essence, not a concept which is hugely abstract; on the contrary, it represents a tension that is very much an integral part of *life* itself. Virtually every day, we find ourselves needing others, indeed working out our individual identities as well as meaning in life from the perspective of our

[63] See generally Hutchinson and Monahan (n 13).

[64] On Marxian legal theory, see the next part of this chapter.

[65] See Hutchinson and Monahan (n 13) 216 and 220–221. Professor Roberto Mangabeira Unger, a prominent member of the Critical Legal Studies Movement, characterises Marxian theory as 'deep structure theory': see RM Unger, *Social Theory: Its Situation and Its Task – A Critical Introduction to Politics* (Cambridge, Cambridge University Press, 1987) 87. And on Unger's work generally, see the text to nn 73–78, below.

[66] See generally above, n 12. See also chs 6, 7 and 8 in this volume.

[67] His most famous work is J Rawls, *A Theory of Justice* (Cambridge, Belknap Press, 1971). See also J Rawls, *Political Liberalism* (New York, Columbia University Press, 1993), amongst his many other works. The literature on Rawls's ideas is – not surprisingly – enormous.

[68] See D Kennedy, 'The Structure of Blackstone's Commentaries' (1979) 28 *Buffalo Law Review* 205, 211–213. However, Kennedy apparently recanted this concept subsequently: see P Gabel and D Kennedy, 'Roll Over Beethoven' (1984) 36 *Stanford Law Review* 1, 15–16 and 24. Kennedy was probably expressing a tongue-in-cheek view here. On related concepts, for example the tension between individualism and altruism, see D Kennedy, 'Form and Substance in Private Law Adjudication' (1976) 89 *Harvard Law Review* 1685 and, by the same author, 'Distributive and Paternalist Motives in Contract and Tort Law, With Special Reference to Compulsory Terms and Unequal Bargaining Power' (1982) 41 *Maryland Law Review* 563. *Cf* Gabel and Kennedy, above, 38–39.

relations with others, especially with regard to those who are particularly close to us, for example, our family members. Yet, we also find ourselves often wanting to *distance* ourselves from others: to have that space in which to realise our own individuality and which resists (even vehemently, on occasion) the attempts (whether intended or otherwise) by society or community to stifle that individuality and creativity in the name of conformity for the greater good. Indeed, it bears repeating that 'the fundamental contradiction' is not an abstruse or arcane concept – it goes (as we have just seen) to the very essence of our lives and being. But it is also a rather curious creature: Janus-faced and even more complexly chameleon-like at many other points in time. Despite its very practical impact and implications, 'the fundamental contradiction' simultaneously manifests itself as an intractable philosophical conundrum. It is manifested in such basic philosophical dilemmas as the tension or conflict between freewill and determinism, between individualism and communitarianism (and the closely related conflict between individual rights on the one hand and countervailing utilitarian goals on the other) – all of which have, to date, not received even close to satisfactory resolutions. But is this intractability itself some evidence, at least in support of the postmodernist stance adopted by the Critical Legal Studies Movement? If the central tenets of that jurisprudential movement are correct, then *no* resolution is ever possible. Indeed, the slogan (already referred to above) that 'law is politics' would 'assault' us with a vengeance: every decision (whether in favour of the individual or the wider community) would be one that is indelibly stained with the blot of arbitrariness – an arbitrariness that we have to accept and are powerless to change. 'Might is right' soon becomes the accompanying slogan, and if 'might' is not on our side (as would, in the nature of things, be the case for the vast, vast majority of people), then our fate is thrown to the waves and the winds, tossed and turned at the whims and fancies of those in power. This is, unfortunately, the logical (and, I might add, inevitable) consequence of accepting the central arguments of the Critical Legal Studies Movement.[69] Ironically, this jurisprudential movement began as one that sought to empower but ends up as something that does the *complete opposite*. Given the *fact* of 'the fundamental contradiction' (particularly as experienced in our daily lives), are we simply to acknowledge that fact and give up on a normative solution?

To return more generally to the Critical Legal Studies Movement, as a result of its approach as briefly described above, it arrives – in the final analysis (albeit via a different route) – at the same 'destination' as American Realism. Put simply, it has (with an exception I will note in the next part of this chapter) *no* positive

[69] Which, as we have seen, are profoundly pessimistic – and which is consistent with the postmodernist approach adopted. And this is so even when (in my view, especially when) it appears in erudite tomes: see, eg, D Kennedy, *A Critique of Adjudication* (Cambridge, Harvard University Press, 1997). And for my critique of that particular work, see A Phang, 'Critical Legal Studies, Economic Development and Human Rights' (1999) 142/143 *Law and Justice* 122, 123–124.

theoretical programme as such.[70] This is not surprising in view of the premise that underlies this particular jurisprudential movement – that 'law is politics'. Whilst it is true that such a skeptical as well as negative approach does arrive at a 'negative' theory of sorts (a kind of 'theory of no theory'), from a practical perspective, the consequences are simply negative and unhelpful – especially if one bears in mind that the adjudicative process is intended to assist courts and judges in arriving at a just and fair decision in the case at hand. Indeed, as we have just noted in the preceding paragraph, the Critical Legal Studies Movement does not accept the idea of objective standards in the first place.

In the circumstances, the difficulties with this jurisprudential movement appear to be clear – and it is to those difficulties that our attention now turns.

B. The Difficulties

As we have seen, the Critical Legal Studies Movement did not constitute a coherent *theory* as such. Its primary message – that 'law is politics' – whilst attractive, did *not* (like American Realism) posit a *coherent positive programme* as such. Even its negative critique of existing legal doctrine and theories was too dispiriting. It is therefore not surprising that (again, like American Realism) Critical Legal Studies also did not take off and fizzled out – despite being a far more contemporary school of legal thought than, for example, American Realism itself. I would suggest a number of reasons why this was the case.

First (and this is a point that was in fact just alluded to), it was too disparate. Perhaps this is not surprising in view of the fact that much of the Critical Legal Studies Movement did not engage with *law* as such – save, perhaps, in its *critique* of the same. The central thread was indeed *critique* – whether in the field of legal theory[71] or legal history.[72] However, it is one thing to critique (which is akin to tearing down an old and allegedly unusable building); something new, however, has to be put in its place (which is akin to constructing a new building). And this leads to my second – and closely related – point.

Second, it is submitted that the Critical Legal Studies Movement did not develop or construct a *positive* programme or theory simply because it was 'trapped' by its own fundamental premises. Put simply, if law is politics and it would therefore be impossible to develop (let alone legitimate) any one theory, then it could be argued (as also alluded to above) that *that* was indeed the *theoretical framework*

[70] On the suggested reasons as to why American Realism fizzled out, see the preceding part of this chapter.

[71] See, eg, RM Unger, *The Critical Legal Studies Movement* (Cambridge, Harvard University Press, 1983) and (by the same author) *What Should Legal Analysis Become* (London, Verso, 1996), as well as Kennedy (n 69).

[72] See, eg, Horwitz (n 6).

that the Critical Legal Studies Movement had mooted. However, if that was the case, it is not surprising that the Movement never progressed because such a 'programme', by arguing that no positive theory could be posited, is *self-defeating*. As I have sought to demonstrate in chapter two of the present book, even such an approach is *itself necessarily* a 'theory' of sorts – albeit one that is, with respect, theoretically stagnant and practically impotent. Indeed, this is why, for example, one of the leading lights in the Critical Legal Studies Movement, Professor Roberto Mangabeira Unger, was compelled to develop – in his social theory – what he terms 'a structure of no structure'. As I have just argued, however, even a 'structure of no structure' is *itself* a 'structure'. Further, as I argue elsewhere,[73] even the aforementioned 'structure of no structure' would nevertheless run into the problem of what I have termed 'solidification' inasmuch as any 'structure of no structure' (no matter how well intentioned it is) would (owing to basic human nature, if nothing else) ultimately succumb to 'capture' by a person or group of persons of bad faith. Indeed, Professor Unger's work in fact leads me to my third (and again, closely related) point. However, before proceeding to consider it, it should be noted that Unger's work[74] is both nuanced and complex, and a detailed critique is outside the purview of the present book. Adjudication is also a subject that is also on the margins or periphery of his work (which is focused on more general political as well as social theory). I have, however, dealt with Unger's work in more detail elsewhere, and the interested reader may refer to those writings.[75]

Third (and this is in fact related to the preceding two points), the leading scholars in the Critical Legal Studies Movement tended to be more concerned about philosophy and/or social theory rather than the law itself. Perhaps this is not surprising in view of the fact that they had rejected legal theory and legal doctrine as having no real legitimacy of their own and as being part of politics (with the attendant struggle for power and ascendency). With respect, however, by discarding existing legal theory and legal doctrine out of hand, the available material to develop or construct an alternative became too abstract and hence too divorced from the nature and role of law that has been developed *and* practised (as well as accepted by the public) for literally centuries. To make matters worse, each of the leading lights of this Movement adopted different approaches and theories. Hence, as we have just seen, Professor Unger, having discarded

[73] See A Phang, 'Roberto Unger and the Politics of Transformation in an Asian Context' [1997] *Tydskrif Vir Die Suid-Afrikaanse Reg (Journal of South African Law)* (published in 3 parts), 45–65, 287–304 and 472–497. See also, by the same author, *Toward Critique and Reconstruction. Roberto Unger on Law, Passion and Politics* (UK, Hull University Law School, 1993, Studies in Law Series).

[74] See the works cited at n 77, below. See also n 71, above.

[75] See the works cited at n 73, above. In those works, I also deal with Unger's earlier works as well as other aspects of his social theory, including his theory of personality (as to which see RM Unger, *Passion – An Essay on Personality* (New York, The Free Press, 1984)) as well as his views on the law itself (see, eg, RM Unger, *The Critical Legal Studies Movement* (n 71) and, by the same author, *What Should Legal Analysis Become* (n 71)).

the then existing views of law and legal theory,[76] developed a far broader and indeed sweeping social theory.[77] Once again, though, these broad theories were not, with respect, anchored in legal reality and indeed provided neither theoretical explanation nor practical guidance for judges sitting on actual cases. This is not surprising – to underscore a fundamental point already made, the Critical Legal Scholars were not interested in providing such explanations or guidance in the first place. Indeed, their approach, whilst disparate, had a common (and negative) thread – that the law as we know it is all about politics and the concomitant power struggle that that entails. It comes very close to a third theory, which I will briefly consider in the next part of this chapter – the Marxian theory of law.

However, before proceeding to do so, the reader would have noticed that, unlike the previous part (dealing with American Realism), I do not have a concluding part which acknowledges the benefits and legacy of the Critical Legal Studies Movement. This is because, with respect, there are none (save perhaps, like American Realism, to underscore, indirectly at least, the importance of the broader extra-legal context). The *negative* critique is without doubt a powerful one. However, it does not provide us with a complete picture of the role of law in general and of adjudication in particular. This is due, in the main, to the fact that it has *no positive programme* as such. The closest approach towards a positive programme is the political and social theory of Unger, which, as I have briefly pointed out above,[78] is not only far too broad but is also (again, with respect) divorced from reality (in particular, the manner in which the law has been developed *and* practised in *actual* cases, as well as the manner in which it has been perceived by the public itself). I therefore turn now to consider briefly the Marxian theory of law.

[76] Unger (n 71).

[77] See RM Unger, *Politics, a Work in Constructive Social Theory* (Cambridge, Cambridge University Press, 1987). This is, in fact, a massive three-volume work, spanning over one thousand pages. The first volume, entitled *Social Theory: Its Situation and Its Task – A Critical Introduction to Politics* (Cambridge, Cambridge University Press, 1987) sketches out the theoretical premises of the entire project. The second volume, entitled *False Necessity – Anti-Necessitarianism Social Theory in the Service of Radical Democracy* (Cambridge, Cambridge University Press, 1987), elaborates (in meticulous detail) on the various institutional element of Unger's project. The third (and final) volume, entitled *Plasticity into Power – Comparative-Historical Studies on the Institutional Conditions of Military Success* (Cambridge, Cambridge University Press, 1987), comprises three essays which are intended to provide the historical focus on, as well as illustration of, the more abstract themes and ideas contained in the preceding two volumes (in particular, the second). There was an extensive consideration of *Politics* in a symposium, the papers of which were published in the Summer 1987 issue of the *Northwestern University Law Review* (vol 81, no 4); all the papers (plus a few more, but minus essays by MS Ball, 'The City of Unger' (1987) 81 *Northwestern University Law Review* 625 and D Cornell, 'Beyond Tragedy and Complacency' (1987) 81 *Northwestern University Law Review* 693) were subsequently published in book form in RW Lovin and MJ Perry (eds), *Critique and Construction – A Symposium on Roberto Unger's Politics* (Cambridge, Cambridge University Press, 1990).

[78] See the text to nn 73–77, above.

IV. The Marxian Theory of Law

I will not dwell at length with the Marxian theory of law. Indeed, by the very nature of both his expertise and (relatedly) his discourse, Karl Marx (and those who followed him) were not really concerned about the law itself. There are at least two reasons. The first has in fact just been alluded to – Marx was concerned with a metatheory in general and the *economic as well as political* implications in particular. The second is a closely related reason: even on Marx's theory of political economy, the law itself played little or no part. If it played a role at all, it was, first, mere *superstructure* (in contrast to *the material base*, which, in his view, ought to constitute the main focus, particularly in relation to the main factors of production (which included capital, land and labour)). Cruder versions (often termed 'vulgar Marxism') view the law as a mere instrument used to maintain the hegemony of the ruling class whilst simultaneously keeping the working class in check.

It will be immediately seen why we need not spend too much time on the Marxian theory of law – in particular, 'vulgar Marxism'. It is too simplistic and betrays an absence of understanding as to the content as well as the role of law in society. Before the reader raises the (Marxian) objection that I am merely repeating the mantra of the ruling class, it is important to note that any judge or lawyer involved in the administration of law (whether in a common law system (which is the primary focus of this book) or a civil law system[79]), will (without any hint of any delusion) inform the reader that what they do is neither sham nor oppression – quite the contrary. Indeed, the following observations by the leftist scholar, EP Thompson,[80] in a quite startling coda to his brilliantly researched book, *Whigs and Hunters – The Origin of the Black Act*,[81] acknowledge (equally startlingly[82]) that the Rule of Law is (contrary to what he has always believed) 'an unqualified human good'; in his own words (which merit setting out *in extenso*):[83]

> [T]he law … may be seen instrumentally as mediating and reinforcing existent class relations and, ideologically, as offering to these a legitimation. But we must press our definitions a little further. … [t]he law, like other institutions which from time to

[79] See generally the classic text by JH Merryman and R Pérez-Perdomo, *The Civil Law Tradition – An Introduction to the Legal Systems of Europe and Latin America*, 4th edn (Stanford, Stanford University Press, 2018).

[80] See generally BD Palmer, *E.P. Thompson – Objections and Oppositions* (London, Verso, 1994).

[81] New York, Pantheon Books, 1975. His classic work for which he is probably the most well known for is *The Making of the English Working Class* (London, Victor Gollancz Ltd, 1963).

[82] Perhaps Thompson's rejection of 'vulgar Marxism' generally (which, in turn, entails a *total* rejection of the Rule of Law) is explicable by his rejection of the events relating to the Hungarian Revolution of 1956 (see Palmer (n 80) 73 as well as ibid ch 4, entitled 'The 1970s: Rethinking Marxism, Returning to 1956, and the Politics of Democracy'). See also generally EP Thompson, *The Poverty of Theory & Other Essays* (London, Merlin Press Ltd, 1978).

[83] Thompson, *Whigs and Hunters* (n 81) 262, 263, 265 and 266 (emphasis in italics in original, emphasis added in quoted italics).

time can be seen as mediating (and masking) existent class relations …, has its own characteristics, its own independent history and logic of evolution.

Moreover, people are not as stupid as some structuralist philosophers suppose them to be. They will not be mystified by the first man who puts on a wig. It is inherent in the especial character of law, as a body of rules and procedures, that it shall apply logical criteria with reference to standards of universality and equity. … Most men have a strong sense of justice, at least with regard to their own interests. If the law is evidently partial and unjust, then it will mask nothing, legitimize nothing, contribute nothing to any class's hegemony. The essential precondition for the effectiveness of law, in its function as ideology, is that it shall display an independence from gross manipulation and shall seem to be just. It cannot seem to be so without upholding its own logic and criteria of equity; indeed on occasion, by actually *being* just. And furthermore it is not often the case that a ruling ideology can be dismissed as mere hypocrisy; even rulers find a need to '*legitimize*' their power, to moralize their functions, to feel themselves to be useful and just. … The law may be rhetoric, but it need not be empty rhetoric.

…

The rhetoric and the rules of society are something a great deal more than sham. In the same moment they may modify, in profound ways, the behaviour of the powerful, and mystify the powerless. They may disguise the true realities of power, but, at the same time, they may '*curb*' that power '*and check*' its intrusions.

…

These reflections lead me on to conclusions which may be different from those which some readers expect. I have shown in this study a political oligarchy inventing callous and oppressive laws to serve its own interests. I have shown judges who, no less than bishops, were subject to political influence, whose sense of justice was humbug, and whose interpretation of the laws served only to enlarge their inherent class bias. … *'But I do not conclude from this that the rule of law itself was humbug. On the contrary, the inhibitions upon power imposed by law seem to me a legacy as substantial as any handed down from the struggles of the seventeenth century to the eighteenth, and a true and important cultural achievement of the agrarian and mercantile bourgeoisie, and of their supporting yeomen and artisans'.*

…

'I am not starry-eyed about this at all. This has not been a star-struck book. I am insisting only upon the obvious point, which some modern Marxists have overlooked, that there is a difference between arbitrary power and the rule of law. We ought to expose the shams and inequities which may be concealed beneath this law. But the rule of law itself, the imposing of effective inhibitions upon power and the defence of the citizen from power's all-intrusive claims, seems to me to be an unqualified human good.' To deny or belittle this good is, in this dangerous century when the resources and pretensions of power continue to enlarge, a desperate '*error of intellectual abstraction*'. More than this, it is a self-fulfilling error, which encourages us to give up the struggle against bad laws and class-bound procedures, and to disarm ourselves before power. It is to throw away a whole inheritance of struggle about law, and within the forms of law, whose continuity can never be fractured without bringing men and women into immediate danger.

Indeed, so startling were the observations just quoted that the leading American legal historian, Professor Morton J Horwitz, took strong issue with them.[84] In particular, he found Thompson's views as constituting, in his words, 'a surprising and disturbing further step';[85] in his view:[86]

> I do not see how a Man of the Left[87] can describe the rule of law as 'an unqualified human good'! It undoubtedly restrains power, but it also prevents power's benevolent exercise. It creates formal equality – a not inconsiderable virtue – but it *promotes* substantive inequality by creating a consciousness that radically separates law from politics, means from ends, processes from outcomes. By promoting procedural justice it enables the shrewd, the calculating, and the wealthy to manipulate its forms to their own advantage. And it ratifies and legitimates an adversarial, competitive, and atomistic conception of human relations.

The views of both Thompson and Horwitz are instructive and merit comment in the context of the present book and the proposed theory of adjudication which I advocate in its final chapter.[88] If I may proceed straight to the point, I agree in part with Thompson and respectfully disagree with Horwitz.

As Thompson himself points out in the extended extract that I have set out above,[89] the rule of law is 'an unqualified human good'.[90] Nevertheless (if I have understood him correctly), its *application* is still flawed. Underlying the alleged flaw is the maintenance by the so-called elite of class structures and the accompanying inequality. This is, of course, entirely consistent with a Marxian view of the law, although Thompson is more nuanced inasmuch as he does not view the law as mere (empty) superstructure, acknowledging that (on occasion at least) the rule of law does prevent the abuse of power. I differ from Thompson inasmuch as the premise which underlies Marxian theory in general and his views in particular is, with respect, flawed – *at least insofar as the courts and their work are concerned.* The *underlying premise*, which constitutes the very pith and marrow of the function of *the courts*, is to attempt their level best to arrive at a *principled* decision that is *consistent with justice and fairness*. This is the complete *antithesis* of Thompson's fundamental premise. As I shall attempt to demonstrate in the final chapter of this book,[91] the *manner as well as the spirit* in which *adjudication* is conducted aids in the aforementioned mission of the courts. Put simply, the rule of law *is* 'an unqualified human good' in *more* than the *occasional* just and fair decision which Thompson refers to. Hence, the concept of *legitimacy* which Thompson refers to is quite *different* from that which I adhere to in this book: the legitimacy of the law

[84] See MJ Horwitz, 'The Rule of Law: An Unqualified Human Good?' (1977) 86 *Yale Law Journal* 561.
[85] ibid 566.
[86] ibid (emphasis in the original text).
[87] Ie, Thompson.
[88] See ch 10 in this volume.
[89] In large part to furnish the reader with an accurate context.
[90] See above, n 83.
[91] See ch 10 in this volume.

is *not* tainted in the least by a need to manipulate the law in order to hoodwink the ordinary citizen; on the contrary, it is a *good faith* effort to achieve the ideals which the rule of law stands for.

I suggest that my critique of Thompson's views applies a fortiori[92] to Horwtiz's views – if nothing else because the latter adopts an even more skeptical approach towards the rule of law. Consistent with his views as a Critical Legal Scholar, Horwitz views law as being nothing more than an exercise in raw power and politics. As I have already attempted to demonstrate in relation to American Realism and Critical Legal Studies in the preceding two parts of this chapter, nothing could be further from the truth, and I will not rehearse the points that I have already made. It is worth reiterating, though, the *disempowering* effect not only on the courts but also on society generally that such a skeptical and cynical view of the law in general and the rule of law in particular can have. To the extent that Thompson does see at least *some* value in the rule of law in its (albeit occasional) constraint on the abuse of power, his view is *less* disempowering than that of Horwitz. Nevertheless, as already explained above, even Thompson's views remain less than satisfactory insofar as they do not acknowledge *fully* what the courts seek their very best to do *everyday*.

The reader would have noticed that, unlike both American Realism *and* the Critical Legal Studies Movement, I have discussed the Marxian theory in a single 'movement', so to speak. I have done this for at least two fundamental reasons.

First, there is, in substance, no real *theory* of *law* as such (and, consequently (as well as logically), no *theory* of adjudication as well).[93] Indeed, Marx himself, as we have briefly seen above, considered law as being mere superstructure. Leaving aside the more general theory that such a dismal view of law is itself a 'theory' of sorts, it can be readily seen – as a matter of pure logic, if nothing else – why I do not consider the Marxian theory of law to be of any assistance in the proposed theory of adjudication which I proffer in the final chapter of the present book.[94]

Second, the central *critique* of the Marxian theory of law as briefly considered earlier in this part of the present chapter demonstrates persuasively (and even powerfully), in my view, that a 'pure' Marxian view of the 'poverty' of law is too crude as well as unrealistic an approach to adopt. And, as also already noted, even Marxian scholars such as Thompson acknowledge that there is at least *some* value in the rule of law.

[92] If I may be forgiven the use of the Latin, as I think it drives home the point I am seeking to make.

[93] *Cf* H Collins, *Marxism and Law* (Oxford, Oxford University Press, 1984). However, although this book attempts (as its title suggests) to relate Marx's ideas to the law, much of it concerns precisely the former rather than the latter. And for an interesting set of readings, see P Beirne and R Quinney (gen eds), *Marxism and Law* (New York, John Wiley & Sons, 1982).

[94] See ch 10 in this volume.

V. Conclusion

As would be evident to the reader by now, apart perhaps from one aspect of American Realism, none of the theories considered in the present chapter is of assistance in the context of the present book simply because they focus almost solely on *negative critique and do not, as a result, set out a positive theory*. There are therefore no useful aspects that can contribute to the main purpose of this book – which is to propose a new theory of adjudication. This is indeed the mission of the final chapter of the book – to which our attention now turns.

PART III

Towards a New Theory of Adjudication

10

A Proposed Theory of Adjudication

I. Introduction

Courts typically proceed to decide cases based on what is essentially a *three-stage approach*. They first ascertain what the relevant *facts* are, evaluating the evidence adduced by the parties to the dispute. They will also ascertain what the applicable law is in the case at hand. They will then proceed to *apply* the applicable law to the relevant facts in order to arrive at their *decision*.[1]

One must not, of course, treat this three-stage approach in a crude or mechanistic fashion. For example, the first and second stages are fairly fluid and, in practice, tend to have an interactional relationship.[2] Further, this approach presents itself typically in first instance cases; in appellate cases, the first stage is fairly well-settled inasmuch as the relevant facts have been ascertained at the trial stage, and, indeed, it is hornbook law that appellate courts will interfere with findings of fact at first instance in only very exceptional circumstances. Put simply, the main concern of the appellate court will traditionally be with the second and third stages.

It is also important to note that the role of the *facts* is of the first importance insofar as the proposed new theory of adjudication mooted in this book is concerned.[3] It is precisely because the fact situations of cases are myriad that it is suggested that it is virtually impossible in all but the most routine or standard fact situations[4] for any given *theory* to assist the court concerned in predicting what the actual *outcome* will be. This particular – and vitally important – point has in fact been covered in an earlier chapter, and I will not re-traverse ground already covered therein.[5]

[1] See also, to like effect, Chief Justice RS French, 'Judicial Activism – The Boundaries of the Judicial Role' (Paper delivered at the Lawasia Conference 2009, Ho Chi Minh City, Vietnam, 10 November 2009) (available at www.hcourt.gov.au/assets/publications/speeches/current-justices/frenchcj/frenchcj10Nov09.pdf (accessed 31 December 2024). Reference may also be made to J McIntyre, *The Judicial Function – Fundamental Principles of Contemporary Judging* (Singapore, Springer, 2019) ch 9, entitled 'Evaluation and the Application of Law to Fact'.

[2] After all, the legal rules contain *factual parameters* that *constitute an integral part of the legal rules* themselves. See also generally McIntyre (n 1) as well as ibid ch 8, entitled 'The Role and Assessment of the Factual Circumstances'.

[3] This was a main contribution of American Realism: see ch 9 in this volume. However, as I also point out in that particular chapter, there should not be such an overemphasis on the importance of facts such as to lead to the jurisprudential malady of 'Fact Skepticism'.

[4] What Professor HLA Hart would term 'core' (as opposed to 'penumbral') cases.

[5] See ch 3 in this volume.

Indeed, as we have also discussed in an earlier chapter, it is not always the case that even the applicable *law* itself is clear – leaving aside, again, the most routine or standard situations.[6] Indeed, in the situation just mentioned (viz, one where even the applicable law is unclear), it would be a fortiori the case that the court concerned would be unable to predict what the actual *outcome* of the case will be.

Looked at in this light, the proposed new theory of adjudication will focus not so much on the actual outcome or result as such but, rather, on the *manner* in which the court concerned approaches its entire process of decision-making. An important point must be made at this juncture. Whilst it might appear that what is being proposed in the present chapter (and, indeed, book) is *procedural* in nature, this is *not (at least entirely)* the case. Let me elaborate.

As we have also seen in an earlier chapter, the line between procedural justice on the one hand and substantive justice on the other is a very fine one – particularly in practice.[7] To recapitulate, ensuring that there is procedural justice tempers the obsession with achieving a substantively fair and just outcome. A *principled* approach is imperative. At the same time a just and fair procedure does not – in and of itself – ensure a just outcome; as has been observed, 'procedural justice is a necessary but not sufficient condition for a fair and just result'.[8] It bears quoting, once again, the following observations that I had made in a judicial capacity:[9]

> 8 The quest for justice, therefore, entails a continuous need to balance the procedural with the substantive. More than that, it is a continuous attempt to ensure that both are *integrated*, as far as that is humanly possible. Both *interact* with each other. One cannot survive without the other. There must, therefore, be – as far as is possible – a fair and just procedure that leads to a fair and just result. This is not merely abstract theorising. It is the *very basis* of what the courts do – and ought to do. When in doubt, the courts would do well to keep these bedrock principles in mind. This is especially significant because, in many ways, this is how, I believe, laypersons perceive the administration of justice to be. The legitimacy of the law in their eyes must never be compromised. On the contrary, it should, as far as is possible, be enhanced.
>
> 9 It is true, however, that in the sphere of practical reality, there is often a *tension* between the need for procedural justice on the one hand and substantive justice on the other. The task of the court is to attempt, as I have pointed out in the preceding paragraph, to *resolve* this tension. There is a *further* task: it is to actually attempt, simultaneously, to *integrate* these two conceptions of justice in order that justice in its fullest orb may shine forth.

In the aforementioned *integration* of procedural justice and substantive justice, the approach proffered in the present chapter seeks, with respect, to avoid the pitfall which the traditional theories of adjudication encounter – the claim to a complete

[6] See n 4, above.

[7] See ch 2 in this volume.

[8] *United Overseas Bank Ltd v Ng Huat Foundations Pte Ltd* [2005] 2 *Singapore Law Reports (Reissue)* 425, [7].

[9] ibid [8]–[9] (emphasis in the original text).

and 'perfect' theoretical framework that purports to encompass *all* manner of cases (*regardless* of their facts and circumstances). What I seek to focus on in this chapter is, instead, the need for (as already mentioned) the correct *attitudinal approach* (which includes what I term as well as elaborate upon below as 'judging in good faith') that is *coupled with* the *requisite judicial action* – the *outcome* of which will result in the *integration* of both procedural justice *and* substantive justice. It will be readily seen that such an approach, whilst clearly concerned with procedure, is *not* one that is *merely* process-oriented. Indeed, as just noted, the *outcome* is *also* impacted as well.

What *is* of the first importance for the present chapter is the normative guidance that can be gleaned not only from the theories considered in the earlier chapters of this book but also from the integration of those elements with others into a proposed theory of adjudication.

To this end, I will deal, first, with the necessary *institutional values* which underlie this theory. Put simply, this is the *spirit* that underlies – and provides the necessary impetus – to the entire theory itself.[10] This is in fact the *first part* of my proposed theory of adjudication.

I then proceed to deal with the *factors* which ought to guide judges and courts in arriving at just and fair decisions in the cases at hand.[11] This is in fact the second part of my proposed theory of adjudication. These factors are, *simultaneously*, both practical *and* theoretical. It is important to note that there is no contradiction involved here inasmuch as the aforementioned factors are not only grounded soundly in theory but are (as, if not more importantly) of immense *practical* guidance to the courts as well. It is hoped that this will be clear in the exposition that follows. Put simply, the aforementioned factors constitute a *concrete outworking* of the *spirit* represented by the *institutional values* in the first part of my proposed theory of adjudication. It is also hoped that the *interactive nature* between procedural justice on the one hand and substantive justice on the other will be demonstrated more clearly as these factors are set out.

Before proceeding to consider the first part of the proposed theory of adjudication (dealing with institutional values), a general note is in order. As I noted at the outset of this book, although none of the theories of adjudication discussed in the preceding six chapters accurately depicts the adjudication process as it occurs in *practice*, each of them does capture accurate facets or aspects of that process. I have therefore not only been guided by but have also integrated – in the present chapter – relevant facets or aspects of those theories into my proposed theory of adjudication insofar as their spirit and/or substance are concerned. Indeed, even when they have not been so integrated, they have nevertheless been extremely useful in provoking much jurisprudential food for thought in relation to my own proposed

[10] See Pt II, below.
[11] See Pt III, below.

theory of adjudication. Finally, I will note, at the appropriate junctures, the debt that is indeed owed in this particular regard.

Let us turn now to the first substantive part of this chapter – that dealing with *institutional values*.

II. The Proposed Theory of Adjudication (1): Institutional Values

A. Introduction

In order to understand fully how the proposed theory of adjudication operates, it is of the first importance to establish *the institutional values* that provide the necessary wisdom as well as guidance to the judges and courts concerned. It may be justifiably stated (as already alluded to above) that this is the *spirit* which is the *attitudinal* aspect that undergirds the elements of the theory proper (which will be the topic of the next part of this chapter).

These (in my view, universal) institutional values may, in turn, be classified under four broad categories – first, the values which judges hold fast to and that are traditionally embodied in the relevant Judicial Oath of Office (viz, the qualities of impartiality and independence, respectively); second, the closely related concept of judging in good faith (drawing upon the judicial values just mentioned); third, the more general (albeit no less important) values of wisdom and humility; and, fourthly, the concept of the separation of powers, which judges need to adhere to. I now turn to consider each in turn.

B. Judicial Values[12]

As just mentioned, the judicial values to which I refer in the present section of this chapter are to be found embodied in the Judicial Oath of Office. Indeed (and

[12] In many ways, it might be said that this section is an at least possible subset of the larger theory centring on *virtue ethics* (I owe this particular point to Rachel Phang). Virtue ethics itself dates back to ancient Greek philosophy focusing on virtue and character which are supposed to be practised in pursuit of a well-lived life. However, the proposed theory of adjudication in the present chapter goes far *beyond* the topic of judicial values although it might be justifiably said that these values are an extremely important part of the theory itself. On virtue ethics generally see, eg, DC Russell (gen ed), *The Cambridge Companion to Virtue Ethics* (Cambridge, Cambridge University Press, 2013) as well as L Besser-Jones and M Slote (gen eds), *The Routledge Companion to Virtue Ethics* (New York, Routledge, 2015). An important study, in my view at least, is AC MacIntyre's seminal book, entitled *After Virtue: A Study in Moral Theory*, 3rd edn (Notre Dame, University of Notre Dame Press, 2007). It might be noted that one of the most significant difficulties with virtue ethics is to locate – with precision and persuasiveness – its ultimate source. This difficulty is akin to that in the context of natural law to which virtue ethics does (in some respects at least) bear an affinity to (as to which see generally

in the Singapore context), this Oath of Office is one which every Judge or Judicial Commissioner or Senior Judge of the Supreme Court of Singapore must take pursuant to Article 97(1) of the Constitution of the Republic of Singapore,[13] which is to be found in the First Schedule of the same, as follows:[14]

> 6. *Oath of Office of Chief Justice, a Judge of the Supreme Court and a Judicial Commissioner and a Senior Judge of the Supreme Court*
>
> I, ……………………………………………………………………………., having been appointed to the office of……………………………………………………………., do solemnly swear (or affirm) that I will faithfully discharge my judicial duties, and I will do right to all manner of people after the laws and usages of the Republic of Singapore without fear or favour, affection or ill-will to the best of my ability, and will preserve, protect and defend the Constitution of the Republic of Singapore.

The reader would immediately discern the quintessential judicial values contained in the Judicial Oath of Office set out above – in particular, those relating to impartiality and independence (which all fall under the larger umbrella concept of objectivity discussed in an earlier chapter of this book[15]). Indeed, the qualities of *impartiality* and *independence* are fundamental to the adjudicative process.

It bears, at this juncture, repeating a couple of concrete examples, which I had also mentioned in an earlier chapter in relation to the need for – and ability to achieve (in practice) – *impartiality*.[16] Hence, to take a concrete example (which I, like many other judges, have experienced at one time or another), if a claimant has a right to win, then the fact that he or she may appear to the judge to be an

ch 5 in this volume). Indeed, it might be said that this particular difficulty (of the ultimate source of a theory) is one that is common to all theories. That having been said, I think that there would be little quarrel with the topic of judicial values (notwithstanding the fact that I cannot *demonstrate* with absolute certainty why it is both objectively true and (more importantly) valuable). There is, in fact, a remarkable similarity (often even coincidence) in the respective contents of the Judicial Oath of Office in various jurisdictions. Again, whilst not a knock-down argument that these contents are objectively true, I think that (as already mentioned) there would be little (or no) quarrel or disagreement with them. And for a similar approach (albeit at a more general level and in relation to legal interpretation), see A Amaya, 'Virtuous Adjudication; or the Relevance of Judicial Character to Legal Interpretation' (2019) 40 *Statute Law Review* 87, where the learned author mentions moral virtues (including honesty, magnanimity, courage, open-mindedness, perseverance, intellectual autonomy, intellectual sobriety, intellectual sobriety, practical wisdom, justice and loyalty); there is also fleeting mention to the judicial oath which is said to formalise the idea of fidelity to law (ibid 91). In this last-mentioned respect, the reader will notice that I place much greater emphasis on this oath. Reference may also be made to LB Solum, 'Virtue Jurisprudence A Virtue-Centred Theory of Judging' (2003) 34 *Metaphilosophy* 178, where the learned author advocates (as the title of the article itself suggests) a virtue-centred theory of judging that includes qualities such as judicial temperance, judicial courage, judicial temperament, judicial intelligence, judicial wisdom impartiality and (perhaps above all) justice (the last-mentioned of which is concretised, so to speak, in the form of qualities such as judicial impartiality, judicial integrity as well as legal vision) – all of which are consistent with what has been advocated in the present chapter.

[13] 1985 Rev Edn. See now the First Schedule of the Constitution of the Republic of Singapore (2020 Rev Edn).

[14] Italics to designate the relevant heading in the original text.

[15] See ch 3 in this volume.

[16] ibid.

unpleasant and even otherwise exploitative person does not alter the fact that the decision must be given in his or her favour. Likewise, a witness who is extremely unpleasant on the witness stand but who is nevertheless telling the truth must be believed regardless of how repugnant he or she presents themselves on a personal level to the court. The reader will immediately discern – even with these very simple, yet commonplace, examples – how fundamentally important an objective and impartial approach is. Putting aside for the moment the actual decision of the court, without an objective and impartial *process*, a just and fair *result or outcome* would not (save for the occasional happenstance) be possible. Indeed, the concept of 'process' is, in my view, also helpful in understanding 'objectivity *in action*', so to speak.

The above examples also illustrate the fact that it *is* realistic to expect a judge to put aside his or her *personal* views so long as his or her focus is on the indispensable requirement to fulfil his or her Judicial Oath of Office – in particular, the part in which the judge solemnly undertakes that he or she will 'faithfully discharge [his or her] judicial duties, and [that he or she] will do right to all manner of people after the laws and usages of the Republic of Singapore *without fear or favour, affection or ill-will* to the best of [his or her] ability'.[17]

In order to be able to decide *impartially*, the judge must also be accorded the *independence* which enables him or her to do so. Hence, most (if not all) constitutions (or equivalent documents) will ensure that the judge is not beholden to anyone (in particular, the Executive) for his or her salary. Traditionally (at least in the higher judiciary), there is also security of tenure. Judges can generally be removed from office for significant misconduct, but the procedures concerned are generally detailed and provide the right to a fair hearing.

Indeed, so fundamental to the judicial office are the qualities of impartiality and independence that we will find them embodied in every judicial code of conduct.[18]

[17] Emphasis added; see also above, n 14. See also the Rt Hon B Dickson, 'A Life in the Law: The Process of Judging' (2000) 63 *Saskatchewan Law Review* 373, 375, where the learned author observed thus:

> Once on the bench the trial judge does not simply and automatically turn into an impartial being. That is a quality that a judge must cultivate through hard work. This is by no means an easy task. Judges are human. They are shaped by all sorts of experiences before elevation to the bench. The challenge is to leave preconceptions behind and to show, to the extent possible, open-mindedness, courtesy and patience. The task is to preside with the dignity and thoroughness that the privilege of the position demands.

[18] See, eg, the Singapore Judicial Code of Conduct for the Judges and Judicial Commissioners of the Supreme Court of Singapore (available online at www.judiciary.gov.sg/docs/default-source/who-we-are-docs/judicial-code-of-conduct.pdf?sfvrsn=360bf6b7_3 (accessed 2 January 2025)); the United Kingdom Supreme Court Guide to Judicial Conduct 2019 (available online at www.jcpc.uk/uploads/uksc_guide_to_judicial_conduct_a456af62f8.pdf (accessed 2 January 2025)); the Australian and New Zealand Guide to Judicial Conduct, 3rd edn (Revised) (The Australasian Institute of Judicial Administration Incorporated, 2023) (available online at aija.org.au/wp-content/uploads/2024/04/Judicial-Conduct-guide_revised-Dec-2023-formatting-edits-applied.pdf (accessed 2 January 2025)); and the Hong Kong Guide to Judicial Conduct (The Judiciary of the Hong Kong Special Administrative Region of the People's Republic of China, 2022) (available online at www.judiciary.hk/en/publications/

Needless to say (and contrary to skeptical theories such as the Marxian theory of law[19]), the assumption is that judges practise these qualities *in good faith* (which is a factor that I discuss separately in the next section of this chapter, although the interactive overlap between good faith on the one hand and impartiality as well as independence on the other is obvious).

C. Judging in Good Faith[20]

Although this may appear to be an obvious point, it is nevertheless extremely important. Indeed, the reader may have noticed some (perhaps even substantial) *overlap* between this particular factor and the *judicial values* (of impartiality and independence) just dealt with. This is not surprising because, as is the case with the relationship between procedural justice and substantive justice, there is an inevitable overlap between the institutional values that judges hold and the *practical outworking* of such values in the form of the (good faith) reasoning as well as ultimate decisions arrived at by the same. One might even venture to state that both are mirror images of each other.

Therefore, in proceeding to judge 'in good faith', judges ought in fact to draw on the *judicial values* which we have considered in the preceding section of this

gjc_e.pdf (accessed 2 January 2025)). Reference may also be made generally to McIntyre (n 1) ch 10, entitled 'Principles of Judicial Impartiality: Threats to the Independence and Impartiality of Judges', ch 11, entitled 'Dispute-Specific Threats to Impartiality' and ch 12, entitled 'Structural Threats to Impartiality'. In particular, the learned author distinguishes between a 'valid' decision and one that is in 'error' (ibid 159–160) and, as he puts it, an impartial judicial decision-making process 'means that it delivers "valid" rather than "correct" decisions' (ibid 160). And insofar as independence is concerned, McIntyre observes that '[j]udicial independence does not place the judge in a privileged position, isolated and aloof, but instead *ensures that they exercise their judicial functions impartially, protected against improper pressures or influences*' (ibid 169; emphasis added). All this is consistent with the focus more on *procedure* that is advocated by the proposed theory of justice proffered in the present chapter of this book (see also ibid 170 (where the focus is on the proper 'method')).

[19] As to which see ch 9 in this volume.

[20] And see SJ Burton, *Judging in Good Faith* (Cambridge, Cambridge University Press, 1992). Despite the similarity in terminology, Burton's approach in his book is somewhat different from that proffered in the present book. There is some similarity though inasmuch as the learned author emphasises that the legitimacy of adjudication does not necessarily rely upon the *outcome* of the case concerned but, instead, on the provision of *legal reasons* for the decision (ibid xii, 28, 237 and 256). Indeed, such an approach leads the learned author to reject the concept of determinacy in legal decisions (which leads him, in turn, to reject Dworkin's theory of adjudication (as to which see ch 6 in this volume as well as chs 7 and 8.)). However, the focus of his good faith thesis on legal reasons only (see, eg, ibid 36–37) may, with respect, be too akin to legal positivism (as to which see generally ch 4 in this volume). Indeed, Burton accepts that, on occasion at least, if the judge concerned desires to do the morally right thing, he or she may have to depart from his good faith thesis simply because the judge will need to depart from or ignore the relevant legal reasons (see, generally, ibid ch 7, entitled 'Legal and moral duties'). As he acknowledges, '[t]he good faith thesis does not claim that the law is always just or that judges should never disobey it' (ibid 221). But *cf* the proposed theory of adjudication proffered in this chapter which would aid the judge concerned in arriving (as far as is possible) at a just and fair decision in the case at hand.

chapter. In particular, they should hold fast to the values of independence and impartiality.[21]

D. Wisdom and Humility

Wisdom and humility are – from my own personal experience – utterly essential to good and fair judging. Indeed, these two essential qualities are not mere personal preferences inasmuch as my personal experience merely served to *confirm* the *objective value* that both wisdom and humility bring to the adjudicative process. A further – and preliminary – note is necessary at this juncture: these qualities, whilst an integral part of both the practice and theory of adjudication, are *simultaneously* part of *the institutional values* which were the subject of this part of the chapter. However, there are two reasons why I have dealt with them separately.

The first is, admittedly, a rather technical one: wisdom and humility, whilst arguably part of the *legal* process (in particular that pertaining to adjudication), are, strictly speaking, *also more general and, indeed, permeate (or ought to permeate) the practice and theory of other institutions as well.* Put simply, wisdom relates to *sound judgment* in the *application* of relevant knowledge.[22] Hence, wisdom would, in my view, be necessary with regard to all walks of life and disciplines. However, a moment's reflection would reveal that it is *especially* important in the context of adjudication. It was, however, interesting that some reviewers of an earlier manuscript of this book had differing views of the *nature* of wisdom itself. One was of the view that wisdom is an inherent quality which one either possesses or does not possess. Another was of the view that wisdom is not a quality that is (as I allude to in the next paragraph) exercised as such but is, instead, a quality that is something that must be *acquired* over time. Life and individuals are complex, and, hence, all of the above views on wisdom apply to specific individuals and/or specific contexts. To some, for example, wisdom is indeed a quality that is naturally inherent within the individual concerned. However, it is my respectful view that, barring extreme individuals, wisdom can indeed be acquired and developed (as well as exercised) over time. Indeed, even individuals who are 'naturally' wise learn to become even wi*ser* over time.

[21] Discussed above under the rubric of 'Judicial Values'. A closely allied quality is that of 'honesty' (I owe this point to Justice Michelle Gordon and Justice Kenneth Hayne, present as well as former Justices of the High Court of Australia, respectively).

[22] *Cf* the *The Oxford English Dictionary*, where 'wisdom' is defined as follows (see the *The Oxford English Dictionary*, 2nd edn (Oxford, Clarendon Press, 1989) vol XX, 421):

> Capacity of judging rightly in matters relating to life and conduct; soundness of judgement in the choice of means and ends; sometimes, less strictly, sound sense, esp. in practical affairs: opp. to *folly*.

The second reason is more practical: it has always been my view that an excellent judge needs to constantly remind himself or herself of the *utter necessity* to *constantly* exercise wisdom *and* humility. Indeed, I would go so far as to state that even if a particular judge fulfils all the other requirements set out in the present chapter, he or she will never be an *excellent* judge if he or she neglects or (worse still) lacks these two qualities.

To these reasons, the reader may conceivably have two responses. The first is that the need for wisdom and humility is *obvious*. This may well be the case – albeit often only with regard to those who *already subscribe* to these values. The reader may be surprised that – as is often said of common sense as well – the qualities of wisdom and humility are (unfortunately) often not that common. In any event, given their signal importance, there is every justification for emphasising them in the context of the present book.

The second response is, in a way, a contrast to the first. And it is that the need for wisdom and humility is too *simple*. Nothing, with respect, could be further from the truth. The qualities of wisdom and humility, as already mentioned in the preceding paragraph, are often not that common. Yet, they are absolutely essential. A clever judge is not necessarily a wise judge. Being replete with legal learning does not *necessarily* result in the *wise application* of that learning. Indeed, a judge who is of the view that he or she is extremely learned in the law might (even subconsciously) become arrogant – which is the precise opposite of the humility that is required.[23] Indeed, the quality of humility manifests itself in the acceptance that, no matter how well schooled in the law and/or other knowledge we think we are, there is always something new or more that can be learnt. I have always subscribed to that view. As a sitting judge, it was humbling to realise that there was so very much to learn – even in, for example, the field of law which (as a legal academic of many decades standing) I was considered to be an expert. The quality of humility also manifests itself in the willingness to listen to the parties or to counsel – to be patient and to be open. This prevents one from jumping to conclusions, which, more often than not, results in the wrong decision, thus resulting in injustice and unfairness – the very *antithesis* of the ultimate mission of the adjudicative process.

I would go so far as to state that the qualities of wisdom and humility in a judge are what *bind together* all the other factors and qualities that I consider in the present chapter. It should also be acknowledged, however, that there may be other qualities that may lay claim to being included as well. These include the quality of

[23] It has been argued that this is what perhaps prevented Sir Thomas Scrutton, one of the (if not the) foremost commercial lawyers and judges of his time, from being elevated to the House of Lords: see D Foxton, *The Life of Thomas E Scrutton* (Cambridge, Cambridge University Press, 2013), especially 169–173, 295–296 and 298–299. See also generally A Phang, 'A Legal Giant Revisited – Thomas Edward Scrutton and the Development of English Commercial Law' (2015) 32 *Journal of Contract Law* 119, 128–130 as well as T Bingham, *The Business of Judging: Selected Essays and Speeches* (Oxford, Oxford University Press, 2000) 82.

courage.[24] Indeed, courage is inextricably linked not only to wisdom and humility but also to the judicial virtues of impartiality and independence as well as to the need to judge in good faith.[25] All these entail the judge being able to deliver just but unpopular decisions as well as having the courage to risk being wrong and even being found to be wrong.[26]

Finally, it should be noted that the various qualities do in fact overlap with each other. For example, a wise person will tend to be humble as well. In point of fact, the 'journey' of a judge is, in many ways, a microcosm of the (more general) 'journey of life' itself. Nothing worthwhile remains static. We are constantly learning and honing the various qualities (in particular, wisdom and humility) that are so vital to the task of adjudication.[27]

E. The Separation of Powers

The concept of the separation of powers is inextricably linked to the concept of judicial independence, which we considered in an earlier section of this part of the present chapter. Indeed, the separation of powers requires, amongst other things, that judges exercise the independence that they have been accorded in a responsible manner. This means that they ought to observe the relevant boundaries between the various institutions; in particular, they must not arrogate to themselves the power to make laws that are appropriately within the province of the legislature. Put simply, courts cannot – and must not – become 'mini-legislatures'. There is in fact a theoretical underpinning to this, and it is best

[24] I owe this point to Justice David Foxton, Justice of the High Court of England and Wales, and former Judge in Charge of the Commercial Court. See also Solum (n 12) 190–191.

[25] As discussed earlier in the present chapter.

[26] Once again, this point is owed to Justice Foxton.

[27] One personal illustration (centring on humility in general and the need for openness in particular) relates to the contrast between my views as a legal academic on the one hand and as a judge on the other on the practical viability of an umbrella doctrine of unconscionability (which would merge the doctrines of duress, undue influence and unconscionability). As a legal academic, I *endorsed* such an umbrella doctrine (see A Phang, 'Undue Influence – Methodology, Sources and Linkages' [1995] *JBL* 552). However, in delivering the judgment of the Singapore Court of Appeal in *BOM v BOK* [2019] 1 *Singapore Law Reports* 349 [167], I expressed a *completely different* view (which *rejected* the aforementioned umbrella doctrine of unconscionability, inter alia, on the basis that, whilst such a doctrine was *theoretically* elegant, there did not exist practical legal criteria that would enable such a doctrine to function in a coherent as well as *practical* manner), observing (with regard to the article just mentioned) as follows (emphasis in the original text):

> Undoubtedly, the article concerned would ***not*** be binding on the court; it would not even be influential by dint of its provenance alone, save to the extent that it contained persuasive arguments that might be of assistance to the court. Therefore, it cannot be begun to be argued that the views expressed in an *extra*judicial context in [the article] (to the effect that there ought not only be a broad doctrine of unconscionability but also that that doctrine ought to constitute an umbrella doctrine subsuming the doctrines of duress and undue influence) are inconsistent with the views of this court.

exemplified (as we have seen) in Professor Dworkin's theory of adjudication.[28] In particular, Dworkin distinguished between principle on the one hand and policy on the other. Courts were concerned with principle, whilst policy was within the purview of the legislature. However, I differed from Dworkin's view in this particular regard in relation to the power of the courts to develop the law in areas where what I termed 'judicial public policy' was necessary. This last-mentioned conception of the concept of 'policy' is different from the conception which relates to '*legislative* policy'.[29] Indeed, without the invocation of 'judicial public policy', many developments in private law (including that relating to the duty of care in negligence for pure economic loss (as opposed to physical damage)) would not have been possible. I will not rehearse the analysis which I have proffered in a previous chapter, and the reader is referred to it for a more detailed rendition of the various points.[30]

III. The Proposed Theory of Adjudication (2): Practical and Theoretical Factors

A. Introduction

Having considered the *spirit*, so to speak, that undergirds as well as animates the theory of adjudication proposed in the present book, it is now apposite to consider the various factors that are not only grounded in theory but also provide *practical* guidance to the judges and courts concerned. This is important because the various theoretical writings have, in the main at least, been pitched at a very high level of abstraction and do not really relate to what actually transpires in the courts themselves. This book in general and the present chapter in particular aim to *integrate* both theory and practice, thus furnishing the reader with a more holistic

[28] As to which see ch 6 in this volume. See also Bingham (n 23) 72.

[29] Although, as in life generally, the lines are not always that clear: see, eg, the situation relating to contractual illegality (where the public policy involved does not quite correspond to the manner in which 'judicial public policy' has operated in the case law).

[30] See ch 6 in this volume. See also Dickson (n 17) 384, where it is observed by the former Chief Justice of the Supreme Court of Canada as follows:

> [T]he Supreme Court of Canada must display sensitivity to the limits of the court's ability to effect major legal change. Frequently, the kind of change that is needed calls for a process that is far better able to read the pulse of the nation and to ensure that society's norms are accurate translated into laws. This is precisely why we have elected legislatures. And it is why we in Canada have long adhered to the doctrine of parliamentary supremacy. That doctrine does not mean that courts are subservient to the legislature, for they are not. They will apply the law as they interpret it and not necessarily as the government of the day would like to see it interpreted. But at the end of the day courts must recognise that the legislature is best equipped to set down guiding principles designed to address some of our most complex social problems.

and accurate picture as to why what judges and courts do is not only theoretically sound but *also* practical as well. To this end, I will (as already mentioned) draw on what is useful from the theories considered in the earlier chapters as well as *integrate* them with other elements in order to provide a *new as well as holistic theory of adjudication* (that also includes the *institutional values* considered in the preceding part of this chapter).

Let us now turn to the first factor, which relates to the judicial process itself and comprises, as it were, a number of sub-factors. It bears reiterating that these factors constitute the *practical outworking* of the institutional values discussed in the preceding part of this chapter.

B. The Judicial Process

i. Reason and Logic

It ought to come as no surprise to the reader that reason and logic constitute the foundation of the judicial process. Whilst the primary focus is on *legal* reasoning and logic, it is clear from even a cursory reading of common law judgments (regardless of the jurisdiction concerned) that *general* reasoning and logic are also deployed in the writing of judgments. Indeed, it might be said that legal reasoning and logic, whilst necessarily specialised, are consistent with (and, generally speaking, are also developed from) general reasoning and logic. This focus on *rationality* is wholly consistent with, for example, Professor Fuller's internal morality of law[31] although it would not, strictly speaking, be accurate to classify it as 'morality' – at least in the sense that a layperson would construe the term.

However, it should also be noted that although reason and logic are an essential as well as integral part of the adjudicative process, there is a sense in which an overemphasis on these qualities (in particular, a literal and/or mechanistic approach towards them) may lead to the very *antithesis* of what the adjudicative process seeks to achieve – a just and fair decision in the case at hand. Put simply, reason and logic constitute a necessary but not sufficient condition for the attainment of a just and fair decision. They are nevertheless a large part of what the adjudicative process is about as any judge or lawyer will tell you. Indeed, they are essential elements of what we would characterise as the *doctrinal* part of that process – especially given that reason and logic constitute a large part of the contents of the *legal rules* themselves.[32] However, when reason and logic are in fact that sole – or even main – focus of the adjudicative process, what we are likely to end up with is something very akin to *legal positivism*.[33] This is because, like legal

[31] See generally the discussion of Fullerian theory in ch 5 in this volume.

[32] And principles as well – especially if we accept Dworkin's theory of adjudication: see ch 6 in this volume.

[33] As to which see ch 4 in this volume.

positivism, courts which adopt such a (narrow) focus will necessarily understate – or even exclude – moral considerations, at least insofar as they are considered as *necessarily* connected to the law.

ii. Precedent

The doctrine of precedent – or, more accurately, binding precedent – is an integral part of the adjudicative process at common law.[34] Indeed, this doctrine is to be found – to a greater or lesser extent – in every common law jurisdiction (including Singapore[35]).

It is important to note that, on a more *theoretical* level, this doctrine is also significant. Professor Dworkin, for example, refers to the concept of precedent throughout his work – presumably on the basis (which he also endorses) that like cases should be treated alike. Indeed, such a reference corresponds (in large part at least) to the (*first*) dimension of 'fit' in Dworkin's theory of adjudication.[36]

However, like the requirements of reason and logic (which were discussed in the preceding section of this part of the present chapter), the doctrine of binding precedent is just an element (albeit an important one) of the adjudicative process. Looked at in one sense, it complements the requirements of reason and logic by helping to *channel* them, thereby assisting in aiding the court concerned in arriving at a just and fair decision in the case concerned. It should also be noted that the doctrine of precedent is also an integral part of the operation of legal doctrine itself.[37]

iii. Substance

This particular factor has its closest correspondence to Dworkin's *second* dimension of 'substance' in his theory of adjudication. As we have seen, it is also one

[34] The classic work in the field is R Cross and JW Harris, *Precedent in English Law*, 4th edn (Oxford, Clarendon Press, 2012). See also N Duxbury, *The Nature and Authority of Precedent* (Cambridge, Cambridge University Press, 2008) and, by the same author, *The Intricacies of* Dicta *and Dissent* (Cambridge, Cambridge University Press, 2021).

[35] See, eg, W Woon, 'Precedents that Bind – A Gordian Knot: *Stare Decisis* in the Federal Court of Malaysia and the Court of Appeal, Singapore' (1982) 24 *Malaya Law Review* 1 and, by the same author, 'Stare Decisis and Judicial Precedent in Singapore' in ch 4 of AJ Harding (gen ed), *The Common Law in Singapore and Malaysia* (Singapore, Butterworths, 1985) as well as 'The Doctrine of Judicial Precedent' in ch 8 of KYL Tan (gen ed), *The Singapore Legal System*, 2nd edn (Singapore, Singapore University Press, 1999). See also ABL Phang, '*Stare Decisis* in Singapore and Malaysia: A Sad Tale of the Use and Abuse of Statutes' (1983) 4 *Singapore Law Review* 155 and, by the same author, '"Overseas Fetters": Myth or Reality?' (1983) 2 *Malayan Law Journal* cxxxix as well as ABL Phang, VK Rajah and KWK Tan, 'The Case for a Re-Appraisal and Re-Statement of the doctrine of Stare Decisis in Singapore' (1990) 2 *Malayan Law Journal* at lxxi, xcvii and cxiii, respectively and, by the same authors, 'The Case for a Re-Appraisal and Re-Statement of the doctrine of Stare Decisis in Singapore – An Overview" (1990) 6 *Law Society's Journal* 22. See also *Practice Statement (Judicial Precedent)* [1994] 2 *Singapore Law Reports* 689.

[36] See generally chs 6, 7 and 8 in this volume.

[37] And *cf* ch 4 in this volume (which, however, acknowledges the importance that *legal rules* play in the actual practice of law).

of the most problematic elements in that theory.[38] This is not surprising as it relates to the *substantive merits* of the case itself and can therefore engender a variety of views. Put simply, unless it is a so-called 'easy case', it might well be controversial as to what the correct answer is. However, I included this particular factor because it does in fact relate directly to the ultimate goal of the court – to arrive (as best as it can) at a just and fair result based on the application of the relevant law to the relevant facts in the particular case itself. Indeed, this factor is often exemplified by the question which courts not infrequently ask themselves (often implicitly): 'Where does the justice of this case lie?' The reader will now appreciate why I just used the word 'implicitly'. Indeed, shorn of its context, an external observer might well be under the mistaken impression that this statement means that the court concerned is deciding based on its own *subjective preferences*. Nothing could be further from the truth – especially if one takes into account the factor referred to in the preceding part of the present chapter, which is that judges must decide in good faith (having regard, of course, to reason and logic as well as precedent, which has just been referred to).

It is suggested that this particular factor – relating to 'substance' – represents (in practice) *an umbrella of sorts under which the court concerned, utilising all the various other factors set out in the present chapter, arrives at what the substantive merits of the case are, thereafter arriving (in turn) at what it considers a just and fair decision in that particular case.* However, it is also important to note that the utilisation of the aforementioned factors does not – and cannot – occur in a vacuum. These factors operate in the context of the relevant law *and* the relevant facts.

If what has just been stated in the preceding paragraph appears 'messy', the truth of the matter is that the adjudicative process is not (save perhaps in so-called 'easy cases') a mechanistic one – if nothing else, because life itself is far more complex than we could ever predict. And this takes us back *full circle*, so to speak, to the importance of ensuring that, *at the very least*, both the *attitudinal values and factors* canvassed in the present chapter are *observed and applied scrupulously*. This is *especially important* in the context of 'hard cases' where adherence to *principle* is of the first importance. Indeed, adherence to principle is so important that it applies to *both* 'hard cases' *and* 'easy cases' alike. This is in fact the next factor to which our attention now turns. However, before proceeding to do so, I would like to touch briefly upon the nature – as well as limits – of 'judicial creativity'.

C. 'Judicial Creativity' and the Adherence to Principle

I have, in fact, touched on the role of 'judicial creativity' in earlier chapters discussing Dworkin's theory of adjudication,[39] and the reader is referred

[38] See generally chs 6, 7 and 8 in this volume.
[39] ibid.

to the analysis therein. By way of brief summary, whilst 'judicial creativity' is in fact an integral part of the manner in which the common law as well as principles of equity have developed over the centuries, there are nevertheless limits to the extent to which the courts can legitimately develop the law. In theory at least, the line is clear: as was emphasised in the chapters just mentioned, it was argued that, whilst under a duty to develop common law and equity, courts cannot – and must not – become 'mini-legislatures'. This limit is inextricably related to that institutional value considered in the preceding part of this chapter, centring on the concept of the separation of powers. It is admitted, however, that in the real world, the situation is (understandably) far more complex and that the line just referred to, whilst clear in theory, might not be so clear in practice. In order to refine the aforementioned approach, it was suggested that one has to distinguish between two conceptions of the concept of 'policy' (a point in fact alluded to in an earlier part of this chapter). This is because, on occasion, the court does have to resort to policy in order to develop the law (for example, in relation to the duty of care in negligence[40]).[41]

However, what is the situation when courts are faced with 'hard cases' (cases in which no legal answer is immediately discernible)? The quintessential example is a novel case for which there is no established legal rule covering the fact situation at hand. This is the issue to which our attention now turns.

D. Hard Cases

By definition, 'hard cases' are rare. However, they do in fact occur from time to time. And when they do, they pose – by their very nature – an extremely difficult situation for the court concerned. The question that then arises is this: how is the court to proceed in order to arrive at a fair and just decision? Notwithstanding the fact that there is, *ex hypothesi*, no established legal rule covering the fact situation concerned, are there (as, most notably, Professor Dworkin argues) nevertheless legal *principles* that can be called in aid to arrive at a fair and just decision? Or (as, for example, Professor Hart argues), is the judge concerned free to exercise his or her (*unbridled*) discretion to make *new* law to decide the case at hand? I have in fact explored these questions in detail in previous chapters of this book,[42] and will therefore not rehearse the arguments as well as analyses contained therein.

Suffice it to state that I suggested – using the Singapore Court of Appeal decision of *ACB v Thomson Medical Pte Ltd*[43] as an illustration – to argue that to the

[40] This is what I have termed 'judicial public policy'. And see, eg, the Singapore Court of Appeal decision of *Spandeck Engineering (S) Pte Ltd v Defence Science & Technology Agency* [2007] 4 *Singapore Law Reports (Reissue)* 100 (discussed in ch 6 in this volume).

[41] And see generally the discussion in ch 6 in this volume. See also PS Atiyah, 'Judges and Policy' (1980) 15 *Israel Law Review* 346, 370–371.

[42] See generally chs 6, 7 and 8 in this volume.

[43] *ACB v Thomson Medical Pte Ltd* [2017] 1 *Singapore Law Reports* 918.

extent that the court in this case developed the law *incrementally and consistently with (as well as from) existing legal rules*, it cannot be said that it had created new law in the *broad* sense which legal positivists are said to do in 'hard cases' (at least according to Dworkin); in particular, the court in the *Thomson Medical* case did *not* have to resort to *extra*legal considerations, *except* to the extent that they *aided* it in *formulating* a new *(legal)* head of damages (viz, damages for *loss of genetic affinity*). So the reader will see that the approach in the *Thomson Medical* case was in fact consistent with *both* legal positivism *and* Dworkinian theory (or, more accurately, with *specific aspects* of *both* theories). All this also illustrates a *central theme* of the present book – that *no single theory* can capture accurately as well as completely the *actual process of adjudication*, but that many *aspects* of many of such theories *do* capture various *aspects* of what transpires during the *actual* process of adjudication itself. Indeed, this last-mentioned reference to *aspects* of *theories of adjudication* has also been illustrated earlier in this chapter when I considered Dworkin's distinction between principle and policy (in particular, that the courts cannot be 'mini-legislatures') as well as the concept of '*judicial public* policy' – all as they operated in the context of the *actual practice of adjudication* itself. Most importantly, perhaps, the court in the *Thomson Medical* case adopted throughout the approach advocated above as one of the practical as well as theoretical factors – that of judging *in good faith*. Indeed, all this demonstrates that the various factors considered in the present part of this chapter of the book are not writ in stone – they operate *interactively* and depend very much upon the precise facts and circumstances of the case at hand.

This would be an appropriate juncture at which to conclude the present chapter and, indeed, this book.

IV. Conclusion

As I mentioned in the *Preface* to this book, this entire project has been a labour of love. I spent almost a quarter of a century in legal academia and a further 18 years or so on the Bench, having had the distinct privilege and honour to serve on the highest appellate court in Singapore. It was a wholly unexpected honour to have been afforded the opportunity to serve my country in a judicial capacity. Upon my retirement at the end of 2022 from the Bench, it occurred to me that my experience was almost unique. Indeed, although a number of judges have written in the context of jurisprudence and legal theory,[44] there are virtually none who have had the experience of lengthy stints in both legal academia and in the highest appellate

[44] See, eg, EW Thomas, *The Judicial Process – Realism, Pragmatism, Practical Reasoning and Principles* (Cambridge, Cambridge University Press, 2005) and NH Chan, *How to Judge the Judges*, 2nd edn (Petaling Jaya, Sweet & Maxwell Asia, 2009). The former is a lawyer as well as a retired judge of the New Zealand Court of Appeal and a former acting judge of the Supreme Court of New Zealand, whilst the latter was a lawyer as well as a former judge of the Malaysian Court of Appeal.

courts of their respective jurisdictions.[45] Indeed, I continue to serve, part-time, as both a judge[46] and a legal academic.[47]

As I elaborate upon in the *Preface* of this book, it occurred to me that the major theories of adjudication at common law did not fully capture what *actually*

In the first book (reference may also be made to his earlier monograph, entitled *A Return to Principle in Judicial Reasoning and an Acclamation of Judicial Autonomy* (Monograph 5, Wellington, Victoria University of Wellington Law Review, 1993)), Thomas appears, with respect, to have adopted a rather extreme jurisprudential approach in his book inasmuch as he argues that judges 'make law – endlessly' as well as 'policy – regularly' (above, 3 and 4, respectively). Whilst endorsing 'principle', his critique of Dworkin's theory of adjudication (in contrast to that adopted in the present book) is trenchant (see especially ibid ch 8, entitled 'There is no personal law'), as is his critique of both legal positivism as well as natural law theory (the latter of which is described as 'a mix of superstition and speculation' (ibid 43)). He is also highly critical of the doctrine of binding precedent (see especially ibid ch 6, entitled 'The piety of precedent' and ch 7, entitled 'The foibles of precedent – a case study'; though *cf* ibid 251–254) as well as of the concept of separation of powers (and insofar as the latter is concerned, the learned author observes that '[p]olitical scientists have long since exposed the doctrine of separation of powers as an illusion' (ibid 77); though *cf* the learned author's admission that 'this does not mean that the court should behave like "little legislatures"' (ibid 259), a view that is consistent with that advocated in the present book (see especially ch 6 in this volume) – although he then proceeds to observe that 'undue deference to Parliament in changing the law retards the courts' ability to reform the law long before it has become an embarrassment requiring legislative intervention' (ibid) (though *cf*, in turn, ibid 260 and 262)). In his view, '[r]ealism, pragmatism, practical reasoning and principles will become the order of the judicial day', [o]r so that is [his] hope' (ibid 23; see also generally ch 11, entitled 'Towards a new judicial methodology'). The reader will discern from even this very brief summary of this particular book that the views expressed therein are quite different from those expressed in the present book. Although I do agree with some of the learned author's views (for example, the uncertainty surrounding fact-finding, that judges do consider policy, and that law is essentially a process), his general approach is, with respect, far too broad and freewheeling. His seeming dismissal of the Judicial Oath of Office (ibid 238–239) is also too sweeping. However, there is no denying Thomas's very practical approach. This is evident, for example, from his survey of the various constraints on the judiciary (see generally ibid ch 10, entitled 'The constraints of the judiciary') – comprising external constraints (including the appellate process, the need to give reasons for the decision, the effect of legal education training and experience as well as comment and criticism of judgments) as well as internalised constraints (in particular, the judge's own sense of the proper judicial role).

The second book (by Chan) is, in the main, one that critiques many specific judgments in the Malaysian context although the learned author does also focus (consistently with what is advocated in the present chapter) on the need for integrity and impartiality on the part of the judge. There is also reference to the views of the late Lord Denning (whose series of books, beginning with *The Discipline of Law* (London, Butterworths, 1979), also provides us with insights into the judicial process).

[45] One such individual is Aharon Barak who was not only Professor of Law and Dean at the Hebrew University of Jerusalem and subsequently Attorney-General of Israel and Justice as well as President of the Supreme Court of Israel. He is presently Professor of Law at Reichman University in Herzliya. And see generally A Barak, *Judicial Discretion* (New Haven, Yale University Press, 1989) and, by the same author, *Purposive Interpretation in Law* (Princeton, Princeton University Press, 2005) as well as *The Judge in A Democracy* (Princeton, Princeton University Press, 2006). Reference may also be made to his article, 'Foreword: A Judge on Judging: The Role of a Supreme Court in a Democracy' (2002) 116 *Harvard Law Review* 19. With respect, whilst perceptive and thought-provoking, the views expressed in these works are relatively general and abstract although there are specific points that are consistent with those proffered in the present book (for example, that judges do give effect to the policies of the legal system, the need for judicial impartiality and objectivity as well as independence, the need to achieve justice, the avoidance of undermining the legislature, as well as the importance of comparative law).

[46] As a Senior Judge of the Supreme Court of Singapore.

[47] As Distinguished Professor of Law at the Yong Pung How School of Law at the Singapore Management University and also as Distinguished Honorary Professor of Law at the Faculty of Law at the National University of Singapore and as Visiting Professor of Law at the University of Reading.

happens in the adjudicative process. There were nevertheless facets or aspects of many of these theories that capture – in *part* at least – what in fact transpires in the adjudicative process. I have therefore sought to incorporate and integrate them into a new proposed theory of adjudication in the present book. Indeed, this chapter expounds on the various elements of this proposed theory. As this book concludes, I now draw the various threads together in a summary of this theory in both its main elements and how it relates contextually to the other major theories of adjudication at common law, which were canvassed in the preceding six chapters of the present book. However, a caveat is in order: this summary cannot be a substitute for actually reading as well as engaging with the detailed arguments set out in the various chapters of this book (including this final chapter).

From the most *general* perspective, I begin with the argument that although objectivity in the law is not only theoretically coherent but also practically necessary, there is no 'perfect' theoretical framework as such that would enable us to justify as well as predict the *substantive outcomes* in every case).[48] Hence, the approach of the proposed theory of adjudication proffered in this book in general and the present chapter in particular presents an *objective* approach that focuses upon the *actions* by the court in relation to the *process* of ascertaining the relevant facts and circumstances of each case in as objective a manner as possible in order to arrive at a just and fair result after applying the relevant law to these relevant facts and circumstances. Put simply, the focus of the proposed theory is upon the *process* as opposed to the *substantive outcome* of the case concerned. It is nevertheless important to reiterate – yet again – the extremely important point that there is an inevitable as well as inextricable *interaction* between procedural justice and substantive justice and that the focus on process in general and procedural justice in particular in the proposed theory of adjudication is not only consistent with but also tends to aid in achieving a substantively just and fair *outcome*.[49]

Insofar as the *elements* of the proposed theory themselves are concerned, we have seen that they fall under *two* main – albeit closely related – categories.

The *first* may be said to be *the attitudinal* aspect (the *spirit*, so to speak) of the proposed theory itself. However, notwithstanding its intangible nature, it is no less *real*, particularly when viewed in the context of the practical *reality* which it can aid in achieving. I have in fact termed this first category as encompassing four broad – and inextricably related topics – under the umbrella concept of *institutional values*: (1) the *judicial values* of *impartiality and independence*, (2) the requirement of *judging in good faith*, (3) the need for *wisdom and humility*, as well as (4) the *separation of powers*. The former three topics relate more to the individual judge, whereas the final topic relates more to the appropriate

[48] See generally ch 3 in this volume.
[49] See also the text to nn 7–9, above. See also generally ch 2 in this volume.

institutional boundaries, although, as in life generally, there is an overlap amongst the aforementioned topics.

The *second* main element of the proposed theory of adjudication may be said to relate to the *requisite judicial action* which gives *concrete expression* to the *attitudinal* aspect referred to in the preceding paragraph (and which is the *first part* of the proposed theory of adjudication). Such judicial action depends on a number of practical and theoretical *factors*.

The first factor relates to *the judicial process*, which has (in turn) several sub-factors: (1) reason and logic; (2) precedent; and (3) substance. The first two are closely related to legal *rules* (which are, in turn, closely related to legal positivism[50]), whilst the third raises issues with regard to the need to arrive at a just and fair decision,[51] having regard to all the various factors set out in the present chapter of this book. Both the second and third also relate to Professor Dworkin's dimensions of 'fit' and 'substance', respectively, in his theory of adjudication.[52]

The second factor relates to *'judicial creativity' and (more importantly) its limits* (in particular, the need to adhere to principle,[53] although I have argued that, on occasion at least, the courts may need to have recourse to policy as well[54]).

The third – and final – factor relates to the approach that ought to be adopted when facing a *'hard case'*.[55] I have argued that the courts adopt an approach that draws from various appropriate aspects of the various theories of adjudication considered in the preceding six chapters of the present book. In particular, such an approach is consistent with specific aspects of *both* legal positivism *and* Dworkinian theory.

In conclusion, the present book has sought to set out, analyse as well as draw from the most useful aspects of the various major theories of adjudication and integrate them into a proposed theory of adjudication that has, however, more modest aims than the theories just mentioned. In particular, it focuses on the *procedural* aspects of theory that (in turn) *interact* with as well as impact the *substantive* outcomes of cases. It is, in other words, a proposed theory that *integrates both theory and practice* in a manner that is at once intellectually stimulating and practically relevant.

What is clear, however, is that a truly *effective* theory of adjudication depends, in the final analysis, upon *the actual judge concerned*. He or she must always bear in mind that each case matters – because it matters to the litigants concerned (whether in terms of livelihood, reputation, liberty or even life itself). In some cases, the decision in a case might even contribute simultaneously to the broader development of the law. Indeed, it is one thing to theorise about the law in general

[50] As to which see generally ch 4 in this volume. It might even be argued that there ought to be adherence to legal *principles* as well (as to which see generally ch 6 in this volume).

[51] *Cf* ch 5 in this volume.

[52] See generally chs 6, 7 and 8 in this volume.

[53] And see generally ibid.

[54] ibid.

[55] And see generally ibid.

and adjudication in particular. It is a quite different situation altogether when real-life decisions need to be made in such a way as to demonstrate simultaneously the objectivity and principled basis underlying a particular decision. This is no mean feat, although the judge today is equipped – more than ever before – to achieve this (bearing in mind the fact that technology in general and Artificial Intelligence in particular are not ends in themselves but merely aids to be harnessed wisely to facilitate the adjudicative process[56]).

What has been discussed and (more importantly) advocated in this book[57] can truly be confirmed in its actual *practice*. We tend to think of individual experience as being merely subjective in nature. Paradoxically, however, it is submitted that it is only through the individual judge's experience that theoretical approaches can either be confirmed or discarded. This is best achieved by an approach akin to what Professor John Rawls has termed a 'reflective equilibrium' in which an individual's own experience figures prominently as well.[58] For all the skepticism that has been levelled against the law,[59] the institution of the law remains as noble as it is necessary. It is this integration of ideal and necessity that the judge in any and all jurisdictions practises in his or her ultimate quest for justice and fairness. This is the underlying spirit as well as substance which a theory of adjudication must embody, and it is hoped that this book has contributed in some small way towards the development of a theory of adjudication that is not only conceptually sound but also of practical relevance as well.

[56] And see generally Chief Justice Sundaresh Menon, 'Keynote Speech at the Inaugural Singapore-India Conference on Technology' (delivered on 15 April 2024, and available online at www.judiciary.gov.sg/news-and-resources/news/news-details/chief-justice-sundaresh-menon--keynote-speech-at-the-inaugural-singapore-india-conference-on-technology (accessed 3 January 2025)).

[57] Especially in this final chapter.

[58] See J Rawls, *A Theory of Justice* (Cambridge, Belknap Press, 1971) 19–21. Briefly put, Rawls argues that the principles of justice chosen should match our own individual convictions of justice and that a certain back and forth movement might be necessary before an equilibrium is achieved.

[59] See, eg, ch 9 in this volume.

INDEX

www.ingramcontent.com/pod-product-compliance
Ingram Content Group UK Ltd.
Pitfield, Milton Keynes, MK11 3LW, UK
UKHW020802290926
15470UKWH00003B/906

9 781509 976959